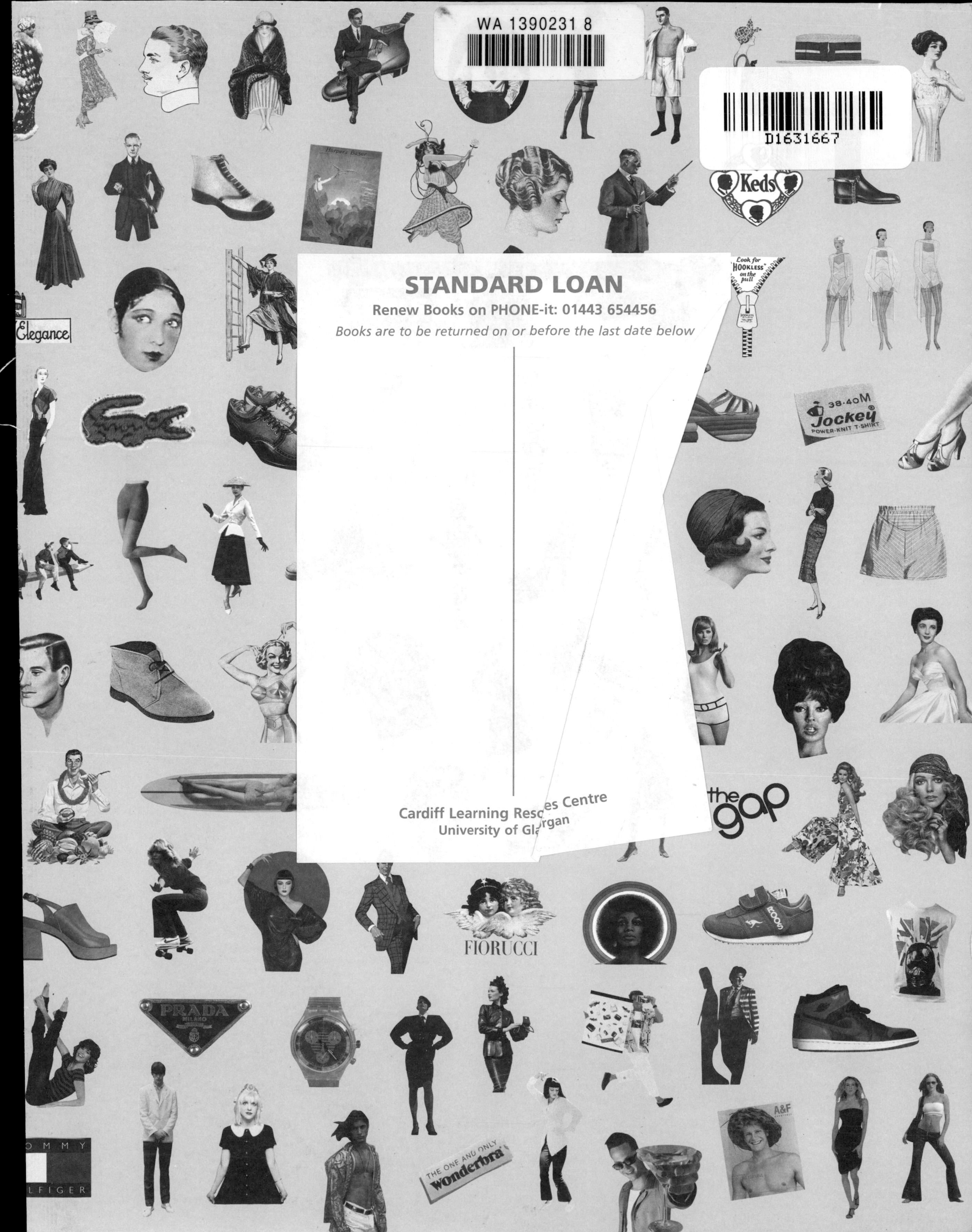
Harpers Bazar
Keds
Elegance
Look for HOOKLESS on the pull
38-40M
Jockey
POWER-KNIT T-SHIRT
the gap
FIORUCCI
KOOS
PRADA
MILANO
OMMY
LFIGER
THE ONE AND ONLY
wonderbra
A&F

EXTRA
THE DAILY TRIBUNE
FINAL MARKETS SPECIAL SPORTS REVIEW
BEAUTY DISAPPEARS !
MYSTERY FIGURE HIDES
Outposts of Atomic Age Now Encircle Globe

JIM HEIMANN · ALISON A. NIEDER

100 YEARS OF APPAREL ADS
100 JAHRE MODE IN DER WERBUNG
100 ANS DE PUBS DE MODE

TASCHEN

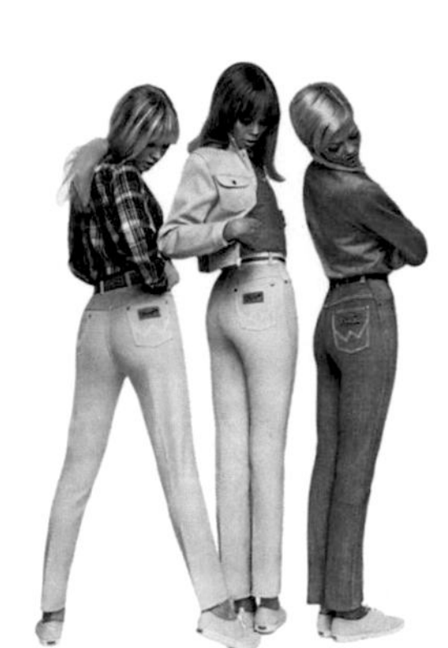

THE BIRTH OF COUTURE COINCIDES WITH THE INVENTION OF THE SEWING MACHINE AND THE BEGINNING OF THE INDUSTRIAL AGE. MECHANIZATION AND AUTOMATION WERE CREATING MASS-PRODUCED CLOTHING FOR A BURGEONING MIDDLE CLASS.

DIE GEBURTSSTUNDE DER COUTURE FÄLLT MIT DER ERFINDUNG DER NÄHMASCHINE UND DEM BEGINN DES INDUSTRIEZEITALTERS ZUSAMMEN. MECHANISIERUNG UND AUTOMATION BRACHTEN KLEIDUNG ALS MASSENWARE FÜR DIE AUFSTREBENDE MITTELSCHICHT AUF DEN MARKT.

LA NAISSANCE DE LA HAUTE COUTURE COÏNCIDA AVEC L'INVENTION DE LA MACHINE À COUDRE ET LES DÉBUTS DE L'ÈRE INDUSTRIELLE. LA MÉCANISATION ET L'AUTOMATISATION PERMIRENT DE PRODUIRE DES VÊTEMENTS EN MASSE POUR LA CLASSE MOYENNE ÉMERGENTE.

INTROD

FASHION FORWARD

MODE IM ZEITRAFFER

EN AVANT LA MODE !

UCTION

"WITHOUT FOUNDATION THERE CAN BE NO FASHION." —CHRISTIAN DIOR

IN SEPTEMBER 1947, THE QUEEN ELIZABETH OCEAN LINER DOCKED IN NEW YORK HARBOR WITH A PASSENGER LIST THAT INCLUDED CHRISTIAN DIOR and Salvatore Ferragamo, both en route to Dallas, Texas, to receive Neiman Marcus fashion awards. Six months before, Dior had released his first solo collection. Dubbed the New Look by *Harper's Bazaar* editor Carmel Snow, Dior's silhouette was a radical departure from the austere, masculine, wartime styles of the decade's early years.

"We want to forget all about the war," Dior told a *New York Times* reporter on the dock that day. After being told that some American women did not like his new silhouette, with its long, full skirts and hourglass shape, Dior replied, "Once they have seen it, they are convinced. From the male point of view, long skirts are much more feminine." Despite the *Times* reporter's questions on that autumn day in 1947, Dior's redefinition of the female form was already evident.

In reviving the feminine silhouette, Dior also revived the French fashion industry, which had suffered considerably during World War II. Designers like Mainbocher left for America, and others, like Coco Chanel, simply shut their doors. During the war, fabric and metal trim was in short supply in many European countries due to strict rationing. In America the shortages were less severe, but they still brought an end to such high-yardage styles as long skirts, bias cuts, and shawl collars.

The New Look was not just a reaction to an earlier silhouette and the end of the deprivations of war—it was also the result of a very fortuitous partnership. Dior, who had worked with couturiers Robert Piguet and Lucien Lelong before the war, struck out on his own with the backing of his business partner, French cotton millionaire Marcel Boussac.

The partnership and the resulting collection echoed the 19th-century collaboration between Charles Frederick Worth, the first couturier, and French empress Eugénie Bonaparte, who together popularized numerous trends, including the voluminous hoopskirt. Replacing layers of bulky petticoats, the hoopskirt, or crinoline, provided a large canvas for Worth's ideas and for the conspicuous consumption of Napoléon III's court. But it also bolstered the French textile industry. The exaggerated silhouette used upwards of 10 yards of fabric at the hem, helping to turn the fortunes of struggling silk weavers in Lyon.

The collaboration also marked the beginning of the partnership between designers and members of high society, an association which escalated in the 20th century as photography became more prevalent and society coverage found a home in newspapers and magazines. Decades before icons like Grace Kelly, Jacqueline Kennedy, and Princess Diana, American Wallis Simpson became an international obsession after her marriage to the former King of England, Edward VIII. Later known as the Duke of Windsor, Edward was also a trendsetter, eschewing formal dress for business suits and adopting casual, sportswear-like plus fours and V-neck sweaters for everyday attire. In the 1930s, American debutantes began embracing their roles as style leaders and started working with designers to make sure they were spotted wearing the latest styles when they were out on the town. The fashion magazines joined in, using society women as models in fashion spreads and editorial features.

At the same time, consumers were taking their fashion cues from the stars of the silver screen, mimicking looks seen in films or in the pages of fan magazines and gossip columns. Recognizing the influence of celebrities, some advertisers signed them on to endorse their products and appear in their ads. One of the first companies to recognize the potential of a celebrity spokesperson was Portland, Oregon-based swim label Jantzen, whose models ranged from Olympic champions Johnny Weissmueller and Duke Kahanamoku to actors Loretta Young, Joan Blondell, Ginger Rogers, and Dick Powell.

As the century progressed, celebrities eclipsed high society as the driving force for fashion trends. And by the 1950s, models began coming to the fore, achieving celebrity in their own right. Dorian Leigh, Suzy Parker, Jean Shrimpton, Twiggy, Brooke Shields, Cheryl Tiegs, Christie Brinkley, Iman, Cindy Crawford, Kate Moss—they all personified the look of their eras, and their activities, opinions, and love lives became as closely watched as any debutante or Hollywood starlet.

1900

1900 S-bend health corset defines the Edwardian hourglass silhouette

Das s-förmige Gesundheitskorsett erzeugt die edwardianische Sanduhr-Silhouette

Le corset en « S » définit la silhouette en sablier de la Belle Epoque

1900 Straw boater hats, formerly worn by British Navy, become popular summer headwear

Matrosenhüte aus Stroh, die vormals die britische Marine trug, werden zur beliebten sommerlichen Kopfbedeckung

Jusqu'alors réservé à la British Navy, le canotier devient le chapeau d'été à la mode

1900 Upswept pompadour hairstyles achieved with false hair and "transformation" frame

Hochgebürstete Pompadour-Frisuren erzielte man mit Haarteilen und entsprechenden Gestellen

Les coiffures à la Pompadour incluent de faux cheveux et une armature de « transformation »

1900 First patented in 1868, union suit still most popular form of underwear for men

Der 1868 patentierte Union Suit bleibt die beliebteste Herrenunterwäsche

D'abord brevetée en 1868, la combinaison longue reste le sous-vêtement le plus porté par les hommes

The advent of the so-called supermodel put the spotlight on the relationship between designer and muse. But that symbiotic relationship stretches back to Empress Eugénie and Worth, the British designer acknowledged to be the first couturier.

BORN IN 1826, IN BOURNE, LINCOLNSHIRE, ENGLAND, CHARLES FREDERICK WORTH WORKED AS A FABRIC SALESMAN FROM AN EARLY AGE, first in England and later in Paris. By 1858, he'd established the House of Worth on Paris's rue de la Paix. Before Worth, wealthy women's clothing was designed by female dressmakers, designing with considerable input from their clientele. Only menswear was designed by male tailors. The birth of couture coincides with the invention of the sewing machine and the beginning of the industrial age. Mechanization and automation were creating mass-produced clothing for a burgeoning middle class. In America, catalog merchants like Montgomery Ward and Sears, Roebuck and Co. began delivering everyday products — as well as the latest fashions — to America's most remote regions. Meanwhile, European designers had already taken steps to preserve the art of handcraftsmanship, and, in 1868, the French government stepped in, forming the Chambre Syndicale de la Haute Couture in Paris, a trade organization strictly regulated by the French Department of Industry.

Like Dior, many of the Chambre Syndicale's members can be credited with revolutionary designs that significantly altered the look of fashion of the day. In America, those who could afford to travel to Europe to buy couture, did. Others purchased "licensed" reproductions of couture pieces from upscale department stores. And within a few seasons, details culled from couture collections were adapted for lesser-priced lines, reaching far wider audiences. Thus, Chanel's wool jersey pieces with details borrowed from menswear have become synonymous with the look of the modern 1920s woman. Elsa Schiaparelli's highly tailored looks and strong, padded shoulders became a mainstay of the 1930s and '40s. Cristobal Balenciaga's architectural designs provided a counterbalance to Dior's structured glamour. And Pierre Cardin's modern designs, with their emphasis on clean, graphic shapes, ushered in the space-age styles of the 1960s.

But the person credited with the first fashion shift of the 20th century is Paul Poiret, a French designer who left the House of Worth with a concept for Oriental-inspired fashion designed for a completely new body type. The Victorian aesthetic locked the ideal woman in a rigid corset that lifted her bust while constricting her waist to tiny proportions. Poiret had another idea about beauty. Using his wife, Denise, as his muse and model, the designer began with a slender, athletic body, which he then draped in column-like dresses and kimono-style robes that gave the wearer the appearance of being wrapped in a luxurious cocoon. His designs were exotic and radical, and they helped to transform the body's silhouette.

Madeleine Vionnet's bias-cut gowns evoked the image of blonde bombshell Jean Harlow and the escapist glamour depicted in Hollywood films of the early 1930s. But the glamour reflected on the screen belied the harsh reality of the Great Depression. Women's magazines still ran fashion spreads showing the latest styles, but many also published tips for altering and updating existing pieces from one's wardrobe.

The look of fashion advertising also changed in the 1930s, as magazines and advertisers relied less on well-known illustrators to attract attention and underscore the quality of the product and more on photography and less costly in-house artists. The shift marked an end to a rich history of ads using such name artists as J. C. Leyendecker, whose artwork for Arrow shirts and Interwoven socks conveyed sophistication and panache; the Art Nouveau–style illustrations of Maxfield Parrish; the pinup girls drawn by Coles Phillips for Holeproof Hosiery; or George Petty, whose long-limbed Petty Girl was first featured as the Jantzen Diving Girl logo.

And while magazines and advertisers were downsizing, cash-strapped American consumers were looking for economical alternatives, as well. Considered the progenitor of what came to be known as the American Look, Claire McCardell designed everything from everyday apparel to outerwear,

1905

1905 Illustrator J. C. Leyendecker creates Arrow Collar Man campaign

Der Illustrator J. C. Leyendecker entwirft die Kampagne Arrow Collar Man

L'illustrateur J. C. Leyendecker crée la campagne Arrow Collar Man

1908 S-bend gives way to long-line corset, which slims hips as well as waist

Das S-Korsett wird von einem länger geschnittenen Modell verdrängt, das nicht nur die Taille, sondern auch die Hüftpartie verschlankt

Le corset en S est remplacé par le corset long qui affine les hanches et la taille

1910 Paul Poiret's inspired hobble skirts become short-lived fad

Paul Poirets Humpelrock bleibt eine kurzlebige Modeerscheinung

Les jupes dites « entravées » de Paul Poiret remportent un bref succès

1910 Gabrielle "Coco" Chanel opens first store in Paris

Gabrielle "Coco" Chanel eröffnet ihren ersten Laden in Paris

Gabrielle « Coco » Chanel ouvre sa première boutique à Paris

Onyx Hosiery/Lord & Taylor Department Store, 1907 ◂◂

Luxite Hosiery, 1917

▸▸ National Lamp Co., 1927

skiwear, and wedding dresses. From the 1930s through the '50s, McCardell's mix-and-match separates became a mainstay of women's wardrobes. Denim, calico, and madras plaid became signature fabrics for the designer, who also favored such details as topstitching, hoods, spaghetti ties, and patch pockets, as well as leotards and pedal pushers.

While McCardell was designing in New York, California's West Coast casual style was beginning to influence trends in sportswear. Costume designer Bonnie Cashin was "discovered" by Carmel Snow to head design for women's suit maker Adler & Adler. In her 40-year career, Cashin designed everything from Adler & Adler's suits and coats to costumes for the 1944 film *Laura* and accessories for Coach and Hermès.

The West Coast was also home to the swimwear industry, where brands like Jantzen, Catalina, and Cole of California thrived. Evolving from heavy woolen knits, swimwear's foundation was rocked by the invention of the bikini in 1946. The daring new style had a starring role throughout the 1950s and '60s in popular beach- and surf-themed movies, which helped drive swim trends beyond their seaside roots.

DESPITE THE RAPID AND UNIVERSAL SUCCESS OF DIOR'S NEW LOOK, HIS TENURE COINCIDED WITH OTHERS, LIKE CARDIN AND BALENCIAGA, whose ideas of beauty helped pave the way for the space-age styles of the 1960s. One of the first proponents of ultramodern design was André Courrèges, who created deceptively simple pieces in stark colors that looked more stamped in hard plastic than cut from fabric. His short hemlines and white go-go boots were both iconic to the decade and inspirational to a generation of designers. Courrèges' Los Angeles-based contemporary Rudi Gernreich also hewed to the modernist approach, but his design philosophy was even more conceptual. Remembered best for his topless "monokini" swimsuit, Gernreich also created the soft bralette, which complemented his whimsical designs. Using his favorite model, Peggy Moffitt, as his muse, Gernreich helped craft the mod look, and Moffitt's husband, photographer William Claxton, helped preserve it. While Courrèges and Gernreich were raising hemlines to new heights, British designer Mary Quant and her Chelsea Look took the mini to the masses.

In the late '60s, former Dior designer Yves Saint Laurent struck out on his own, creating a label that at once defined trends and defied convention. Saint Laurent's creations were quickly adopted into mainstream fashion. From the classic men's tuxedo—known as Le Smoking—to fashions inspired by Russian, Gypsy, and African garments, his influence can be clearly seen in the street trends of the 1960s and '70s.

The 1970s also saw blue jeans evolve from the uniform of the working man, counterculture, and kids to a legitimate fashion essential. Denim's dominance—and the importance of branding—continued throughout the century, as labels like Levi's, Lee, and Wrangler saw new competition from designer brands like Jordache, Calvin Klein, Guess, and Diesel.

1911 Triangle Shirtwaist Factory fire in New York City leads to sweeping labor reform

Das Feuer in der Triangle Shirtwaist Factory in New York führt zu weitreichenden Reformen für die Arbeiter

L'incendie de la Triangle Shirtwaist Factory à New York entraîne une grande réforme du travail

1912 Millions copy bobbed hair of dancer Irene Castle

Millionen Frauen kopieren den Bob der Tänzerin Irene Castle

Des millions de femmes copient la coupe au bol de la danseuse Irene Castle

1914 Coco Chanel popularizes loose-fitting chemise dresses

Coco Chanel macht locker sitzende Hemdblusenkleider populär

Coco Chanel lance la mode des robes-chemises amples

1914 World War I begins

Der I. Weltkrieg beginnt

Début de la Première Guerre mondiale

"IT WASN'T ME WHO WAS AHEAD OF MY TIME, IT WAS MY TIME THAT WAS BEHIND ME." —ANDRÉ COURRÈGES

To move denim from its utilitarian past to its fashionable future required new cuts, new washes, and a new marketing message. Klein, one of the first designers to recognize that fact, put his brand and Brooke Shields on the fashion map with his landmark 1980 ad, shot by photographer Richard Avedon, that featured the 15-year-old Shields declaring that nothing came between her and her Calvins.

THROUGHOUT THE 1980s, LUXURY FASHION BRANDS – NOTABLY CALVIN KLEIN – worked with an ever-expanding roster of fashion photographers, including Steven Meisel, Patrick Demarchelier, Mario Testino, and Helmut Newton. Following the success of the Brooke Shields ad, Klein continued to use controversial imagery to market his underwear and jeans. Photographer Bruce Weber created many of his memorable campaigns featuring chiseled male models in various stages of undress, and Herb Ritts, whose 1992 Calvin Klein ad featuring a young white rapper named Marky Mark (aka Mark Wahlberg) in his underwear, shocked tourists and locals when it appeared as a giant billboard looming over New York's Times Square.

Similarly, jeans maker Guess updated the pinup for the modern era with a mix of supermodels (Claudia Schiffer and Naomi Campbell were both Guess girls) and celebrity (Anna Nicole Smith, who got her start as a Guess girl).

The silhouette shifted again in the '80s. As more women entered the workforce and began achieving positions of power, designers like Giorgio Armani, Donna Karan, and Claude Montana responded with strong-shouldered, tailored fashions. There was an avant-garde wave of design coming from Japan, led by Comme des Garçons designer Rei Kawakubo. Meanwhile, music-inspired fashions from punk to pop to new wave were broadcast into people's homes through the new MTV cable channel.

In the 1990s, street- and music-inspired fashion took center stage with grunge-inspired anti-fashion and oversize urban streetwear. Several New York designers — including Anna Sui, Christian Francis Roth, and Marc Jacobs, then designing for Perry Ellis — attempted to incorporate grunge trends into their collections, all with mixed results. But by the end of the decade, the look changed again, with new designers Miuccia Prada and Gucci's Tom Ford offering divergent takes on new luxury: Prada's highlighted minimalist sophistication, while Ford's look was sexy and indulgent. Early on, both designers showed a keen understanding of branding and the potential of using accessories to reach a wider audience — the consumer who couldn't afford a Gucci or Prada ensemble might be able to project the glamour of the label by buying Gucci sunglasses or a Prada backpack. Other high-end and haute-couture labels joined in with their own luxury accessories, and soon brands were vying for their latest clutch, tote, or "baguette" to be declared the "it" bag of the season.

As the decade and the millennium came to a close, fashion companies vied for ways to set their brands apart. For some, that meant injecting a little shock value into their marketing. Benetton became the subject of controversy when the Italian brand addressed the AIDS crisis, racism, and ethnic violence in its ads. And Diesel, ever the provocateur, scandalized the editors at *Mother Jones* magazine with a 1998 ad that featured bound and submerged men and women, with the tag line, "At least you'll leave a beautiful corpse."

Meanwhile, the House of Dior — now owned by French conglomerate Moët Hennessey–Louis Vuitton — made its own shocking announcement, naming John Galliano as head of design. He wasted no time in putting his iconoclast imprint on the label, drawing inspiration from a romantic mélange that included the English countryside, pinup girls, Maasai beadwork, Casanova, and the homeless. Still, the enfant terrible has been credited with instilling in the House of Dior — and the art of haute couture — a newfound sense of fun and youthful artistry. Indeed, the *New York Times*, in reviewing Galliano's first collection for Dior, wrote, "Mr. Galliano's show was a credit to himself, to Mr. Dior, whose name is on the door, and to the future of the art, which is always in question."

1915 Artist and costume designer Erté lands cover contract with *Harper's Bazaar*

Der Künstler und Kostümbildner Erté schließt mit *Harper's Bazaar* einen Vertrag über Titelbilder ab

L'artiste et costumier Erté signe un contrat avec *Harper's Bazaar* pour créer toutes les couvertures du magazine

1917 Demand increases for athletic shoes

Steigende Nachfrage nach Sportschuhen

La demande en chaussures de sport augmente

1920 American women gain right to vote in national elections

Amerikanische Frauen erringen auf nationaler Ebene das Wahlrecht

Les Américaines obtiennent le droit de vote aux élections nationales

1920 Lean lines of flapper styles achieved with bust-reducing brassieres

Die schmalen Konturen der Flapper-Mode erzielt man mit Büstenhaltern, die den Brustumfang verringern

Les lignes élancées des vêtements des années folles reposent sur des soutiens-gorge qui compriment la poitrine

COLES PHILLIPS

IM SEPTEMBER 1947 DOCKTE DIE QUEEN ELIZABETH MIT CHRISTIAN DIOR UND SALVATORE FERRAGAMO AUF DER PASSAGIERLISTE IM HAFEN VON NEW YORK AN. Die beiden waren auf dem Weg nach Dallas, Texas, um die Neiman Marcus Fashion Awards entgegenzunehmen. Sechs Monate zuvor hatte Dior seine revolutionäre erste Solo-Kollektion vorgestellt. Die Herausgeberin von *Harper's Bazaar*, Carmel Snow, taufte Diors neue Silhouette, die sich so radikal von den nüchternen, maskulinen Trends der Kriegsjahre zu Beginn des Jahrzehnts unterschied, „The New Look".

„Wir wollen alles, was mit dem Krieg zusammenhängt, vergessen", erklärte Dior an jenem Tag noch am Kai einem Reporter der New York Times. Nachdem man ihm mitgeteilt hatte, dass manche Amerikanerinnen seine neue Silhouette mit den langen, weiten Röcken und der Sanduhr-Figur nicht goutierten, erwiderte Dior: „Sobald sie es gesehen haben, werden sie überzeugt sein. Vom männlichen Standpunkt aus gilt, dass lange Röcke sehr viel weiblicher wirken." Trotz der Fragen des Times-Reporters an jenem Herbsttag 1947 war Diors Neubestimmung der weiblichen Figur bereits offensichtlich.

Mit der Wiederbelebung der femininen Silhouette gab Dior auch der französischen Modeindustrie neuen Auftrieb, die während des Zweiten Weltkriegs beträchtlich gelitten hatte. Designer wie Mainbocher waren damals nach Amerika ausgewandert, andere wie Coco Chanel hatten ihre Läden einfach dicht gemacht. Während des Krieges waren Stoff und Zubehör aufgrund der strikten Rationierungsmaßnahmen in vielen europäischen Ländern Mangelware. In den USA war die Verknappung weniger schlimm, bedeutete aber dennoch das Ende meterverschlingender Trends wie lange Röcke, Schrägschnitt und Schalkragen.

Der New Look war nicht nur eine Reaktion auf frühere Silhouetten und das Ende des kriegsbedingten Mangels – er war auch das Ergebnis einer ganz zufälligen Verbindung. Dior, der vor dem Krieg mit den Couturiers Robert Piguet und Lucien Lelong gearbeitet hatte, wurde mit Unterstützung seines Geschäftspartners, des französischen Baumwollmillionärs Marcel Boussac, selbst kreativ.

Die Partnerschaft und die daraus resultierende Kollektion erscheint wie eine Wiederholung der Kooperation zwischen dem ersten Couturier Charles Frederick Worth und der französischen Kaiserin Eugénie Bonaparte im 19. Jahrhundert; die beiden sorgten für die Verbreitung zahlreicher Moden, darunter der voluminöse Reifrock. Der Reifrock, auch Krinoline genannt, machte die vielen Schichten bauschiger Unterröcke überflüssig und sorgte für den richtigen Hintergrund zu Worths Ideen und dem aufwändigen Lebensstil am Hof von Napoléon III. Das Ganze förderte zugleich die französische Textilindustrie. Für die auffällige Silhouette wurden am Saum mindestens zehn Laufmeter Stoff benötigt, was den darbenden Seidenwebern in Lyon sehr zupass kam.

Diese Kooperation markierte aber auch den Beginn der Partnerschaften zwischen Designern und bedeutenden Mitgliedern der Gesellschaft; wobei diese Zweckbeziehung erst im 20. Jahrhundert ihren Höhepunkt erreichte, als die Fotografie immer mehr Verbreitung fand und Gesellschaftsreportagen zum festen Bestandteil von Zeitungen und Magazinen wurden. Jahrzehnte vor Ikonen wie Grace Kelly, Jacqueline Kennedy und Lady Diana gab es einen internationalen Hype um die Amerikanerin Wallis Simpson, nachdem diese den ehemaligen König von England, Edward VIII., geheiratet hatte. Der fortan nur noch als Herzog von Windsor betitelte Edward war ebenfalls ein Trendsetter, der formelle Kleidung als Business-Outfit mied und lässige Sportswear mit Knickerbocker und V-Ausschnitt-Pullover als Alltagsgarderobe salonfähig machte. In den 1930er Jahren begannen amerikanische Debütantinnen ihre stilbildenden Rollen anzunehmen und die Dienste von Designern in Anspruch zu nehmen, um sicherzugehen, dass man sie in den neuesten Trends sah, wenn sie sich ins Licht der Öffentlichkeit begaben. Die Modezeitschriften griffen das auf und begannen, Damen der Gesellschaft als Models in Modebeilagen und redaktionellen Beiträgen zu präsentieren.

Gleichzeitig holten sich die Konsumenten Modetipps bei den Leinwandstars und ahmten Outfits nach, die sie in Filmen, Fanzeitschriften und Klatschkolumnen gesehen

1920

1920 Society Brand Clothing begins air-shipping orders to communities not accessible by rail

Society Brand Clothing beginnt Lieferungen in Orte, die nicht per Bahn erreichbar sind, auf dem Luftweg durchzuführen

Society Brand Clothing commence à livrer par avion les communautés non desservies par le train

1925 Exposition Internationale des Arts Décoratifs et Industriels Modernes, Paris

Exposition Internationale des Arts Décoratifs et Industriels Modernes in Paris

Exposition Internationale des Arts Décoratifs et Industriels Modernes, Paris

1926 Josephine Baker performs in Paris with hair cut in Eton crop bob

Josephine Baker tritt in Paris mit Bubikopf-Frisur auf

Josephine Baker apparaît sur les scènes parisiennes avec une coupe de garçonne

1926 Movies add sound

Aufkommen des Tonfilms

Début du cinéma parlant

„KEINE MODE OHNE MIEDER.“ —CHRISTIAN DIOR

hatten. Nachdem sie den Einfluss der Prominenten erkannt hatten, nahmen einige Werbekunden diese unter Vertrag, damit sie Produkte empfahlen und in Annoncen auftraten. Eine der ersten Firmen, die das Potenzial eines berühmten Fürsprechers erkannten, war die Bademodenmarke Jantzen mit Sitz in Portland, Oregon; zu ihren Modellen zählten die Olympiasieger Johnny Weissmueller und Duke Kahanamoku, aber auch Schauspieler wie Loretta Young, Joan Blondell, Ginger Rogers und Dick Powell.

Im weiteren Verlauf des Jahrhunderts verdrängten Prominente die Angehörigen der besseren Gesellschaft als Vorreiter für modische Trends. Etwa ab den 1950er Jahren rückten schließlich die Models selbst in den Vordergrund und besaßen fortan ebenfalls den Status von Berühmtheiten. Dorian Leigh, Suzy Parker, Jean Shrimpton, Twiggy, Brooke Shields, Cheryl Tiegs, Christie Brinkley, Iman, Cindy Crawford und Kate Moss – sie alle personifizierten den Look ihrer jeweiligen Ära, während ihre Aktivitäten, Ansichten und Liebschaften so aufmerksam verfolgt und dokumentiert wurden wie bis dato bei Debütantinnen oder Hollywood-Sternchen.

Das Aufkommen sogenannter Topmodels brachte die Beziehung zwischen Designer und Muse ins Rampenlicht. Doch auch diese Symbiose lässt sich schon Kaiserin Eugénie und dem britischen Modeschöpfer Worth, der als erster Couturier gilt, attestieren.

DER 1826 IN BOURNE, LINCOLNSHIRE, ENGLAND GEBORENE CHARLES FREDERICK WORTH ARBEITETE SCHON IN JUNGEN JAHREN ALS TEXTILKAUFMANN, ZUNÄCHST IN ENGLAND, SPÄTER IN PARIS. 1858 eröffnete er in der Pariser Rue de la Paix sein House of Worth. Vor ihm war die Garderobe betuchter Damen von Schneiderinnen und maßgeblich nach den Wünschen der Klientel entworfen worden. Schneider waren damals nur für Herrenmode zuständig. Die Geburtsstunde der Couture fällt mit der Erfindung der Nähmaschine und dem Beginn des Industriezeitalters zusammen. Mechanisierung und Automation brachten Kleidung als Massenware für die aufstrebende Mittelschicht auf den Markt. In Amerika begannen Versandhändler wie Montgomery Ward und Sears, Roebuck and Co. Alltagsprodukte – wie auch die neuesten modischen Errungenschaften – in die entlegensten Regionen des Landes zu liefern. Inzwischen hatten europäische Modeschöpfer bereits Maßnahmen er-

1928

1928 Zipper trademarked by Talon

Talon lässt sich den Reißverschluss patentieren

La société Talon fait breveter la fermeture à zip

1933 Parisian designer Elsa Schiaparelli charms Hollywood royalty on trip to U.S.

Die Pariser Designerin Elsa Schiaparelli bezaubert auf ihrer Amerikareise ganz Hollywood

La couturière parisienne Elsa Schiaparelli charme l'élite d'Hollywood lors d'un voyage aux Etats-Unis

1933 Depression-era magazines publish tips for altering existing clothes to current style

Amerikanische Zeitschriften veröffentlichen während der Depression Tipps zum Umarbeiten vorhandener Kleidung nach aktuellem Trend

Pendant la Grande Dépression, les magazines américains publient des conseils pour adapter les vêtements à la mode du moment

1933 Tennis star René "le Crocodile" Lacoste designs popular line of tennis shirts

Tennisstar René „le Crocodile“ Lacoste entwirft eine erfolgreiche Kollektion von Tennishemden

La star du tennis René « le Crocodile » Lacoste lance une ligne de chemises à succès

Jantzen Skiwear, 1947 ◄◄

Dr. Jeanne Walter's Rubber Garments, 1912 ◄

Munsingwear Skit-Suit Undergarments, 1937

griffen, um die Kunst ihres Handwerks zu schützen. Bereits 1868 war die französische Regierung auf den Plan getreten und hatte in Paris das Chambre Syndicale de la Haute Couture gegründet, einen vom französischen Industrieministerium streng regulierten Händlerverband.

Wie Dior zeichneten auch viele andere Mitglieder des Chambre Syndicale für revolutionäre Kreationen verantwortlich, die das Bild der Mode in der jeweiligen Zeit maßgeblich bestimmten. Wer es sich leisten konnte, reiste aus den USA nach Europa, um dort Haute Couture zu erstehen. Andere kauften „lizensierte" Reproduktionen von Couture-Modellen in gehobenen Warenhäusern. Innerhalb weniger Saisonen wurden ausgewählte Details aus Couture-Kollektionen in günstigere Linien übernommen und erreichten so ein weit größeres Publikum. Auf diese Weise wurden etwa Chanels Kostüme aus Wolljersey mit aus der Herrenmode entlehnten Details zum Synonym des modischen Erscheinungsbilds der modernen Frau in den 1920er Jahren. Elsa Schiaparellis anspruchsvoll geschneiderte Outfits und die betonten, gepolsterten Schultern wurden zum Hauptmerkmal der 1930er und 1940er. Cristobal Balenciagas geometrische Entwürfe lieferten ein Gegengewicht zu Diors wohlgesetztem Glamour. Pierre Cardins moderne Kreationen mit ihren betont klaren, grafischen Silhouetten leiteten die spacigen Trends der 1960er ein.

Die erste große modische Veränderung des 20. Jahrhunderts muss man jedoch Paul Poiret zugute halten. Der französische Modeschöpfer verließ das House of Worth mit einem Konzept für orientalisch-inspirierte Mode, die er für einen ganz neuen Körpertyp entworfen hatte. Während die viktorianische Ästhetik die Idealfrau in ein starres Korsett gezwängt hatte, das ihre Büste hob und ihre Taille möglichst eng zusammenschnürte, hing Poiret einem ganz anderen Schönheitsideal an. Mit seiner Frau Denise als Muse und Modell ging er von einem schlanken, athletischen Körper aus, den er sodann in säulenförmige Kleider und kimonoartige Roben kleidete, die ihre Trägerin wie in einen kostbaren Kokon gehüllt erscheinen ließen. Seine Kreationen waren so exotisch wie radikal und trugen dazu bei, die weibliche Silhouette grundlegend zu verändern.

Madeleine Vionnets schräg geschnittene Abendkleider wecken Erinnerungen an das blonde Gift Jean Harlow und den irrealen Glamour der Hollywoodfilme der frühen Dreißigerjahre. Dabei strafte der Leinwandglanz die harte Realität der Großen Depression Lügen. Damals gab es in Frauenzeitschriften zwar immer noch Modebeilagen, die die neuesten Trends präsentierten, viele veröffentlichten aber auch Tipps zum Ändern und Auffrischen bereits vorhandener Teile der eigenen Garderobe.

Das Erscheinungsbild der Modewerbung änderte sich in den 1930ern ebenfalls, denn Zeitschriften wie Werbemacher

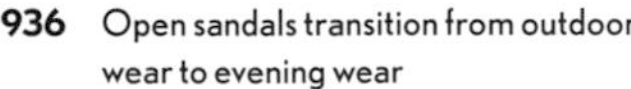

1936 Open sandals transition from outdoor wear to evening wear

Offene Sandalen schaffen den Schritt von der Freizeit- zur Abendmode

Les sandales ouvertes délaissent les activités de plein air pour s'intégrer aux tenues de soirée

1939 World War II begins

Der II. Weltkrieg beginnt

Début de la Seconde Guerre mondiale

1940 Turbans become popular accessory

Turbane werden zum gefragten Accessoire

Les turbans deviennent un accessoire très tendance

1942 American women serve war effort as Women Airforce Service Pilots (WASPs)

Amerikanerinnen leisten Kriegsdienst als Women Airforce Service Pilots (WASPs)

Les Américaines participent à l'effort de guerre en tant que pilotes WASP (Women Airforce Service Pilots)

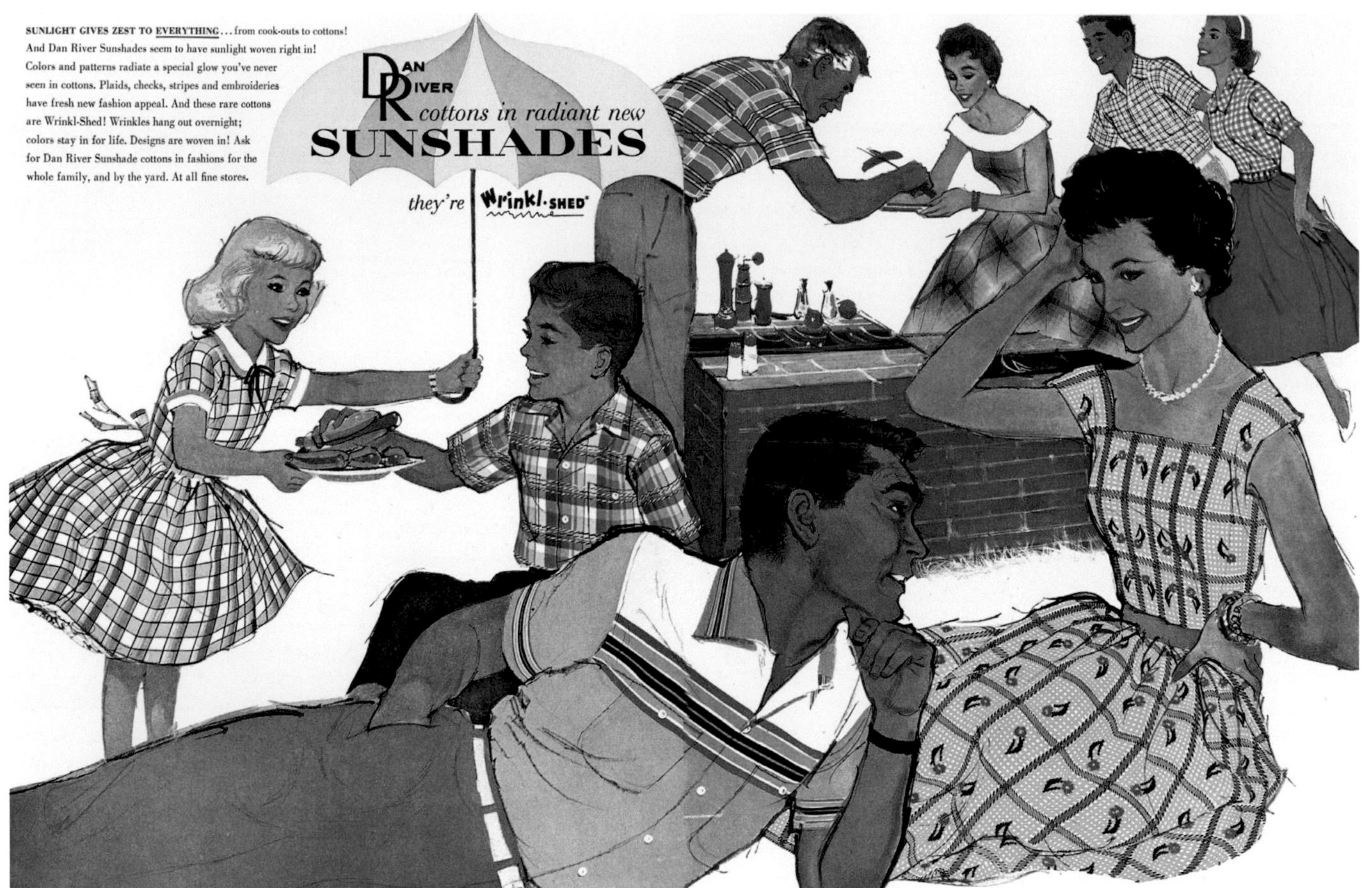

SUNLIGHT GIVES ZEST TO EVERYTHING... from cook-outs to cottons! And Dan River Sunshades seem to have sunlight woven right in! Colors and patterns radiate a special glow you've never seen in cottons. Plaids, checks, stripes and embroideries have fresh new fashion appeal. And these rare cottons are Wrinkl-Shed! Wrinkles hang out overnight; colors stay in for life. Designs are woven in! Ask for Dan River Sunshade cottons in fashions for the whole family, and by the yard. At all fine stores.
DAN RIVER
cottons in radiant new
SUNSHADES
they're Wrinkl-SHED

setzten nicht mehr so stark auf bekannte Illustratoren, um Aufmerksamkeit zu erregen und die Produktqualität zu betonen, sondern stärker auf Fotografie und weniger kostspielige hauseigene Künstler. Der Wandel bedeutete das Ende der Werbeanzeigen von Künstlern wie J. C. Leyendecker, dessen Illustrationen für die Hemdenmarke Arrow und den Sockenhersteller Interwoven Raffinesse und Flair ausstrahlten, der Jugendstil-Illustrationen von Maxfield Parrish, der von Coles Phillips für Holeproof Hosiery gezeichneten Pin-up-Girls oder des Petty Girls von George Petty, das zunächst als Diving-Girl-Logo für Jantzen fungierte.

Und während Zeitschriften und Werbeleute den Gürtel enger schnallten, sahen sich die amerikanischen Konsumenten, die knapp bei Kasse waren, ebenfalls nach kostengüns-

1947 Carmel Snow dubs Christian Dior's collection the "New Look"

Carmel Snow tauft Christian Diors Kollektion "New Look"

Carmel Snow qualifie la collection de Christian Dior de « New Look »

1947 Baby boom begins

Der Babyboom beginnt

Début du baby-boom

1948 Sonja de Lennart debuts capri pant

Sonja de Lennart führt die Caprihose ein

Sonja de Lennart lance le corsaire

1950 Hawaiian shirt boom

Das Hawaii-Hemd boomt

La mode de la chemise hawaïenne déferle sur les Etats-Unis

„NICHT ICH WAR MEINER ZEIT VORAUS, SONDERN DIE ZEIT KAM NICHT HINTER MIR HER.“ – ANDRÉ COURRÈGES

tigen Alternativen um. Als Vorreiterin des späteren American Look entwarf Claire McCardell schlichtweg alles – von Alltagskleidung bis zu Skianzügen, von Unterwäsche bis zu Brautmoden. Von den 1930ern bis in die 1950er waren McCardells perfekt kombinierbare Einzelteile ein Hauptbestandteil der Damenmode. Denim, Kattun und Schottenkaro waren die Lieblingsstoffe der Designerin, die außerdem eine Vorliebe für Details wie Abnäher, Kapuzen und aufgesetzte Taschen, aber auch für Trikots und Caprihosen hatte.

Während McCardell in New York designte, begann der lässige Stil der kalifornischen Westküste die Trends der Sportmode zu beeinflussen. Bonnie Cashin war eine Kostümbildnerin, die Carmel Snow für den Damenkostüm-Hersteller Adler & Adler „entdeckte“. In ihrer 40-jährigen Karriere entwarf auch Cashin praktisch alles, von Kostümen und Mänteln bis zur Ausstattung des Films *Laura* von 1944 oder Accessoires für Coach und Hermès.

Die Westküste war die Heimat der Bademodenindustrie, wo Marken wie Jantzen, Catalina und Cole of California florierten. Nachdem man ursprünglich mit dickem wollenen Strickstoff begonnen hatte, kam die Erfindung des Bikinis 1946 einem Erdbeben gleich. Diese gewagte neue Mode spielte eine Hauptrolle in den beliebten Strand- und Surferfilmen der 1950er und 1960er, die Bademodentrends auch über den Strand hinaus förderten.

TROTZ DES RASCHEN UND WELTWEITEN ERFOLGS VON DIORS NEW LOOK FIEL SEINE ZEIT MIT DEM ERFOLG ANDERER WIE CARDIN UND BALENCIAGA ZUSAMMEN, deren Schönheitsideale dazu beitrugen, den Weg für die spacigen Trends der 1960er zu bereiten. Einer der ersten Verfechter ultramodernen Designs war André Courrèges, der scheinbar simple Kleidungsstücke in kräftigen Farben kreierte, die wie aus Hartplastik gestanzt wirkten. Seine kurzen Säume und weißen Go-go-Stiefel avancierten zu Ikonen jenes Jahrzehnts wie auch zur Inspirationsquelle einer ganzen Generation von Designern. Courrèges' in Los Angeles arbeitender Zeitgenosse Rudi Gernreich war zwar auch ein Vertreter des modernistischen Ansatzes, doch war seine Design-Philosophie noch konzeptioneller. Am bekanntesten ist er für seinen Oben-ohne-Badeanzug namens Monokini. Gernreich entwarf aber auch die weiche Bralette, die seine skurrilen Entwürfe perfekt ergänzte. Unter Mitwirkung seines Lieblingsmodels Peggy Moffitt als Muse trug Gernreich zur Erfindung des Mod-Looks bei, den Moffitts Ehemann, der Fotograf William Claxton, für die Nachwelt dokumentierte. Während Courrèges und Gernreich die Säume zu neuen Höhen steigen ließen, machte die britische Designerin Mary Quant mit ihrem Chelsea Look den Minirock zu einem Massenphänomen.

In den späten Sechzigern wagte der vormalige Dior-Designer Yves Saint Laurent den Schritt in die Selbstständigkeit und gründete ein Label, das Trends setzte und mit Konventionen brach. Saint Laurents Kreationen wurden schnell für die Mainstream-Mode adaptiert. Angefangen beim klassischen Smoking für den Herrn bis hin zu Trends, die von russischer, afrikanischer und Zigeuner-Kleidung inspiriert waren, lässt sich Saint Laurents Einfluss auf die Mode für die breite Masse in den 1960ern und 1970ern deutlich ablesen.

In den Siebzigern entwickelte sich auch die Bluejeans von der Uniform des amerikanischen Arbeiters, vom Symbol der Gegenkultur zu einem vollwertigen modischen Basic. Die Dominanz von Denim – und die wichtige Rolle der jeweiligen Marken – sollte das gesamte Jahrhundert hindurch andauern, während altehrwürdige Marken wie Levi's, Lee und Wrangler sich neuer Konkurrenz in Gestalt von Designerlabels wie Jordache, Calvin Klein, Guess und Diesel gegenüber sahen. Um sich von der funktionalen Vergangenheit zu lösen, benötigte man neue Schnitte, Waschverfahren und eine neue Marketing-Message für den Jeansstoff. Klein erkannte diese Tatsache als einer der ersten Designer und platzierte in seiner legendären Anzeige seine Marke zusammen mit Brooke Shields auf der modischen Landkarte. Das Foto von Richard Avedon zeigt die 15-jährige, die erklärt, ihr käme nichts zwischen sie und ihre Calvins.

1952 Teen boys embrace Converse All-Star basketball shoe

Männliche Teenager favorisieren den Basketballschuh Converse All-Star

Les adolescents adoptent les baskets Converse All-Star

1952 Trendy teens dance on Dick Clark's *American Bandstand*

Trendbewusste Teenies tanzen nach Dick Clarks *American Bandstand*

L'émission *American Bandstand* animée par Dick Clark présente les dernières danses à la mode chez les ados

1953 Marilyn Monroe's cat's-eye glasses lampooned in *How to Marry a Millionaire*

Marilyn Monroes Katzenaugen-Brille wird in *Wie angelt man sich einen Millionär* veralbert

Les lunettes « œil de chat » de Marilyn Monroe font sensation dans *Comment épouser un millionnaire*

1954 TV sales surpass radio

Werbeumsätze im Fernsehen übertreffen die des Radios

Les ventes de téléviseurs dépassent celles des radios

Dan River Sunshade Cottons, 1957 ◂◂

▸ Cutex Nail Polish, 1946

IM LAUFE DER 1980ER ARBEITETEN LUXUSLABELS – ALLEN VORAN CALVIN KLEIN – MIT EINER STÄNDIG WACHSENDEN SCHAR VON MODEFOTOGRAFEN, darunter Steven Meisel, Patrick Demarchelier, Mario Testino und Helmut Newton. Nach dem Erfolg der Brooke-Shields-Anzeige setzte Klein die Verwendung kontroverser Bilder fort, um seine Dessous und Jeans zu bewerben. Der Fotograf Bruce Weber schuf viele der Calvin-Klein-Anzeigen, die Männermodels beim Ausziehen zeigten. Herb Ritts Anzeige von 1992 präsentierte einen jungen weißen Rapper namens Marky Mark (alias Mark Wahlberg) in Unterwäsche, der auf einem Riesenplakat am New Yorker Times Square die Passanten schockte.

Auf ähnliche Weise aktualisierte der Jeanshersteller Guess die Idee des Pin-ups, und zwar mit einer Mischung aus Supermodels (sowohl Claudia Schiffer als auch Naomi Campbell waren Guess-Girls) und anderen Prominenten (so begann etwa Anna Nicole Smith ihre Karriere als Guess-Girl).

Die 1980er brachten mal wieder eine neue Silhouette in die Mode. Nachdem immer mehr Frauen auf den Arbeitsmarkt drängten und zunehmend begannen einflussreiche Positionen zu erklimmen, reagierten Designer wie Giorgio Armani, Donna Karan und Claude Montana mit betonten Schultern und maßgeschneiderter Mode darauf. Aus Japan kam eine avantgardistisch geprägte Design-Welle, angeführt von Comme des Garçons' Designerin Rei Kawakubo. Inzwischen erreichten von der Musik inspirierte Modeströmungen – von Punk über Pop bis hin zu New Wave – über den neuen Kabelkanal MTV die Menschen im eigenen Wohnzimmer.

In den 1990ern stand vom Alltag und der Musik inspirierte Mode ebenso im Mittelpunkt wie die grungeartige Anti-Mode und bewusst überschnittene urbane Streetwear. Einige New Yorker Designer – darunter Anna Sui, Christian Francis Roth und Marc Jacobs, der damals für Perry Ellis entwarf – versuchten mit gemischtem Erfolg Grunge-Trends in ihre Kollektionen zu integrieren. Zum Ende des Jahrzehnts änderte sich der Look abermals, als neue Designer wie Miuccia Prada und Tom Ford von Gucci divergierende Interpretationen des neuen Luxus offerierten: Pradas betont minimalistische Raffinesse und Fords sexy Überfluss. Von Anfang an bewiesen beide Designer kluges Markenverständnis und erkannten das Potenzial von Accessoires, um ein breiteres Publikum zu erreichen – wer sich kein komplettes Outfit von Gucci oder Prada leisten konnte, der wollte vielleicht mit einer Gucci-Sonnenbrille oder einem Prada-Rucksack etwas vom Glamour dieser Labels auf sich projizieren. Andere Nobel- und Haute-Couture-Labels sprangen mit eigenen Luxus-Accessoires auf denselben Zug auf. Und bald wetteiferten die Marken darum, dass ihre neuesten Clutch-, Tote- oder Baguette-Modelle zur „It"-Bag der Saison würden.

Als Jahrzehnt und Jahrtausend sich dem Ende zuneigten, rangen die Modefirmen darum, ihre Marken voneinander abzugrenzen. Einige taten dies, indem sie ihre Marketingkampagnen mit einer gewissen Schockwirkung versahen. So geriet etwa Benetton in die Kontroverse, weil die italienische Marke in ihren Anzeigen AIDS, Rassismus und Gewalt gegen Minderheiten thematisierte. Als Provokateur schlechthin sorgte Diesel 1998 für einen Skandal in der Redaktion der Zeitschrift *Mother Jones*, und zwar mit einer Anzeige, die gefesselte Männer und Frauen unter Wasser zeigte, versehen mit dem Slogan „At least you'll leave a beautiful corpse".

Etwa zur gleichen Zeit gab das Haus Dior – inzwischen im Besitz des französischen Marken-Konglomerats Moët Hennessey/Louis Vuitton – die schockierende Nachricht bekannt, John Galliano als Chefdesigner ernannt zu haben. Dieser vergeudete keine Zeit, sondern drückte dem Hause Dior seinen ikonoklastischen Stempel auf; dabei bezog er seine Inspiration aus einer romantischen Melange von englischem Landleben, Pin-up-Girls, Massai-Perlen, Casanova und Obdachlosen-Chic. Dennoch attestierte man dem Enfant terrible, dem Hause Dior – und der Kunst der Haute Couture an sich – einen neuen Sinn für Spaß und jugendliche Kunstfertigkeit zurückgegeben zu haben. In einer Kritik der ersten Galliano-Kollektion für Dior schrieb die *New York Times*, „Mr. Gallianos Show habe ihm selbst, Mr. Dior, dessen Name an der Tür steht, ebenso zur Ehre gereicht wie der Zukunft seiner Kunst, die schließlich stets zur Disposition stünde".

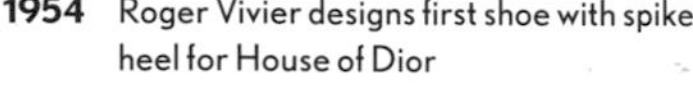

1954

1954 Roger Vivier designs first shoe with spike heel for House of Dior

Roger Vivier entwirft den ersten Schuh mit Pfennigabsatz für das Haus Dior

Roger Vivier conçoit les premières chaussures à talons aiguilles pour la maison Dior

1959 Nudie's Rodeo Tailors make Elvis Presley $10,000 custom gold lamé tuxedo

Nudie's Rodeo Tailors kreiert Elvis Presleys 10,000 $ teuren Maß-Smoking aus Goldlamé

Pour Elvis Presley, Nudie's Rodeo Tailors crée un smoking lamé or sur mesure d'une valeur de 10 000 dollars

1961 American women mimic iconic style of First Lady Jacqueline Kennedy

Amerikanerinnen kopieren den Stil von First Lady Jacqueline Kennedy, der bald Kultstatus erreicht

Les Américaines copient le style élégant de leur première dame, Jacqueline Kennedy

1961 London's music and fashion scene dubbed "Youthquake" by Diana Vreeland

Diana Vreeland nennt die Londoner Musik- und Modeszene "Youthquake"

Diana Vreeland qualifie de « séisme jeune » le milieu londonien de la musique et de la mode

Wool Bureau/Dalton of America, 1964 ◂

QUAND LE PAQUEBOT QUEEN ELIZABETH JETA L'ANCRE À NEW YORK EN SEPTEMBRE 1947, IL COMPTAIT PARMI SES PASSAGERS CHRISTIAN DIOR ET SALVATORE FERRAGAMO, tous deux en route vers Dallas, Texas, pour recevoir leurs prix Neiman Marcus. Six mois plus tôt, Dior avait provoqué une petite révolution en lançant sa première collection à son nom. Etiquetée de « New Look » par la rédactrice en chef d'*Harper's Bazaar* Carmel Snow, la silhouette Dior représentait un changement radical par rapport aux modèles austères et masculins des années de guerre.

« Nous voulons tout oublier de la guerre », expliqua Dior à un reporter du *New York Times* présent sur le port ce jour-là. Après s'être entendu dire que certaines Américaines n'aimaient pas sa nouvelle silhouette en forme de sablier et ses longues jupes amples, Dior répondit : « L'essayer, c'est l'adopter. Aux yeux d'un homme, les jupes longues sont beaucoup plus féminines. » Malgré les questions du journaliste du *Times* en ce jour d'automne 1947, il semblait évident que Dior avait déjà redessiné les formes féminines.

En redynamisant la silhouette féminine, Dior insuffla aussi une nouvelle vie à l'industrie de la mode française qui avait considérablement souffert pendant la Seconde Guerre mondiale. Certains couturiers, comme Mainbocher, s'étaient exilés aux Etats-Unis, tandis que d'autres, notamment Coco Chanel, avaient tout simplement fermé boutique. Tout au long de la guerre, de nombreux pays européens avaient été confrontés à une pénurie de tissu et d'articles de mercerie en raison de politiques de rationnement très rigoureuses. Bien que la pénurie fût moins sévère outre-Atlantique, on avait également interrompu la production des vêtements nécessitant beaucoup de tissu, comme les jupes longues, les coupes en biais et les cols châles.

Le New Look n'était pas qu'une réaction à la silhouette précédente et à la fin des privations de la guerre : il fut aussi le fruit d'un partenariat absolument improbable. Dior, qui avait travaillé avec des couturiers tels Robert Piguet et Lucien Lelong avant la guerre, finit par lancer sa propre maison grâce au soutien financier de son associé Marcel Boussac, un millionnaire français du coton.

Ce partenariat et la collection à laquelle il donna lieu rappelaient la collaboration entre Charles Frederick Worth, le tout premier couturier, et l'impératrice française Eugénie Bonaparte, qui avaient tous deux lancé de nombreuses tendances au 19ème siècle, notamment celle de la volumineuse jupe à cerceaux, ou crinoline. En remplaçant les nombreuses et inconfortables couches de jupons, la crinoline offrait plus de place aux idées de Worth et à la consommation ostentatoire qu'en faisait la cour de Napoléon III. Cependant, la crinoline avait aussi soutenu l'industrie française du textile. Nécessitant plus de neuf mètres de tissu à l'ourlet, cette silhouette demesurée avait relancé les soieries de Lyon alors menacées de banqueroute.

Cette collaboration marqua aussi le début des partenariats entre couturiers et membres de la haute société, une forme d'association qui prit tout son essor au 20ème siècle quand la photographie devint omniprésente et que la jet-set se retrouva dans les journaux et les magazines. Bien longtemps avant des icônes comme Grace Kelly, Jacqueline Kennedy et Lady Diana, le monde entier avait les yeux braqués sur l'Américaine Wallis Simpson, qui venait d'épouser l'ex-roi d'Angleterre, Edouard VIII. Plus tard connu sous le nom de duc de Windsor, Edouard lança de nombreuses tendances. Délaissant les tenues officielles au profit des costumes, il adopta le sportswear décontracté au quotidien sous la forme de culottes de golf et de pulls à col V. Pendant les années 30, les débutantes américaines commencèrent à assumer leur rôle de figures de mode et collaborèrent avec les couturiers pour être sûres d'être vues dans leurs modèles les plus récents lors de leurs sorties en ville. Les magazines de mode suivirent le pas, transformant les femmes de la haute société en mannequins dans leurs photos de mode et leurs éditoriaux.

A la même époque, les femmes s'inspirèrent des stars du grand écran en reproduisant les tenues repérées dans les films ou dans les pages des magazines de fans et les chroniques mondaines. Conscients de l'influence exercée par les

1961

1961 Following president John F. Kennedy's lead, millions of men stop wearing hats

Nach dem Vorbild von Präsident John F. Kennedy hören Millionen von Männern auf, Hüte zu tragen

A l'instar du président John F. Kennedy, des millions d'hommes renoncent au port du chapeau

1963 Peggy Moffitt appears in Rudi Gernreich's monokini

Peggy Moffitt präsentiert Rudi Gernreichs Monokini

Peggy Moffitt pose dans le monokini de Rudi Gernreich

1966 Miniskirt goes mainstream

Der Minirock wird zum Massentrend

La minijupe se démocratise

1966 Mary Quant's "Chelsea Look" is British Invasion of fashion world

Mary Quants „Chelsea Look" ist die britische Invasion in die Modewelt

Le « Chelsea Look » de Mary Quant traduit l'invasion de la mode par les Britanniques

« SANS SOUS-VÊTEMENTS, IL N'Y A PAS DE MODE. » — CHRISTIAN DIOR

célébrités, certains annonceurs leur firent signer des contrats pour promouvoir leurs produits et apparaître dans leurs publicités. L'une des premières marques à avoir exploité le potentiel d'un interprète célèbre fut le fabricant de maillots de bain Jantzen, basé à Portland dans l'Oregon, qui compta parmi ses égéries les champions olympiques Johnny Weissmuller et Duke Kahanamoku, mais aussi les actrices Loretta Young, Joan Blondell, Ginger Rogers et le comédien Dick Powell.

Au fil du siècle, les célébrités prirent la place de la haute société pour lancer les tendances. A partir des années 50, les mannequins commencèrent à occuper le devant de la scène et devinrent des stars à part entière. Dorian Leigh, Suzy Parker, Jean Shrimpton, Twiggy, Brooke Shields, Cheryl Tiegs, Christie Brinkley, Iman, Cindy Crawford et Kate Moss : elles ont toutes incarné le look de leurs époques respectives. Leurs activités, opinions et vies sentimentales ont été scrutées et documentées comme celles de n'importe quelle débutante ou starlette hollywoodienne.

L'arrivée de celles qu'on appelle les top-modèles vit renaître la relation entre le créateur et sa muse, un rapport symbiotique qui remontait déjà à l'époque de l'Impératrice Eugénie et de Worth, le styliste anglais reconnu comme le premier grand couturier de l'histoire.

NÉ EN 1826 À BOURNE DANS LE LINCOLNSHIRE, L'ANGLAIS CHARLES FREDERICK WORTH COMMENÇA À TRAVAILLER TRÈS TÔT COMME VENDEUR DE TISSU, D'ABORD EN ANGLETERRE PUIS À PARIS. En 1858, il ouvrit la maison Worth rue de la Paix à Paris. Avant Worth, les femmes riches commandaient leurs vêtements à des couturières qui suivaient leurs ordres à la lettre. Seule la mode pour homme était conçue par des tailleurs. La naissance de la haute couture coïncida avec l'invention de la machine à coudre et les débuts de l'ère industrielle. La mécanisation et l'automatisation permirent de produire des vêtements en masse pour la classe moyenne émergente. Aux Etats-Unis, les vendeurs par correspondance, comme Montgomery Ward et Sears, Roebuck and Co., se mirent à commercialiser des produits d'usage quotidien – dont les derniers vêtements à la mode – dans les régions les plus reculées du pays. Pendant ce temps, les couturiers européens avaient déjà pris des mesures pour préserver l'artisanat fait main et, en 1868, le gouvernement français s'engagea en fondant la Chambre Syndicale de la Haute Couture de Paris, une organisation strictement réglementée par le Ministère de l'Industrie.

Comme Dior, de nombreux membres de la Chambre Syndicale inventèrent des créations révolutionnaires qui influencèrent considérablement le look de l'époque. Les Américaines les plus fortunées se rendaient en Europe pour acheter des pièces de haute couture, les autres se contentant de leurs reproductions fabriquées « sous licence » et vendues dans les grands magasins de luxe. En l'espace de quelques saisons, les détails repérés dans les collections de haute couture furent repris dans des gammes plus accessibles destinées à une clientèle beaucoup plus large. Voilà comment les tailleurs Chanel en jersey de laine et leurs détails empruntés à la mode masculine devinrent synonymes du look de la femme moderne des années 20. Les tailleurs très structurés d'Elsa Schiaparelli et leurs épaules carrées avec épaulettes s'imposèrent comme le pilier de la mode des années 30 et 40. Les créations architecturales de Cristobal Balenciaga apportèrent un contrepoint au glamour étudié de Dior. Les tenues modernes de Pierre Cardin, qui mettaient l'accent sur les formes pures et graphiques, lancèrent la mode des tenues « space age » dans les années 60.

1972

1972 Catherine Deneuve lends face to Chanel No. 5 throughout '70s

Catherine Deneuve ist in den 70ern das Gesicht zu Chanel N° 5

Catherine Deneuve prête son visage à Chanel N° 5 tout au long des années 70

1972 L'eggs, first pantyhose brand sold in mass retailers, introduces Sheer Energy

L'eggs, die erste im Einzelhandel verkaufte Strumpfhosenmarke, bringt das Modell Sheer Energy auf den Markt

L'eggs, première marque de collants vendue en grande surface, lance son modèle Sheer Energy

1975 Vivienne Westwood and Malcolm McLaren dress Sex Pistols; dawn of punk era

Vivienne Westwood und Malcolm McLaren statten die Sex Pistols aus; Anbruch der Punk-Ära

Vivienne Westwood et Malcolm McLaren habillent les Sex Pistols aux tout débuts du punk

1976 Farrah Fawcett in *Charlie's Angels*, inspires feathered-hair look

Mit *Drei Engel für Charlie* macht Farrah Fawcett den Löwenmähnen-Look populär

Dans *Drôles de dames*, Farrah Fawcett lance la mode du brushing « à la lionne »

C'EST TOUTEFOIS À PAUL POIRET QUE L'ON DOIT LA PREMIÈRE RÉVOLUTION DE LA MODE AU 20ÈME SIÈCLE. Ce couturier français avait quitté la maison Worth avec un concept de mode d'inspiration orientale pour une toute nouvelle silhouette. L'esthétique victorienne avait verrouillé l'idéal féminin dans un corset rigide qui rehaussait la poitrine tout en réduisant le tour de taille à des proportions minuscules. Poiret avait une autre idée de la beauté. Avec son épouse Denise comme muse et mannequin, le couturier travailla sur un corps athlétique plus élancé qu'il drapait dans des robes-colonnes et des manteaux kimonos donnant l'impression que la femme était enveloppée dans un cocon. Exotiques et radicales, ses créations transformèrent la silhouette du corps féminin.

Les robes taillées en biais de Madeleine Vionnet évoquent aujourd'hui l'image de la sulfureuse blonde Jean Harlow et le glamour dépeint par Hollywood au début des années 30 pour faire oublier la dure réalité de la Grande Dépression. Les magazines féminins publiaient encore des pages de mode sur les dernières tendances, mais la plupart d'entre eux proposaient des conseils pour modifier et remettre au goût du jour les vêtements de votre garde-robe.

La publicité de la mode changea de look dans les années 30 : pour attirer l'attention et mettre en avant la qualité des produits, les magazines et les annonceurs comptaient plus sur la photographie et leurs dessinateurs maison moins onéreux que sur les illustrateurs célèbres. Cette transition marqua la fin d'un patrimoine de publicités faisant appel à des artistes aussi connus que J. C. Leyendecker, dont le travail pour les chemises Arrow et les chaussettes Interwoven véhiculait sophistication et panache, Maxfield Parrish et ses illustrations Art Nouveau, Coles Phillips et les pin-up qu'il dessinait pour Holeproof Hosiery, ou George Petty, dont la femme aux longues jambes avait fait sa première apparition en tant que plongeuse du logo Jantzen.

Alors que les magazines et les annonceurs licenciaient à tour de bras, les Américains à court d'argent recherchaient des alternatives de consommation. Considérée comme la mère de ce qui allait devenir le « look américain », Claire McCardell conçut toutes sortes de modèles, des tenues de tous les jours aux vêtements de ski et de plein air en passant par les robes de mariée. Des années 30 à la fin des années 50, ses ensembles coordonnés s'imposèrent dans la plupart des garde-robes féminines. Le denim, le calicot et les carreaux madras devinrent ses tissus signature, la styliste privilégiant également les détails comme les surpiqûres, les capuches, les bretelles spaghettis et les poches plaquées, mais aussi les collants de danse et les corsaires.

Pendant que Claire McCardell s'activait à New York, le style décontracté de la côte ouest californienne commença à influencer les tendances du sportswear. Carmel Snow de *Harper's Bazaar* « découvrit » la costumière Bonnie Cashin, destinée à devenir directrice de la création chez le fabricant de tailleurs Adler & Adler. En quarante ans de carrière, Bonnie Cashin a tout fait, des tailleurs et manteaux d'Adler & Adler aux costumes du film *Laura* (1944) en passant par des accessoires pour Coach et Hermès.

La côte ouest, également berceau de l'industrie des vêtements de plage, vit prospérer des marques comme Jantzen, Catalina et Cole of California. Abandonnant les maillots

1977 Men's leisure-suit trend reaches height of popularity

Der Trend zum Freizeitanzug für Männer erreicht seinen Höhepunkt

Le costume disco pour homme atteint des sommets de popularité

1977 Studio 54 opens in New York, soon becoming the epicenter of disco chic

In New York öffnet das Studio 54 und avanciert bald zum Epizentrum des Disco-Chic

Ouverture du Studio 54 à New York, qui devient rapidement l'épicentre du disco chic

1977 Roy Halston Frowick defines disco era as designer for Studio 54 crowd

Roy Halston Frowick prägt als Designer für das Studio 54-Publikum die Disco-Ära

Le tailleur Roy Halston Frowick incarne l'ère du disco auprès des habitués du Studio 54

1978 Gianni Versace launches in Milan

Gianni Versace gibt in Mailand sein Debut

Gianni Versace fait ses débuts à Milan

en laine trop lourds, la structure du maillot de bain fut révolutionnée par l'invention du bikini en 1946. Dans les années 50 et 60, cette nouveauté audacieuse joua un rôle de premier plan dans les films à succès sur les thèmes de la plage et du surf qui contribuèrent à exporter les tendances de la mode nautique bien au-delà du littoral.

MALGRÉ LE SUCCÈS RAPIDE ET UNIVERSEL DU NEW LOOK DE DIOR, SON RÈGNE COÏNCIDA AVEC CELUI D'AUTRES COUTURIERS TELS CARDIN ET BALENCIAGA, dont la vision de la beauté permit l'avènement de la mode « space age » dans les années 60. Pionnier de cet ultramodernisme, André Courrèges créa des vêtements faussement simples aux couleurs soutenues qui avaient l'air taillés dans du plastique rigide et non dans du tissu. Ses jupes courtes et ses bottes blanches à talons plats furent à la fois l'emblème de la décennie et une source d'inspiration pour toute une génération de créateurs. Rudi Gernreich, contemporain de Courrèges vivant à Los Angeles, adopta aussi l'approche moderniste, mais avec une philosophie créative encore plus conceptuelle. Surtout connu pour son monokini « topless », Gernreich inventa également la brassière souple pour compléter ses créations farfelues. Avec sa muse et mannequin préférée Peggy Moffitt, Gernreich participa à l'élaboration du look Mod, tandis que le mari de Peggy, le photographe William Claxton, l'aida à l'immortaliser. Pendant que Courrèges et Gernreich hissaient l'ourlet des robes vers de nou-

1978

1978 Miuccia Prada takes helm at Prada

Miuccia Prada übernimmt die Leitung von Prada

Miuccia Prada reprend la direction de Prada

1979 Sasson launches "Oo la la!" campaign

Sasson startet die Kampagne "Oo la la!"

Sasson lance sa campagne « Oo la la! »

1980 Brooke Shields appears in Calvin Klein jeans campaign

Brooke Shields posiert für die Jeans-Kampagne von Calvin Klein

Brooke Shields pose pour la campagne publicitaire des jeans Calvin Klein

1980 PETA begins to give furs bad name

PETA beginnt mit Anti-Pelz-Aktionen

Le PETA commence à ternir l'image de la fourrure

Dexter Shoes, 1971 ◂◂

Kenzo Menswear, 1985 ◂

▸▸ Guess Lingerie, 1992

veaux sommets, la styliste anglaise Mary Quant et son « Chelsea Look » firent descendre la minijupe dans la rue.

A la fin des années 60, Yves Saint Laurent, ex-styliste de Dior, lança une griffe qui remettait en question les conventions tout en définissant les tendances. Les créations de Saint Laurent furent rapidement reprises par la mode grand public. Du smoking classique pour homme, appelé « Le Smoking », aux pièces inspirées des vêtements russes, tsiganes et africains, Saint Laurent influença clairement la mode de la rue des années 60 et 70.

Les années 70 virent aussi évoluer le jean – jusqu'alors réservé aux ouvriers, à la contre-culture et aux ados – au rang de véritable basique de mode. La domination du denim, et l'importance du branding, se poursuivit tout au long du siècle, de vénérables marques comme Levi's, Lee et Wrangler entrant en concurrence avec des griffes de créateurs telles que Jordache, Calvin Klein, Guess et Diesel. Pour faire oublier le passé utilitaire du denim et le faire entrer dans la mode du futur, il fallait de nouvelles coupes, de nouveaux délavages et un nouveau message marketing. Calvin Klein fut l'un des premiers à en prendre conscience. Il fit la réputation de sa marque, et celle de Brooke Shields au passage, grâce à son inoubliable visuel publicitaire de 1980 photographié par Richard Avedon, sur lequel la jeune mannequin de quinze ans déclarait qu'il n'y aurait jamais rien entre elle et son Calvin.

TOUT AU LONG DES ANNÉES 80, LES GRIFFES DE LUXE – EN PARTICULIER CALVIN KLEIN – TRAVAILLÈRENT AVEC UN NOMBRE DE PHOTOGRAPHES SANS CESSE CROISSANT, notamment Steven Meisel, Patrick Demarchelier, Mario Testino et Helmut Newton. Face au succès de son affiche avec Brooke Shields, Calvin Klein continua de recourir aux images controversées pour vendre ses sous-vêtements et ses jeans. Le photographe Bruce Weber signa un grand nombre de pubs mémorables pour Calvin Klein qui présentaient des hommes aux corps sculptés plus ou moins dévêtus, tandis qu'Herb Ritts, toujours pour Calvin Klein en 1992, mit en scène un jeune rappeur blanc en slip nommé Marky Mark (alias Mark Wahlberg) dans une affiche géante qui, une fois placardée au-dessus de Times Square, choqua les touristes et les New-Yorkais.

De même, le spécialiste du jean Guess modernisa la pin-up d'autrefois grâce à un mélange de top-modèles (Claudia Schiffer et Naomi Campbell furent toutes deux des Guess girls) et de célébrités (Anna Nicole Smith, qui doit sa renommée à Guess).

La silhouette changea à nouveau dans les années 80. Alors que plus de femmes entraient dans le monde du travail et commençaient à occuper des postes à responsabilités, des créateurs tels Giorgio Armani, Donna Karan et Claude Montana leur proposèrent des tailleurs aux épaules très marquées. Menée par la styliste Rei Kawakubo de Comme des Garçons, une vague avant-gardiste déferla aussi sur le Japon. Au même moment, la nouvelle chaîne câblée MTV popularisait les tendances inspirées par la scène musicale, du punk à la pop en passant par la new wave.

Dans les années 90, les looks de la rue et les fans de musique occupèrent une place centrale grâce au mouvement anti-mode du grunge et aux vêtements surdimensionnés du streetwear urbain. Plusieurs créateurs de New York – Anna Sui, Christian Francis Roth et Marc Jacobs, qui travaillait alors pour Perry Ellis – tentèrent d'intégrer les tendances grunge dans leurs collections, mais avec des résultats mitigés. Vers la fin du siècle, le look changea encore une fois avec l'arrivée des stylistes Miuccia Prada et Tom Ford (chez Gucci) qui proposèrent des visions divergentes du nouveau luxe : Prada mit l'accent sur la sophistication minimaliste, tandis que Tom Ford inventa un look sexy et décadent. Ces deux créateurs comprirent très rapidement les stratégies de branding et exploitèrent tout le potentiel des accessoires pour toucher un plus large public : le consommateur qui n'avait pas les moyens de s'offrir un ensemble Gucci ou Prada pouvait s'approprier le glamour de la marque en achetant des lunettes de soleil Gucci ou un

1982 Oliviero Toscani launches controversial "United Colors" campaign for Benetton

Oliviero Toscani präsentiert die umstrittene Kampagne "United Colors" für Benetton

Oliviero Toscani crée « United Colors », la campagne controversée de Benetton

1982 Jane Fonda's workout video sparks excercise craze

Jane Fondas Workout-Video löst einen Fitness-Wahn aus

La vidéo d'aérobic de Jane Fonda déclenche la folie du fitness

1983 Power suits from Claude Montana, YSL, and Donna Karan sport XL shoulder pads

Power Suits von Claude Montana, YSL und Donna Karan bringen Schulterpolster im XL-Format in Mode

Les power suits de Claude Montana, d'YSL et de Donna Karan affichent des épaulettes extra larges

1985 Nike introduces Air Jordan model

Nike stellt sein Modell Air Jordan vor

Nike lance son modèle Air Jordan

« CE N'EST PAS MOI QUI ÉTAIS EN AVANCE SUR MON TEMPS, MAIS MON TEMPS QUI ÉTAIT EN RETARD SUR MOI. » — ANDRÉ COURRÈGES

sac à dos Prada. Les autres marques de luxe ou de haute couture rejoignirent le mouvement en lançant leurs propres accessoires, rêvant toutes de voir leur dernier modèle de sac à main, de cabas ou de pochette être déclaré « it bag » de la saison.

A l'approche du troisième millénaire, les griffes de mode rivalisèrent d'inventivité pour se distinguer. Pour certaines, cela revenait à injecter un peu de provocation dans leur communication marketing. Benetton suscita la controverse quand la marque italienne aborda les problèmes du sida, du racisme et des violences ethniques dans ses publicités. En 1998, l'éternel provocateur Diesel scandalisa les journalistes du magazine *Mother Jones* avec une publicité présentant des hommes et des femmes sous l'eau enchaînés à des parpaings, assortie du slogan : « Au moins, vous ferez un beau cadavre ».

A la même époque, la maison Dior – désormais propriété du groupe français LVMH – décida aussi de choquer en nommant John Galliano à la direction de la respectable marque. Ce dernier ne perdit pas de temps pour imprimer sa patte iconoclaste aux collections Dior, puisant son inspiration dans un cocktail romantique de campagne anglaise, de pin-up, de perles massaï, de Casanova et de SDF.

On reconnaît à l'enfant terrible l'exploit d'avoir insufflé un nouveau sens de l'humour et une créativité débordante de jeunesse à la maison Dior, mais aussi à l'art de la haute couture en soi. En effet, dans sa critique de la première collection de Galliano pour Dior, *The New York Times* écrivait : « Le défilé de M. Galliano est tout à son honneur, à celui de M. Dior, dont le nom est écrit sur la porte, et à l'avenir de l'art, sans cesse remis en question. »

1990

1990 International celebrity models dubbed "supermodels"

International berühmte Fotomodels heißen fortan "Topmodels"

Les mannequins mondialement célèbres sont surnommés les « top-modèles »

1994 Tommy Hilfiger gets boost from Snoop Dogg appearance on *Saturday Night Live*

Tommy Hilfiger profitiert von Snoop Doggs Auftritt bei *Saturday Night Live*

Snoop Dogg donne un coup de pouce à Tommy Hilfiger en portant ses vêtements au *Saturday Night Live*

1994 Courtney Love brings back baby-doll dress

Courtney Love bringt das Babydoll-Kleid wieder in Mode

Courtney Love remet les robes babydoll à la mode

1999 Daniella Clarke launches Frankie B. and low-rise premium-denim market

Daniella Clarke führt Frankie B. ein und öffnet damit den Markt für tief geschnittene Nobeljeans

En lançant sa griffe Frankie B., Daniella Clarke invente le marché du jean taille basse en denim de qualité supérieure

GEORGES MARCIANO

DRESSED IN THE STYLES OF THE DAY, THE GIBSON GIRL WORE LONG SKIRTS AND SHIRTWAIST TOPS OVER A TIGHTLY CORSETED FIGURE ... BY MID-DECADE, THE SEARS, ROEBUCK AND CO. CATALOG WAS ADVERTISING 150 STYLES OF SHIRTWAIST.

NACH DER AKTUELLEN MODE GEKLEIDET TRUG DAS GIBSON GIRL LANGE RÖCKE UND HEMDBLUSENOBERTEILE AN IHREM VON EINEM KORSETT STRAMM GESCHNÜRTEN KÖRPER ... DIESER LOOK WAR EIN SO DURCHSCHLAGENDER ERFOLG, DASS DER KATALOG VON SEARS, ROEBUCK UND CO. UM DIE MITTE DES JAHRZEHNTS SAGE UND SCHREIBE 150 VARIANTEN VON HEMDBLUSEN ANBOT.

TOUJOURS À LA POINTE DE LA MODE, LA GIBSON GIRL PORTE DE LONGUES JUPES ET DES CORSAGES SUR UNE SILHOUETTE FERMEMENT CORSETÉE ... CE LOOK SE RÉPAND SI VITE QUE, VERS 1905, LE CATALOGUE SEARS, ROEBUCK AND CO. FAIT LA PROMOTION DE 150 MODÈLES DE CORSAGES.

1900

A BELLE-ÉPOQUE BREAK WITH THE PAST
DIE BELLE ÉPOQUE BRICHT MIT VERGANGENEM
LA BELLE ÉPOQUE : RUPTURE AVEC LE PASSÉ

-1909

Colgate's Talc Powder, 1908 ◂

Royal Worcester Corsets, 1902

THE FIRST DECADE OF THE NEW CENTURY WAS FILLED WITH HOPE, ANTICIPATION, AND INNOVATION. The effects of the Industrial Revolution spreading across Europe and North America had radically shifted Western society from an agrarian culture to a modern, urban one. With it came the new middle class—filled with upwardly mobile businessmen and their families, ready to consume the goods the marketplace could now deliver.

It would be a decade of firsts. The Exposition Universelle in Paris in 1900 publicized talking movies, diesel engines, and telescopes, but it also gave visitors a glimpse of Art Nouveau, whose sensuous, rounded shapes and curving lines were a dramatic departure from the Victorian emphasis on minute details and exaggerated adornment. The Wright brothers first took flight in Kitty Hawk, North Carolina, in 1903. That same year, the first movie—*The Great Train Robbery*, which had a running time of 12 minutes—debuted in America. Within five years, 10,000 stores had been converted to nickelodeons, and the modern film age had begun.

Before the widespread adoption of the camera (soon to take off with Kodak's inexpensive and easy-to-use Brownie model) the turn-of-the century ideal of beauty was propagated by the illustrators of the day. Chief among them was Charles Dana Gibson, who popularized his version of the ideal woman—shapely, with large eyes, delicate features, and a pile of luxurious, dark hair. The "Gibson Girl" became so popular that, in 1900, *Life* magazine began running a serial cartoon featuring her daily adventures. Dressed in the styles of the day, the Gibson Girl wore long skirts and shirtwaist tops over a tightly corseted figure. A wide-brimmed hat—sometimes trimmed in exotic bird feathers—was perched atop her upswept hair. The look was so pervasive that, by mid-decade, the Sears, Roebuck and Co. catalog was advertising 150 styles of shirtwaist. The prodigious use of feathers—from exotic ostriches and egrets to more commonplace skylarks, pigeons and wrens—led the to the formation of the National Audobon Society, which protested the slaughter of birds for the sake of fashion.

Men wore the slim-suited look, often topped with a bowler in the daytime, sticking to formal attire for evening. Chicago suitmaker Hart Schaffner & Marx began introducing suits in "basic body" types. Menswear's looks were rapidly heading for the mass market.

Womenswear, on the other hand, was heading for revolutionary changes, due, in large part, to Paul Poiret, a former protégé of Paris couturier Charles Worth. Poiret opened his Paris salon in 1903 with a new vision for women's apparel. Inspired by Orientalism, Poiret's designs were truly radical. Kimono-style opera coats, turbans, harem pants, and, perhaps most shocking of all, the appearance of an uncorseted shape. Still considered avant-garde in most circles, it would be another 10 years until the corset began to fall from popularity. In fact, due to concerns that the tight-lacing models popularized in the mid-1800s could be harmful, the "S-bend" or "health" corset—which thrust the torso forward and hips back, therefore putting less pressure on the abdomen—was introduced in 1900, only to be replaced by the long-line corset. The girdle would soon follow.

1900

1900 Art Nouveau peaks at Universal Expo, Paris, signaling end of Victorian Era styles

Höhepunkt des Jugendstils auf der Pariser Weltausstellung und Signal für das Ende der Mode viktorianischen Stils

l'Art Nouveau connaît son apogée lors de l'Exposition Universelle de Paris et signe la fin du style de l'ère victorienne

1900 Charles Dana Gibson's "Gibson Girl" appears weekly in *Life* magazine serialization

Charles Dana Gibsons „Gibson Girl" erscheint allwöchentlich als Serienfigur in der Zeitschrift *Life*

La « Gibson Girl » de Charles Dana Gibson apparaît chaque semaine en bande dessinée dans le magazine *Life*

1901 Booming sales of shirtwaist blouse

Der Verkauf von Hemdblusen boomt

Les ventes de corsages explosent

1901 Height of womens' heels lowers to under three inches; Louis XIV heel popular

Die Absatzhöhe für Damen sinkt unter 7,5 Zentimeter; Louis-XIV-Absatz ist gefragt

Le talon des chaussures pour femme descend sous la barre des huit centimètres ; c'est la mode du talon Louis XIV

DIE ERSTE DEKADE DES NEUEN JAHRHUNDERTS WAR EINE ZEIT DER HOFFNUNG, ERWARTUNG UND ERNEUERUNG. Die Auswirkungen der Industriellen Revolution, die in ganz Europa und Nordamerika spürbar waren, hatten aus der bis dato landwirtschaftlich geprägten westlichen Gesellschaft auf radikale Art eine modern-urbane gemacht. Im Zuge dieser Entwicklung entstand auch eine neue Mittelschicht – aufstrebende Geschäftsleute und deren Familien, die nur zu bereit waren, all die Waren zu konsumieren, die der Markt plötzlich zu bieten hatte.

Es sollte ein Jahrzehnt der „Ersten" werden. So wurden 1900 auf der Weltausstellung in Paris der Öffentlichkeit erstmals Tonfilme, Dieselmotoren und das größte Linsenfernrohr vorgestellt, zugleich bekamen die Besucher aber auch einen Eindruck vom Jugendstil, der sich mit seinen sinnlichen runden Formen und geschwungenen Linien auf geradezu dramatische Weise von der viktorianischen Vorliebe für winzigste Details und übertriebenes Dekor unterschied. 1903 unternahmen die Gebrüder Wright in Kitty Hawk, North Carolina, ihren ersten Flug. Im selben Jahr hatte der erste Kinofilm – *The Great Train Robbery*, mit einer Länge von 12 Minuten – sein Amerikadebüt. Innerhalb von fünf Jahren wurden 10.000 Geschäfte zu Nickelodeons (Vorläufern der späteren Kinos) umgebaut; damit hatte das moderne Kinozeitalter begonnen.

Vor dem verbreiteten Einsatz von Fotoapparaten (der mit Kodaks preiswertem und leicht zu bedienendem Brownie seinen Anfang nehmen sollte) wurde das Schönheitsideal der Jahrhundertwende von den Illustratoren der Tagespresse verbreitet. Der wichtigste unter ihnen war Charles Dana Gibson, der sein Idealbild einer Frau – wohlgeformt, mit großen Augen, feinen Zügen und einer prachtvollen dunklen Haarflut – popularisierte. Das „Gibson Girl" war schließlich so berühmt, dass die Zeitschrift *Life* ihr für ihre Alltagsabenteuer eine eigene Cartoon-Serie zubilligte. Nach der aktuellen Mode gekleidet trug das Gibson Girl lange Röcke und Hemdblusenoberteile an ihrem von einem Korsett stramm geschnürten Körper. Ein breitkrempiger Hut – manchmal mit exotischen Vogelfedern geschmückt – thronte auf ihrer Hochsteckfrisur. Dieser Look war ein so durchschlagender Erfolg, dass der Katalog von Sears, Roebuck and Co. um die Mitte des Jahrzehnts sage und schreibe 150 Varianten von Hemdblusen anbot. Die maßlose Verwendung von Federn – angefangen bei exotischen Straußen- und Reihern- bis hin zu gewöhnlicheren wie Lerchen-, Tauben- und Zaunkönigfedern – führte zur Gründung der National Audobon Society, die sich gegen die Tötung von Vögeln zu Modezwecken engagierte.

Die Herren trugen tagsüber schmale Anzüge, oft mit einem Filzhut und hielten sich abends nach wie vor an die traditionellen Kleidervorschriften. Der Anzughersteller Hart Schaffner & Marx aus Chicago brachte als erster Anzüge für unterschiedliche „Körpertypen" auf den Markt. Überhaupt strebten die Trends der Herrenmode rasch nach dem Massenmarkt.

Die Damenmode hatte dagegen revolutionäre Veränderungen im Sinn, was sie größtenteils Paul Poiret, dem ehemaligen Schützling des Pariser Couturiers Charles Worth verdankte. 1903 eröffnete Poiret seinen Pariser Salon mit einer neuen Vision für die Damenbekleidung. Seine orientalisch inspirierten Kreationen waren geradezu radikal. Opernmäntel im Kimonostil, Turbane, Pluderhosen und das vielleicht Schockierendste überhaupt: eine weibliche Silhouette ohne Korsett. Das galt in den meisten Kreisen lange als avantgardistisch, und es sollte noch weitere zehn Jahre dauern, bis die Popularität des Korsetts nachließ. Man führte im Jahr 1900, nachdem gesundheitliche Bedenken gegen die seit Mitte des 19. Jahrhunderts beliebten eng geschnürten Modelle aufgekommen waren, sogar noch ein „s-förmiges" oder „Gesundheits"-Korsett ein, das den Brustkorb nach vorn und die Hüften nach hinten drückte und dadurch den Druck auf den Bauch verringerte. Darauf folgte ein längeres Modell und schließlich bald der Hüfthalter.

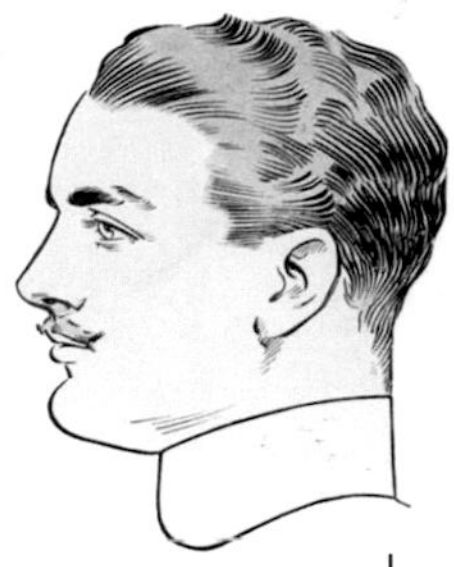

1901

1901 With over 25 collar manufacturers, Troy, NY, becomes known as "Collar City"

Über 25 Kragen-Manufakturen sichern Troy im Bundesstaat New York den Spitznamen „Collar City"

Avec plus de 25 fabricants de cols, la ville de Troy dans l'Etat de New York devient célèbre en tant que « Collar City »

1903 First World Series played: Boston Americans 5, Pittsburgh Pirates 3

Die ersten World Series werden gespielt: Boston Americans 5, Pittsburgh Pirates 3

Première World Series de baseball : Boston Americans 5, Pittsburgh Pirates 3

1903 Couturier Paul Poiret opens salon in Paris

Couturier Paul Poiret eröffnet seinen Pariser Modesalon

Le couturier Paul Poiret ouvre un salon à Paris

1904 Brown Shoe adopts Buster Brown name and character at St. Louis World's Fair

Brown Shoe setzt bei der Weltausstellung in St. Louis auf den Namen und die Figur Buster Brown

A l'Exposition Universelle de Saint-Louis, la société Brown Shoe adopte le nom et le personnage de Buster Brown

American Lady
American Lady

Butterick Dress Patterns, 1906 ◄◄

American Lady Shoes, 1906 ◄

LA PREMIÈRE DÉCENNIE DU NOUVEAU SIÈCLE EST UNE PÉRIODE PLEINE D'ESPOIRS, D'ATTENTES ET D'INNOVATIONS. A travers toute l'Europe et l'Amérique du Nord, les effets de la révolution industrielle transforment radicalement la société occidentale, la culture rurale cédant du terrain à la culture urbaine moderne. Ils provoquent l'émergence de la nouvelle classe moyenne – composée d'hommes d'affaires ambitieux et de leurs familles – prête à consommer les produits que le marché est désormais en mesure de lui proposer.

Ce devait être la décennie des premières. En 1900, l'Exposition Universelle de Paris présente les films parlants, les moteurs diesel et les télescopes, mais permet aussi aux visiteurs de découvrir l'Art Nouveau, dont les formes rondes voluptueuses et les lignes arrondies tranchent de façon spectaculaire avec l'insistance victorienne sur les petits détails et l'ornementation chargée. En 1903, les frères Wright effectuent leur premier vol en avion à Kitty Hawk, Caroline du Nord. La même année, *Le Vol du grand rapide* – le tout premier film de cinéma, d'une durée de 12 minutes seulement – sort sur les écrans américains. En l'espace de cinq ans, 10 000 boutiques se reconvertissent en salles de projection, annonçant les débuts de l'ère cinématographique moderne.

Bien avant la démocratisation de l'appareil photo (qui devait connaître un essor rapide grâce au modèle Brownie, pratique et bon marché, de Kodak), ce sont les illustrateurs qui véhiculent l'idéal de beauté en ce début de siècle. Parmi les plus éminents, Charles Dana Gibson popularise sa propre version de la femme idéale : bien faite, avec de grands yeux, des traits fins et une épaisse et luxueuse crinière brune. La « Gibson Girl » remporte un tel succès qu'en 1900 le magazine *Life* lance un feuilleton en bande dessinée racontant ses aventures quotidiennes. Toujours à la pointe de la mode, la Gibson Girl porte de longues jupes et des corsages sur une silhouette fermement corsetée. Ses cheveux remontés sont coiffés d'un chapeau à larges bords, parfois décoré de plumes d'oiseaux exotiques. Ce look se répand si vite que, vers 1905, le catalogue Sears, Roebuck and Co. fait la promotion de 150 modèles de corsages. L'utilisation prodigue des plumes – d'autruches et d'aigrettes exotiques aux espèces plus courantes comme l'alouette, le pigeon et le roitelet – mène à la fondation de la National Audobon Society, une association qui proteste contre le massacre des oiseaux au profit de la mode.

Les hommes portent des costumes près du corps, souvent avec un chapeau melon la journée, s'en tenant aux habits classiques pour le soir. Hart Schaffner & Marx, un tailleur de Chicago, commence à proposer des modèles de costumes « standard ». La mode pour homme s'oriente rapidement vers le marché de masse.

A l'opposé, la mode pour femme s'apprête à connaître des changements révolutionnaires principalement dus à Paul Poiret, un ancien protégé du couturier parisien Charles Worth. Fort d'une nouvelle vision de la mode féminine, Poiret ouvre son salon à Paris en 1903. Inspirées par l'orientalisme, ses créations sont vraiment radicales : manteaux de soirée en forme de kimono, turbans, pantalons de harem et – sans doute le plus grand choc – l'introduction d'une silhouette sans corset. Poiret étant encore considéré comme un avant-gardiste dans la plupart des milieux, il faudra attendre dix ans de plus pour que le corset commence à perdre en popularité. En raison des inquiétudes suscitées par les modèles à laçage très serré qui étaient en vogue au milieu du 19ème siècle, le corset « en S » – qui projette le torse vers l'avant et les hanches vers l'arrière en exerçant donc moins de pression sur l'abdomen – avait été lancé en 1900, avant d'être remplacé par le corset long. La gaine n'allait pas tarder à suivre.

1906

1906 Men offered wider variety of footwear styles

Das Angebot der Schuhmodelle für den Herrn vergrößert sich

Les hommes disposent d'un plus grand choix de chaussures

1907 Annette Kellerman performance in one-piece bathing suit leads to athletic styles

Annette Kellermans Auftritt im einteiligen Badeanzug setzt den Beginn sportlich-athletischer Trends

Les exploits de la nageuse Annette Kellerman en maillot de bain une pièce lancent la mode du sportswear

1908 B.V.D. introduces loose-fitting underwear for men

B.V.D. führt locker sitzende Herrenunterwäsche ein

B.V.D. commercialise des sous-vêtements amples pour homme

1908 Ford's open Model T brings cars—and motor robes—to masses

Fords offenes Model T macht Autos – und Autofahrer-Garderobe – zum Massenartikel

La Model T décapotable de Ford démocratise la voiture – et les vêtements automobiles – auprès du grand public

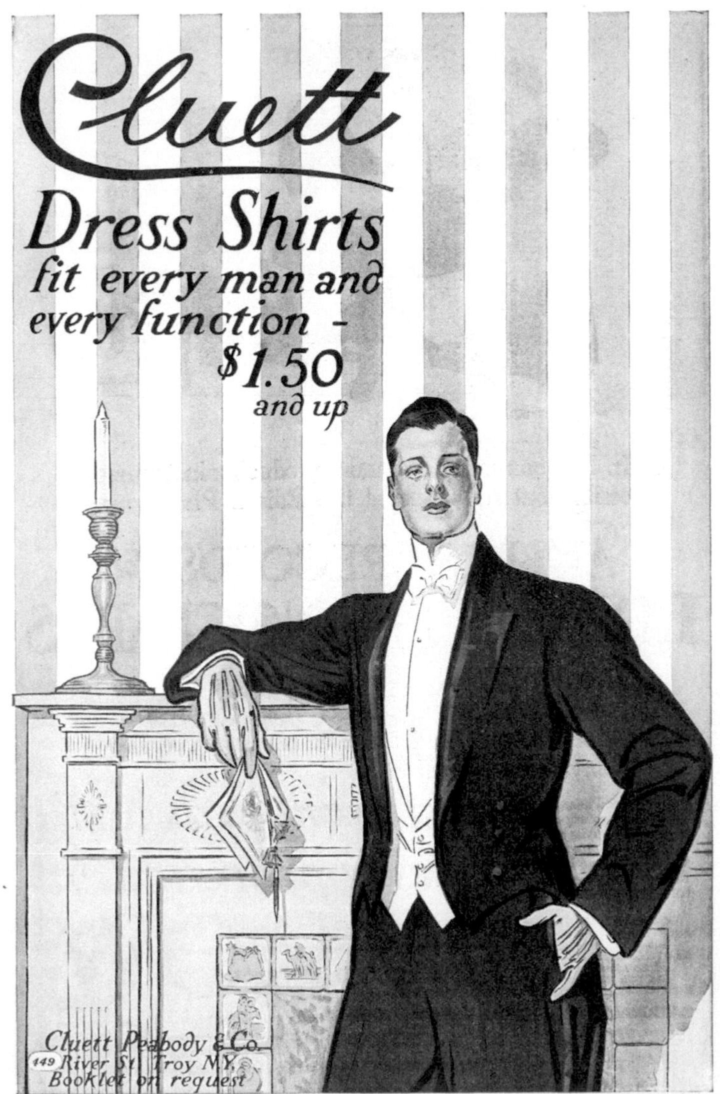

Arrow Collars, 1909

Cluett Shirts, 1909

► Cluett Shirts, 1904

Warner's
Rust-Proof
Corsets

►► Kuppenheimer Menswear, 1907

The lounge suit, precursor to the modern business suit, was an alternative to the more formal morning coat, and was being adopted by men of the emerging middle class.

Der Gesellschaftsanzug, Vorläufer des modernen Straßenanzugs, war eine Alternative zum formelleren Stresemann, und vor allem bei den Herren der aufkeimenden Mittelschicht gefragt.

Le « lounge suit », précurseur du costume masculin moderne, offrait une alternative au peignoir plus formel et fut adopté par les hommes de la classe moyenne émergente.

R & G Corsets, 1904

Warner's Rust-Proof Corsets, 1909 ◄

℄ The constant advance in culture and good taste is but another argument for the wearing of Kuppenheimer Clothes. ℄ You'll find exclusive fabrics and styles in our garments—effects which have always placed Kuppenheimer suits and overcoats beyond the commonplace.

In almost every community where there is a good clothier—a particular merchant—there is a representative of The House of Kuppenheimer who has a complete array of the authoritative styles for Fall and Winter. We'll gladly send you a book of authentic fashions, "Styles for Men," merely for the asking.

THE HOUSE OF KUPPENHEIMER

CHICAGO NEW YORK BOSTON

THE reasons for buying Hart Schaffner & Marx clothes are the same for full dress and Tuxedo as for business suits and overcoats. Correct style, exact tailoring, rigid honesty in all-wool fabrics, perfect fit.
For six cents we'll send our new Style Book; very artistic cover; a new subject, powerfully treated, in rich colors. The book shows many clothing styles
Hart Schaffner & Marx

On Fifth Avenue, New York
Copyright by Hart Schaffner & Marx
MEN who are most particular about style, whoever or wherever they are, find our clothes wholly satisfactory, in fit, fabric, finish. Our mark in clothes is a sign of quality.
See it before you buy; a small thing to look for, a big thing to find. Send for the new Style Book.
Hart Schaffner & Marx
Good Clothes Makers
New York
Boston
Chicago

THE important thing with us is to make clothes as good as we know how; and to know how. We learn every day; our full-dress clothes are the latest and highest expressions of our skill.
Send six cents for the Spring Style Book; handsome poster cover with many styles illustrated.
Hart Schaffner & Marx
Good Clothes Makers

Copyright 1909 by Hart Schaffner & Marx
CRITICAL dressers will find nothing to criticise in the evening and dinner clothes we make; in richness of fabrics; silk linings; perfection of style and finish; fit; they are right.
When you buy dress clothes look for our mark; it's a big thing to find. Send six cents for the Style Book.
Hart Schaffner & Marx
Good Clothes Makers

Hart Schaffner & Marx Menswear, 1909 Hart Schaffner & Marx Menswear, 1909 Hart Schaffner & Marx Menswear, 1908 Hart Schaffner & Marx Menswear, 1908

44

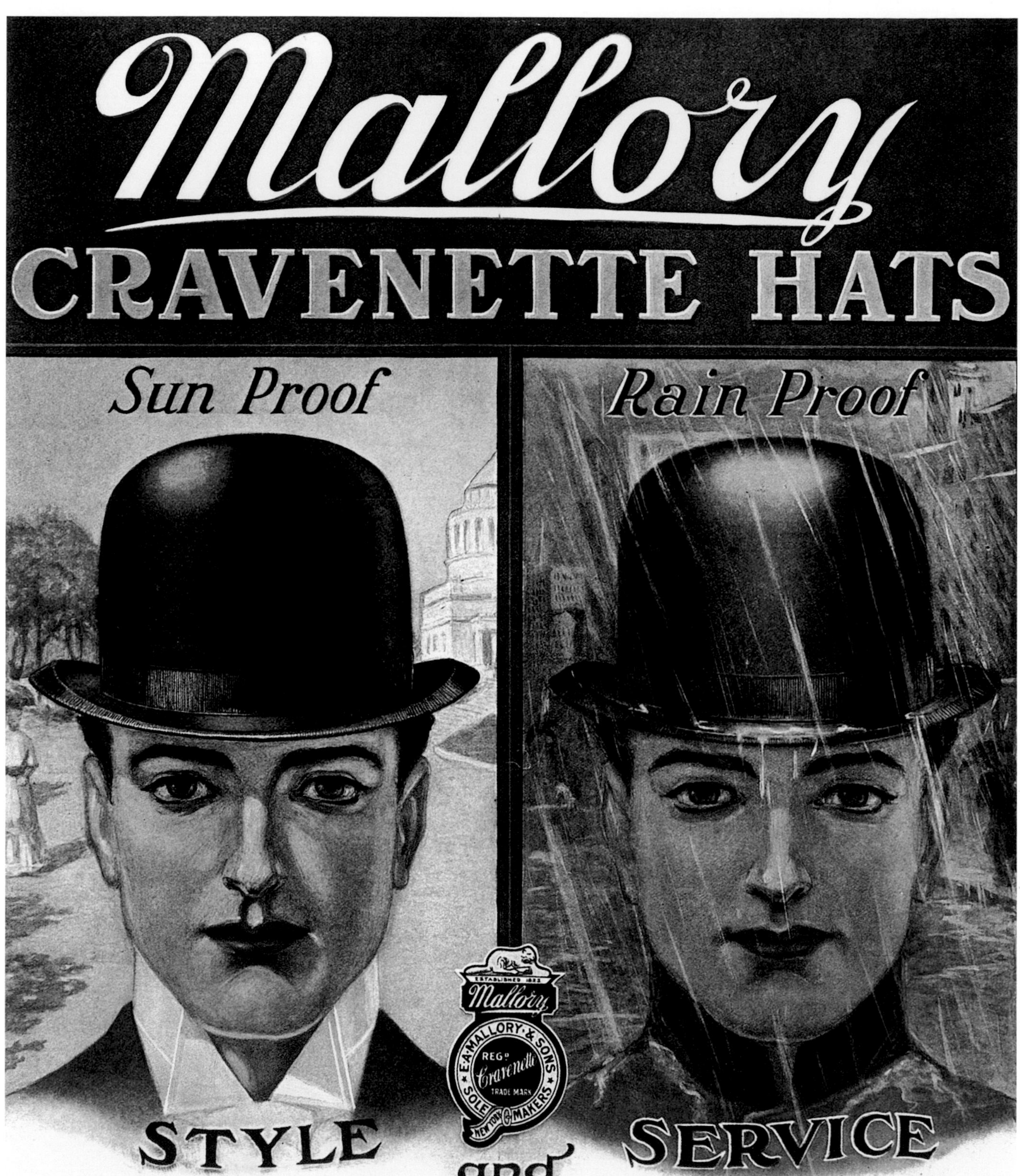

Mallory Hats, 1907

Named for William Bowler, a 19th-century London hat manufacturer, the bowler hat – also called the derby or the coke – continued to be in vogue in the early years of the 20th century.

Der nach William Bowler, einem Londoner Hutmacher aus dem 19. Jahrhundert, benannte Bowler – in England auch Coke, im deutschen Sprachraum Melone oder Koks genannt – war bis zu Beginn des 20. Jahrhunderts in Mode.

Nommé d'après William Bowler, un chapelier londonien du 19ème siècle, le « bowler », chapeau melon en français, était encore à la mode au début du 20ème siècle.

► Fred Kauffmann Tailor, 1903

FRED KAUFFMANN'S

BUILT TO ORDER GARMENTS

UNION MADE

Are ***better*** than others, even if produced from the ***same materials.*** It's the skill in drafting and cutting, the care in putting them together, the constant watchfulness and attention to the smallest details that makes the difference. You'll appreciate how ***great*** this difference ***really is*** when Kauffmann becomes your Tailor.

Suits $14 to $35

Pants $4 to $9

Made in ***any style*** from your own choice of 500 or more new Fall and Winter Fabrics. Kauffmann probably has a representative in your town. If not, he will be pleased to arrange with a reputable merchant.

UNIFORMS

We claim to be the largest house producing **Built-to-Order Uniforms** in the United States. If you want anything in the Uniform line, it may pay you to write to us.

FRED KAUFFMANN

The American Tailor

Nos. 180-186 Market Street, Chicago, Ill.

Established 1880

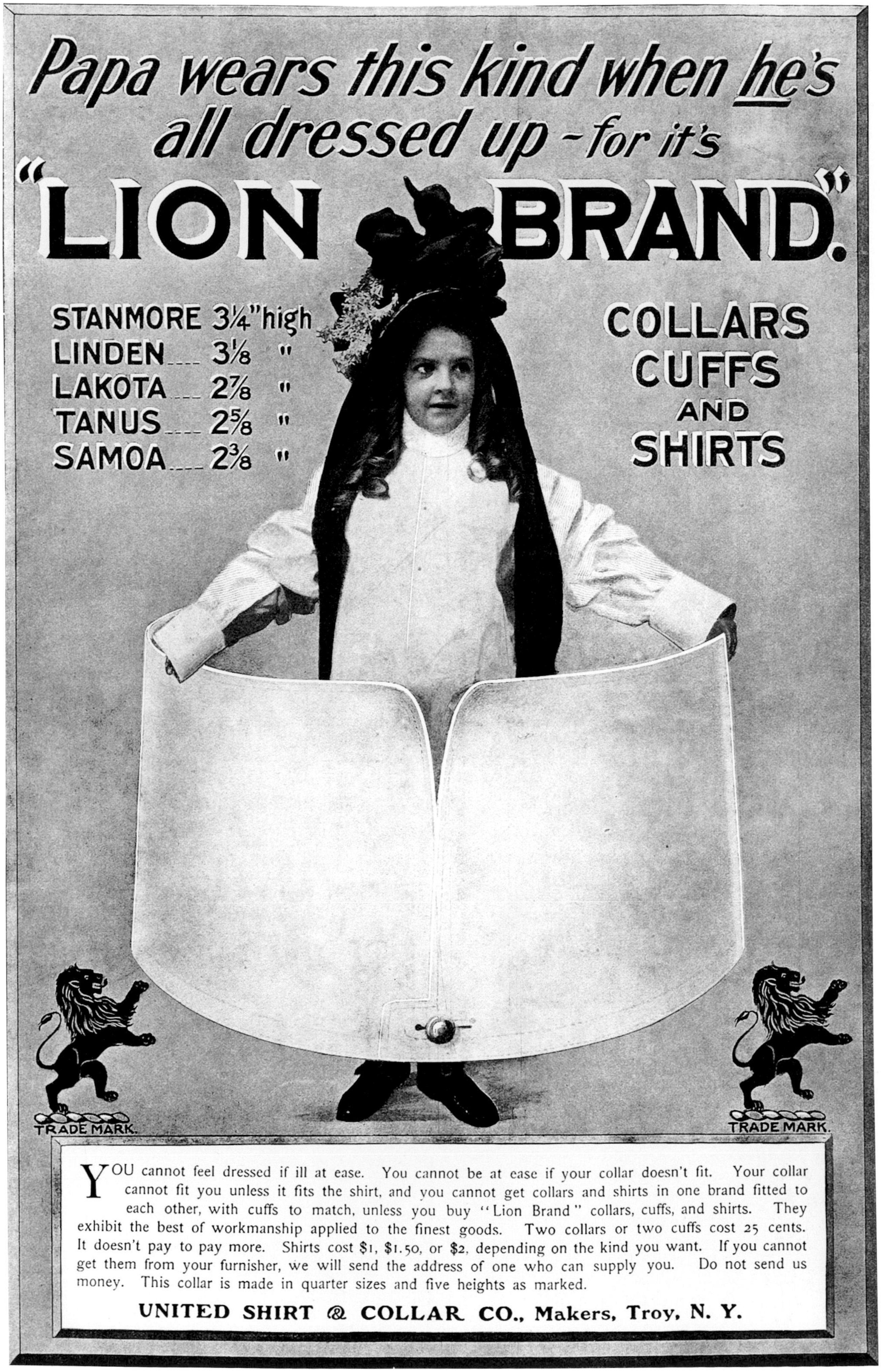

Papa wears this kind when *he's* all dressed up – for it's "LION BRAND."

STANMORE 3¼" high
LINDEN ..... 3⅛ "
LAKOTA ..... 2⅞ "
TANUS ..... 2⅝ "
SAMOA ..... 2⅜ "

COLLARS
CUFFS
AND
SHIRTS

TRADE MARK.

TRADE MARK.

YOU cannot feel dressed if ill at ease. You cannot be at ease if your collar doesn't fit. Your collar cannot fit you unless it fits the shirt, and you cannot get collars and shirts in one brand fitted to each other, with cuffs to match, unless you buy "Lion Brand" collars, cuffs, and shirts. They exhibit the best of workmanship applied to the finest goods. Two collars or two cuffs cost 25 cents. It doesn't pay to pay more. Shirts cost $1, $1.50, or $2, depending on the kind you want. If you cannot get them from your furnisher, we will send the address of one who can supply you. Do not send us money. This collar is made in quarter sizes and five heights as marked.

UNITED SHIRT & COLLAR CO., Makers, Troy, N. Y.

A MAN likes to appear at his very best when he is in evening dress. A bulging, creased bosom will spoil his most painstaking efforts. Avoid it—get a

Donchester Dress Shirt

a Cluett Dress Shirt that has a bosom that slides over the trouser band instead of bulging out of the waistcoat. $2 *to* $3

Lion Brand Collars, 1900 ◂

Until World War I, men's shirts featured detachable collars that could removed to be cleaned and heavily starched, separately from the shirt. The style carries into modern dress in formalwear, particularly for White Tie, which features a stiffly starched collar.

Bis zum 1. Weltkrieg hatten Herrenhemden abnehmbare Kragen, die separat gewaschen und steif gestärkt wurden. Bis heute hat man diesen Stil in der Abendkleidung beibehalten, insbesondere zum Frack gehört ein ordentlich gestärkter Kragen.

Jusqu'à la Première Guerre mondiale, les chemises pour homme comportaient des cols amovibles qui pouvaient être détachés pour être lavés et amidonnés séparément de la chemise. Ce style est toujours d'actualité pour les tenues de soirée, surtout les chemises à col rigide amidonné.

Cluett Shirts, 1909

MUNSING UNION SUITS

FOR ALL AGES

B. V. D. Underwear, 1906

Munsingwear Union Suits, 1909 ◂

Pat. 535 — Any Combination of Colors — 50 cents
Pat. 527 — Any Combination of Colors — 50 cents
Pat. 450 — Any Combination of Colors — 50 cents
Pat. 1606 — Any Combination of Colors — 50 cents
Pat. 1621 — Any Combination of Colors — 50 cents
Pat. 1512 — Any Combination of Colors — 50 cents
Pat. 550 — Any Combination of Colors — 50 cents
Pat. 1666 — Any Combination of Colors — 50 cents
Pat. 622 — Any Combination of Colors — 50 cents
Pat. 569 — Any Combination of Colors — 50 cents
WICK FANCY HAT BANDS
Tone up Your Hat with a Fancy Band
Fashion declares for the cheery hat. A black band suggests mourning. Be sure of the correct thing. Get the WICK Band—"the band with hooks" (all rights reserved)—sold by up-to-date stores everywhere. Exclusive and distinctive designs. The Swastika, Spear-head, Polka Dot, and raised figure effects, smart Fraternity Idea Bands (shown below)—swagger bands for young men, neat patterns in black and white or browns and greys for the quiet dressers. There's only one band that gives you choice of 1600 individual patterns *actually in stock*. The only band that fastens in an instant, snug and smooth — never gets loose or baggy, wrinkles or slips out of place.
These Bands Two Inches Wide
(They're shown here reduced in size)
Wick Fancy Hat Bands fit any hat of any size—straw, panama, slouch, or telescope. Go right on over the old band. Fasten with the unique little hooks. Make any hat into a Club or Varsity Hat.
College and Club combinations, Stripes, Bars, Cords, genuine Scotch plaids, quiet greys, browns, and black and white effects. All 2 inch bands 50 cents at any of the 10,000 Wick hatters and haberdashers in every corner of the country.
Send 50c in Coin or Stamps
For Each 2-inch Band
Tell us what you want—or leave it to us to send you the latest thing, together with our book of color combinations. A copy of our dashing College poster, by Edward Penfield, four feet long, in five colors, sent free with each mail order for two or more bands.
We are the world's authorities in fancy hat bands. We carry a hundred thousand dollar stock of bands all the time—operate our own looms—originate the up-to-date ideas—export to Europe and Spanish America.
Look for the WICK LABEL, stitched inside every genuine Wick Band—your guarantee of hat band satisfaction.
WICK NARROW FABRIC CO., Producers of Specialties, PHILADELPHIA
Pat. 1642 Any Combination of Colors 50 cents

Wick Hat Bands, 1908 ◂

By 1909, the boater hat's origin as part of the uniform of the British navy was a thing of the past. Queen Victoria popularized the style for childrenswear, and, eventually, the hat became a favored summer hat for middle-class gentlemen on both sides of the Atlantic.

Im Jahre 1909 war der Strohhut schon nicht mehr Teil der Uniform britischer Marinesoldaten. Queen Victoria machte ihn als Accessoire der Kindermode wieder beliebt. Und schließlich wurde der Strohhut zur beliebten sommerlichen Kopfbedeckung bei Herren der Mittelschicht zu beiden Seiten des Atlantiks.

En 1909, le canotier n'était plus un élément de l'uniforme de la marine anglaise, la reine Victoria l'ayant mis à la mode pour les enfants. Des deux côtés de l'Atlantique, le canotier finit par devenir le chapeau de prédilection des messieurs de la classe moyenne.

Knapp-Felt Hats, 1908

NOW is Soft-hat time. A picturesque Knapp-Felt harmonizes with the early fall attire and is an agreeable change from the straw hat—the Knapp-Felt derby comes later.

A variety of appropriate shapes of noticeable elegance of style and superb quality.

Knapp-Felt DeLuxe, Six Dollars. Knapp-Felt, Four Dollars—everywhere.
Write for The Hatman.

THE CROFUT & KNAPP CO., Broadway, cor. Thirteenth Street, New York.

$3.00 to $15.00 per pair

The Standard of Corset Fashion

The Foundation of a Perfect-Fitting Gown

Security Rubber Button Hose Supporters
Attached to all
Redfern Whalebone Corsets

Sold at all High-Class Shops

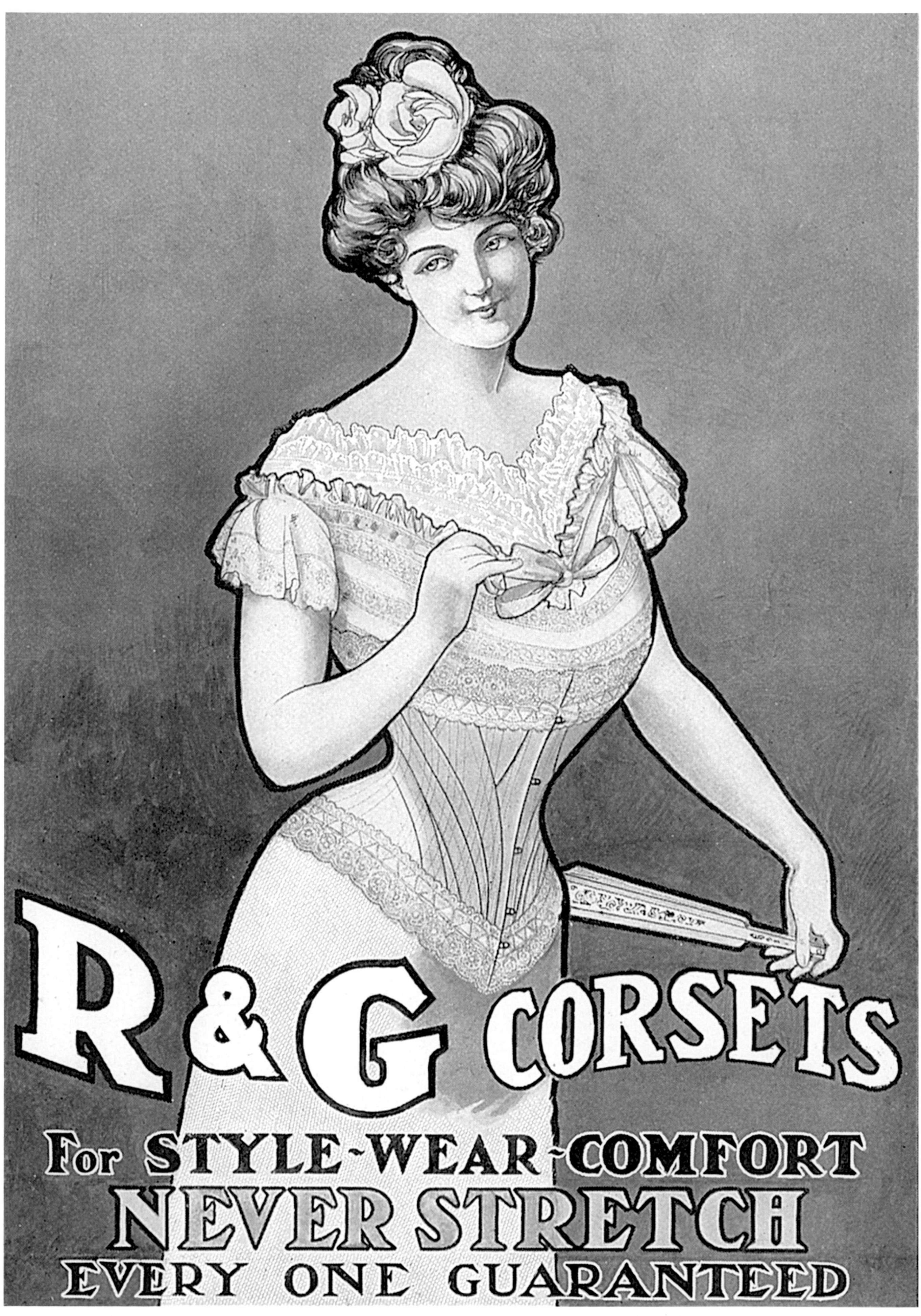

R & G Corsets, 1902

Redfern Corsets, 1909 ◂

54

SAFE SHOES

SOROSIS Safe Shoes are so fashioned that they cannot injure the feet that wear them when properly fitted. Some shoes are really **dangerous** because they do not conform to natural lines of normal feet but do conform to eccentric lines and oddities of shape that happen to be considered highly fashionable.

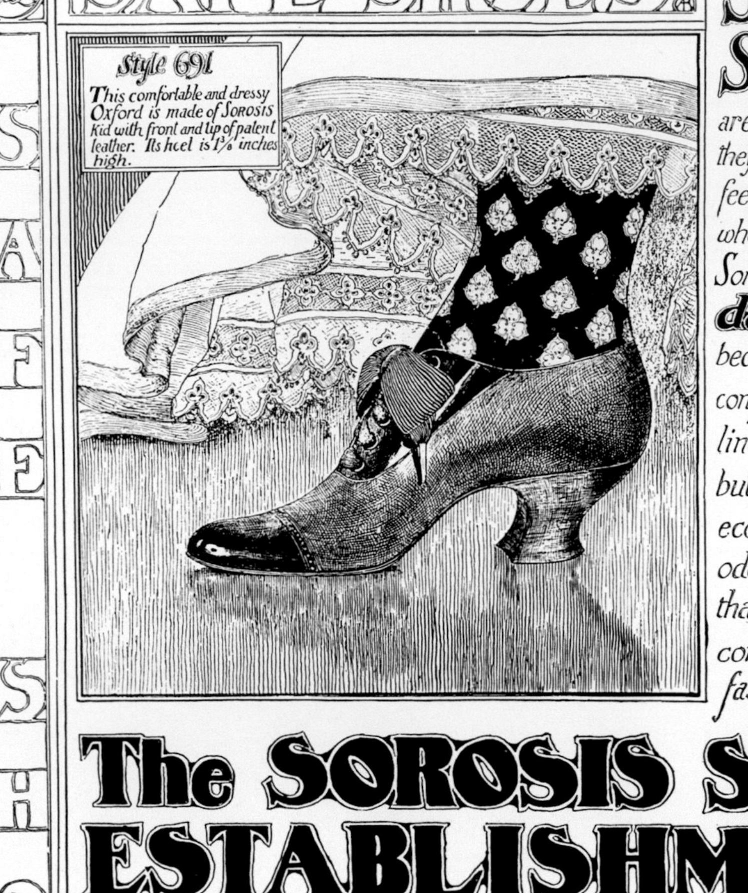

The SOROSIS SHOE ESTABLISHMENT produces many millions of the most intelligently made **Safe Shoes** and it also produces the most distinctly fashionable shoes that are in the market.

Sorosis Stores and Departments:

New York: James McCreery & Co., 23rd St.
Brooklyn: Cor. Fulton & Hoyt Sts.
Baltimore: 19 Lexington St., W.
Washington: 1213 F St.
Boston: 20 Temple Place & 176 Boylston St.
Chicago: 34 Washington St.
Cincinnati: 6 West Fourth St.
Detroit: Newcomb-Endicott Co.
San Francisco: 216 Post St., & 50 Third St.
Buffalo: H. A. Meldrum Co.
Philadelphia: 1314 Chestnut St.
Pittsburg: Penn Ave. & 5th St. & 214 6th St.

Cleveland: 177 Euclid Ave.
Milwaukee: 93 Wisconsin St.
St. Paul: Field, Schlick & Co.
Denver: 626 16th St.
Hartford: 945 Main St.
Providence: The Shepard Co.
St. Louis: Scruggs, Vandervoort & Barney D. G. Co.
Minneapolis: 700 Nicollet Ave.

London Shops: Regent House, Regent Street, W.; 19 Westbourne Grove, W.; 83 Brompton Road, S. W.; all large cities in Europe and America.

Sorosis Safe Shoes, 1905

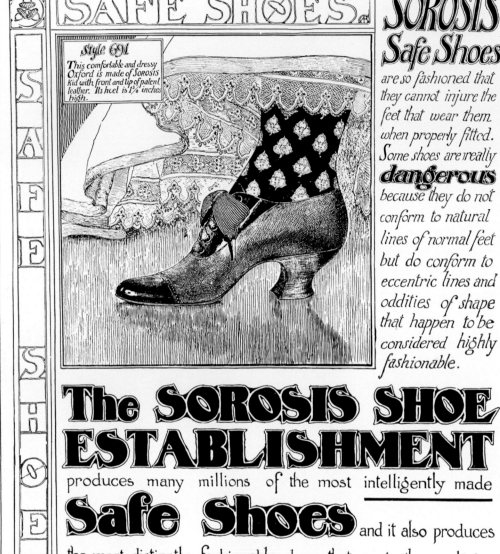

Early patent medicine ads employed an alarmist tone and used faux-medical jargon to sell their products. Similarly, this ad warns of the dire – but not very specific – health consequences of being "highly fashionable."

Frühe, offenkundig medizinische Inserate schlugen einen alarmierenden Ton an und benutzten einen pseudowissenschaftlichen Jargon, um ihre Produkte zu verkaufen. Auf ähnliche Weise warnt diese Anzeige vor den gefährlichen – aber nicht weiter ausgeführten – gesundheitlichen Folgen extremen Modebewusstseins.

Les premières réclames pour spécialités pharmaceutiques employaient un ton alarmiste et un jargon pseudomédical pour éconter leurs produits. Cette publicité avertit les consommateurs des risques terribles – mais pas vraiment spécifiés – pour la santé quand on est « très à la mode ».

▸ O' Sullivan's Rubber Heels, 1908

▸▸ Chalmers "Porosknit" Union Suits, 1909

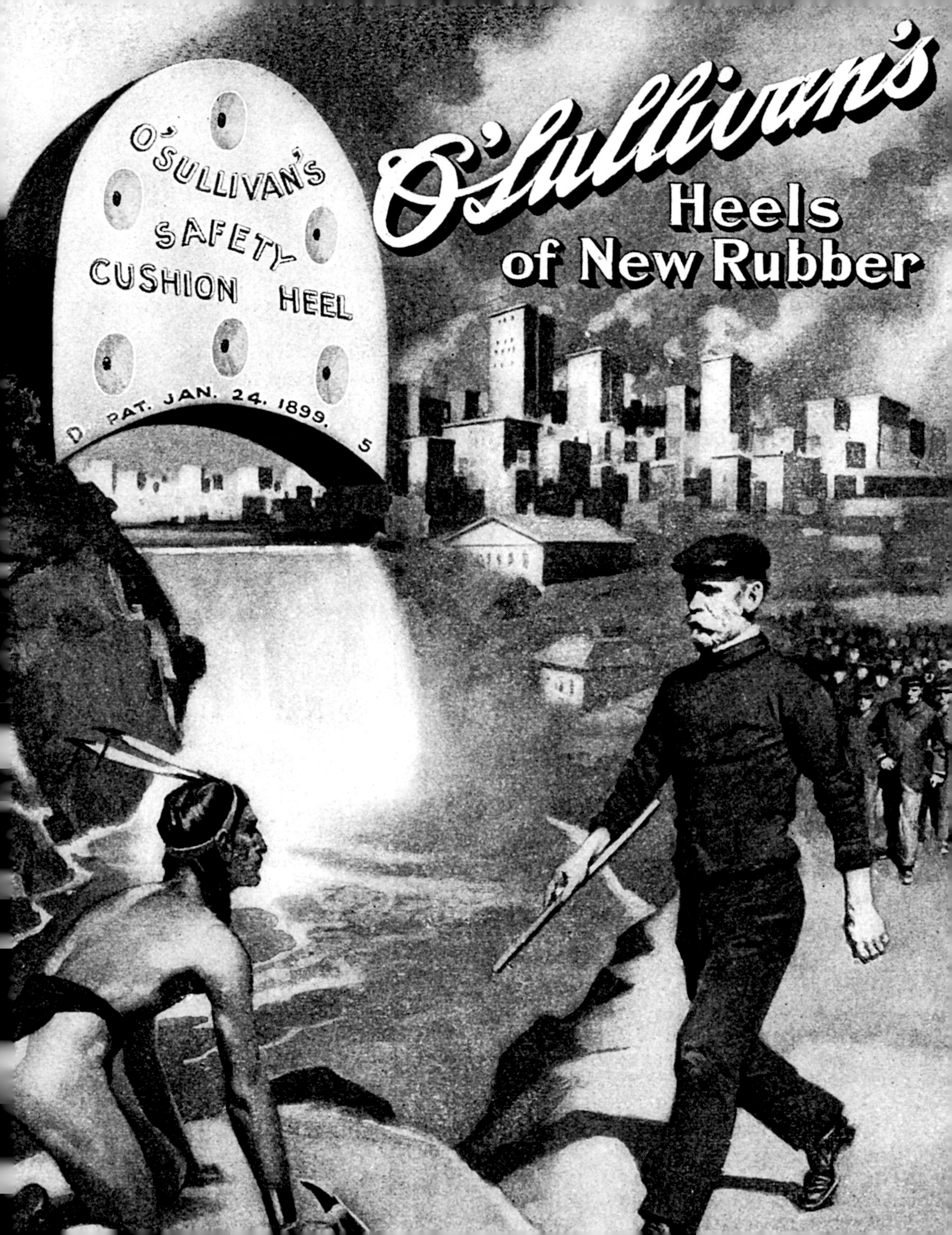
O'Sullivan's
Heels
of New Rubber
O'SULLIVAN'S
SAFETY
CUSHION HEEL
PAT. JAN. 24. 1899.
D
5

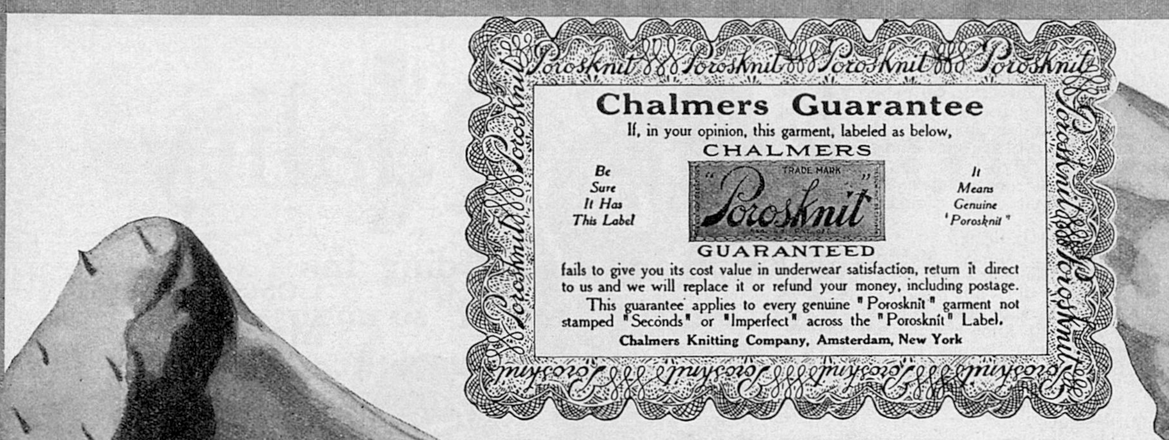

The

For Men
For Boys

Did *You* Ever
Union Suit Cut

The Chalmers "Poroskniṫ
which the elasticity of the
allows it to "give" instead
waisted" feeling and "cutti

Remember also that it is
buttons, no cumbersome fl

Chalmers "Poroskniṫ" is
the fabric keeps your bod
use of the best (high-priced

Try a suit of elastic, light,

Men's Mercerized "Poros

CHALMERS K

roof of "Porosknit" Quality

No word could be said — no argument made — regarding the good quality, durability, fit and comfort of genuine "Porosknit" so unanswerable as this: It is absolutely guaranteed. Read the Guarantee Bond.

Try Chalmers "Porosknit." A trial will mean one of two things to you. Either you will find a summer underwear that will thoroughly please you — a source of delight in the years to come — or, if not satisfied, you need be at no loss. With every Chalmers "Porosknit" garment there is a Guarantee Bond (reproduced here).

To you the importance of becoming acquainted with our label is: that you may continue to buy the Chalmers "Porosknit" Underwear if it satisfies you or avoid it if it is not what we claim it to be.

the Crotch?

ıas solved this. The elastic fitting back, in
nade to run up and down as well as across the back,
ery turn and bend of the body, and thus prevents "short-

ch garment that you really enjoy. No gaping between
ke the ¾ length with covered knee and free ankle.

yles — for man, for boy. It is hygienic. The texture of
ption and evaporation of perspiration. Made possible by
. The softness of this yarn saves your skin from irritation.
e, healthful "Porosknit" (Union Suit or separate garments).
ke silk) for $1.00 per garment, or $2.00 per Union Suit.

Write for Handsome Book of all Styles

For MEN		For BOYS
50c	Any Style Shirts and Drawers per garment	25c
For MEN $1.00	Union Suits Any Style	For BOYS 50c

G COMPANY 1 Washington Street Amsterdam, N. Y.

Ask Your Dealer

POIRET'S INFLUENCE WAS STILL APPARENT IN THE 1910s. HIS DESIGNS SPARKED A FAD FOR HOBBLE SKIRTS IN THE UNITED STATES, AS AMERICAN DRESSMAKERS MISINTERPRETED THE NARROW LINES OF THE DESIGNER'S LOOK.

POIRETS EINFLUSS WAR IN DER MODE NACH 1910 DURCHAUS NOCH SPÜRBAR. SEINE ENTWÜRFE LÖSTEN IN DEN USA DIE MODETORHEIT HUMPEL-ROCK AUS, NACHDEM AMERIKANISCHE SCHNEIDER DIE SCHMALEN SCHNITTE DES DESIGNERS FALSCH INTERPRETIERT HATTEN.

L'INFLUENCE DE POIRET SE FIT ENCORE RESSENTIR APRÈS 1910. AUX ETATS-UNIS, LES ESQUISSES DES MODÈLES DE CE COUTURIER LANCENT LA GRANDE MODE DES JUPES DITES « ENTRAVÉES », LES COUTURIÈRES AMÉRICAINES INTERPRÉTANT MAL LES LIGNES ÉTROITES DU LOOK POIRET.

1910-

DEFENDING THE HOME FRONT
AN DER HEIMATFRONT
SUR LE FRONT

-1919

Arrow Collars/Cluett Shirts, 1911 ◄◄

Kenyon Coats and Suits, ca. 1918 ◄

Luxite Hosiery, 1918

PROMPTED IN PART BY THE MASSIVE IMMIGRATION IN THE PRECEDING DECADE, many Americans in the 1910s took an isolationist, nativist stance, and nostalgia for small-town living began to grow. Meanwhile, dissent was brewing abroad; within a few years, Europe — and, soon after, America — would be thrown into World War I. For many companies, war meant a shift in business. Chicago-based men's apparel manufacturer and retailer B. Kuppenheimer & Co. was among many that began manufacturing uniforms for the U.S. Army. Once the war ended, the president of another apparel maker and retailer, Society Brand Clothing, looked to the skies — and the newly decommissioned fighter planes and pilots — to pioneer a new means of distribution for his products: air delivery.

Into the midst of growing international conflict, Gabrielle "Coco" Chanel opened a hat shop in Paris, followed shortly by dress shops in Deauville and Biarritz, where she began using wool jersey, a fabric previously used for men's underwear, to create comfortable, chic, modern women's apparel. Chanel's was a departure from both the corseted Gibson Girl of the first decade and the kimono-clad Poiret ideal, but Poiret's influence was still apparent in the 1910s. His designs sparked a fad for hobble skirts in the United States, as American dressmakers misinterpreted the narrow lines of the designer's look.

In 1907, Australian swimming star Annette Kellerman performed the first water ballet at New York's Hippodrome. Her one-piece bathing suit scandalized a public accustomed to seeing women dressed in cumbersome swimming-dresses — but it was also trendsetting. Soon new swimming styles were introduced by knitters Jantzen and Bentz Knitting Mills (later renamed Catalina). Indeed, athleticism was on the rise. The Converse Rubber Shoe Company had been founded in 1908, and by the century's second decade, rival U.S. Rubber began mass-marketing its own Keds brand athletic shoes.

Inspired by the New York debut of husband-and-wife ballroom dancers Vernon and Irene Castle, women began bobbing their hair like Irene's while men began wearing theirs slicked back like Vernon's. Both began to learn the pair's signature dances, the Castle Walk and the fox-trot.

Meanwhile, the nascent film industry was leaving New York for the warm climate and cheap land of Southern California, and soon Hollywood was churning out feature-length films, turning its actors into overnight stars and influencing fashion trends around the world. Mack Sennett's *Bathing Beauties* provided a little cheesecake for Keystone comedies; Gloria Swanson cemented her place as Hollywood's glamour queen; and, with a cascade of blonde ringlets, Mary Pickford, "America's Sweetheart," was the most popular and highest-paid movie star of the decade.

In 1913, the New York Armory Show introduced the United States to Symbolism, Impressionism, Post-Impressionism, Neo-Impressionism, and Cubism. While some were shocked by Marcel Duchamp's *Nude Descending a Staircase* and Henri Matisse's distorted female forms, others were inspired. New York's Wanamaker's department store featured "Cubist-inspired" fashion in its window displays, and *Vogue* magazine began incorporating "Cubist fashion" into its editorials. The Armory Show began traveling around the country, and New York's Gimbel Brothers department store followed with a companion Cubist-fashion exhibition that ran in several major cities around the country.

1910

1910 Lampshade hats reach new heights

Lampenschirm-Hüte erreichen neue Dimensionen

Les chapeaux en forme d'abat-jour atteignent de nouvelles hauteurs

1910 B. Kuppenheimer & Co. employs nearly 2,000 people in shops in Chicago

B. Kuppenheimer & Co. beschäftigt in seinen Läden in Chicago knapp 2000 Leute

B. Kuppenheimer & Co. emploie près de 2 000 personnes dans ses points de vente de Chicago

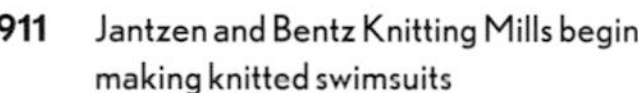

1911 Jantzen and Bentz Knitting Mills begin making knitted swimsuits

Jantzen und Bentz Knitting Mills beginnen mit der Produktion gestrickter Badeanzüge

Jantzen et Bentz Knitting Mills commencent à produire des maillots de bain en tricot

1912 Brown Shoe Company goes public

Die Brown Shoe Company geht an die Börse

La société Brown Shoe Company est introduite en bourse

TEILWEISE BEDINGT DURCH DIE GROSSE EINWANDERUNGSWELLE IM VORANGEGANGENEN JAHRZEHNT, nahmen viele Amerikaner nach 1910 einen isolationistischen, nativistischen Standpunkt ein. Eine Nostalgie hinsichtlich des Lebens in der Kleinstadt kam auf. Inzwischen wuchs die Krisenstimmung im Ausland. Schon wenige Jahre später sollte Europa – und bald darauf auch Amerika – in den Ersten Weltkrieg schlittern. Für viele Unternehmen bedeutete der Krieg eine geschäftliche Veränderung. So zählte etwa der Herrenbekleidungshersteller und Einzelhändler B. Kuppenheimer & Co. zu den zahlreichen Firmen, die Uniformen für die U.S. Army erzeugten. Nach Kriegsende besann sich der Vorsitzende einer anderen Textilkette, Society Brand Clothing, auf die soeben stillgelegten Kampfflugzeuge und die dazugehörigen Piloten und wurde zum Pionier einer neuen Vertriebsform seiner Produkte: der Zustellung auf dem Luftweg.

Während sich die internationale Lage bereits wieder gefährlich zuspitzte, eröffnete Gabrielle „Coco" Chanel ihr Pariser Hutgeschäft, dem bald Modeläden in Deauville und Biarritz folgten; dort begann sie mit der Verarbeitung von Wolljersey, das bislang nur für Herrenunterwäsche Verwendung gefunden hatte, zu bequemer, schicker und moderner Damenbekleidung. Chanels Ideal war eine Abkehr sowohl vom korsetttragenden Gibson-Girl des ersten Jahrzehnts wie auch von Poirets Dame im Kimono. Wobei Poirets Einfluss in der Mode nach 1910 durchaus noch spürbar war. Seine Entwürfe lösten in den USA die Modetorheit Humpelrock aus, nachdem amerikanische Schneider die schmalen Schnitte des Designers falsch interpretiert hatten.

1907 brachte der australische Schwimmstar Annette Kellerman im New Yorker Hippodrome das erste Wasserballett zur Aufführung. Ihr einteiliger Badeanzug schockte ein Publikum, das bis dato nur an Frauen in schwerfälligen Badekostümen gewohnt war – und wirkte zugleich als Trendsetter. Bald wurden neue Bademoden von der Strickwarenfirma Jantzen und Bentz Knitting Mills (später umbenannt in Catalina) präsentiert. Sportlichkeit war zunehmend gefragt. Die Converse Rubber Shoe Company wurde 1908 gegründet; ab den 1920er Jahren trat die Konkurrenzfirma U.S.Rubber mit der Massenproduktion ihrer Sportschuhe der Marke Keds auf den Plan.

Nach dem Vorbild des New Yorker Tanz- und Ehepaares Vernon und Irene Castle begannen Frauen wie Irene einen Kurzhaar-Bob zu tragen, während die Herren ihr Haar wie Vernon zurückgelten. Beide Geschlechter eigneten sich außerdem die typischen Tänze des Paares an: den Castle Walk und den Foxtrott.

Inzwischen kehrte die noch im Werden begriffene Filmindustrie New York den Rücken und strebte nach dem warmen Klima und den billigen Grundstücken Südkaliforniens; schon bald produzierte Hollywood am laufenden Band abendfüllende Spielfilme, machte seine Schauspieler über Nacht zu Stars und beeinflusste damit Modetrends in aller Welt.

Mack Sennetts *Bathing Beauties* waren der Augenschmaus bei den Komödien von Keystone; Gloria Swanson sicherte sich ihren Status als Hollywoods Glamourqueen; und mit ihrer blonden Lockenpracht war Mary Pickford „America's Sweetheart" und der beliebteste wie auch bestbezahlte weibliche Kinostar des Jahrzehnts.

1913 machte die New York Armory Show die Vereinigten Staaten erstmals mit Symbolismus, Impressionismus, Post-Impressionismus, Neo-Impressionismus und Kubismus bekannt. Und während einige sich von Marcel Duchamps *Nackter, die eine Treppe hinabsteigt*, und Henri Matisses verzerrten weiblichen Formen schockiert zeigten, fühlten sich andere davon inspiriert. Das New Yorker Kaufhaus Wanamaker's zeigte in seinen Schaufenstern sogar kubistisch-inspirierte Mode, und auch die Zeitschrift *Vogue* begann „kubistische Mode" in ihren redaktionellen Teil zu integrieren.

Die Armory Show tourte durchs Land, und das New Yorker Kaufhaus Gimbel Brothers schloss sich ihr mit einer begleitenden Ausstellung zum Thema kubistische Mode an, die in mehreren Großstädten der USA gezeigt wurde.

1913

1913 Influence of Orientalism seen in Poiret designs and beyond

Orientalische Einflüsse sind unter anderem in Poirets Kreationen sichtbar

L'Orientalisme influence les créations de Poiret et d'autres couturiers

1913 Grecian hairstyles conform more to natural shape of the head

Frisuren im griechischen Stil folgen stärker der natürlichen Kopfform

Les coiffures à la grecque épousent mieux la forme naturelle de la tête

1914 Mack Sennett's "Bathing Beauties" debut in Keystone comedies

Mack Sennetts „Bathing Beauties" geben ihr Debut in den Keystone-Komödien

« Les jolies baigneuses » de Mack Sennett font leurs débuts dans les comédies produites par Keystone

1915 Spectacles with large round frames become fashionable

Brillen mit großen runden Gestellen kommen in Mode

Les lunettes à gros verres ronds deviennent à la mode

Naiad Dress Shields, 1912 ◄◄

Cluett Shirts, 1911 ◄

EN PARTIE À CAUSE DE L'IMMIGRATION MASSIVE DE LA PRÉCÉDENTE DÉCENNIE, DE NOMBREUX AMÉRICAINS ADOPTENT PENDANT LES ANNÉES 1910 UNE POSITION ISOLATIONNISTE ET NATALISTE QUI VOIT CROÎTRE LA NOSTALGIE DE LA VIE DE PROVINCE. Pendant ce temps, les tensions s'intensifient à l'étranger; en quelques années, l'Europe, suivie par les Etats-Unis, se jette dans la Première Guerre mondiale. Pour de nombreuses entreprises, la guerre implique un changement d'activité. Le fabricant et vendeur de vêtements pour homme B. Kuppenheimer & Co. de Chicago compte parmi ceux qui commencent à manufacturer des uniformes pour l'armée américaine. Après la fin de la guerre, le directeur de Society Brand Clothing, un autre fabricant et détaillant du secteur, tourne son regard vers le ciel – les avions de combat récemment démobilisés – et invente un nouveau moyen de distribution pour ses produits : le transport aérien.

Au milieu des tensions internationales croissantes, Gabrielle « Coco » Chanel ouvre une boutique de chapeaux à Paris, puis des boutiques de vêtements à Deauville et à Biarritz. Elle commence à utiliser le jersey de laine, un tissu autrefois réservé aux sous-vêtements pour homme, pour créer des tenues confortables, chics et modernes à l'intention des femmes. L'idéal Chanel n'a plus rien à voir avec la Gibson Girl corsetée des années 1900 ni avec la femme en kimono de Poiret, bien que l'influence de ce dernier se fasse encore ressentir. Aux Etats-Unis, les modèles de ce couturier lancent la grande mode des jupes dites « entravées », les couturières américaines interprétant mal les lignes étroites du look Poiret.

En 1907, la star de la natation australienne Annette Kellerman présente le tout premier ballet aquatique à l'Hippodrome de New York. Son maillot une pièce scandalise un public habitué à voir les femmes dans d'encombrantes combinaisons de bain, mais la nageuse réussit néanmoins à lancer la tendance. Rapidement, des fabricants de maille tels Jantzen et Bentz Knitting Mills (rebaptisé plus tard Catalina) proposent de nouveaux modèles de bain, l'athlétisme étant en plein essor. Rejointe vers 1915 par son concurrent U.S. Rubber, la Converse Rubber Shoe Company fondée en 1908 commence à commercialiser ses propres chaussures de sport sous la marque Keds.

Inspirées par les débuts new-yorkais du couple de danseurs Vernon et Irene Castle, les femmes adoptent progressivement la coupe au bol d'Irene et les hommes peignent leurs cheveux vers l'arrière, comme Vernon. Hommes et femmes apprennent les danses emblématiques du duo, le Castle Walk et le fox-trot.

Pendant ce temps, l'industrie cinématographique naissante quitte New York pour le climat chaud et les terrains bon marché de la Californie du Sud. Hollywood ne tarde pas à produire des longs métrages en série, hisse ses acteurs au rang de stars, du jour au lendemain, et influence les tendances de la mode à travers le monde entier. Les jolies baigneuses de Mack Sennett jouent les pin-up dans les comédies produites par Keystone ; Gloria Swanson assoit son statut de reine du glamour hollywoodien ; sous une cascade de boucles blondes, la « petite chérie de l'Amérique » Mary Pickford devient la star de cinéma la plus adulée et la mieux payée de la décennie.

En 1913, le salon artistique Armory Show de New York initie les États-Unis au symbolisme, à l'impressionnisme, au post-impressionnisme, au néo-impressionnisme et au cubisme. Si certains sont choqués par *Nu descendant un escalier* de Marcel Duchamp ou par les formes féminines distordues d'Henri Matisse, d'autres s'en inspirent. Le grand magasin new-yorkais Wanamaker's garnit ses vitrines de vêtements « d'inspiration cubiste » et le magazine *Vogue* commence à intégrer la « mode cubiste » dans sa ligne éditoriale. L'Armory Show part en tournée dans tout le pays, tandis qu'à New York, le grand magasin Gimbel Brothers reprend le flambeau avec une exposition de vêtements cubistes qui visitera plusieurs grandes villes des Etats-Unis.

1915

1915 Front-laced boots popular for women during WWI

Während des 1. Weltkriegs in Mode: vorne gebundene Schnürstiefel für Damen

Pendant la Première Guerre mondiale, les femmes portent toutes des bottes à lacets

1915 Mary Pickford most popular and highest-grossing movie star in Hollywood

Mary Pickford, der beliebteste und bestbezahlte Kinostar Hollywoods

Mary Pickford devient la star de cinéma la plus adulée et la mieux payée d'Hollywood

1917 Converse and Keds begin mass-producing athletic shoes

Converse und Keds beginnen mit der Massenproduktion von Sportschuhen

Converse et Keds se lancent dans la production en masse de chaussures de sport

1918 As more Americans begin to drive, sales of accessories like driving gloves boom

Weil immer mehr Amerikaner Auto fahren, steigen die Verkaufszahlen von entsprechenden Accessoires wie Handschuhen sprunghaft an

Alors que de plus en plus d'Américains achètent des voitures, les ventes d'accessoires comme les gants de pilote explosent

—for dress wear

"HOLEPROOF" for men and for women are soft—light weight—stylish—attractive—and perfection in fit.

They are made in twelve colors, ten weights and five grades for men—two colors, two weights and three grades for women.

The best of these grades will grace any ball room. They are sheer, silky and soft as any cotton hose ever made, yet six pairs are guaranteed six months.

Holeproof in Silk for Men and Women—Guaranteed

Holeproof for men may be had in silk at $2 for three pairs guaranteed three months—and in silk for women at $3 for three pairs, guaranteed three months.

Don't judge Holeproof by common guaranteed hosieries. Holeproof is the *original.* Thirty-eight years of hose-making experience go into every pair.

Are Your Hose Insured?

The genuine bear the trade mark and the signature of Ca Freschl, Pres., shown below. Always look for this identification. If it is not on the toe of each pair the hose are not genuine —no matter who says so.

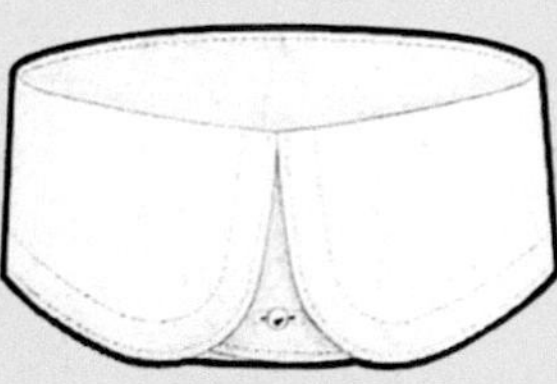

BERWICK
2½ inches

Curve cut to fit over the bones and muscles of the shoulder. Means greater comfort and at the same time improves the sit of the collar.

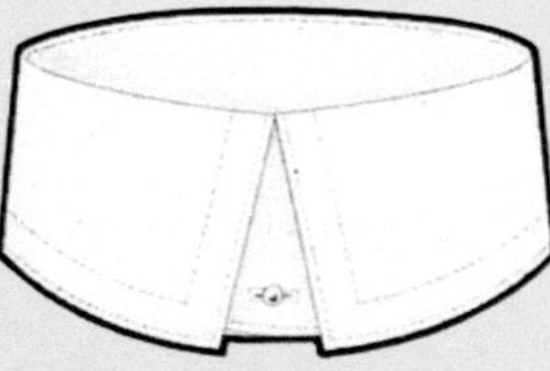

TALBOT
2⅜ inches

It is an exclusive Arrow feature

15c each 6 for 90c

CLUETT, PEABODY & CO. INC.

Makers TROY, NEW YORK, U. S. A.

Arrow Collars, 1916

Holeproof Hosiery, 1911 ◂

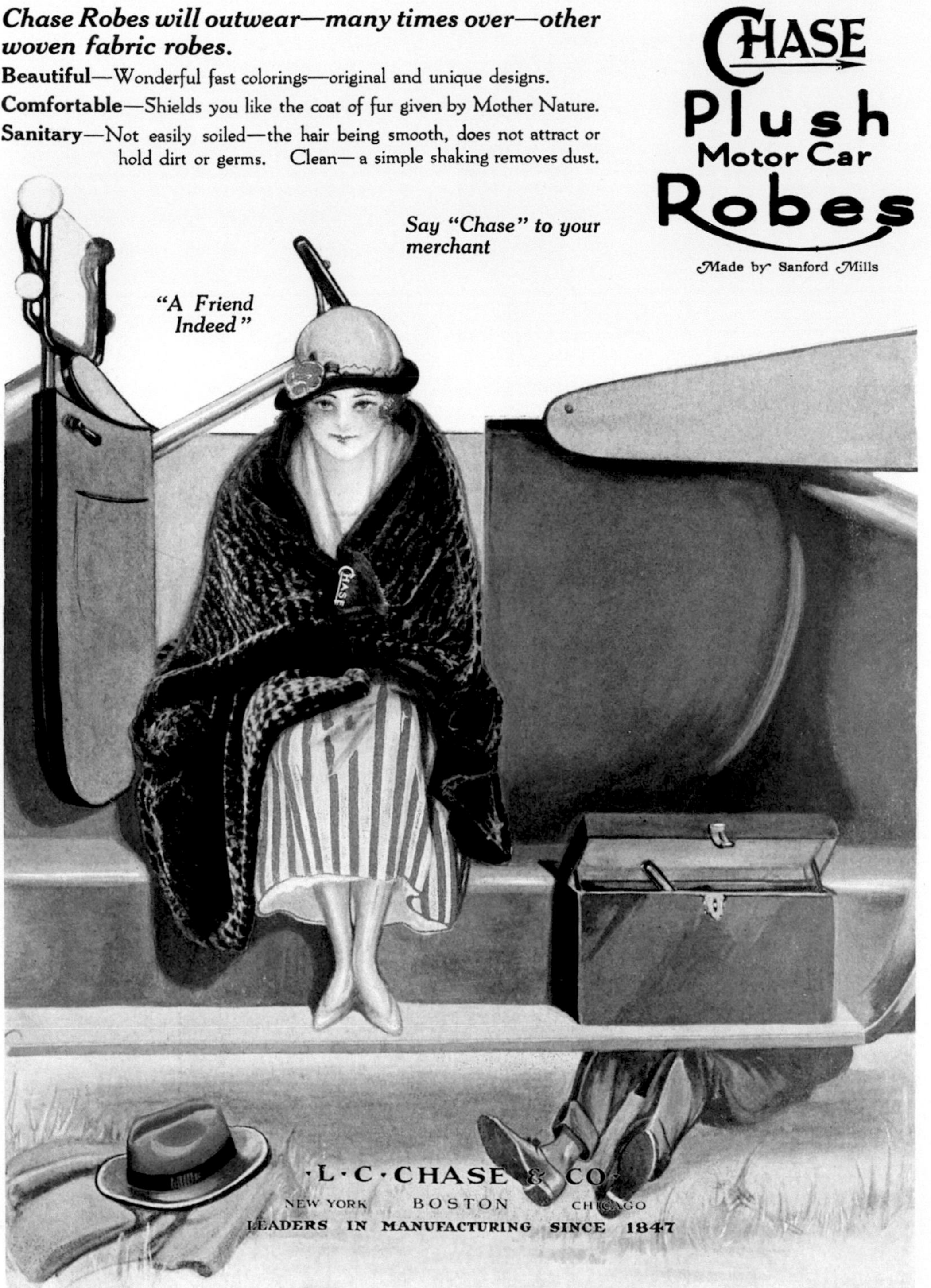

Chase Robes will outwear—many times over—other woven fabric robes.
Beautiful—Wonderful fast colorings—original and unique designs.
Comfortable—Shields you like the coat of fur given by Mother Nature.
Sanitary—Not easily soiled—the hair being smooth, does not attract or hold dirt or germs. Clean—a simple shaking removes dust.
CHASE
Plush
Motor Car
Robes
Made by Sanford Mills
Say "Chase" to your merchant
"A Friend Indeed"
L·C·CHASE & CO
NEW YORK BOSTON CHICAGO
LEADERS IN MANUFACTURING SINCE 1847

Chase Motor Car Robes, 1917

When Henry Ford introduced the affordable Model T automobile in 1908, the price was $850. By 1914, Ford was producing nearly 250,000 Model Ts, and, by 1916, the price had dropped to $360. With the newfound passion for driving came accessories – both automotive and sartorial – to go with the cars.

Als Henry Ford 1908 das erschwingliche Model T auf den Markt brachte, kostete es 850 $. 1914 produzierte Ford an die 250.000 Exemplare der Tin Lizzy, im Jahr 1916 war der Preis auf 360 $ gefallen. Mit der neu entdeckten Leidenschaft für das Autofahren kamen auch passende Accessoires – sowohl für das Automobil wie für dessen Insassen – in den Handel.

Quand Henry Ford lança son abordable Model T en 1908, son prix était de 850 dollars. En 1914, Ford produisait près de 250 000 Model T par an, et en 1916, le prix tomba à 360 dollars. La passion de la route entraîna la création d'accessoires automobiles comme vestimentaires.

► Niagara Maid Underwear, ca. 1910

Women to whom smartness of design is as important as dainty luxury of fabric highly prize
"Niagara Maid"
UNDERWEAR
of silk

► W. B. Reduso Corsets, 1911

The straight-front corset was a departure from the hourglass shape of the previous decade. The style created a small waist and flat stomach, dropped the bust into a "monobosom" silhouette, and curved the body into the new, S-shaped ideal. By the early 1910s, the long-line or "tubular" model – which also slimmed the hips and thighs – briefly came into fashion.

Das S-Korsett war eine Weiterentwicklung der Sanduhrform des vorangegangenen Jahrzehnts. Dieser Schnitt ezeugte eine schmale Taille und einen flachen Bauch, brachte den Busen in eine hochgeschnürte Silhouette und den ganzen Rumpf in die neue, angestrebte S-Form. Nach 1910 kam für kurze Zeit ein längeres „röhrenförmiges" Modell in Mode – das auch Hüften und Oberschenkel schlanker erscheinen ließ.

Le corset droit sur le devant tranchait avec la forme en sablier de la décennie précédente. Ce modèle affinait la taille et aplatissait le ventre, rehaussait les seins sous la forme d'une poitrine pigeonnante et donnait au corps sa nouvelle courbe idéale en S. Au début des années 1910, le modèle long ou « tubulaire » – qui amincissait aussi les hanches et les cuisses – connut un bref succès.

Wolfhead Undergarments, 1918

Wolfhead Undergarments, 1919

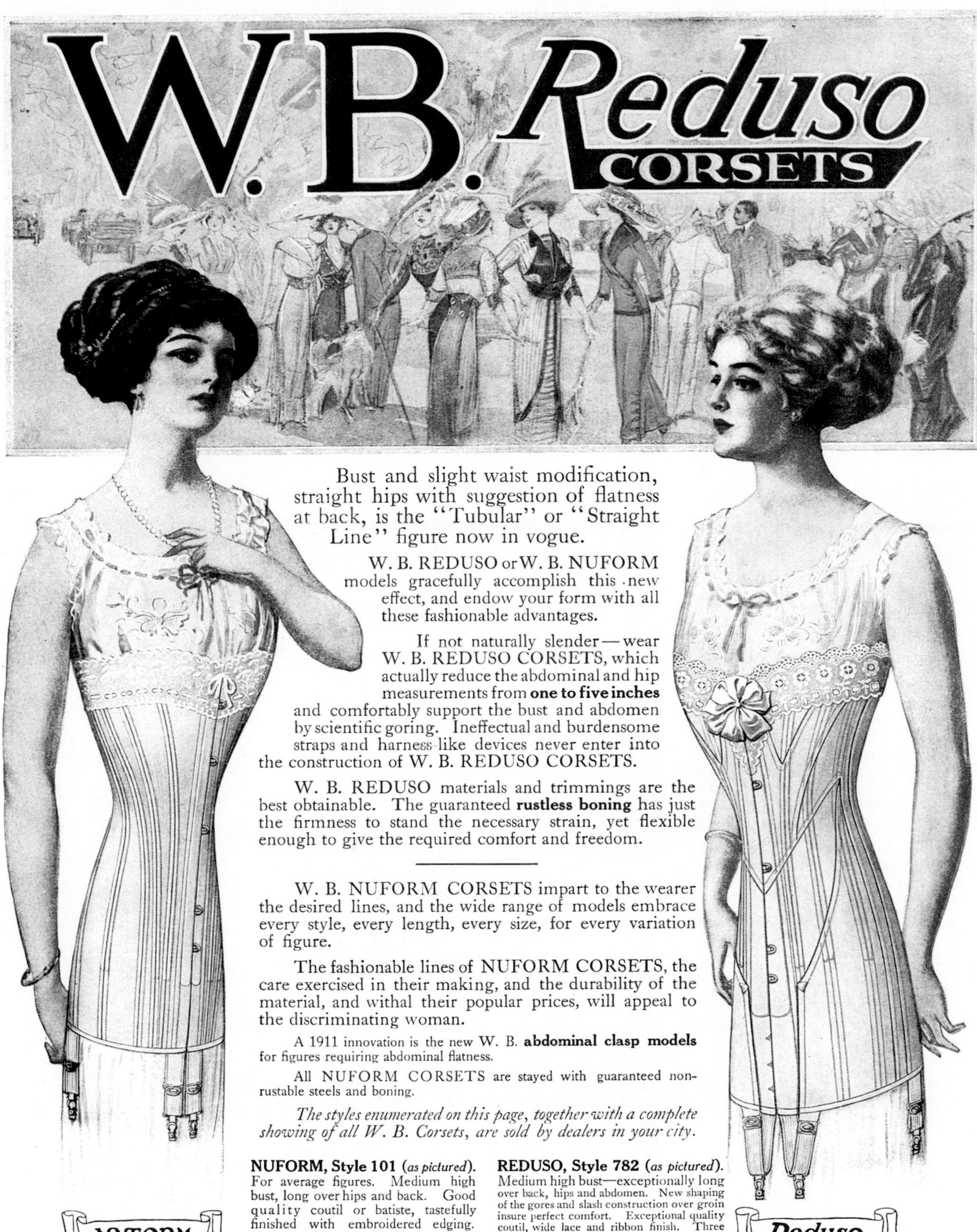

W. B. Reduso
CORSETS
Bust and slight waist modification, straight hips with suggestion of flatness at back, is the "Tubular" or "Straight Line" figure now in vogue.
W. B. REDUSO or W. B. NUFORM models gracefully accomplish this new effect, and endow your form with all these fashionable advantages.
If not naturally slender—wear W. B. REDUSO CORSETS, which actually reduce the abdominal and hip measurements from **one to five inches** and comfortably support the bust and abdomen by scientific goring. Ineffectual and burdensome straps and harness-like devices never enter into the construction of W. B. REDUSO CORSETS.
W. B. REDUSO materials and trimmings are the best obtainable. The guaranteed **rustless boning** has just the firmness to stand the necessary strain, yet flexible enough to give the required comfort and freedom.
W. B. NUFORM CORSETS impart to the wearer the desired lines, and the wide range of models embrace every style, every length, every size, for every variation of figure.
The fashionable lines of NUFORM CORSETS, the care exercised in their making, and the durability of the material, and withal their popular prices, will appeal to the discriminating woman.
A 1911 innovation is the new W. B. **abdominal clasp models** for figures requiring abdominal flatness.
All NUFORM CORSETS are stayed with guaranteed non-rustable steels and boning.
The styles enumerated on this page, together with a complete showing of all W. B. Corsets, are sold by dealers in your city.
NUFORM, Style 101 (*as pictured*). For average figures. Medium high bust, long over hips and back. Good quality coutil or batiste, tastefully finished with embroidered edging. Hose supporters attached.
Sizes 18 to 30. **Price $1.50**
REDUSO, Style 782 (*as pictured*). Medium high bust—exceptionally long over back, hips and abdomen. New shaping of the gores and slash construction over groin insure perfect comfort. Exceptional quality coutil, wide lace and ribbon finish. Three pairs supporters.
Sizes 19 to 36. **Price $5.00**
NUFORM
№ 101 $1.50
Reduso
№ 782 $5.00

NUFORM, Style 123. For average or full figures. Low bust and low under arms. Made with new broadened abdominal support clasp, which gives the fashionable flat effect. Very long over hips and back. Exceptional quality coutil or batiste, finished with embroidered edging. Hose supporters.
Sizes 18 to 30. **Price $2.00**

NUFORM, Style 114. Splendid model for average figures. High bust, long over hips and back. Modish straight lines, slashed both sides of front steel. Fine imported coutil or batiste, finished with dainty embroidered edging. 3 pairs supporters.
Sizes 18 to 30. **Price $3.00**

REDUSO, Style 781. For short, large figures. Low bust and low under arms. Long over hips, back and abdomen. Firm, durable, coutil and batiste lace trimmed. Three pairs supporters.
Sizes 19 to 36. **Price $3.00**

REDUSO, Style 770. For average large figures. Medium high bust, long over hips and abdomen. Durable, coutil or batiste. Lace and ribbon trimming. Three pairs supporters.
Sizes 19 to 36. **Price $3.00**

NUFORM, Style 478. For average figures. Medium low bust, extra length over hips and abdomen. Durable, coutil or batiste, with lace and ribbon finish. 3 pairs supporters.
Sizes 18 to 30. **Price $1.00**

Numerous other Nuform models upwards to $5.00

W. B. FORMU CORSETS give a beautifully modeled full bust effect to the figure, enabling the slender woman to appear to the same advantage as her more fully developed sisters.
Style 107—$2.00 **Style 112—$2.50** **Style 113—$3.00**

REDUSO, Style 776. For tall, well-developed figures. High bust and extra long over hips and back. General construction, trim and material similar to Style 770. Three pairs hose supporters.
Sizes 19 to 36. **Price $3.00**

Other Reduso models upwards to $10.00

WEINGARTEN BROS., Inc., Makers, Broadway and 34th Street, New York City

Everwear Hosiery, 1911

Fleisher Yarns, 1919

► Boston Garter, 1911

Boston Garter
Cord Type
Boston Garter
Pad Type
C. COLES PHILLIPS
Boston Garter
At Stores Everywhere
Lisle, 25 cents; Silk, 50 cents
George Frost Company
Makers Boston

Luxite
Hosiery

Luxite Hosiery, 1919 ◂

Illustrator Coles Phillips, who also produced images for other hosiery brands, blended the look of a pinup — pretty girl in a diaphanous dress — with the sentimental image of an injured veteran. Phillips became known for the "fade away," in which the main figures' clothing is the same color as the background, allowing the elements to partially blend.

Der Illustrator Coles Phillips, der auch Bilder für andere Strumpfmarken produzierte, kombinierte den Anblick eines Pin-ups – hübsches Mädchen in durchsichtigem Kleid – mit dem sentimentalen Bild eines verletzten Veteranen. Phillips wurde mit dem Effekt des „Verblassens" bekannt, bei dem die Kleidung der Hauptfigur dieselbe Farbe aufweist wie der Hintergrund, so dass beide teilweise ineinander übergehen.

L'illustrateur Coles Phillips, qui travailla aussi pour d'autres marques de bonneterie, associait le look de la pin-up (jolie fille en robe diaphane) à l'image sentimentale d'un vétéran blessé. Phillips se fit connaître pour ses « fondus » où les vêtements des personnages principaux se fondaient partiellement dans un arrière-plan de la même couleur.

Luxite Hosiery, 1918

Painted by Coles Phillips for Luxite Textiles, Inc.   © L. T. Inc.

Luxite Hosiery

For Men, Women and Children

SELDOM does your hosiery escape the attention of others, and if it be this captivating Luxite, wherever you go admiration follows.

Luxite has proved that silk hose will wear splendidly when made as we make Luxite, using the finest Japanese silk thread of many tightly spun strands, and pure dyes that cannot injure either the silk or your feet.

Men's Silk Faced 50c, and Pure Thread Silk 75c and $1.00. Other styles at 35c up. Women's Pure Thread Silk $1.10 to $2.50. Other styles 50c up. Children's 50c per pair and up.

Ask for Luxite Hosiery in the stores. If you cannot conveniently get it, write us for directions and illustrated book and prices.

LUXITE TEXTILES, Inc., 654 Fowler Street, Milwaukee, Wis.

Makers of High Grade Hosiery Since 1875

New York   Chicago   San Francisco   Liverpool, England   Sydney, Australia

LUXITE TEXTILES OF CANADA, Limited, London, Ont.

(975)

INDIAN HEAD

Reg. U. S. Pat. Off.

Use It Instead of Linen

Not a Fad but a Fashion

Just as really smart women adopt not the newest of the new fashions, but rather the best of the new fashions—because such garments look best first and last—so you will find the cleverest suits and sport clothes for summer made of Indian Head. It is the white wash-fabric that stays good looking. Garments made of it have a lasting atmosphere of style that is possible only with a very well-made fabric.

Indian Head helps the kiddies to look spick and span longer than seems possible. In it they are clad for any call of fun or fashion.

Many ready-to-wear clothes made of Indian Head are now shown in the shops. If the label is sewn in the garment you will know that it is the real Indian Head.

Made in one unchanging quality for 80 years, Indian Head may now be had in two finishes—soft or linen finish, each made in four widths, 27, 33, 36, and 44 inches.

Some stores sell Indian Head in the Wash Goods Department, others in the Domestics. The Linen Finish is usually sold in the Linen Department. Wherever you find it, the name INDIAN HEAD *must* appear on the selvage, or you are not getting Indian Head at all.

Amory, Browne & Co. Dept. 44, Box 1206 Boston, Massachusetts

FOR YOUR LITTLE GIRL

Send 6 cents for a sample of INDIAN HEAD cut out ready to sew with simple directions into a dress for an 18" dolly.

INDIAN HEAD

25¢
40¢
CHENEY SILKS
SPRING and its awakening colors—the shimmer of warm sunshine—at no time in the year does womanhood so wish to look her prettiest as in Spring.
A Cheney Silk Foulard
expresses Spring!—the ripple and soft fall of it, the beauty and smart newness of it. Here is one of the many new Cheney originations. All of them true in fashion, distinctive, shower-proof and of excellent quality. They are desired by most women who prefer and know the best. Look for a showing of Cheney Silks and take advantage of their many suggestions.
* * *
SOMEWHERE along the silken thread Cheney craftsmanship comes in—and gives you Elegance of Weaving.
* * *
CHENEY SILKS
Foulards

Cheney Silks, 1918

Indian Head Fabrics, 1918 ◄

Kleinert's
Millinery for Mermaids
WHAT captivating bits of mermaid millinery are these gaily-bobbing caps and bonnets that enchant feminine hearts with their becomingness.
Fashion's most exclusive bathing beaches are colorful with Kleinert caps, hats and bonnets, in styles to suit every bathing costume.
Insist on the Kleinert name for service.
I. B. KLEINERT RUBBER CO.
719-727 Broadway New York
Canadian Office:
84 Wellington St., W., Toronto
Makers of Dress Shields, Bathing Caps, Hose Supporters, Baby Pants, etc.

Kleinert's Swim Caps, 1919

▸ McCallum Hosiery, 1917

Mc Callum
Silk Hosiery

Kilburnie
Zephyr
Fast Color
32 inches wide

Bulloz of Paris, 1917

Even if many of his styles were considered extreme, couturier Paul Poiret's design ideas – including relaxed silhouettes, natural waistlines, and such exotic details as turbans and tasseled sleeves – were widely copied by other fashion houses of the era and filtered into everyday dress. By the early part of the decade, he had also experimented with the "lampshade" tunic and the "hobble" skirt.

Obwohl viele seiner Einfälle als extrem galten, wurden die Designideen des Couturiers Paul Poiret – darunter fließende Silhouetten, ungeschnürte Taillen und exotische Details wie Turbane und Ärmel mit Quasten – von anderen Modehäusern jener Ära vielfach kopiert und tauchten selbst in der Alltagskleidung auf. Zu Beginn des Jahrzehnts hatte er auch mit einer Tunika in Lampenschirmform und dem Humpelrock experimentiert.

Bien que ses vêtements fussent considérés comme extrêmes, les créations du couturier Paul Poiret – notamment ses silhouettes décontractées, les tailles naturelles et les détails exotiques comme les turbans et les manches à pompons – ont été largement copiées par les autres maisons de mode de l'époque, jusqu'à s'infiltrer dans l'habillement quotidien. Au début des années 1910, il avait aussi inventé la tunique « abat-jour » et la jupe dite « entravée ».

Kilburnie Zephyr Fabrics, 1918 ◄

Created by Bulloz of Paris
COLES PHILLIPS
For description see page 57

THE AMERICAN MEN ARE THE
Most of them Wear
Cluett
SHIRTS
On and off like a coat
Because
THEY approach so very closely in quality, style and in appearance the best productions of the custom shop.
Because
They are made in color fast fabrics in exclusive designs.
Because
They have revealed all that is best and all that is new in shirt construction, and all that is scientific in pattern draughting during a period of almost fifty years.
Because
They have demonstrated the fact that they fit as well, wear as well and look as well as any shirts regardless of cost.
Made under our own label.
$1.50 and more.
Send for "Today's Shirt," a booklet of more than usual interest.
And These Are Some
CLUETT · PEABODY · & · CO · Largest Makers
River Street,

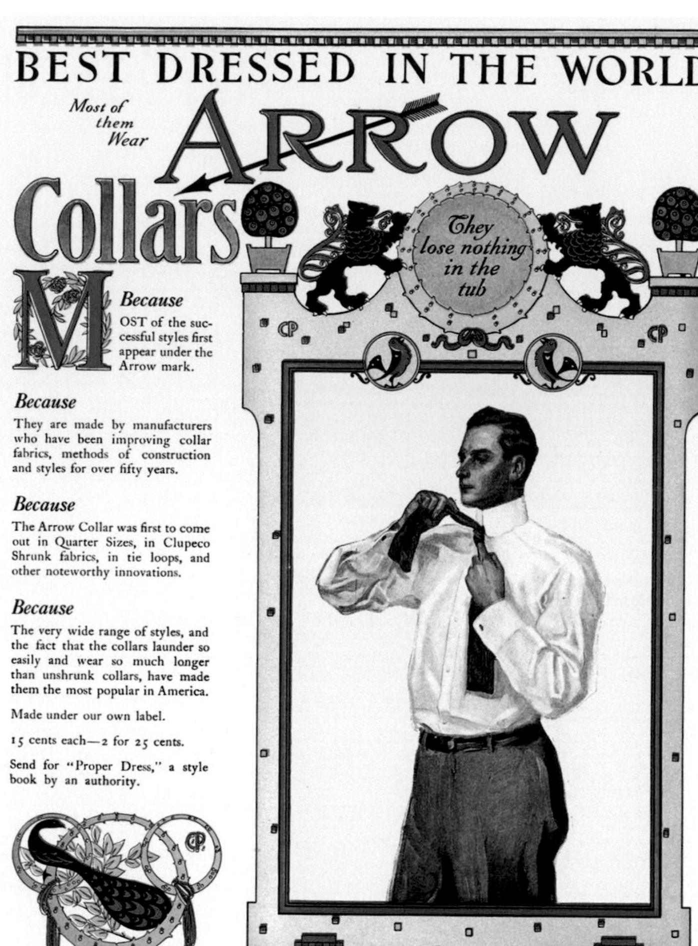

BEST DRESSED IN THE WORLD
Most of them Wear
ARROW
Collars
They lose nothing in the tub
Because
MOST of the successful styles first appear under the Arrow mark.
Because
They are made by manufacturers who have been improving collar fabrics, methods of construction and styles for over fifty years.
Because
The Arrow Collar was first to come out in Quarter Sizes, in Clupeco Shrunk fabrics, in tie loops, and other noteworthy innovations.
Because
The very wide range of styles, and the fact that the collars launder so easily and wear so much longer than unshrunk collars, have made them the most popular in America.
Made under our own label.
15 cents each—2 for 25 cents.
Send for "Proper Dress," a style book by an authority.
of The Reasons Why
of · COLLARS · and · SHIRTS · in · the · World
TROY, N.Y.

Cluett Shirts/Arrow Collars, ca. 1916

Advertising boomed with the proliferation of new magazines and new printing techniques, and advertisers found themselves in the position of having to differentiate their products from those of their competitors. This ad uses color illustrations to draw the reader in, and then lists the reasons its products are superior.

Das Werbegeschäft blühte mit dem Aufkommen neuer Zeitschriften und Drucktechniken, und die Reklamemacher waren bald gezwungen, ihre Produkte von den Erzeugnissen der Konkurrenz abzugrenzen. Diese Annonce benutzt farbige Illustrationen, um die Aufmerksamkeit des Lesers zu gewinnen, und listet Gründe für die Überlegenheit der eigenen Produkte auf.

Face au boom de la publicité engendré par la prolifération de nouveaux magazines et de nouvelles techniques d'impression, les annonceurs se virent contraints de différencier leurs produits par rapport à ceux de leurs concurrents.
Cette publicité utilise des illustrations en couleurs pour attirer l'attention du lecteur, puis énumère les raisons pour lesquelles ses produits sont les meilleurs.

► McCallum Hosiery, 1914

"Silk Stockings?"

Of course, some beautiful silk stockings would be just the thing! Something a little better than she would buy herself. She'd like McCallum's No. 113—very fine black all silk hose, known to be the most satisfactory silk stocking made. Or, No 201—very sheer, with hand embroidered clocks. McCallum's No. 153 are made in any color to match shoes or gown on a few days' notice.

McCallum
Silk Hosiery

If you're making gifts of men's hose—ask for McCallum's No. 326—pure thread silk, heavy weight, black and colors. And No. 329—rib-shot silk, the most distinctive hose on the market.

Sold at the Best Shops Everywhere

McCallum Hosiery Company, Northampton, Mass.

Mary MacKinnon
Tom Wye
TRADE MARK
TW
TOM WYE has caught the brightness of the sunshine, the freedom of the great out-of-doors, the smartness of the Avenue and the sturdiness of his native English hills and knitted them into the very fabric of the Swimming-Suits he makes for women.
Ask for them today in your favorite shop. Study their clever cut. Admire their rich coloring. Select your favorite.
If your dealer is out of them write to
TOM WYE of Winchendon, Mass.

Tom Wye
KNIT JACKET

TOM WYE Knit Utility Jackets combine custom-tailored smartness with the comfort of an old shooting-coat; they have a golfy knock-about quality without losing their air of swagger; they give warmth without bulk. Exclusive haberdashers everywhere carry them and will show them to you in blurry Heather mixtures that will make you think of the wind-swept uplands.

TOM WYE WINCHENDON, MASS.

Tom Wye Knits, 1919

Tom Wye Swimwear, ca. 1919 ◂

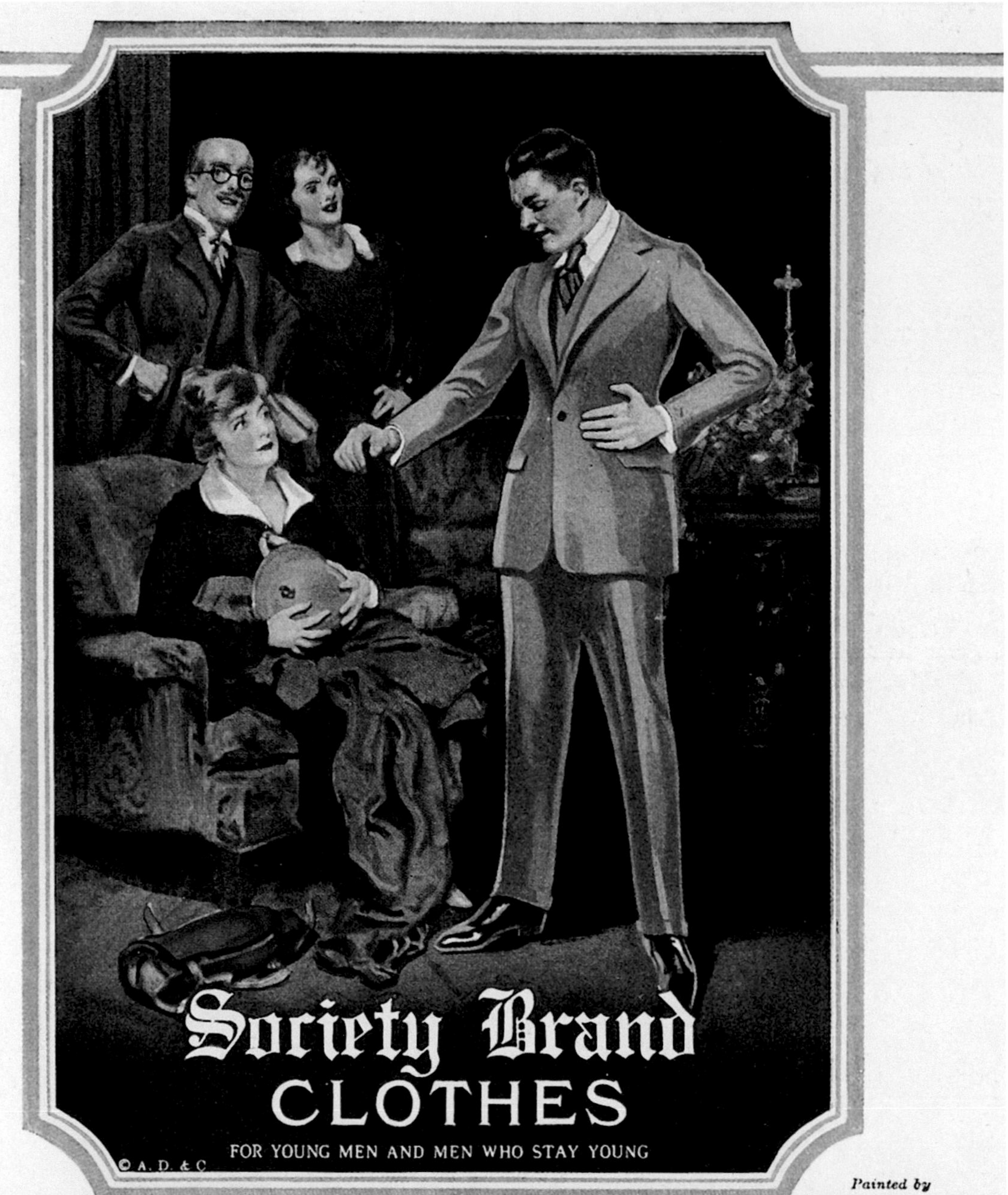

Society Brand Clothes, 1919

Alfred Decker, president of Society Brand Clothing, saw a business opportunity in the thousands of decommissioned fighter planes flown in the war. In 1920, the businessman purchased several planes, created an airfield outside of Chicago, and began air-shipping products to the company's retailers in large Midwestern cities and to smaller communities that were less accessible by rail or truck.

Alfred Decker, Präsident der Society Brand Clothing, sah eine geschäftliche Chance in den Tausenden von stillgelegten Kampfflugzeugen aus dem Krieg. 1920 kaufte der Geschäftsmann einige Flugzeuge, ließ außerhalb von Chicago einen Flugplatz anlegen und begann auf dem Luftweg Ware zu den Einzelhändlern in Großstädten des Mittleren Westens und zu kleineren Gemeinden, die via Bahn oder Lkw nur schwer erreichbar waren, zu transportieren.

Alfred Decker, le président de Society Brand Clothing, vit une opportunité commerciale dans la démobilisation des milliers d'avions de combat envoyés à la guerre. En 1920, l'homme d'affaires acheta plusieurs avions, fit construire un aérodrome à l'extérieur de Chicago et commença à envoyer ses produits par voie aérienne vers ses points de vente situés dans les grandes villes du Midwest et les petites communautés mal desservies par le train ou le réseau routier.

► Kuppenheimer Menswear, 1914

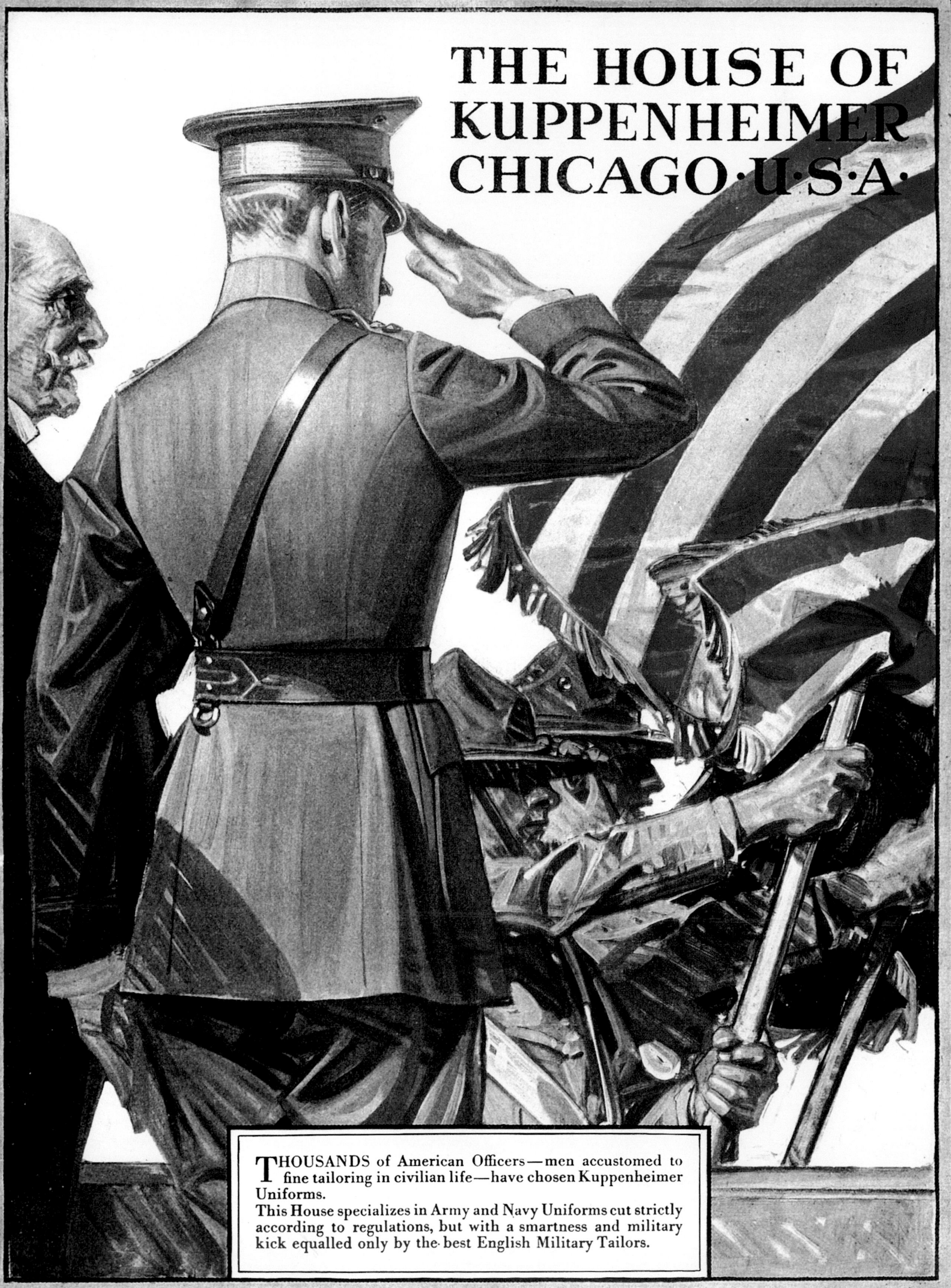
THE HOUSE OF
KUPPENHEIMER
CHICAGO·U·S·A·
THOUSANDS of American Officers—men accustomed to fine tailoring in civilian life—have chosen Kuppenheimer Uniforms.
This House specializes in Army and Navy Uniforms cut strictly according to regulations, but with a smartness and military kick equalled only by the best English Military Tailors.

Kuppenheimer Uniforms, 1918 ◂

During the Great War, Chicago-based suitmaker Kuppenheimer was one of many companies that manufactured uniforms for American soldiers.

Im Ersten Weltkrieg zählte die Anzugfabrik Kuppenheimer mit Sitz in Chicago zu den vielen Firmen, die Uniformen für die amerikanischen Soldaten nähten.

Pendant la Grande Guerre, le fabricant de costumes Kuppenheimer de Chicago compta parmi les nombreuses entreprises produisant des uniformes pour les soldats américains.

Kuppenheimer Menswear, 1919

▸▸ Hart Schaffner & Marx Menswear, 1916

New Styles with the Old Integrity
You'll find more men this Fall waiting to buy good clothes than there are clothes, or good woolens to make them.
Stick to the staunch, reliable make that you know or you'll find yourself paying full price for less than full standard of service and quality.
Kuppenheimer Clothes mean the new styles with the old integrity of all-wool fabric and sound tailoring.
THE HOUSE OF KUPPENHEIMER
A National Clothes Service
The HOUSE OF KUPPENHEIMER

Hart Schaffner & Marx

New Varsity Fifty Five designs for Spring have the style that young men want.

Look for this picture in color, in the window of the store that sells these clothes

SKIRTS GREW SHOCKINGLY SHORT. ONLY THE MOST DARING WORE THEM ABOVE THE KNEE, BUT EVEN MID-CALF STYLES WERE SHORTER THAN EVER BEFORE, AND WITH THAT MUCH LEG SHOWING, STOCKINGS AND SHOES WERE GAINING NEW ATTENTION.

DIE ROCKSÄUME RUTSCHTEN IN SCHOCKIERENDE HÖHEN. NUR DIE MUTIGSTEN TRUGEN KNIEKURZ, ABER SELBST HALBE WADE WAR NOCH KÜRZER ALS JE ZUVOR, UND WEIL MAN DABEI SO VIEL BEIN ZEIGTE, ERHIELTEN STRÜMPFE UND SCHUHWERK UNVERSEHENS NEUE AUFMERKSAMKEIT.

LES JUPES CHOQUENT EN NE CESSANT DE RACCOURCIR. SEULES LES PLUS AUDACIEUSES OSENT LES PORTER AU-DESSUS DU GENOU, MAIS MÊME LES MODÈLES TOMBANT À MI-MOLLET PARAISSENT PLUS COURTS QUE JAMAIS. COMME LES JAMBES S'EXPOSENT, LES BAS ET LES CHAUSSURES SUSCITENT SOUDAIN UN NOUVEL INTÉRÊT.

1920

JAZZ BABIES AND COLLEGE BOYS
JAZZ BABIES UND COLLEGE BOYS
JAZZEUSES ET ÉTUDIANTS

-1929

McCallum
Silk Hosiery

Aberfoyle Fabrics, 1928 ◄◄

Mc Callum Hosiery, 1922 ◄

Cutex Nail Polish, 1929

THE 1920s WAS A DECADE OF CONTRADICTIONS. EUROPE, STILL RECOVERING FROM THE DEVASTATION OF THE GREAT WAR, SUFFERED A SERIES OF ECONOMIC CRISES. Yet it was an age of cultural high points, with great literary works coming from authors D. H. Lawrence, Marcel Proust, Virginia Woolf, and James Joyce, and an expansion of both modern and commercial art.

In America, the era opened with the passage of women's suffrage and Prohibition. It closed with the Wall Street stock-market collapse of 1929. In between, there was the flapper.

It was the Jazz Age, marked by an air of frivolity and an emphasis on youth. More and more people were flocking to the movies to see stars like Joan Crawford dance the Charleston in *Our Dancing Daughters*, or reading about her literary counterparts in F. Scott Fitzgerald's *The Great Gatsby*.

Young people flocked to colleges, sparking an interest in collegiate trends. Some were short-lived, like raccoon-skin coats, rolled-down stockings, and "Oxford bags"—extra-wide trousers with pleats and cuffs, worn with spectator shoes and cardigans. Bobbed hairstyles for women inspired new hat styles, including the popular, close-fitting cloche. And, of course, the skirts grew shockingly short. Only the most daring wore them above the knee, but even mid-calf styles were shorter than ever before, and with that much leg showing, stockings and shoes were suddenly gaining new attention. Most women wore sensible oxford shoes during the day, but favored beautiful dancing shoes with dainty straps and Louis XIV heels in the evening.

England's Prince of Wales became a trendsetter, as men emulated his elegant, casual style: pullover sweaters worn under a jacket, belted trousers, and the so-called American collar. Collars had in fact become a subject of debate, with the older generation preferring a detachable, starched collar worn upright, and younger men preferring the attached collar worn folded over the tie. In 1924, American tailor Jesse Langsdorf patented a new construction of tie. Made from three pieces and cut on the bias, Langsdorf's ties retained their shape without the need of ironing.

Sports clothes also became fashionable, championed by athletes and celebrities. Golf's plus fours—baggy knickers that took their name from the length of fabric that fell below the knees—and the V-neck, cable-knit tennis sweater soon made their ways off the courses and courts and into men's casual wardrobes. French tennis star René Lacoste began capitalizing on his nickname, "Le Crocodile," by designing and then selling pique golf shirts with embroidered crocodile logos.

On the economic front, business was booming and credit was easy to get. Improvements in manufacturing and new innovations in retailing gave rise to the chain store, which offered a large selection and cheap prices. It was an advertiser's paradise. Advertisers shifted from quasi-scientific and testimonial-driven copy to the employment of psychological techniques to convey emotional attachment to a specific brand. And when it came to playing up snob appeal—and marketing styles as "chic"—no other sector could hold a candle to the fashion industry.

1920

1920 Johnston & Murphy markets equestrian boots to country-club set

Johnston & Murphy bietet Reitstiefel für den Country-Club

Johnston & Murphy commercialise les bottes d'équitation dans les country clubs

1920 Jantzen introduces Diving Girl logo, designed by George Petty

Jantzen präsentiert sein von George Petty entworfenes Logo Diving Girl

Jantzen introduit son logo avec nageuse, dessiné par George Petty

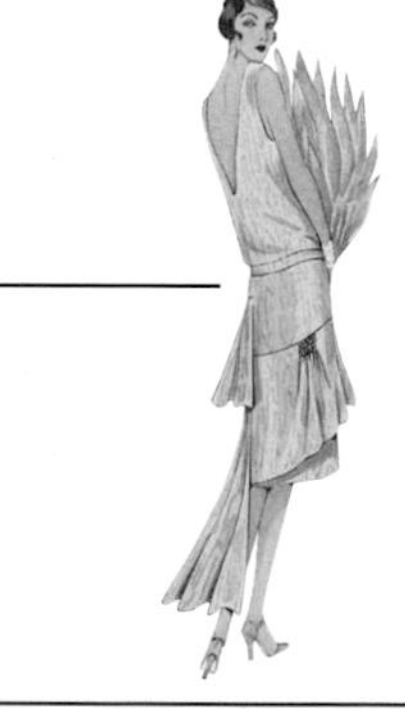

1920 Jazz Age woman introduced to world in silent film, *The Flapper*

Im Stummfilm *The Flapper* wird die typische Frau der Jazz-Ära präsentiert

Le monde découvre les jazzeuses dans le film muet *The Flapper*

1921 Men emulate Rudolph Valentino's shiny, slicked hair in *The Sheik*

Männer nehmen sich Rudolph Valentinos glänzend glatte Frisur aus *Der Scheich* zum Vorbild

Les hommes copient la coiffure lissée à la brillantine qu'arbore Rudolph Valentino dans *Le Cheik*

DIE 1920ER JAHRE WAREN EIN JAHRZEHNT DER WIDERSPRÜCHE. EUROPA WAR DAMALS NOCH DABEI, SICH VON DEN VERWÜSTUNGEN DES ERSTEN WELTKRIEGS ZU ERHOLEN UND ERLITT EINE REIHE VON WIRTSCHAFTSKRISEN. Dennoch handelte es sich um eine Epoche kultureller Höhepunkte mit großartigen literarischen Werken von Autoren wie D. H. Lawrence, Marcel Proust, Virginia Woolf und James Joyce sowie zunehmender Verbreitung sowohl der modernen wie auch der kommerziellen Kunst.

In Amerika begann die Ära mit der Durchsetzung des Frauenwahlrechts und der Prohibition. An ihrem Ende stand der Börsencrash der Wall Street von 1929. Dazwischen gab es den „flapper" genannten Backfisch.

Es war das Jazz Age, geprägt von einer gewissen Frivolität und Betonung der Jugend. Die Menschen strömten in immer größerer Zahl in die Kinos, um Stars wie Joan Crawford in *Our Dancing Daughters* Charleston tanzen zu sehen. Oder sie lasen in F. Scott Fitzgeralds *Der große Gatsby* von ihren literarischen Pendants.

Die Jugend drängte in die Colleges und entwickelte zunehmend Interesse an dort herrschenden Trends. Einige davon erwiesen sich als sehr kurzlebig, etwa Mäntel aus Waschbärenfell, hinuntergerollte Strümpfe und „Oxford bags" – extrem weite Hosen mit Bügelfalte und Aufschlag, zu denen man zweifarbige Schuhe und Strickjacken trug. Die kinnlangen Frisuren der Damen brachten neue Hutmoden zutage, darunter der beliebte, eng anliegende Glockenhut. Und natürlich rutschten die Rocksäume in schockierende Höhen. Nur die Mutigsten trugen kniekurz, aber selbst halbe Wade war noch kürzer als je zuvor, und weil man dabei so viel Bein zeigte, erhielten Strümpfe und Schuhwerk unversehens neue Aufmerksamkeit. Die meisten Frauen wählten für tagsüber praktische Schnürschuhe, bevorzugten für den Abend jedoch schöne Tanzschuhe mit zierlichen Riemchen und Louis-XIV-Absätzen.

Der englische Prince of Wales wurde zum Trendsetter, als die Männerwelt begann, seinen elegant-lässigen Stil zu kopieren: Pullover unterm Jackett, Hosen mit Gürtel und den sogenannten amerikanischen Kragen. Kragen wurden ohnehin zum Gegenstand der Diskussion, weil die ältere Generation die abnehmbare, gestärkte Variante bevorzugte, die aufrecht getragen wurde, während jüngere Herren lieber fest angenähte Kragen trugen, die man über die Krawatte klappte. 1924 ließ sich der amerikanische Schneider Jesse Langsdorf eine neue Krawattenform patentieren. Sie war aus drei Teilen genäht, schräg geschnitten und behielt ihre Form auch ohne Aufbügeln.

Von Athleten und anderen Prominenten bevorzugte Sportbekleidung kam ebenfalls in Mode. Weite Knickerbocker aus dem Golf und Strickpullover mit Zopfmuster und V-Ausschnitt, wie man sie zum Tennis trug, fanden bald ihren Weg von den Golf- und Tennisplätzen in die Freizeitgarderobe der Herren. Der französische Tennisstar René Lacoste begann aus seinem Spitznamen „Le Crocodile" Kapital zu schlagen, indem er Golfhemden aus Piqué, die mit einem gestickten Krokodil als Logo versehen waren, entwarf und verkaufte.

In wirtschaftlicher Hinsicht boomte der Markt und Kredite waren leicht zu bekommen. Verbesserungen in der Massenproduktion und Innovationen im Einzelhandel ermöglichten den Aufstieg von Handelsketten, die eine große Auswahl zu günstigen Preisen boten. Für die Reklamebranche war es das Paradies. Man wandte sich ab vom pseudo-wissenschaftlichen Abbild nach Art eines Empfehlungsschreibens und hin zur Verwendung psychologischer Methoden, um einer bestimmten Marke quasi einen emotionalen Zusatznutzen zu verpassen. Und wo es um vermeintlichen Snobismus und die Vermarktung bestimmter Trends als „chic" ging, da konnte keine andere Branche der Modeindustrie das Wasser reichen.

1922 Cloche hat with narrow brim popular for women with shorter hairstyles

Glockenhut mit schmaler Krempe beliebt bei Frauen mit Kurzhaarfrisur

Les femmes aux cheveux courts adoptent le chapeau cloche à bord étroit

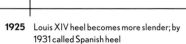

1924 American tailor Jesse Langsdorf patents Resilient Construction necktie

Der amerikanische Schneider Jesse Langsdorf lässt sich das Krawattenmodell Resilient Construction patentieren

Le tailleur américain Jesse Langsdorf fait breveter la cravate souple

1925 Louis XIV heel becomes more slender; by 1931 called Spanish heel

Louis-XIV-Absätze werden schmaler und heißen ab 1931 spanischer Absatz

Le talon Louis XIV s'affine ; il sera rebaptisé talon espagnol en 1931

1926 Garters hold up stockings and hide small flasks of liquor during Prohibition era

Strumpfbänder halten Strümpfe und während der Prohibition auch kleine Schnapsflaschen

Sous la Prohibition, les jarretières ne servent pas qu'à fixer les bas : on y cache aussi de petites flasques d'alcool

Chimin

Bradley Knitwear, 1926 ◂◂

Stehli Silks, 1929 ◂

LES ANNÉES 20 REPRÉSENTENT UNE DÉCENNIE DE CONTRADICTIONS. A PEINE REMISE DES RAVAGES DE LA GRANDE GUERRE, L'EUROPE FAIT FACE À UNE SÉRIE DE CRISES ÉCONOMIQUES. L'époque connaît toutefois de grands moments culturels grâce aux chefs-d'œuvre littéraires d'auteurs tels D. H. Lawrence, Marcel Proust, Virginia Woolf et James Joyce, et à l'expansion de l'art moderne et commercial.

Aux Etats-Unis, la décennie s'ouvre sur le droit de vote des femmes et la Prohibition, et s'achève sur l'effondrement de la Bourse de Wall Street en 1929. Entre-temps, la jeune femme des années 20 est née.

L'ère du jazz est marquée par une certaine frivolité qui accorde la priorité à la jeunesse. Les foules sont de plus en plus nombreuses à fréquenter les cinémas pour voir des stars comme Joan Crawford danser le charleston dans *Les Nouvelles Vierges*, ou à lire les histoires de ses homologues littéraires dans *Gatsby le Magnifique* de F. Scott Fitzgerald.

Les jeunes fréquentent l'université en masse et on s'intéresse aux modes lancées sur les campus. Certaines ne sont qu'éphémères, par exemple les manteaux en peau de raton laveur, les bas roulés aux chevilles et le « pantalon Oxford » – ultra large, avec des plis et des revers, porté avec des chaussures bicolores et des cardigans. La coupe au bol des femmes inspire de nouveaux chapeaux, notamment le modèle cloche à succès. Et, bien sûr, les jupes choquent en ne cessant de raccourcir. Seules les plus audacieuses osent les porter au-dessus du genou, mais même les modèles tombant à mi-mollet paraissent plus courts que jamais. Comme les jambes s'exposent, les bas et les chaussures suscitent soudain un nouvel intérêt. La plupart des femmes portent des richelieus confortables en journée, mais privilégient les chaussures de bal aux délicates lanières et à talons Louis XIV pour le soir.

Le prince de Galles devient un précurseur de tendances dans la mesure où les hommes s'approprient son style élégant et décontracté : les pulls portés sous une veste, le pantalon ceinturé et le soi-disant « col américain ». En fait, les cols sont devenus l'objet d'un vrai débat : l'ancienne génération préfère le col montant amidonné et amovible, et les jeunes, le col intégré à la chemise, qui se replie par-dessus la cravate. En 1924, le tailleur américain Jesse Langsdorf fait breveter une nouvelle sorte de cravate. Fabriquée à partir de trois pièces et taillée en diagonale, la cravate de Langsdorf conserve sa forme sans besoin de repassage.

Défendus par les athlètes et les célébrités, les vêtements de sport deviennent à la mode. Les culottes de golf, ou « plus fours » – pantalon court qui doit son nom anglais à la longueur de tissu tombant sous le genou – et les pulls de tennis torsadés à col V se frayent rapidement un chemin en dehors des courts et des parcours dix-huit trous pour devenir des basiques de la garde-robe masculine. Le grand tennisman français René Lacoste mise sur son surnom, « Le Crocodile », en concevant et commercialisant des chemises de golf en coton piqué brodées d'un logo de crocodile.

Dans le domaine des affaires, l'économie est en plein boom et les banques font facilement crédit. Les progrès de l'industrie et les innovations en matière de distribution donnent naissance aux chaînes de magasins qui proposent un large choix de produits à des prix avantageux. C'est une époque bénie pour tous les publicitaires. La publicité délaisse les discours pseudoscientifiques reposant sur les témoignages et recourt aux techniques psychologiques pour que le consommateur s'attache émotionnellement à une marque spécifique. Quand il s'agit d'attirer l'attention des snobs – et de vendre des produits dits « chics » – aucun autre secteur n'arrive à la cheville de l'industrie de la mode.

1927

1927 Hollywood redefines sex appeal in Clara Bow film, *It*

Mit Clara Bows Film *Das gewisse Etwas* definiert Hollywood eine neue Form von Sexappeal

Hollywood redéfinit le sex-appeal à travers le personnage interprété par Clara Bow dans *Le Coup de Foudre*

LEVI'S

1928 Levi Strauss & Co. registers Levi's as trademark

Levi Strauss & Co. lässt Levi's als Markenzeichen eintragen

Levi Strauss & Co. dépose la marque Levi's

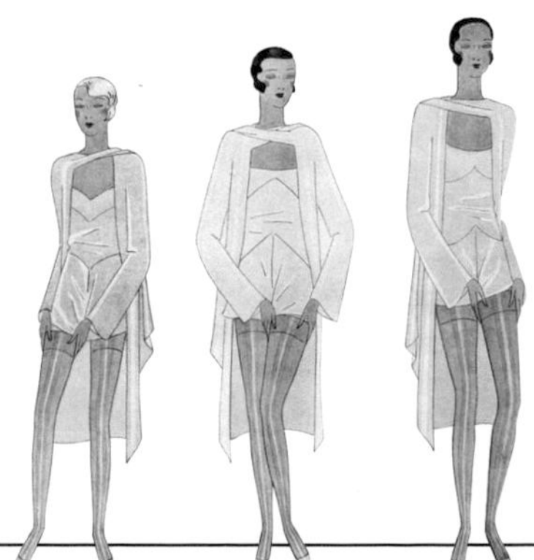

1929 Gordon introduces proportioned stockings

Gordon bringt proportionierte Strümpfe auf den Markt

Gordon lance les bas dits « proportionnés »

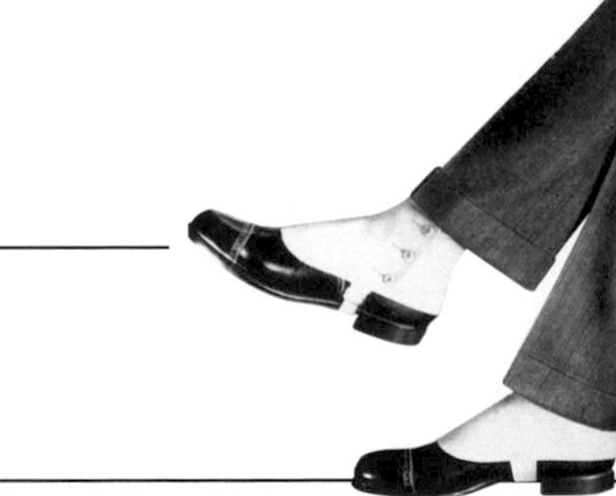

1929 Irving Berlin celebrates spats in song, "Puttin' on the Ritz"

Irving Berlin singt in „Puttin' on the Ritz" ein Loblied auf die Gamasche

Irving Berlin fait l'apologie des guêtres dans sa chanson « Puttin' on the Ritz »

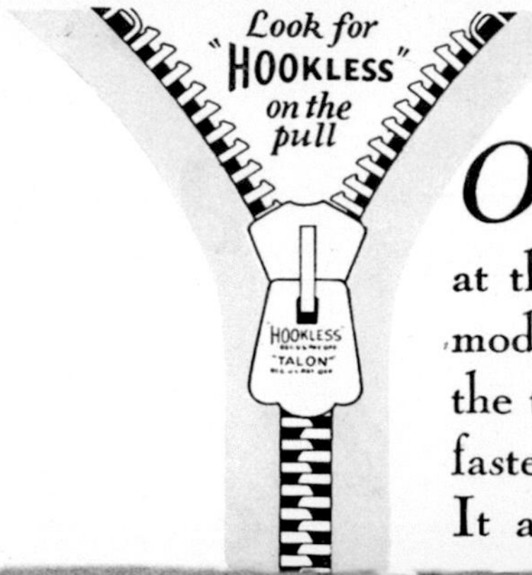

Look for "HOOKLESS" on the pull

On the Shore—or in the Mountains. You see it on fine luggage arriving at the fashionable resorts. You see it at the shore—on smart new bathing suits, on modish shoes, on gayly colored bathing bags. Just glance around the golf links or the tennis court and note the sport clothes, golf bags, racquet covers neatly and securely fastened with the Talon Fastener! . . . Salt water, rain, damp weather cannot rust it. It always opens with an easy pull and always closes quickly, snugly and securely.

How many uses has the Talon Fastener? You liked the speed, the smartness, the convenience of the Talon Fastener on overshoes and youngsters' leggings. Now it's available to you on play suits, riding boots and purses—tents, sleeping bags and lumberjacks—countless items of apparel and equipment . . . Before you buy, be sure to ask "Can I get that fitted with a Talon Fastener?" Then, to make certain that you get the Talon, the original slide-fastener—that always works, never rusts, launders perfectly—look for "Hookless" or "Talon" on the pull.

Write us, the original manufacturer, for the name of companies making articles fitted with the Talon Fastener

HOOKLESS FASTENER COMPANY, MEADVILLE, PENNSYLVANIA

CHICAGO: Lytton Building, 14 East Jackson Boulevard NEW YORK CITY: 393 Seventh Avenue

Bathing bags and bathing shoes, bathing trunks and tennis racquet cover showing the application of the smart, convenient Talon Fastener.

105

Gossard Corsets and Brasseries, 1926

Talon Slide-Fasteners, 1928 ◂

McClelland Barclay
Jantzen
© 1923
SWIMMING SUIT
PAT. SEPTEMBER 6TH 1921

Jantzen Swimwear, 1929

Jantzen Swimwear, 1929

Jantzen Swimwear, 1926 ◂

BLUE MOON
Silk Stockings

New Day in Women's Hosiery!

$1.65 to $2.15

A NEW silk stocking has been made—so beautiful, so durable, that women are amazed to find that the price is only **$1.65 to $2.15**. Not at any price, however high, can you buy silk stockings that are more lovely or more lasting. And the reason is this:

The Blue Moon Company makes nothing but this one brand of *full-fashioned silk hosiery*. On this one product their entire effort is centered

Patented Triple Garter Strip Prevents Runs.

—their great new factory, the latest improved machinery, the highest textile skill. And inspiring all this, is a conscientious pride in doing a fine thing well.

Every Blue Moon Silk Stocking is made of pure Japanese dipped dye silk, which is the longest-wearing fabric known. Delightfully sheer yet substantial and firm. Shimmering, dainty, exquisite!

Blue Moon Silk Stockings come in every smart new shade—for every taste, every occasion. Be sure to ask for the new Blue Moon Silk Stockings next time you go shopping. Don't accept a substitute.

BLUE MOON SILK HOSIERY CO., Philadelphia, Pa. *New York Office:* 389 FIFTH AVENUE

McCallum Hosiery, 1922

Early advertising remained simple: Explain the product, its benefits, and why you need it. The look tended to be text-heavy, with few images, and the copy was straightforward. By the 1920s, new printing techniques and changes in the marketplace led to an advertising boom which would rely more on psychological motivation than literal displays of the product. McCallum had been using the "You just know she wears them" slogan for several years to sell its stockings – but, in this instance, the ad does not even show the product.

Frühe Reklame blieb schlicht: Erkläre das Produkt, seine Vorzüge und warum man es braucht. Das Erscheinungsbild war textlastig, mit wenig Bildern und einfachem Druck. Ab den 1920ern sorgten neue Drucktechniken und Veränderungen des Marktes für einen Werbe-Boom, der stärker auf psychologische Motive als auf die wirklichkeitsgetreue Darstellung des Produkts abzielte. McCallum hatte einige Jahre lang mit dem Slogan „You just know she wears them" für den Verkauf seiner Strümpfe geworben – in diesem Fall zeigt die Annonce das Produkt allerdings nicht einmal.

A ses débuts, la publicité était très simple : présenter le produit, ses avantages et les raisons pour lesquelles on en a besoin. Il y avait beaucoup de texte et peu d'images, et le ton employé était direct. Dans les années 20, les nouvelles techniques d'impression et les évolutions du marché déclenchèrent un boom publicitaire qui reposait plus sur la motivation psychologique que sur la présentation réelle des produits. McCallum utilisait le slogan « You just know she wears them » depuis plusieurs années pour vendre ses bas mais, dans cet exemple, le visuel publicitaire ne montre même pas le produit.

Blue Moon Hosiery, 1926 ◄

McCallum
Silk Hosiery
You just know she wears them
SOMEWHERE in the McCallum line is precisely the silk stocking you want. Numbers 105—113—122—199 in black, and 152—153—199 in colors are the most popular, and can be found in the best shops. You have confidence in wearing silk stockings with a name you are proud to tell your friends.
McCALLUM HOSIERY COMPANY, NORTHAMPTON, MASS.

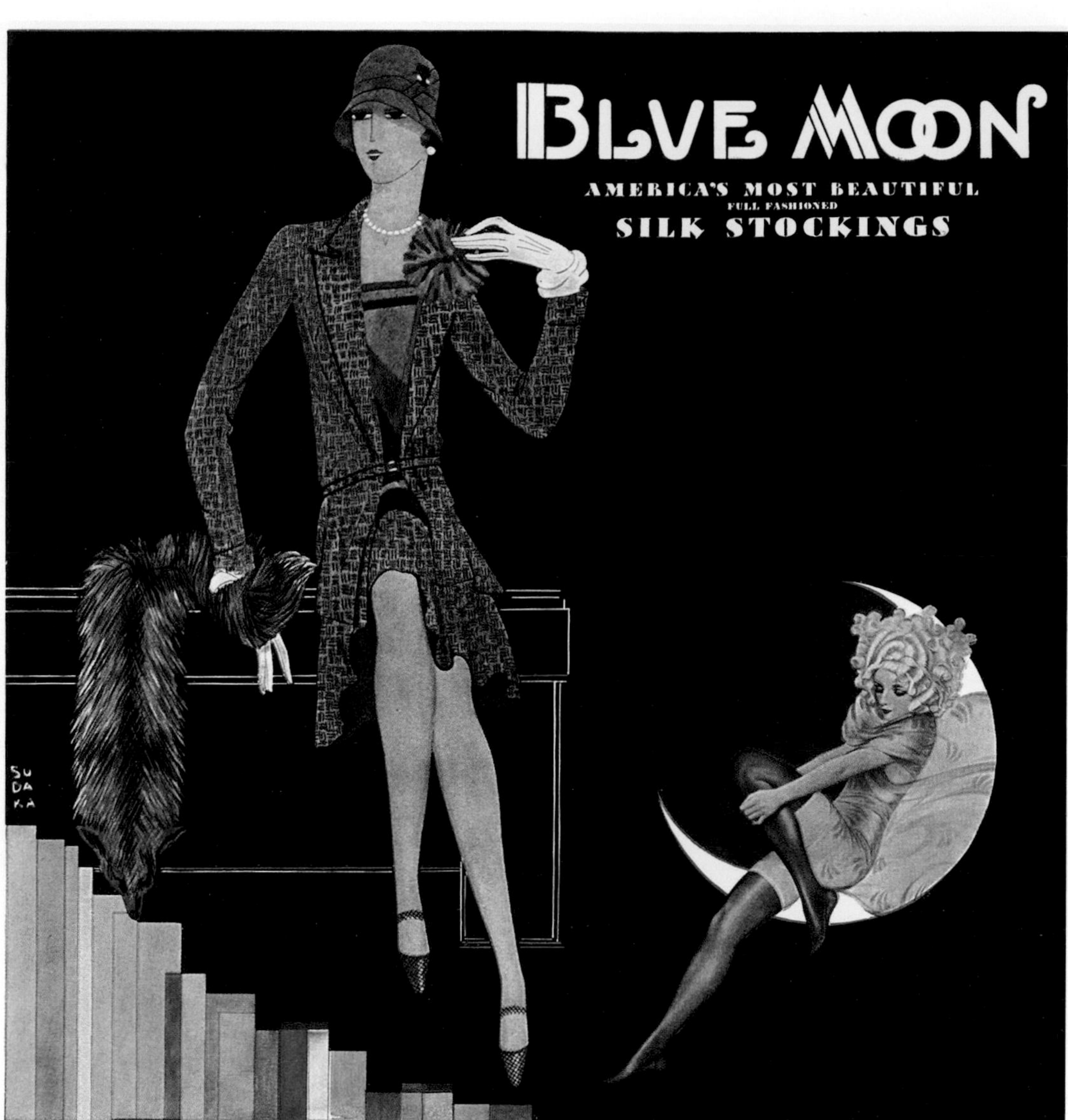

A NEW CREATION *by BLUE MOON*

Think of it . . . exquisite stockings of finely woven chiffon, pure thread silk from top to toe, with a dainty Picot edge, at $1.65! For your smart Fall wardrobe, Blue Moon recommends Style 900, in all the newest shades dictated by Paris . . . Woven into this new creation are hidden reinforcements at toe, sole, heel and top for long life at points of greatest wear.

Woven to fit, Blue Moon Silk Stockings hold their smart shapeliness without strain on the delicate threads, and enhance the beauty of any carefully planned ensemble . . . Other Blue Moon styles, in chiffons and service weights, may be had from $1.35 to $2.50.

LARGMAN, GRAY CO., 389 Fifth Ave., N. Y.

Blue Moon Hosiery, 1929

Blue Moon silk stockings had used the Art Deco girl-in-the-moon image in previous ads. To underscore the "new creation," the old image appears within a more modern layout, featuring a fashionable 1920s woman in a short skirt and cloche hat.

Für die Seidenstrümpfe von Blue Moon hatte man in früheren Annoncen das Art-Deco-Bild vom Mädchen im Mond verwendet. Um die „neue Kreation" zu unterstreichen, erscheint das alte Bild mit einem moderneren Layout und zeigt eine modebewusste Frau in kurzem Rock und mit Glockenhut.

Les précédentes publicités pour les bas de soie Blue Moon utilisaient l'image Art Déco de la fille assise sur un croissant de lune. Pour valoriser la « nouvelle création », l'ancien visuel fut ici repris avec une disposition plus moderne, présentant une femme à la mode des années 20 vêtue d'une jupe courte et coiffée d'un chapeau cloche.

▸ McCallum Hosiery, 1921

McCallum
Silk Hosiery

Gene Pressler

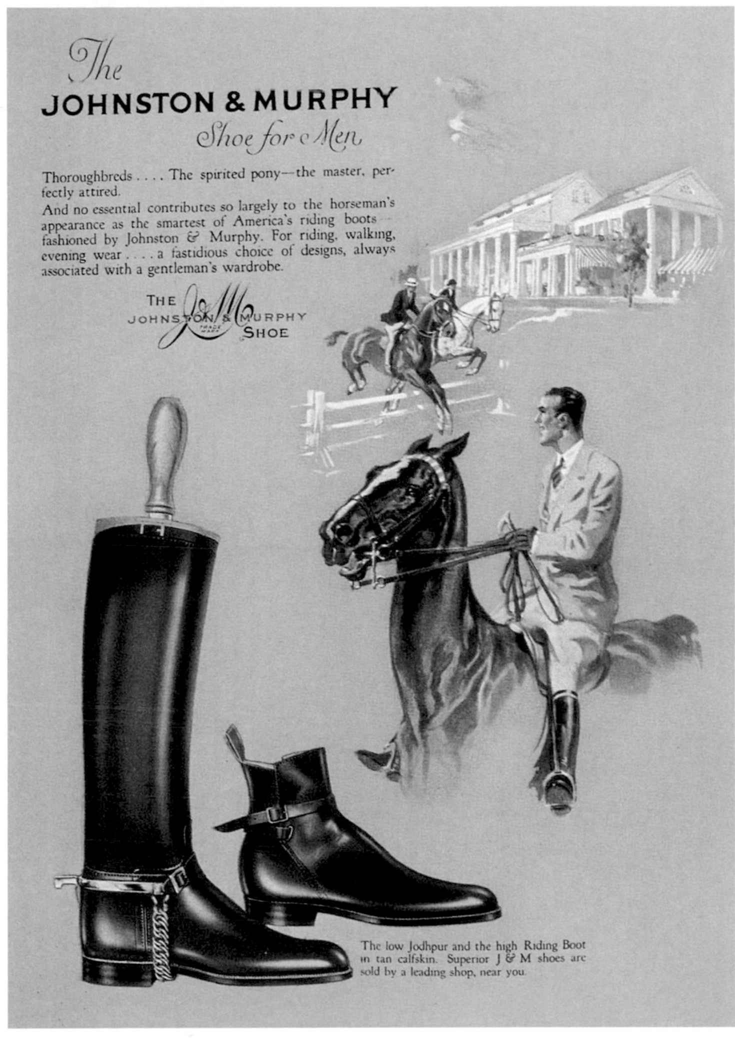

113

▸▸ Buster Brown Shoes, 1920

Early in the century, Brown Shoe Company struck a deal with cartoonist Richard F. Outcault to purchase the Buster Brown name. Outcault had created Buster Brown, a popular cartoon character whose adventures involved his dog, Tige, and sister, Mary Jane. Through the first half of the century, Brown Shoe hired young actors to dress as the character and appear – with dogs playing Tige – at department stores, shoe stores, and theaters across the United States.

Zu Beginn des Jahrhunderts ging die Brown Shoe Company ein Geschäft mit dem Karikaturisten Richard F. Outcault ein und kaufte ihm den Namen Buster Brown ab. Outcault hatte die beliebte Cartoonfigur geschaffen, die mit ihrem Hund Tige und einer Schwester namens Mary Jane allerlei Abenteuer bestand. Im Verlauf der ersten Hälfte des Jahrhunderts engagierte Brown Shoe junge Schauspieler, die wie die Figur gekleidet – mit Hunden in der Rolle von Tige – in Kaufhäusern, Schuhgeschäften und Theatern in ganz Amerika auftraten.

Au début du 20ème siècle, Brown Shoe Company signa un contrat avec le dessinateur Richard F. Outcault pour acquérir le nom de Buster Brown, un personnage de bande dessinée très populaire dont les aventures impliquaient son chien Tige et sa sœur Mary Jane. Pendant la première moitié du siècle, Brown Shoe recruta de jeunes acteurs et leur fit porter le costume du personnage – avec des chiens dans le rôle de Tige – pour des apparitions dans les grands magasins, les boutiques de chaussures et les cinémas à travers tous les Etats-Unis.

Johnston & Murphy Shoes, 1927

Johnston & Murphy Shoes, 1927

Vode Kid Shoes, 1920 ◂

For Girls For Boys of 2 to 16

BUSTER BROWN SHOES

THE Goodyear Welt process of attaching the uppers to the soles adds to the appearance, to the comfort and to the wear of every pair of Buster Brown Shoes. Any shoe merchant will explain why this process excels and what it means to you.

Because they are made upon the famous Brown Shaping Lasts, these shoes fit perfectly, and throughout the growing years keep the feet free from corns, bunions, broken arches, weak ankles and tortured toes. Buster Brown Shoes are the only shoes that combine the important advantages of the Brown Shaping Lasts and

Genuine Goodyear Welt Construction

Good stores everywhere sell Buster Brown Shoes at $4.00, $5.00, $6.00 and up, in button, lace and blucher models—all with genuine Goodyear Welts and Government standard oak-tanned soles.

For detailed information regarding the Brown Shaping Lasts, and positive proof that wearing Buster Brown Shoes insures sound, healthy feet, write today for the free book on "Training the Growing Feet".

Brown Shoe Company, St. Louis, U. S. A.

Manufacturers of White House Shoes for Men, Maxine Shoes for Women, Buster Brown Shoes for Boys and for Girls, and Blue Ribbon Service Shoes

Style No. F-93

This New Galosh sets the season's style!

When the ball is on the two-yard line and wintry blasts are breezing up the stadium, you find a snug *new* galosh setting the season's style—in colors, lightness, warmth and wear.
It's the *new* Hood galosh—feather light and winter warm—in the colors and fabrics of this ultra-smart season . . . . At your dealer's!
Made by HOOD RUBBER COMPANY
Watertown, Mass.
HOOD
RUBBER FOOTWEAR
CANVAS SHOES
PNEUMATIC TIRES
SOLID TIRES
HEELS – SOLES – TILING
HOOD THE SYMBOL OF WORLD WIDE SERVICE IN QUALITY RUBBER PRODUCTS

There's a shoe store in your neighborhood specializing in Athletic Footwear—Look for the oval sign
The HOOD Hyscore
From the Daily Dozen to World's Championships
—the right shoe helps!
Announcing the W.R. Type last
We have had designed by Mr. L. P. Haight, founder of the Walk Straight Club, and noted foot specialist, a foot-fitting type of last upon which we will make the W. R. line of HOOD Athletic Shoes.
These shoes will be similar to those we manufacture for the Walk Straight Club, and may be obtained through our regular dealers in the W. R. Type.
W. R. shoes are easy fitting, allow the utmost use of the foot muscles, and tend to develop a greater length of stride. They are particularly comfortable.
We have also arranged with Mr. Haight, to send his personally developed series of foot exercises to those who send 10 cents in stamps to him, at the address, Mr. L. P. Haight, 80 Boylston, St., Boston, Mass.
Health maintenance in the winter months is receiving nation-wide recognition: Few remain today who are not making some plans to keep vacation fitness throughout the entire year.
From the setting up exercises of the school children, through the period of gymnasium work, to the "keeping fit" exercises of the adult; and from "gym" hand or volley ball to expert basketball, squash or tennis, there is a HOOD Athletic Shoe, properly designed for the work.
It is particularly important for the beginner to start with the shoe which will give him confidence, add to his comfort, and save his strength. It is for these reasons that we have suggested that you go to the store where you will find expert advice and complete stocks to meet your exact needs.
The HOOD Hyscore
A professional basketball shoe. Sole grips and releases instantly. Helps a sure, fast game. Will last through a full playing schedule. Strongly reinforced.
The HOOD Vantage
A fine all-around indoor athletic shoe for men or women. Kendex insole and heavy cushion mid sole absorb the shocks. Tough rubber outsoles for wear.
The HOOD Bayside
Made for all, but recommended for women and children, where the amount and nature or the floor-work does not demand a stronger shoe.
HOOD RUBBER PRODUCTS COMPANY, Inc.
Watertown, Massachusetts
Let us send you the Hood Athletic Footwear Buying Guides
INDOOR ATHLETIC HOOD FOOTWEAR
The HOOD Vantage
The HOOD Bayside
Look for this oval sign it identifies the shoe store in your neighborhood specializing in Athletic Footwear

115

Grinnell Gloves

"Best for every purpose"

Grinnell Driving Gloves Mean Wear and Comfort

The Grinnell Driving Glove illustrated is a favorite because it is cool, comfortable and durable. It is an extremely handsome glove, splendidly made, perfect in every detail.

It appeals to the driver who values not only the appearance of his hands but the real worth of the gloves he wears.

These gloves are made of Grinnell velvet coltskin—soft and pliable, yet wearing like iron.

They are also produced in choicest imported South African cape. We guarantee them not to shrink, peel, crack or harden. They wash in soap and water or gasoline and dry out like new.

This is only one of the 900 styles in Grinnell Gloves. If the Grinnell dealer in your community does not have the style you want write us for our special style book.

MORRISON-RICKER MANUFACTURING COMPANY
(Established 1856)
GRINNELL, IOWA, U. S. A.
200 FIFTH AVENUE, NEW YORK CITY

STYLED AND TAILORED AS ONLY THE ENGLISH KNOW HOW

DO YOU insist on spats that fit snugly over instep and ankle with never a wrinkle? Do you like seams finished and edges bound so that there are apparently no seams or binding at all? Have you wished for soft leather straps that will not curl . . . sewed in so they do not draw the spat at the instep? If you have, you are a man made for BOND STREET spats . . . and BOND STREETS are made for you.

Here are spats with the style and smartness found heretofore only in English spats. Their tailoring, too, conforms to the best English standards in every little detail. Fact is, BOND STREET spats are styled in England by a famous designer of correct anklewear and are equaled only by the finest imported product.

BOND STREET spats are sold at the best shoe stores and men's wear shops. Ask for them by name and look for the BOND STREET label inside. It is a guarantee of superior quality and smartness. The Williams Manufacturing Company, Portsmouth, Ohio, U. S. A.

Four of the many styles of BOND STREET spats are illustrated on this page. They are available in a wide range of prices.

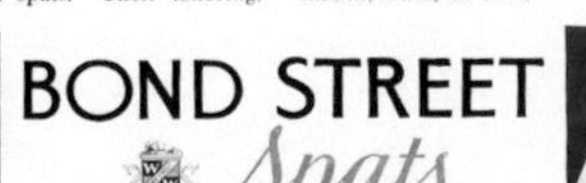

Meticulous and flawless styling and tailoring characterize all BOND STREET spats, regardless of price.

BOND STREET *Spats*

THE *CORRECT* ANKLEWEAR

Hood Rubber Footwear, 1928 Hood Athletic Shoes, 1923 Grinnell Gloves, 1920 Bond Street Spats, 1929

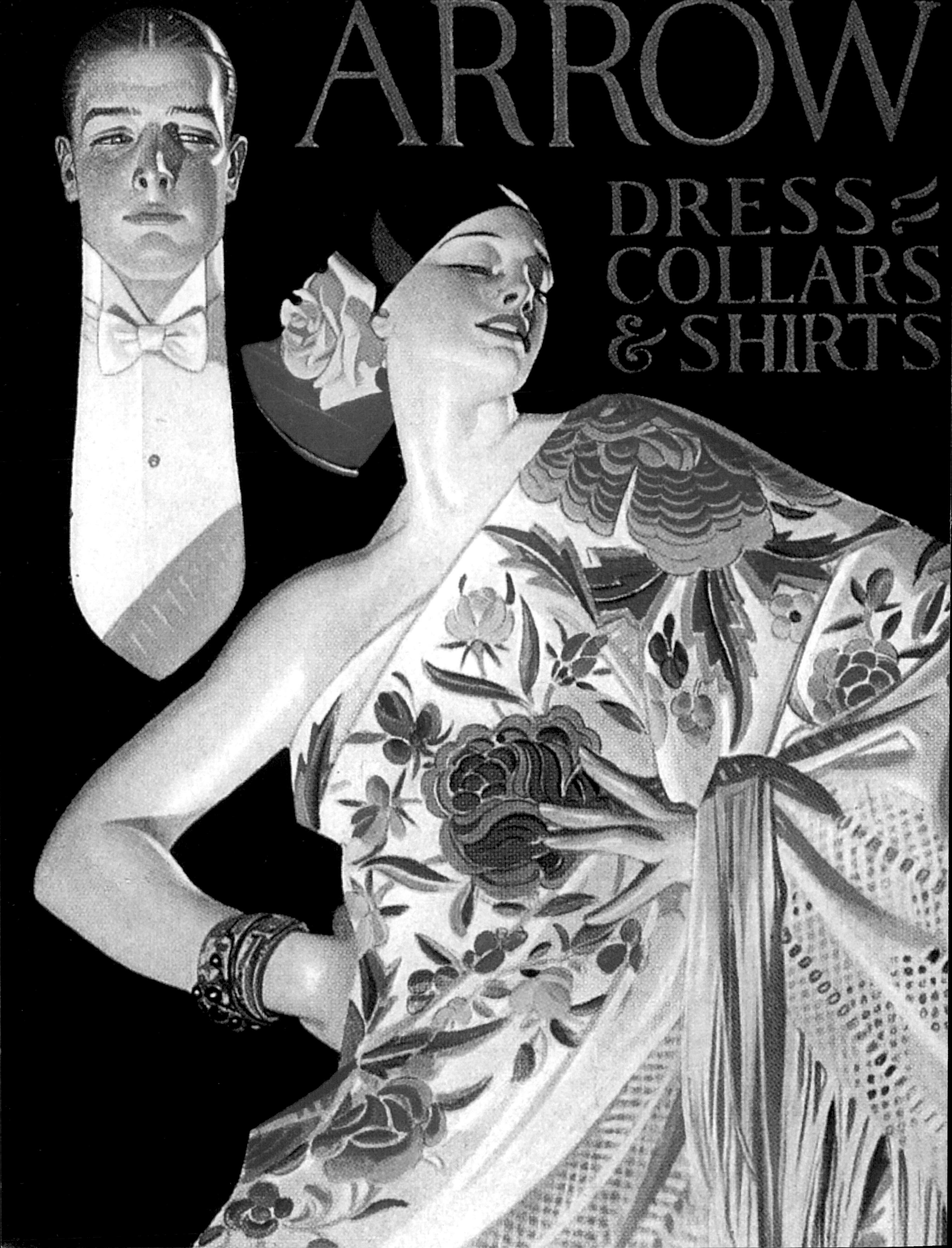
ARROW
DRESS
COLLARS
& SHIRTS

Arrow Shirts, 1929

Illustrator J. C. Leyendecker first began creating advertisements for Arrow shirts in 1906. The men and women depicted were singularly glamorous; in this case, evoking the style of popular husband-and-wife dance team Vernon and Irene Castle.

Der Illustrator J. C. Leyendecker entwarf 1906 die ersten Anzeigen für Arrow-Hemden. Die darauf dargestellten Herren und Damen waren ausgesprochen glamourös. In diesem Fall hat man sich an den Stil des bekannten Tanz- und Ehepaares Vernon und Irene Castle angelehnt.

L'illustrateur J. C. Leyendecker commença à créer des publicités pour les chemises Arrow en 1906. Les hommes et les femmes illustrés étaient particulièrement glamour ; ici, les personnages évoquent le célèbre couple de danseurs Vernon et Irene Castle.

Arrow Collars and Shirts, 1926 ◂

WOMEN who first are attracted to Holeproof Hosiery by its lustrous, sheer appearance, are pleasantly surprised—wearing it—to find that its charming beauty is matched by unusually long service.
It is this combination of style and durability that has made Holeproof the preferred hosiery of millions.
Buy Holeproof and both your hosiery and money will go farther.
HOLEPROOF HOSIERY COMPANY
MILWAUKEE, WISCONSIN
Holeproof Hosiery Company of Canada, Limited
London, Ontario
Holeproof Silk Hosiery for women is offered in Full-Fashioned, High-point Heel, Broadseam Back, Extra-Stretch Ribbed Top, and other popular styles. Holeproof is also made for men and children in all wanted styles and materials. If your dealer cannot supply you, write for price list and illustrated booklet.
© H. H. Co.
COLES PHILLIPS
Holeproof Hosiery

Holeproof Hosiery, 1923 ◂

Coles Phillips's pinup girls for Holeproof Hosiery are lovely in their wispy lingerie, with eyes demurely downcast. But shocking? For their time, they were. Only a few years before Phillips's ads began running, the glimpse of a woman's ankle was considered titillating. But as hemlines rose and rules for appropriate dress relaxed, advertisers had more leeway with what could be shown.

Coles Phillips Pin-up-Girls für Holeproof Hosiery in ihrer zarten Wäsche und mit züchtig niedergeschlagenen Augen sind hübsch anzusehen. Schockierend? Zur damaligen Zeit sehr wohl. Nur wenige Jahre vor der Veröffentlichung von Phillips Anzeigen galt schon der Blick auf eine weibliche Fessel als anzüglich. Doch als die Säume nach oben wanderten und die Regeln für angemessene Kleidung sich lockerten, bekamen auch die Werbeleute mehr Spielraum.

Dans leur lingerie vaporeuse, les yeux pudiquement baissés, les pin-up dessinées par Coles Phillips pour Holeproof Hosiery étaient irrésistibles. Mais étaient-elles choquantes ? Pour leur époque, oui. A peine quelques années avant la diffusion des publicités dessinées par Phillips, apercevoir les chevilles d'une femme suffisait à émoustiller les sens. Avec le raccourcissement des jupes et la décontraction des codes vestimentaires, les annonceurs disposaient néanmoins d'une plus grande marge de liberté.

Holeproof Hosiery, 1923

Holeproof Hosiery, 1921

Gossard
Corsets and Brassieres
The Gossard Line of Beauty
THAT slender line of youth, falling in graceful undulation from armpit to waist and over hip to knee, is the Gossard Line of Beauty. It is the line which two centuries ago, the artist, Hogarth, distinguished as the real secret of figure charm.
Fashions change and styles alter, but wise womanhood does not lose the line of her identity—the Gossard Line of Beauty. In youth it is moulded to perfection; in maturity it is retained with all its pristine charm, and as years advance, remains with stateliness and dignity. The Gossard Line of Beauty is the possession of every woman who wears Gossards. There is a Gossard for each of the nine ideal figure types—your type, your size.
Doubtless your favorite store has an expert corsetiere who will give you a perfect Gossard fitting. For most of the better stores have a Gossard department.
The H. W. Gossard Co., Chicago, New York, Toronto, London, Sydney, Buenos Aires
Copyright 1923

Gossard Corsets and Brassieres, 1924

► Real Silk Hosiery, 1926

My Valentine

REAL SILK HOSIERY MILLS INDIANAPOLIS
REAL SILK
"FROM MILL TO MILLIONS"

This gold button identifies the Bonded Real Silk Representative when he calls at your home or office

REAL SILK

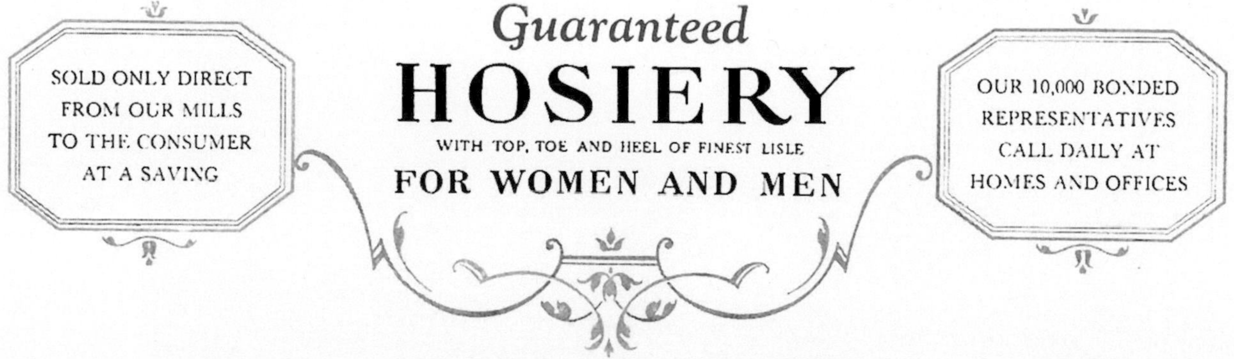

Guaranteed
HOSIERY
WITH TOP, TOE AND HEEL OF FINEST LISLE
FOR WOMEN AND MEN
SOLD ONLY DIRECT FROM OUR MILLS TO THE CONSUMER AT A SAVING
OUR 10,000 BONDED REPRESENTATIVES CALL DAILY AT HOMES AND OFFICES

REAL SILK HOSIERY MILLS · *World's Largest Manufacturers of Silk Hosiery* · INDIANAPOLIS, IND., U. S. A.

250 BRANCH OFFICES IN THE UNITED STATES AND CANADA. CONSULT 'PHONE DIRECTORY FOR YOUR LOCAL OFFICE

Nufashond
TRADE MARK REG. U.S. PAT. OFF.
GARTERS
Fancy garters were never so popular, and Nufashond Garters are the last word.
Nufashond, leading manufacturer of garter elastic, has produced a wonderful assortment of beautiful finished garters in glorious colors. Ask to see them at your store. Though bewitchingly pretty, they're modestly priced.
But the beauty of Nufashond Garters is only one of their virtues. Bear in mind that they are made of the famous Nufashond Elastic, which means more stretch and snap and longer wear.
Or you can buy Nufashond Garter Elastic by the piece and make garters for yourself or your friends.
Dept. L5, Nufashond
READING, PA.
Look for this sign on the dealer's door or window. If he handles the best in little things you can depend upon the quality of all his merchandise.
Nufashond
NOTIONS
For 50c we will send you a pair of beautiful Roll Top Garters, made up with attractive ornaments attached, or, for 25c sufficient material for making a pair of garters. Specify color desired.
Nufashond
TRADE MARK REG. U.S. PAT OFF
GARTER ELASTIC
No. 5101
Frilled Garter Elastic, plain and in patterns; 27-inch lengths.
No. 5123
Roll Top Garters, plain and in patterns; 27-inch lengths and made-up garters.
No. 5126
Shirred ribbon made-up Garters and 27-inch lengths.

DeBevoise Brassieres, 1921

Nufashond Garters, 1925 ◂

65
Faseal
The new idea in
GAITERS
The Faseal Slide always slides; its action is sure and unfailing. "It works like a charm." A light pull up or down—and the Faseal is on or off in a trice!
You get a new idea of ease, convenience and protection in the Faseal Gaiter. It guards your feet against wet and dampness, and yet is light enough for comfortable walking. Made of high-grade jersey, fleece lined. Carefully fitted and smartly tailored as a glove; in fact, a slim ankle loses none of its trim and shapely grace in this Faseal Gaiter.
Firestone Footwear Co.
Chicago HUDSON, MASS. Boston
The Mark of Quality
Firestone
AMERICANS SHOULD PRODUCE THEIR OWN RUBBER . . . Harvey S. Firestone

124

▸ Talon Slide-Fasteners, 1929

The first variation of the zipper dates back to 1851, but the Hookless Fastener Company – later renamed Talon – patented its product in 1913. The B. F. Goodrich Company came up with the "zipper" name for the product, but it wasn't widely used until Hart Schaffner & Marx created the first zip-fly trouser in 1936.

Der erste Reißverschluss stammt zwar aus dem Jahre 1851, allerdings ließ sich die Hookless Fastener Company – später in Talon umbenannt – ihr Produkt 1913 patentieren. Die B. F. Goodrich Company kam auf den Namen „Zipper", der jedoch nicht sehr verbreitet war, bis Hart Schaffner & Marx 1936 die erste „zip-fly trouser" herausbrachte.

Si la première version de la fermeture à zip remontait à 1851, la société Hookless Fastener Company, plus tard rebaptisée Talon, ne fit breveter son produit qu'en 1913. Ce fut B. F. Goodrich Company qui eut l'idée d'appeler ce produit « zipper », mais son usage ne se répandit qu'en 1936, quand Hart Schaffner & Marx créa le premier pantalon à fermeture Eclair.

Firestone Footwear, 1926

Look for
"TALON"
or
"HOOKLESS"
on the
pull
TALON

The lightning rapidity with which Talon Slide-Fasteners open and close, pleases men—and women too—

Speed! Action! You get both in Talon Slide-Fasteners. A swift, gentle pull, and grips, golf-bags, etc., are open, their contents instantly available. You've seen these quick, convenient Talon Slide-Fasteners on bags, luggage, overshoes, etc., but they are not restricted to these alone. Today Talon Slide-Fasteners are the accepted method of fastening on frocks, for women and children; work and sports clothes for men and boys; utility items for household purposes, etc. There are literally hundreds of Talon-fastened articles and garments that you can buy ready-made or make at home yourself, using Talon Slide-Fasteners which you can buy at any notion counter.

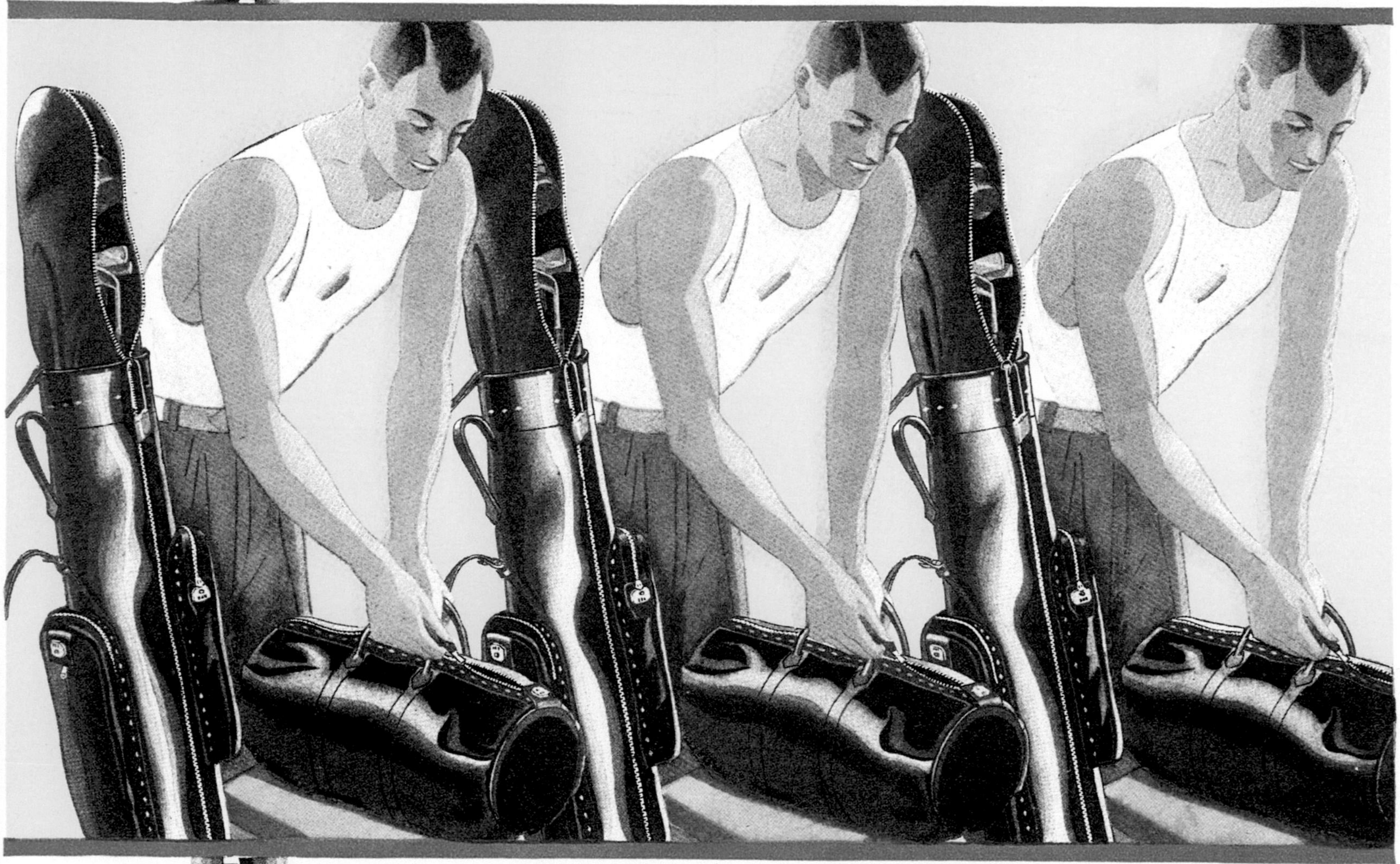

Buy Ready-for-Service Talon-Fastened garments and articles, or make them at home yourself

Trim, convenient, Talon Slide-Fasteners are featured on the clothes smart people wear—on the fashion accessories they use; and now Talon Slide-Fasteners are available for all kinds of home-sewing use. Unlike all old-fashioned fasteners Talon Slide-Fasteners prevent gaping edges, because each tight-gripping coupling is machined and matched with almost a fine watchmaker's care and precision. Flexible, unbreakable, they can be run through a wringer and still they will work smoothly and quickly. Rustless, they launder or dry-clean perfectly.

Identify these fasteners by "Talon" or "Hookless" on the slider-pull. If your department or general store does not stock Talon Slide-Fasteners for home-sewing, write us. Send us your name and address and we will mail you an illustrated catalog giving the names of companies making Talon-fastened articles.

HOOKLESS FASTENER COMPANY, 623 ARCH STREET, MEADVILLE, PENN.

The Pioneer Manufacturers of Slide-Fasteners

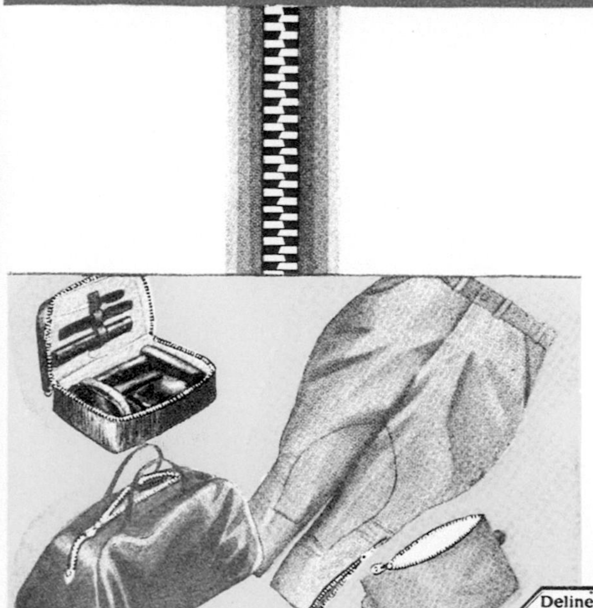

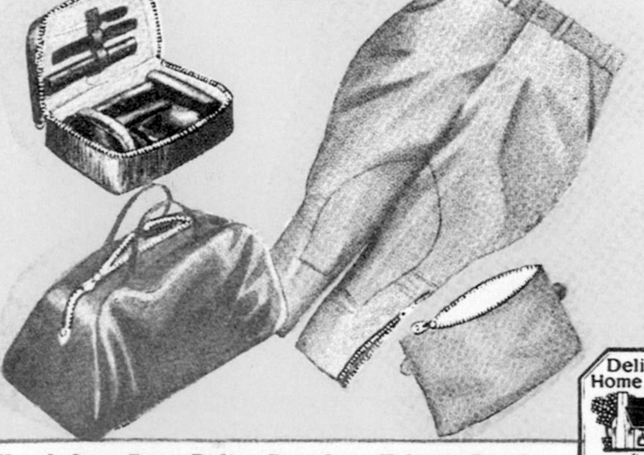

Knockabout Bag; Riding Breeches; Tobacco Pouch; Men's Toilet Kit; equipped with Talon Slide-Fasteners.

Delineator Home Institute
Endorses TALON SLIDE-FASTENERS

TALON
THE ORIGINAL
SLIDE FASTENER . . .
REG. U.S. PAT. OFF
TALON SLIDE FASTENERS

FROM NOW ON—LET
MUNSING WEAR
UNION SUIT YOU
REMEMBER
Don't Say Underwear
ALWAYS SAY
MUNSING WEAR
Munsingwear Garments, because of their fine quality and the satisfactory way in which they fit and cover the form and because of the unusual service they give the wearer, have received the enthusiastic endorsement of discriminating people in all parts of the United States. They are carried in stock by one or more of the leading merchants in practically every town and city of importance in the country. They are made in a great variety of fabrics, in practically all wanted styles, in form-fitting knitted garments, in loose-fitting woven garments, for men, women and children. The children's suits may be had in either knit or woven fabrics, and either with or without tapes and buttons for use in supporting outer garments. Munsingwear is also made in wrappers, bands and binders for infants. Whether you are tall or short, fat or thin, old or young, man, woman, boy or girl, there is a Munsingwear garment that will give you the utmost in service and satisfaction.
It will pay you to find the Munsingwear dealer in your community and let him union suit you in Munsingwear.
Munsingwear Satisfaction Lasts
THE MUNSINGWEAR CORPORATION
Minneapolis New York

FOR EACH . . HER OWN INDIVIDUALLY –PROPORTIONED STOCKINGS by Gordon

NOW . . . for the first time in costume history . . . stockings are made in two varying dimensions—and in four groups—as explained on the opposite page. For these Gordon Individually-Proportioned Stockings are dimensioned for the proportions of individual legs—as well as of individual feet.

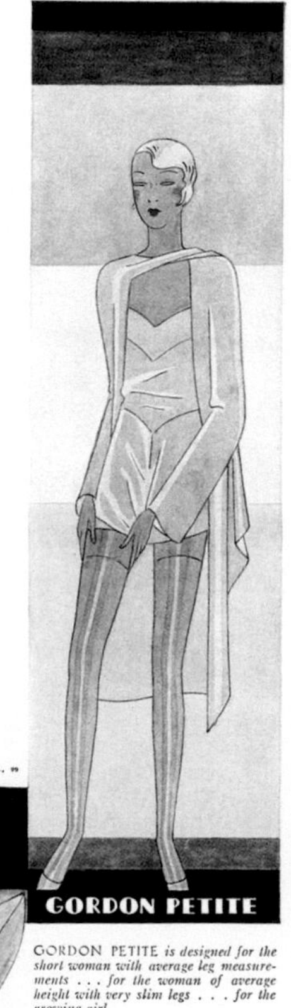

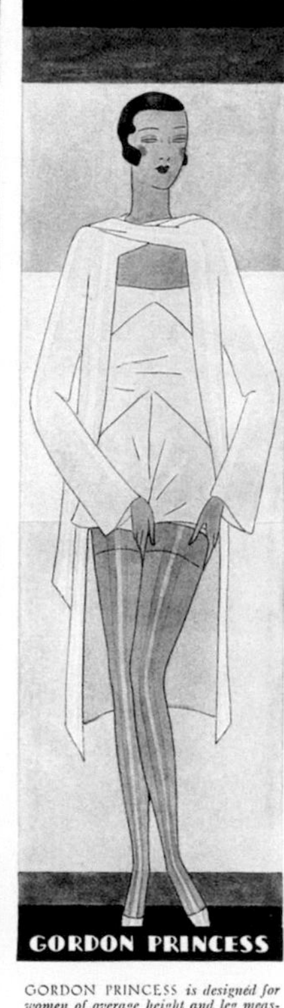

Shoes have always been made—and ordered—in *two* measurements—length and width. But Stockings . . . the important "Third" of the modern woman's ensemble . . . have hitherto concerned themselves with only the *foot* size. Yet . . . some women are diminutive with slim legs. Others . . . just as tiny, and with the same 9 foot-size . . . have wide thighs and thin ankles. Still others . . . wearing the 9 foot-size . . . are tall and regally proportioned.

So—Gordon has designed these Individually-Proportioned Stockings—in four leg-sizes and all foot-sizes. These are so scientifically worked out that . . . whatever your type of figure . . . some one of these proportions will give you stocking-smoothness . . . freedom from strain or binding, from surplus that needs to be rolled . . . and . . . you will enjoy their longer wear.

These new stockings . . . to be found at the shops you prefer . . . are called *Gordon Petite, Gordon Princess, Gordon Regal* and *Gordon Splendide.* The *Gordon Splendide* is particularly designed for the thousands of American women who . . . whether tall or short . . . are *generously proportioned* throughout the lower part of their bodies.

Gordon

GORDON PETITE

GORDON PRINCESS

GORDON REGAL

GORDON PETITE *is designed for the short woman with average leg measurements . . . for the woman of average height with very slim legs . . . for the growing girl.*

GORDON PRINCESS *is designed for women of average height and leg measurements; for the short woman with plump legs and thighs; for the young girl whose skirts are brief.*

GORDON REGAL *is designed for the tall woman with average leg measurements; for the woman of average height with somewhat heavy calves or thighs.*

Gordon Hosiery, 1929

Munsingwear Undergarments, 1921 ◂

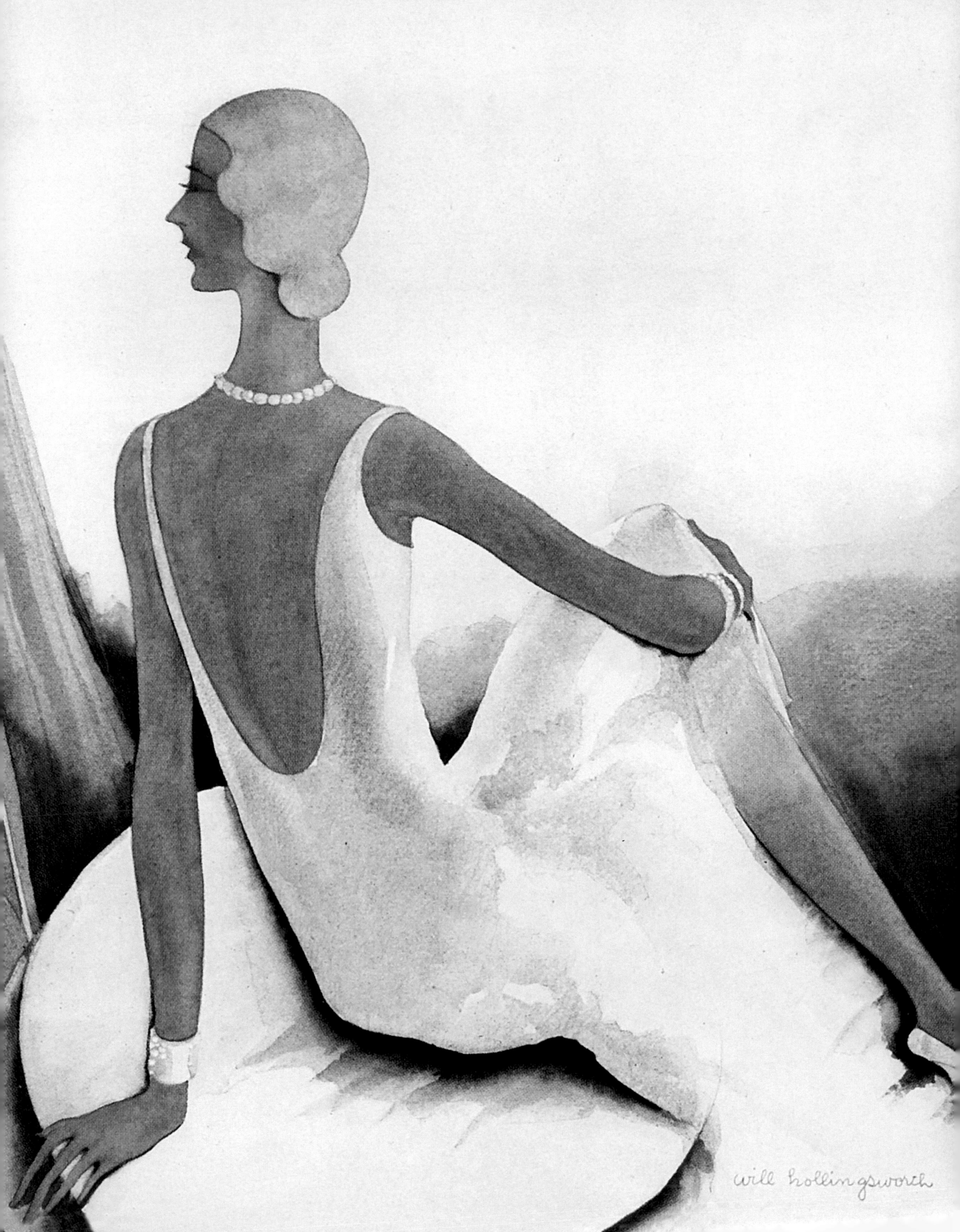
will hollingsworth

svelda

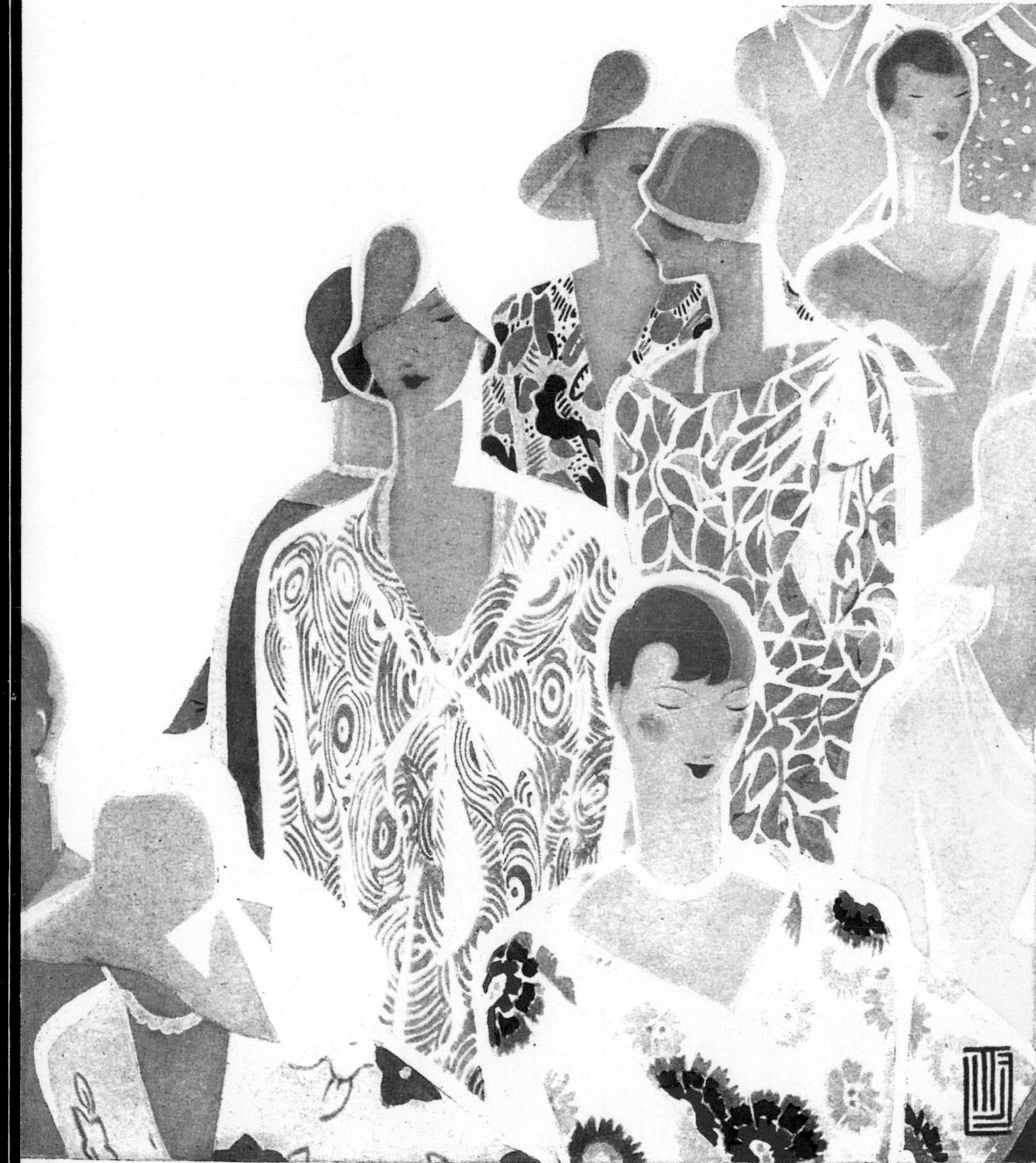

SVELDA FABRICS are modern, distinguished weaves of pure Bemberg. Exclusive shops are showing Svelda in their smartest gowns. Women are making their loveliest frocks of it. For afternoon and evening gowns, they prefer the mist sheer voiles and chiffon crepes in tropical pastels or exquisite prints; for sports, piqué and comparable weaves. Women buy them because they are smart. Later, they discover that Svelda, like all Aberfoyle Fabrics, is washable and fadeless . . . even in the sheerest prints for evening. May we send you fashion folder illustrating Svelda Fabrics? Galey & Lord, Incorporated, 57 Worth Street, New York City.

"MADE BY ABERFOYLE GUARANTEED FAST COLOR" APPEARS ON THE SELVAGE

Svelda Fabrics, 1929

Stehli Silks, 1929 ◂

Now You Can Buy It in Colors

It is made in

Pink	Rose
Helio	Cadet
Biscuit	Tan
Pearl	Linen
Reseda	Ciel
Copen	Brown

Now for the first time you can buy Indian Head in colors, and in colors guaranteed fast. By "fast colors" we mean colors that will hold bright and true through seasons of sun, sea air, dampness, and washing.

We guarantee: If any garment made of Indian Head fails to give proper service because of the fading or running of Indian Head colors, we will make good the total cost of the garment.

Fifty-nine cents a yard is the price of guaranteed fast-color Indian Head, 36 inches wide —a value that you will appreciate more fully after months of wear. If your store does not carry Indian Head in fast colors, write us giving your dealer's name. We will see that you are supplied.

"The Girl Who Loved Pink" tells the story of colored Indian Head and has a sample of the material. It also shows the complete color range. It is sent free upon request.

Amory, Browne & Co., Department 234, Box 1206, Boston, Mass.

Nashua Blankets *Parkhill Fine Ginghams* *Lancaster Kalburnie Gingham* *Gilbrae Gingham*

Copyright, Amory, Browne & Co., Boston and New York

INDIAN HEAD CLOTH
Reg. U.S. Pat. Off.
Always on the Selvage

Indian Head Fabrics, 1922

Textile company Amory Browne & Co., based in Boston, Massachusetts, produced fabrics under a variety of names, including Indian Head cloth, a fine muslin fabric that was said to resemble linen but was less expensive. The fabric became a favorite of quilters. Among Amory Browne's other products were Kalburnie Zephyr ginghams and Nashua Woolnap blankets, which were marketed as being made from "pure cotton to keep you warm."

Das Textilunternehmen Amory Browne & Co. mit Sitz in Boston, Massachusetts, produzierte Stoffe mit einer Vielzahl von Namen, darunter Indian Head, ein feiner Musselin, der Ähnlichkeit mit Leinen hatte, aber preiswerter war. Der Stoff wurde zum Lieblingsmaterial fürs Quilten. Andere Produkte von Amory Browne waren Karostoffe namens Kalburnie Zephyr und Decken unter der Bezeichnung Nashua Woolnap, die, wie es hieß, aus reiner Baumwolle gemacht waren, „um Sie warmzuhalten".

Basé à Boston, Massachusetts, le fabricant textile Amory Browne & Co. produisait des tissus sous une variété de noms, notamment Indian Head, une fine mousseline supposée ressembler au lin tout en étant moins chère, qui remporta un franc succès auprès des quilteurs. Amory Browne proposait aussi le tissu à carreaux vichy Kalburnie Zephyr et les couvertures Nashua Woolnap, vendues avec l'argument du « 100 % coton qui vous tient chaud ».

► Indian Head Fabrics, 1920

Clothes and Summer Fun
THE best times of all are tramps through the woods, a wonderful sail, a clam bake on the beach, or a day at the Army Camp. The girl who has to be too careful of her clothes spoils the fun and is not invited a second time.
The one who dresses in sport clothes of Indian Head looks charming all day, yet can enter into everything without fear of looking crumpled or mussed.
Indian Head is the ideal cloth for white clothes for the whole family. Economical in price and easy to work on, it appeals to the purse and the needle of the woman who does her own sewing. Besides, it launders wonderfully.
INDIAN HEAD
REG. U. S. PAT. OFF.
CLOTH
Use it instead of Linen
All good stores carry Indian Head in one of their white goods departments. Made in 27, 33, 36, 44, and 54 inch widths, name always appears on selvage. Indian Head is sold the world over.
Ready-to-wear clothes of Indian Head are now shown in the smart shops. Identify them by the Indian Head Label sewn in the garment.
Our interesting booklet "The Wash-Fabric for Your Whole Family," sent free upon request.
Amory, Browne & Co. Dept. 48, Box 1206, Boston, Mass.

MISS TOKIO
HOS IERY

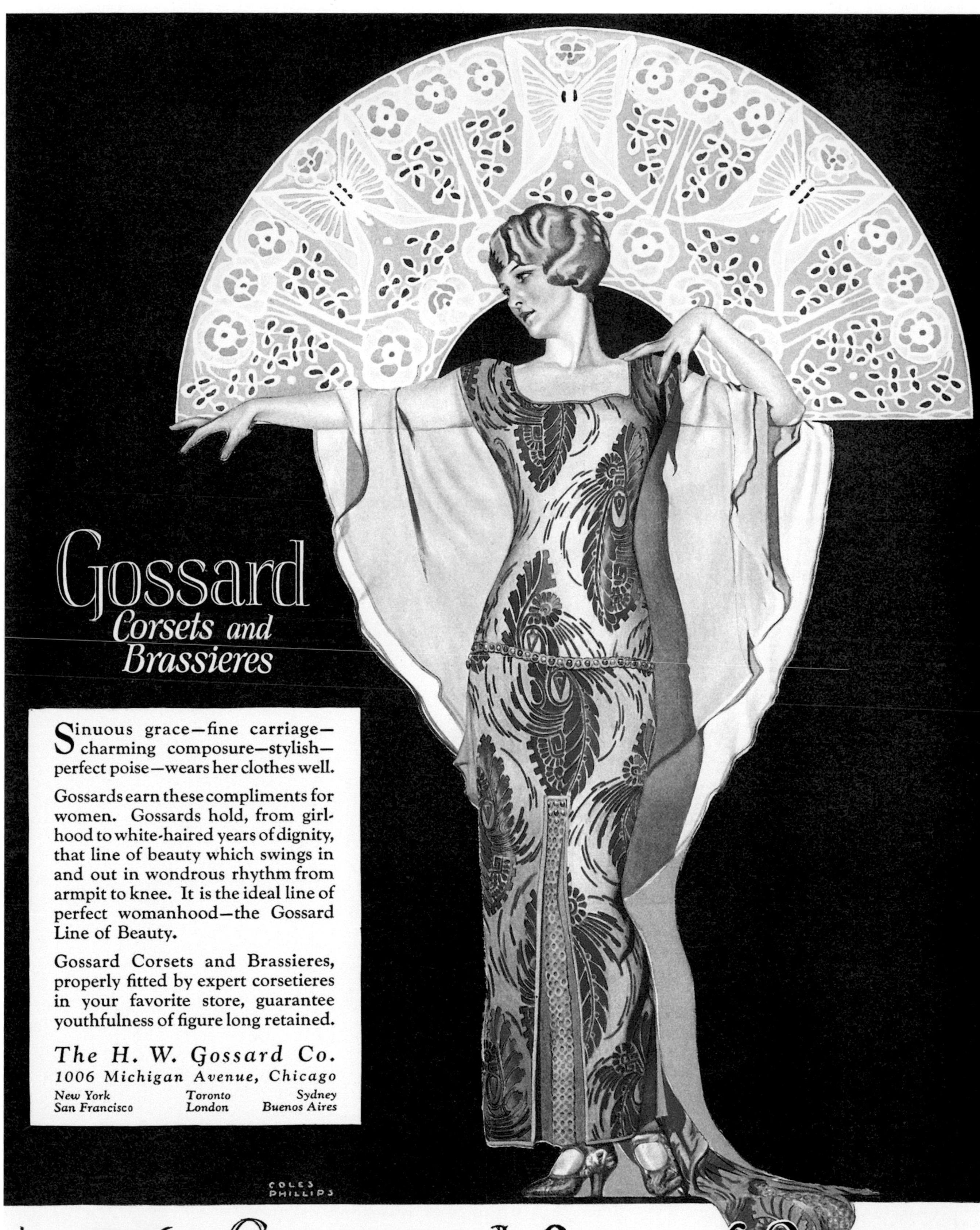

Gossard
Corsets and
Brassieres
Sinuous grace—fine carriage—charming composure—stylish—perfect poise—wears her clothes well.
Gossards earn these compliments for women. Gossards hold, from girlhood to white-haired years of dignity, that line of beauty which swings in and out in wondrous rhythm from armpit to knee. It is the ideal line of perfect womanhood—the Gossard Line of Beauty.
Gossard Corsets and Brassieres, properly fitted by expert corsetieres in your favorite store, guarantee youthfulness of figure long retained.
The H. W. Gossard Co.
1006 Michigan Avenue, Chicago
New York Toronto Sydney
San Francisco London Buenos Aires
COLES PHILLIPS
The Gossard Line of Beauty

Gossard Corsets and Brassieres, 1924

Miss Tokio Hosiery, 1927 ◂

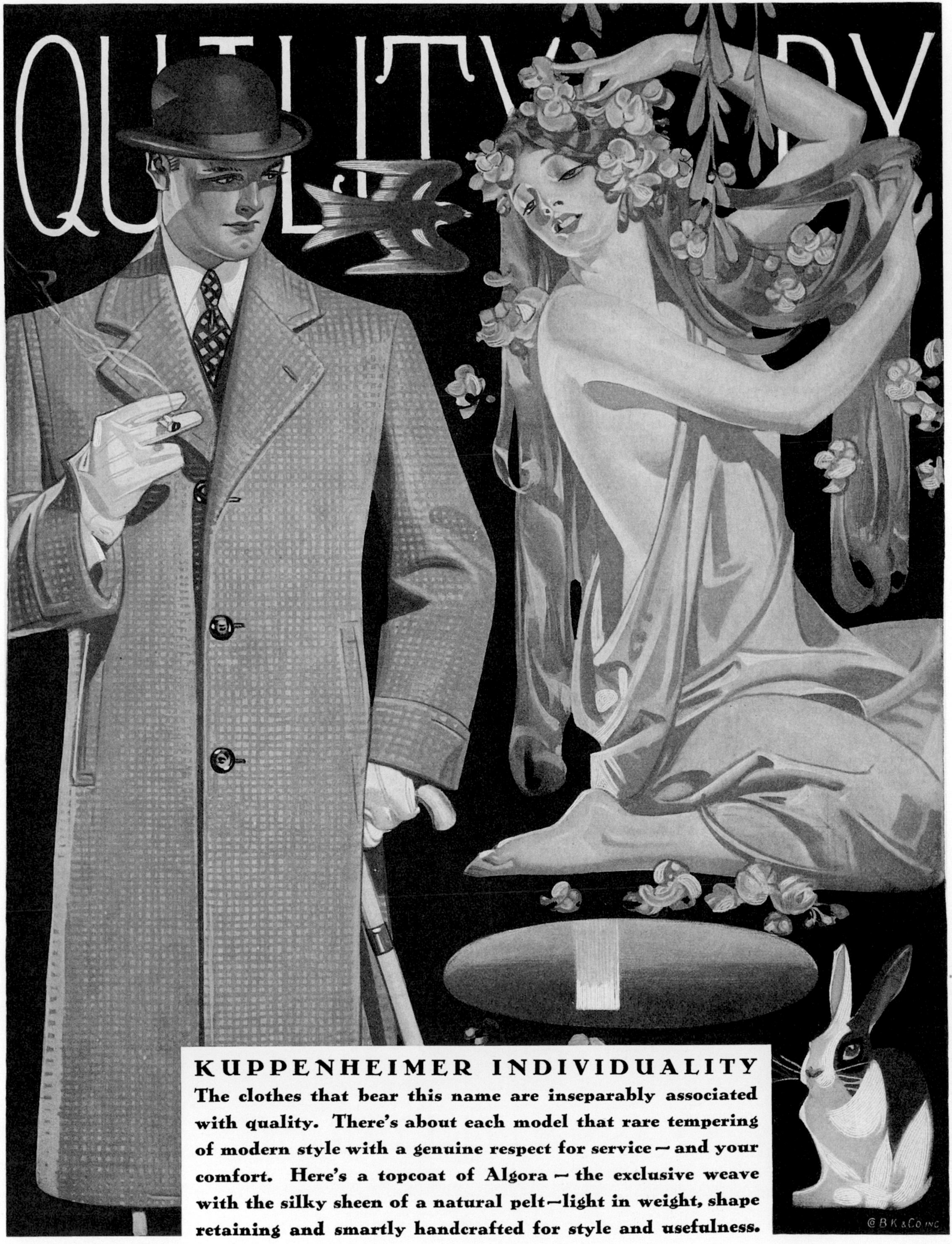

KUPPENHEIMER INDIVIDUALITY
The clothes that bear this name are inseparably associated with quality. There's about each model that rare tempering of modern style with a genuine respect for service — and your comfort. Here's a topcoat of Algora — the exclusive weave with the silky sheen of a natural pelt—light in weight, shape retaining and smartly handcrafted for style and usefulness.
©B K & Co. INC.

Kuppenheimer Menswear, 1929

KUPPENHEIMER
SPRING BRINGS A NEW STYLE
A neater, smoother grace is the new vogue the young men have adopted for spring. This style is given fine expression by worthy fabrics—Tigertwist—Trojan Weave—Castilians, designed and controlled by Kuppenheimer, exclusive woolens enriched by new color and decoration—loomed from long fibered yarns that stoutly resist wear.
© B.K.&Co. INC.

Kuppenheimer Menswear, 1929

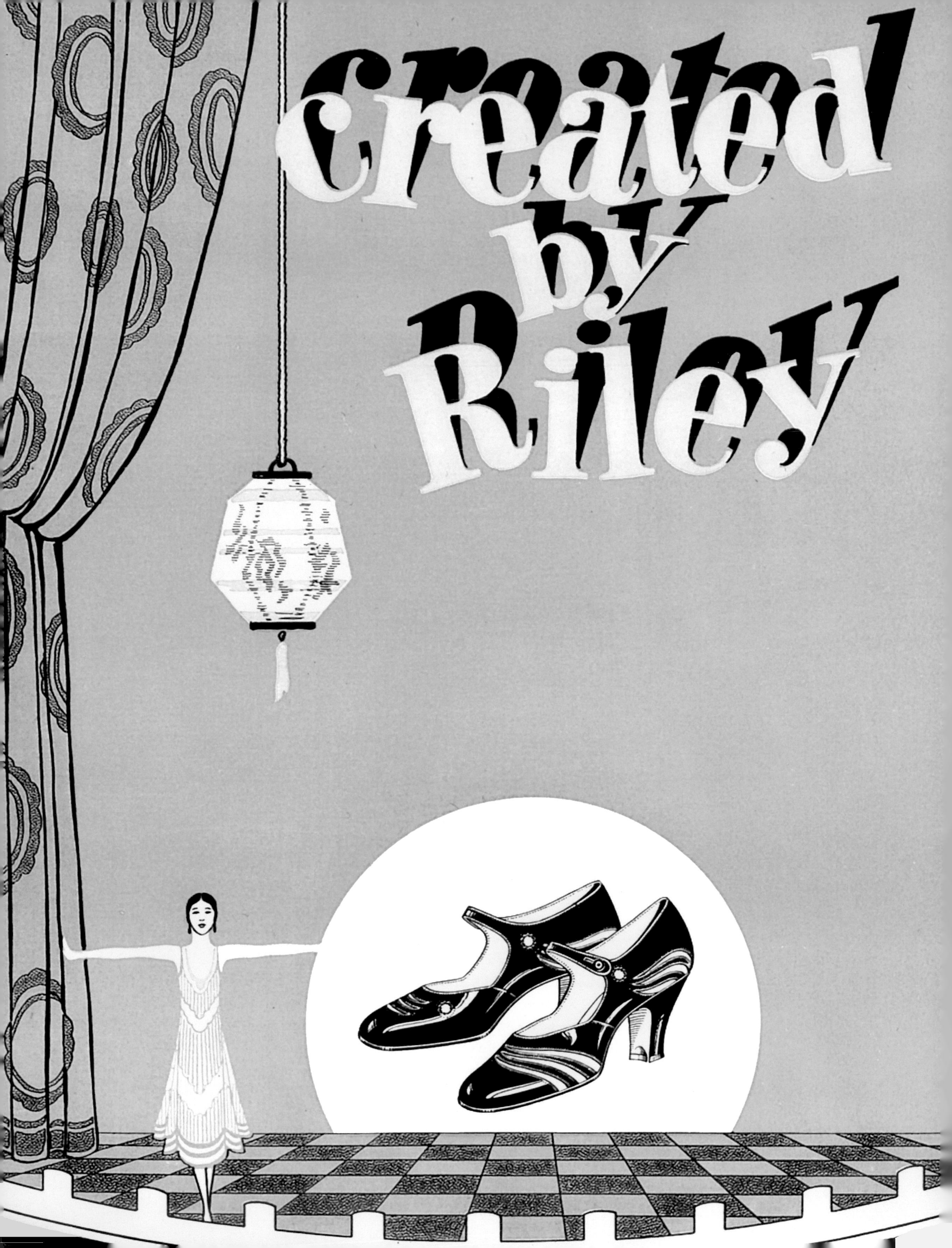
Created by Riley

Selby Shoes, 1929

The 1930s silhouette – long, lean, and graceful – replaced the short, flirty, and freewheeling look of the '20s. New shoe styles followed suit, shifting away from the Louis XIV heel to a slimmer line.

Die Silhouette der 1930er – lang, schmal und graziös – ersetzte den kurzen, koketten und flatterhaften Look der Zwanziger. Neue Schuhmoden folgten und bedeuteten die Abkehr vom Absatz à la Ludwig XIV. hin zu einer schlankeren Form.

La silhouette des années 30 – longue, svelte et gracieuse – remplaça le look court, aguicheur et relâché de la décennie précédente, suivie par de nouveaux modèles de chaussures s'éloignant du talon Louis XIV au profit d'une ligne plus fine.

Riley Shoes, 1927 ◂

HIGH of heel, slender of line, light as a fairy sandal, vivaciously chic — these are the modish charms of Tru-Poise Shoes. And now you can wear these intriguing styles that make your feet and ankles look so trim and slender. For the exquisite Tru-Poise Shoes have patented features that tend to hold the foot in its correct position and give you — for the first time — graceful poise and complete assurance in the airiest, highest-heeled models. Tru-Poise is the only shoe with these exclusive features that make smart footwear so pleasing to active feet.
THE SELBY SHOE COMPANY, 218 Seventh St., Portsmouth, Ohio
Write for name of your nearest Tru-Poise dealer and folder of latest Paris and New York styles.
Selby
TRU-POISE
SHOE
OLIVIA — Brown genuine lizard vamp; brown kid quarter, three eyelet oxford.
MODERNE — Marron kid gored pump; beige kid trim.
CASCADE — Mauve kid one strap button; brown genuine lizard trim.
ILSA—Brown kid, center strap with beaded gore; whippet suede trim.
ROWENA—Dark blue kid vamp and trim, one strap buckle; dark blue suede quarter.

137

▸ Interwoven Socks, 1929

The 1920s was the era of the college man, and this Interwoven ad, illustrated by J. C. Leyendecker, perfectly captures a campus scene. At the time, young men had begun to wear extremely wide-legged trousers called "Oxford bags," in honor of the university where the style originated.

Die 1920er waren die Ära des Collegestudenten, und diese von J. C. Leyendecker illustrierte Interwoven-Anzeige erfasst eine Campus-Szene auf perfekte Weise. Damals hatten junge Männer gerade begonnen, Hosen mit extrem weitem Bein zu tragen, die man zu Ehren der Universität, wo diese Mode aufgekommen war, „Oxford bags" nannte.

Les années 20 mirent l'étudiant d'université à l'honneur et cette publicité pour Interwoven, dessinée par J. C. Leyendecker, illustrait parfaitement le mode de vie sur les campus. A l'époque, les jeunes hommes commencèrent à porter des pantalons à jambe très large, appelés « Oxford bags » en référence à l'université où était né ce modèle.

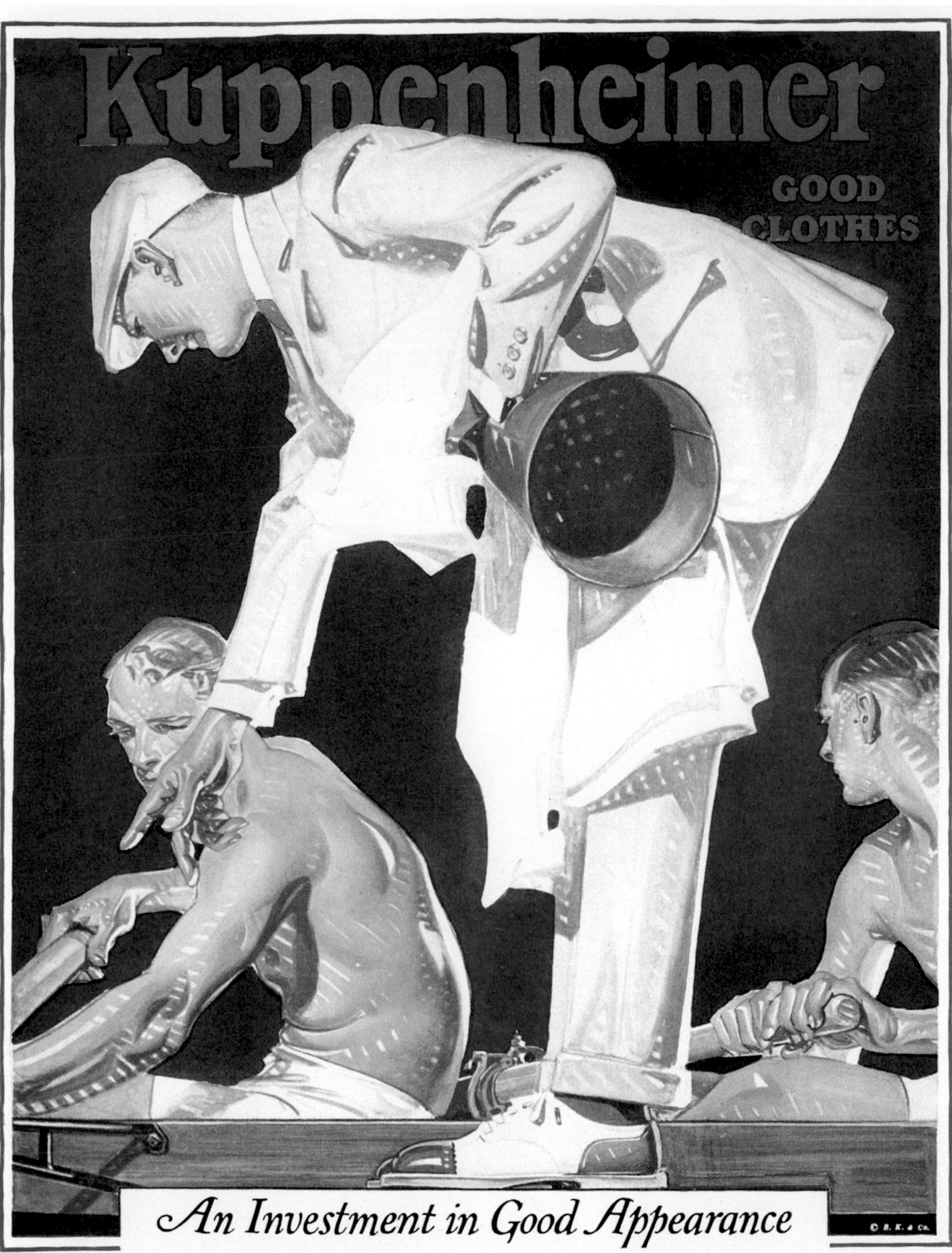

Kuppenheimer Menswear, 1923

Socks by
Interwoven
REG. U.S. PAT. OFF.

THE DECADE HAD A ROMANTIC SCANDAL NON-PAREIL WHEN ENGLAND'S NEWLY CROWNED KING EDWARD ABDICATED HIS THRONE TO MARRY AMERICAN DIVORCÉE WALLIS SIMPSON IN 1936. TAKING THE TITLES DUKE AND DUCHESS OF WINDSOR, THE PAIR'S ARISTOCRATIC STYLE BECAME SYNONYMOUS WITH THE DECADE.

CETTE PÉRIODE CONNAÎT UN SCANDALE ROMANTIQUE SANS PAREIL QUAND, EN 1936, LE ROI EDOUARD D'ANGLETERRE FRAÎCHEMENT COURONNÉ RENONCE AU TRÔNE POUR ÉPOUSER WALLIS SIMPSON, UNE AMÉRICAINE DIVORCÉE. SOUS LES TITRES DE DUC ET DUCHESSE DE WINDSOR, LE COUPE SE DISTINGUE PAR UN STYLE ARISTOCRATIQUE DEVENU SYNONYME DES ANNÉES 30.

EINEN UNVERGLEICHLICH ROMANTISCHEN SKANDAL ERLEBTE DAS JAHRZEHNT, ALS ENGLANDS NEU GEKRÖNTER KÖNIG EDWARD AUF SEINEN THRON VERZICHTETE, UM 1936 DIE GESCHIEDENE AMERIKANERIN WALLIS SIMPSON ZU HEIRATEN. NACHDEM SIE DEN TITEL HERZOG UND HERZOGIN VON WINDSOR ANGENOMMEN HATTEN, WURDE DER ARISTOKRATISCHE LEBENSSTIL DES PAARES ZUM SYNONYM JENER DEKADE.

1930-

ESCAPING ECONOMIC REALITY
DER HARTEN REALITÄT ENTFLIEHEN
UNE DURE RÉALITÉ ÉCONOMIQUE

ARROW

PRIL
APRIL
30
MAY
1
ARROW
MAY
2
MAY

Arrow Shirts, 1935 ◄◄

Hockanum Woolens, 1939 ◄

The French Line, 1933

IN THE 1930s, THE UNITED STATES SLOWLY SANK INTO THE GREAT DEPRESSION WHILE THE SEEDS OF ANOTHER WAR WERE SOWN in a still-recovering Europe and points beyond. Civil war erupted in Spain; India continued its fight for independence; Japan invaded Manchuria; Italy invaded Ethiopia; and Germany had its eye on neighboring countries. In America, Franklin Delano Roosevelt was elected President on his New Deal platform, but on the day he took office, most of the national banks failed.

The radio, a new technology in the '20s, boomed in the '30s, as producers developed sophisticated programming ranging from music and comedy to news and sports. Children tuned in for the ongoing adventures of cowboys, while their mothers listened to the trials and tribulations of characters in soap operas. Sound had been introduced to movies in the late '20s, putting an end to the silent-film era; by 1930, 85 million people were going to the movies weekly. Entertainment remained largely escapist — from Busby Berkeley's elaborately staged musicals to Shirley Temple's cloyingly cute stranglehold on the box office. Greta Garbo made a successful transition to the talkies, and Jean Harlow defined the decade's sex symbol as brash and independent.

The decade had a romantic scandal nonpareil when England's newly crowned King Edward abdicated his throne to marry American divorcée Wallis Simpson in 1936. Taking the titles Duke and Duchess of Windsor, the pair's aristocratic style became synonymous with the decade.

For men, the silhouette became overtly masculine. A good tailor could re-create the broad-shouldered and narrow-hipped look of athlete/actor Johnny Weissmueller. Double-breasted suits became more popular, some with wide-peaked or pointed lapels. For women, skirts were long and slim, jackets were fitted, and accessories were de rigueur: hats, gloves, furs, scarves, handbags, and shoes — low-heeled for day, but towering for evening. Hats evolved from the '20s: brimless styles, and others with a folded brim, framed the face. As the decade progressed, hats grew more structured, with taller crowns and wider brims. Exotic styles featured veils and ribbon trim.

Taking a cue from menswear, designer Elsa Schiaparelli began padding the shoulders of women's suits. In 1931, tennis player Lili de Alvarez wore a Schiaparelli-designed split skirt to play at Wimbledon. A year later, tennis champ Henry "Bunny" Austin wore shorts to play at the U.S. Open Men's Championships in New York City.

The range of women's fashion — from smartly fitted suits to fantasy lingerie and dramatic evening gowns — got the star treatment in the 1939 film *The Women*, which featured the work of Hollywood costume designer Adrian, who often took his cues from French designer Madeleine Vionnet's sensual, bias-cut satin gowns. Starring Norma Shearer, Joan Crawford, and Rosalind Russell, the otherwise black-and-white film included a fashion-show segment filmed in color.

The glamorous fashions on the silver screen, however, did not reflect the wardrobes of mainstream America, as unemployment reached 25%. It was the ads for workwear — touting brands' durability and bargain prices — not dresswear, that reflected the economic reality of the Great Depression.

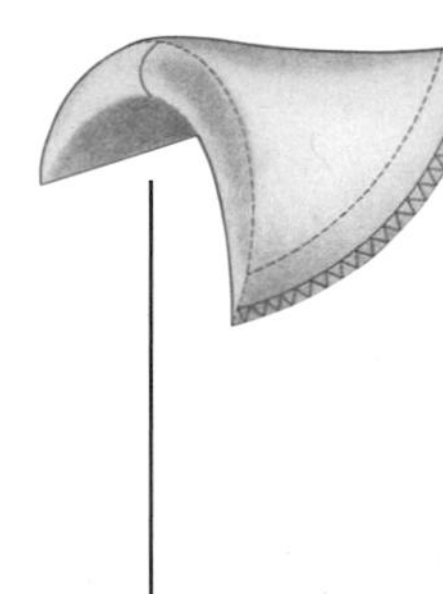

1930

1930 Jean Harlow's platinum-blonde Marcel wave sets trend

Jean Harlows platinblonde ondulierte Welle wird zum Modetrend

Jean Harlow lance la mode des cheveux blond platine coupés courts et ondulés

1930 Madeleine Vionnet's bias-cut dress becomes dominant silhouette of decade

Madeleine Vionnets schräg geschnittenes Kleid ist die dominierende Silhouette des Jahrzehnts

La robe taillée dans le biais de Madeleine Vionnet s'impose comme la silhouette de la décennie

1931 Charlie Chaplin dons signature bowler hat as The Tramp in *City Lights*

Charlie Chaplin trägt als Tramp in *Lichter der Großstadt* die unverwechselbare Melone

Dans *Les Lumières de la ville*, Charlie Chaplin arbore le chapeau melon qui ne quittera plus Charlot le vagabond

1931 Elsa Schiaparelli creates the shoulder-padded power suit

Elsa Schiaparelli entwirft ein Kostüm mit Schulterpolstern

Elsa Schiaparelli crée le tailleur à épaulettes

IN DEN 1930ERN VERSANKEN DIE USA LANGSAM IN DER DEPRESSION, WÄHREND IN EINEM NOCH UNTER DEN KRIEGSFOLGEN LEIDENDEN EUROPA BEREITS DIE SAAT FÜR EINEN NEUEN KRIEG GELEGT WURDE. In Spanien brach der Bürgerkrieg aus; Indien setzte seinen Kampf um Unabhängigkeit fort; Japan besetzte die Mandschurei, Italien okkupierte Äthiopien, während Deutschland seine Nachbarn ins Visier nahm. In Amerika wurde Franklin Delano Roosevelt mit seinem Programm eines New Deal zum Präsidenten gewählt. Allerdings gingen am Tag seiner Amtsübernahme die meisten Banken des Landes bankrott.

Das Radio, eine technische Erfindung der 20er, erlebte in den 30er Jahren einen regelrechten Boom, weil die Produzenten das Programm durchdacht gestalteten und Unterhaltung von Musik und Comedy bis hin zu Nachrichten und Sportberichterstattung anboten. Kinder lauschten den Fortsetzungsabenteuern von Cowboys, während ihre Mütter sich die Probleme und Sorgen der Charaktere von Seifenopern anhörten. In den späten Zwanzigerjahren hatte der aufkommende Ton im Kino die Stummfilmära beendet. Im Jahr 1930 besuchten allwöchentlich an die 85 Millionen Menschen die Kinos. Unterhaltung besaß nach wie vor hauptsächlich realitätsfernen Charakter – ob in Form von Busby Berkeleys erlesenen Bühnenmusicals bis hin zu Shirley Temples süßlichem Würgegriff um die Kinokassen. Greta Garbo gelang der Übergang zum Tonfilm erfolgreich, und Jean Harlow avancierte frech und unabhängig zum Sexsymbol des Jahrzehnts.

Einen unvergleichlich romantischen Skandal erlebte das Jahrzehnt, als Englands neu gekrönter König Edward auf seinen Thron verzichtete, um 1936 die geschiedene Amerikanerin Wallis Simpson zu heiraten. Nachdem sie den Titel Herzog und Herzogin von Windsor angenommen hatten, wurde der aristokratische Lebensstil des Paares zum Synonym jener Dekade.

Die Silhouette der Männer war betont maskulin. Und ein guter Schneider schaffte es, mit breiten Schultern und schmalen Hüften die Figur des Schauspielers und Athleten Johnny Weissmueller nachzuempfinden. Zweireiher waren zunehmend gefragt, teilweise mit spitz zulaufenden Revers. Die Damen trugen lange, schmale Röcke, figurnahe Jacken und obligatorische Accessoires: Hüte, Handschuhe, Pelze, Schals, Handtaschen und Schuhe – tagsüber mit kleinem Absatz, am Abend turmhoch. Seit den 20ern entwickelten sich die Hüte ohne Krempen. Es gab solche ganz ohne und andere mit gefalteter Krempe, die das Gesicht umrahmte. Im weiteren Verlauf des Jahrzehnts wurden die Hüte aufwändiger, mit höherer Krone und breiterer Krempe. Exotischere Modelle waren zusätzlich mit Schleiern und Bändern verziert.

In Anlehnung an die Herrenmode begann die Designerin Elsa Schiaparelli die Schultern von Damenkostümen auszupolstern. 1931 trug die Tennisspielerin Lili de Alvarez einen von Schiaparelli kreierten Hosenrock. Im Jahr darauf spielte der Tennischampion Henry „Bunny" Austin bei den Herrenmeisterschaften der U. S. Open in New York bereits in Shorts.

Das Spektrum der Damenmode – von elegant geschnittenen Kostümen über fantasievolle Dessous bis hin zu dramatischen Abendroben – genoss in dem Film *Die Frauen* von 1939 Starkult. Darin waren die Arbeiten des Hollywood-Kostümbildners Adrian zu sehen, der sich oft Anregungen bei den sinnlichen, schräg geschnittenen Satinroben der französischen Designerin Madeleine Vionnet holte. In dem ansonsten in Schwarzweiß gedrehten Film mit den Stars Norma Shearer, Joan Crawford und Rosalind Russell gab es die in Farbe aufgenommene Sequenz einer Modenschau.

Die glamourösen Trends auf der Leinwand spiegelten aber natürlich nicht den Kleidungsstil der breiten Masse Amerikas wider, wo die Arbeitslosigkeit inzwischen 25 Prozent betrug. In den Anzeigen für Arbeitskleidung – die die Haltbarkeit und den günstigen Preisen der jeweiligen Marke priesen – ließ sich die ökonomische Realität der Großen Depression erkennen.

1932

1932 Athlete Johnny Weissmuller becomes actor, inspiring broad-shouldered cuts

Der Sportler Johnny Weissmueller wird Schauspieler und inspiriert zu schulterbetonten Schnitten

L'athlète Johnny Weissmueller devient acteur et inspire la mode des costumes à épaules larges

1932 Katharine Hepburn wears trousers in debut film role; women wear pants

Katharine Hepburn trägt im Film Hosen; Frauen fangen an, Hosen zu tragen

Katharine Hepburn porte des pantalons dans son premier rôle au cinéma ; les femmes la suivent

1934 Two-tone wing tips favored shoe of dancing star Fred Astaire

Zweifarbige Wing-Tips waren die Lieblingsschuhe des tanzenden Stars Fred Astaire

Star de la danse Fred Astaire privilégie les chaussures bicolores à bout golf

1934 Jockey manufactures first brief underwear for men

Jockey produziert die erste kurze Unterwäsche für Herren

Jockey fabrique le premier slip pour homme

Very Exclusively Yours—
Jantzen
THE LUXURY
DUPONT RAYON
ACELE
REG. U.S. PAT. OFF.
OF FASH

McCall's Patterns, 1933 ◂◂

DuPont Acele Acetate, 1936 ◂

PENDANT LES ANNÉES 30, LES ETATS-UNIS S'ENFONCENT LENTEMENT DANS LA GRANDE DÉPRESSION, TANDIS QUE LES GRAINES D'UNE AUTRE GUERRE GERMENT DANS UNE EUROPE ENCORE FRAGILISÉE PAR LA PRÉCÉDENTE. L'Espagne est en proie à la guerre civile ; l'Inde lutte toujours pour son indépendance ; le Japon envahit la Mandchourie ; l'Italie s'empare de l'Ethiopie ; l'Allemagne a des vues sur ses voisins. Aux Etats-Unis, Franklin Delano Roosevelt est élu président sur la base de son New Deal mais, le jour de son investiture, la plupart des banques nationales font faillite.

Nouvelle technologie inventée dans les années 20, la radio connaît un véritable boom pendant les années 30 quand les producteurs commencent à diffuser des programmes sophistiqués, de la musique à la comédie en passant par les actualités et le sport. Les enfants suivent les feuilletons relatant les aventures des cow-boys, tandis que leurs mères se passionnent pour les épreuves et les tribulations des personnages de soap-opéras. Le son, qui a fait son apparition dans les films à la fin de la décennie précédente, met un terme à l'ère du cinéma muet. En 1930, 85 millions de personnes se rendent au cinéma chaque semaine. Dans une large mesure, le monde du spectacle reste une façon d'échapper au quotidien, des comédies musicales élaborées mises en scène par Busby Berkeley à la prédominance au box-office d'une Shirley Temple à l'écœurante mièvrerie. Greta Garbo réussit le passage au film parlant et Jean Harlow définit les canons du sex-symbol de la décennie en femme effrontée et indépendante.

Cette période connaît un scandale romantique sans pareil quand, en 1936, le roi Edouard d'Angleterre fraîchement couronné renonce au trône pour épouser Wallis Simpson, une Américaine divorcée. Sous les titres de duc et duchesse de Windsor, le couple se distingue par un style aristocratique devenu synonyme des années 30.

Pour les hommes, la silhouette devient ouvertement masculine. Tout bon tailleur est capable de recréer le look du l'athlète sporty et acteur Johnny Weissmueller, avec ses larges épaules et ses hanches étroites. Le costume croisé gagne en popularité, parfois avec de larges revers ou revers à pointes. Pour les femmes, la jupe se porte longue et près du corps, la veste est ajustée et les accessoires sont de rigueur : chapeaux, gants, fourrures, foulards, sacs à main et chaussures, plates en journée, mais à talons hauts le soir. La forme cloche des chapeaux des années 20 évolue. Les visages s'encadrent de modèles sans bords ou à bords pliés. Au fil de la décennie, les chapeaux deviennent plus structurés et plus profonds avec des bords élargis. Les modèles plus exotiques comportent une voilette et sont gansés de ruban.

S'inspirant de la mode pour homme, la styliste Elsa Schiaparelli ajoute des épaulettes à ses tailleurs pour dame. En 1931, la joueuse de tennis Lili de Alvarez dispute le tournoi de Wimbledon dans une jupe fendue signée Schiaparelli. Un an plus tard, le champion de tennis Henry « Bunny » Austin joue en short au championnat des U. S. Open à New York.

Du tailleur ingénieusement flatteur à la lingerie fantaisie en passant par les spectaculaires robes du soir, toute la garde-robe féminine crève l'écran dans *Femmes*, un film de 1939 où s'exprime le talent d'Adrian, le chef costumier d'Hollywood qui s'inspire souvent des robes sensuelles en satin taillés en biais de la créatrice française Madeleine Vionnet. Ce film en noir et blanc avec Norma Shearer, Joan Crawford et Rosalind Russell inclut même une séquence de défilé de mode tournée en Technicolor.

Les tenues glamour du grand écran ne reflètent cependant pas la véritable garde-robe de l'Américaine de la rue, le taux de chômage atteignant 25 %. Faisant la réclame de la longévité des marques et de leurs prix abordables, ce sont les publicités pour les vêtements utilitaires, et non les tenues de soirée, qui reflètent la réalité économique de la Grande Dépression.

1935

1935 Warner Brothers Corset Co. introduces standard A, B, C, and D bra sizes

Die Warner Brothers Corset Co. führt die Standardgrößen A, B, C und D für Büstenhalter ein

Warner Brothers Corset Co. lance les tailles de bonnets de soutien-gorge A, B, C et D

1936 Duke and Duchess of Windsor married; define aristocratic style of decade

Herzog und Herzogin von Windsor prägen frisch getraut den aristokratischen Stil des Jahrzehnts

Le duc et la duchesse de Windsor se marient et incarnent le style aristocratique de la décennie

1937 Salvatore Ferragamo opens shop in Florence, Italy; patents cork wedge heel

Salvatore Ferragamo eröffnet sein erstes Geschäft in Florenz und lässt sich den Keilabsatz aus Kork patentieren

Salvatore Ferragamo ouvre une boutique à Florence en Italie ; il fait breveter le talon compensé en liège

1937 Ray-Ban's aviator sunglasses, developed for U.S. Air Force, released to public

Ray-Bans für die U.S. Air Force entwickelte Piloten-Sonnenbrille wird der Öffentlichkeit vorgestellt

Conques pour l'U.S. Air Force, les lunettes de pilote de Ray-Ban sont commercialisées pour le grand public

"Beau Brummell"

PALM BEACH CRAVATS

Again...America's Smartest Summer Tie!

Style enthusiasts again say . . . Genuine Palm Beach Cravat . . . Summer's fashion "first" in neckwear. The essence o smartness . . . patterns and colors brilliantly conceived b master stylists. Palm Beach Cravats are fashioned fro Genuine Palm Beach Cloth. Their unique, patented four-fol construction provides a perfect knot. They have no inne lining . . . they're easy to tie . . . hard to muss . . . washabl

"Beau Brummell" has taken the 1937 version of the Genuine Palm Beach Cravat and Bow Tie to new heights, along with their latest fashion spark . . . the Palm Beach Handkerchief. Smartness unlimited!

It isn't a Genuine Pal Beach Cravat . . . withou the Palm Beach Label

FOUR-IN-HANDS $1.00 BOWS 75c HANDKERCHIEFS $1.0

THE WEISBAUM BROS., BROWER COMPANY, CINCINNA

"Sure I'm leaving—I can't get used to men without Hart Schaffner & Marx clothes!"

THIS is a free country. If these gentlemen think they're going to enjoy life better without clothes—that's their business. But as long as most men have to wear clothes—that's our business!

And candor certainly compels us to admit that—much as we admire the American male—he looks a lot better *with* smart clothes than without them; and smart clothes naturally mean Hart Schaffner & Marx clothes! So no matter if you're trying to impress blonde, brunette or boss, take a lesson from the little lady above; drop in today and inspect the great collection of new, up-to-the-minute styles now on display at your local Hart Schaffner & Marx dealer!

★ The growing demand by well dressed men for a plainer back sport suit was a feature of the Palm Beach season. According to Robert Surrey, famed Hart Schaffner & Marx style scout, it gained momentum as fashion leaders moved northward with Spring through Augusta, Aiken, Pinehurst and the Virginia fox hunting country. This beltless model, the Ascot, with gussets at the shoulder for freedom of movement and the new side vents, has become a prime favorite at all the smart country clubs.

HART SCHAFFNER & MARX

THE TRUMPETER LABEL

A SMALL THING TO LOOK FOR  *...A BIG THING TO FIND*

Hart Schaffner & Marx Menswear, 1936

Weisbaum Bros. Ties, 1937◄

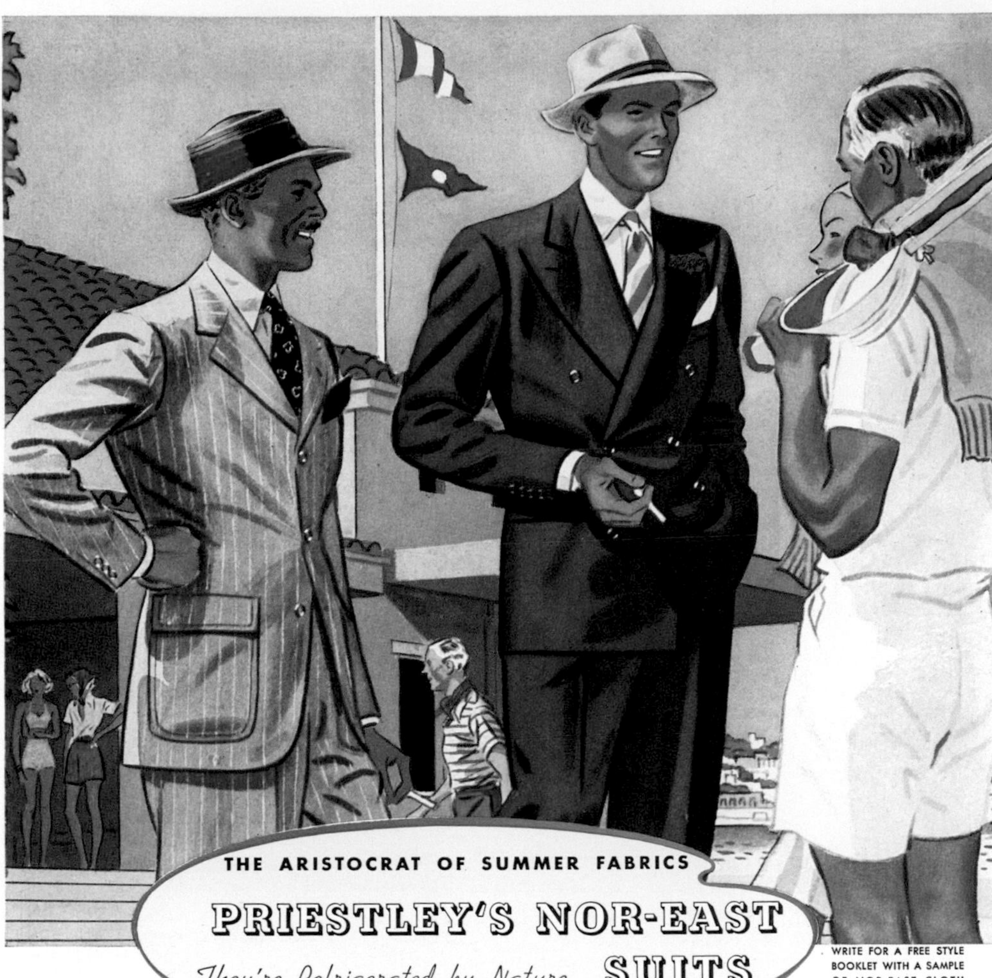

THE ARISTOCRAT OF SUMMER FABRICS
PRIESTLEY'S NOR-EAST
They're Refrigerated by Nature SUITS
WRITE FOR A FREE STYLE BOOKLET WITH A SAMPLE OF NOR-EAST CLOTH

Priestley's IMPORTED NOR-EAST NON-CRUSH* *REG.U.S.PAT.OFF.

At Better Men's Stores Everywhere

$29.75

Here, at last, is the summer suit that makes LIFE worth living.

It's Priestley's Nor-East, the original worsted and mohair blend—the fabric that's refrigerated by Nature! It is actually *cool to the touch,* in addition to being feather-light and tissue-thin, yet holds its shape and style.

The cloth is imported—because only Priestley of England knows the secret of weaving this most luxurious of summer fabrics; the suits are styled and tailored by America's foremost maker of summer clothes. Your clothier can show you Nor-East in both light and dark colors, in plain shades and patterns. Ask for it!

★ TAILORED FOR READY-TO-WEAR EXCLUSIVELY BY L. GREIF & BRO., BALTIMORE ★

Priestley's Nor-East Suits, 1939

The 1930s saw the birth of the summer-weight suit, called the Palm Beach suit, in honor of the resort town in Florida. Made of seersucker, linen, shantung, or other light-weight fabrics, these suits tended to be double-breasted and featured open-notch lapels.

In den 1930ern kam erstmals der sommerlich leichte sogenannte Palm-Beach-Anzug auf, der nach dem Urlaubsort in Florida benannt war. Aus Seersucker, Leinen, Shantung oder anderen leichten Stoffen gefertigt waren diese Anzüge meist zweireihig und mit eingeschnittenem Revers versehen.

Les années 30 virent la naissance du costume estival léger, baptisé le Palm Beach en hommage à la station balnéaire de Floride. Taillés dans du seersucker, du lin, de la soie shantung ou d'autres tissus légers, ces costumes comportaient en général une veste croisée avec revers à crans ouverts.

► Priestley's Nor-East Suits, 1938

Promise....

and fulfillment await the woman just discovering the telling power of figure beauty. For her, the modern way of youthful figure discipline... Foundettes.

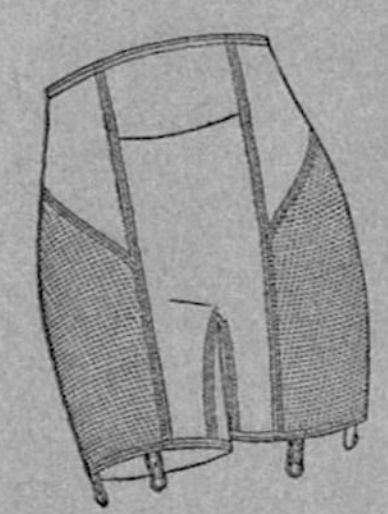

There are glamour and good form for figures in this new Foundette *pantie-girdle by* MUNSINGWEAR. *The new feature "Lastex"* batiste panel stretches up and down... extends into a horizontal-stretch yoke over the hips. Zipper in back; net fabric sides of "Lastex"* and "Cordura" Rayon.* Style 4215. *At all better stores. *Woven or knit of "Lastex" yarn.*

Foundettes
BY MUNSINGWEAR

Minneapolis New York Chica

RIDING HABIT AND ACCESSORIES BY ABERCROMBIE & FITCH CO. PHOTOGRAPH BY LOUISE

C.M.O. Womenswear, ca. 1938

Although Katharine Hepburn is the best-known actress to introduce trousers into the mainstream, many other Hollywood actresses were known for wearing pants, including Jean Harlow and Marlene Dietrich. The real world, however, was still far behind the silver screen, and it was uncommon for everyday women to don slacks for anything other than sporting occasions for several decades to come.

Obwohl Katharine Hepburn die wohl bekannteste Schauspielerin ist, die Hosen für die breite Masse tragbar machte, gab es auch viele andere Hollywood-darstellerinnen, die Hosen trugen, u. a. Jean Harlow und Marlene Dietrich. Die Realität blieb allerdings weit hinter der Leinwand zurück, und es sollte noch einige Jahrzehnte lang als unüblich gelten, dass normale Frauen zu anderen Anlässen als zum Sport lange Hosen anzogen.

Si l'on se souvient de Katharine Hepburn comme l'actrice qui a démocratisé le pantalon pour femme, bien d'autres comédiennes d'Hollywood étaient connues pour en porter, notamment Jean Harlow et Marlene Dietrich. La mode de la rue accusait néanmoins un grand retard sur celle du grand écran, et il fallut attendre plusieurs décennies avant que les femmes arborent le pantalon en dehors des activités sportives.

Munsingwear Foundettes Undergarments, 1939 ◂

MUNSING Wear presents Foundettes

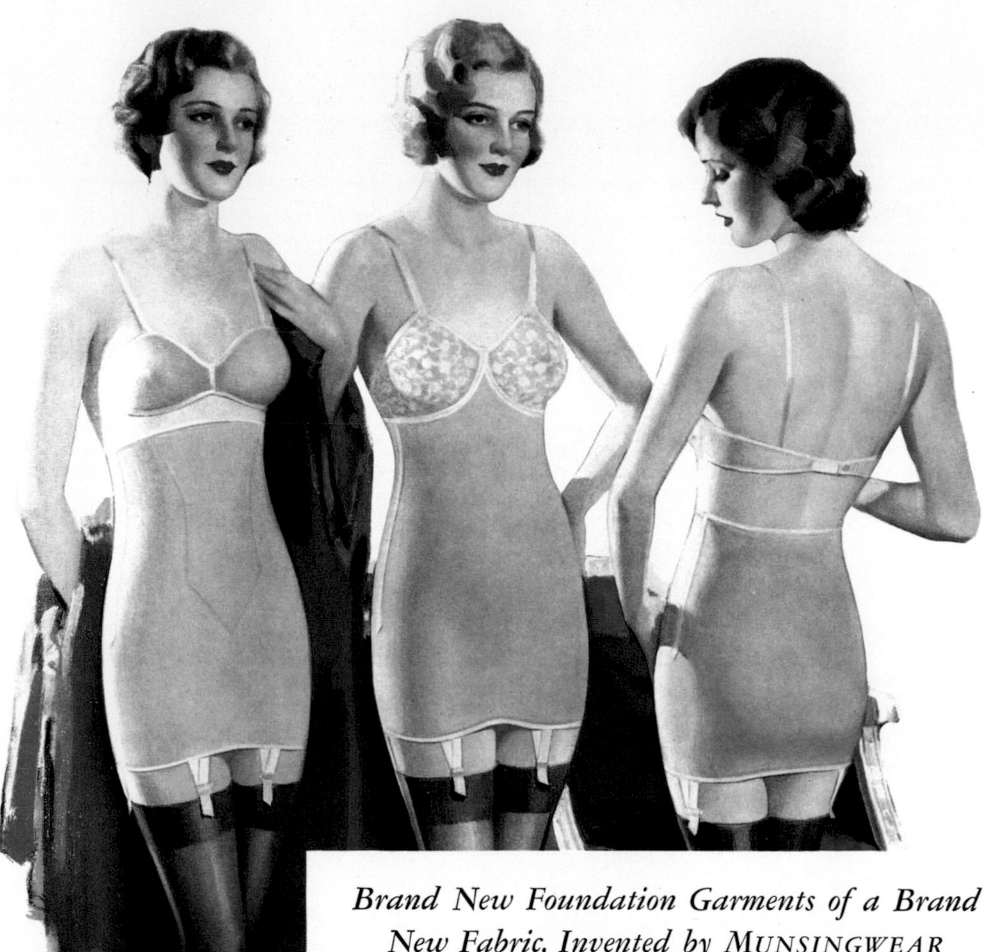

Brand New Foundation Garments of a Brand New Fabric, Invented by MUNSINGWEAR

YOU'VE never seen step-in girdles and foundation garments quite like these . . . for nothing like them has ever been created! Foundettes slim the hips, trim the waist, flatten the diaphragm and smooth the silhouette into smart and lovely lines. Yet, you've never worn anything quite so comfortable! Fashioned of specially processed two-way-stretch fabric . . . invented by Munsingwear . . . Foundettes will wash marvelously and wear wonderfully. They won't pull away from the seams or ravel back or curl. You'll like Munsingwear Foundettes for slimmer figures. And they're priced for slimmer purses. See these new Foundettes at a Munsingwear dealer near you. Munsingwear, Minneapolis.

Munsingwear makes all styles of smart undergarments in all types of fabrics. For men, women and children.

UNDERWEAR · WATERWEAR · HOSIERY
SLEEPING AND LOUNGING GARMENTS · KNIT COATS
PULL-ONS · FOUNDATION GARMENTS

LET MUNSINGWEAR COVER YOU WITH SATISFACTION

Munsingwear Foundettes Undergarments, 1933

Famous for its men's one-piece union suits, Minneapolis-based Munsingwear Inc. was founded in 1886 as Northwestern Knitting Company. The company changed its name in 1923 and went on to grow its business though a series of acquisitions of other knitting mills and apparel makers. Eventually, the company grew to produce men's and children's underwear, sleepwear, and sportswear; and women's lingerie and sleepwear.

Die für ihre einteilige Herrenunterwäsche berühmte Munsingwear Inc. mit Sitz in Minneapolis wurde 1886 als Northwestern Knitting Company gegründet. 1923 änderte das Unternehmen seinen Namen und erweiterte sein Sortiment durch den Zukauf anderer Strickereien und Bekleidungshersteller. Schließlich umfasste die Produktion Unterwäsche, Nachtwäsche und Sportbekleidung für Herren und Kinder sowie Dessous und Nachtwäsche für Damen.

Réputée pour ses combinaisons longues pour homme, la société Munsingwear Inc. de Minneapolis fut fondée en 1886 sous le nom de Northwestern Knitting Company. Rebaptisée Munsingwear Inc. en 1923, elle diversifia ses activités en rachetant plusieurs manufactures de tricot et fabricants de vêtements. L'entreprise finit par produire des sous-vêtements, des pyjamas et du sportswear pour homme et pour enfant, ainsi que de la lingerie et des vêtements de nuit pour femme.

► Foot Saver Shoes, 1939

Exciting, unexpected perforations, bracelet buckles, sudden color at your instep! Foot Saver dramatizes the classics, makes your walking shoes gay shoes—lighter, softer, smarter. All made over Foot Saver's wonderful Shortback* Last that fits your foot like a stocking. No gap, no slip, no pinch! Write for our Spring Fashion Folio and name of the store nearest you. The Julian & Kokenge Company, makers of Foot Saver Shoes and Foot Saver Skuffies, 61 W. Main Street, Columbus, Ohio.

SIMPLICITY PATTERN 1776—15c complete. Shorts with button-on top, of seersucker gingham. Separate wrap-around skirt of white linen tweed.

SIMPLICITY PATTERN 1773—15c complete. Tie-around and bareback play-dress of bright cotton-print with amusing laundry rope suspenders.

Nunn-Bush

Ankle fashioned Oxfords

Nunn-Bush Genuine White Buck Styles $8.50 to $10.50

Your PERSONAL APPEARANCE
Deserves the Difference Ankle-Fashioning Makes
If every man knew what every Nunn-Bush salaried craftsman knows—every man would be wearing Nunn-Bush shoes.
You wear sports oxfords for better appearance. Treat yourself to the finest money can buy! Learn why Ankle-Fashioning is winning the *Lifetime* loyalty of innumerable men.
$7.85 *to* $12.50
NUNN-BUSH SHOE COMPANY
MILWAUKEE NEW YORK SAN FRANCISCO
Ask your local Nunn-Bush merchant about the built-in Nunn-Bush Weight Distributor Arch.

Nunn-Bush Shoes, 1937

Simplicity Patterns, 1935 ◄

PETTY
Perfectly suited
BY JANTZEN
Suited for stunning appearance, for perfect fit, for glorious comfor
Briefly, skillfully cut, the new Jantzens give you a world of sun exposur
and free-as-a-breeze action for swimming, diving and beach fun. Kav
Knit fabrics of luxurious quick-to-dry wool in fresh new versions hav
magical knitted-in qualities through the magic of Jantzen-Stitch th
mean figure-control for women and trim athletic smartness for men.
the water and out, you are assured a perfect, permanent fit. See the ne
Jantzens at your favorite store or shop. Jantzen Knitting Mills, Portlan
Oregon; Vancouver, Canada; London, England; Sydney, Australia.
The Swing
The "Swing" (illustrated) in tune with the rhythm of Youth! Gay three-color contrast—or in solid colors—created of whipcord Kava Knit fabric. Tailored-in elastic Brä-Lift for youthful uplift. $6.95
Other Jantzen Creations $4.50 to $10.95
De Luxe Half-Hitch
De Luxe Half-Hitch (illustrated) The Trunks of the Year! Superbly tailored from a rope-stitch Kava Knit. Hawaiian beach-patrol side stripes. $3.95
Other Jantzen Trunks $2.95 to $4.95
A reproduction of this Petty painting without descriptive copy will be sent on receipt of 10c in stamps or coins.
Jantzen
JANTZEN KNITTING MILLS, Dept. 301, Portland, Oregon
Send me style folder in color featuring new 1937 models.
WOMEN'S ☐ MEN'S ☐
Name
Street
City

A Jantzen always attracts attention! Because it's America's finest fitting swimming suit! It's the best precaution against a distressing appearance—in the sea or on the sands. Cruise into any good shop and see the new models in the fashionable Kava-Knit fabrics. Upon receipt of 10c in coin or stamps we'll gladly send you a reproduction of this Petty painting without advertising. Address Dept. 241, Jantzen Knitting Mills, Portland, Oregon.
"One of us must flag that ship with our Jantzen"

"RUNNING IMPROVES MY FIGURE?— SILLY, IT'S JUST MY JANTZEN!"
Presenting the new Jantzen Glamour Fabrics
VELVA-LURE ☆ SUEDE-SHEEN
SATIN-KNITS ☆ KNIT-IN PRINTS
the most radiant stars of summer's bright stage. Their creation is unquestionably the outstanding swim suit news of the year. They are new, amazingly new. They were developed by Jantzen exclusively and are made only by Jantzen. Gorgeous textures have been developed in these luxurious Glamour Fabrics. Velva-Lure and Suede-Sheen are soft, gleaming, velvety; Satin-Knits are rich, radiant, lustrous; Knit-in-Prints, of vibrant color and gaiety. The miracle of Lastex yarn has been added for just the right amount of two-way stretch that holds the body in youthful sculptured lines. These astonishing tailored Jantzens with Positive Uplift give a new meaning to figure-control in a swim suit for women and set a new standard of trim athletic appearance for men. In the water and out they fit with wrinkle-defying perfection. See these new Jantzen Glamour Swim Suits at your favorite shop or store. Note their rich sheen and beauty of texture. Feel their appealing softness. Test their amazing elasticity. Jantzen Knitting Mills, Portland, Oregon; Vancouver, Canada; Sydney, Australia; London, England.
Left: The ZIP-IN, a sparkling new Jantzen half-skirt model tailored in gorgeous "Velva-Lure", $7.95. Skirtless model in "Satin-Knit", $5.95. Other Jantzen models, $4.95 to $7.95.
Right: Tops in design, tailoring, fit and fabric is the new STREAMLINER in Suede-Sheen, luxuriously soft and rich. $4.95. Other Jantzen trunks $2.95 to $4.95.
Jantzen
MOLDED-FIT SWIM SUITS
JANTZEN KNITTING MILLS, Dept. 281, Portland, Oregon.
Send me style folder in colors, featuring new 1939 models. Women's Men's
Name
Street
City

Jantzen Swimwear, 1936

Jantzen Swimwear, 1939

Jantzen Swimwear, 1937 ◂

EXQUISITE colors . . wondrously lovely details of texture and finish . . Realsilk Hosiery pleases more women than any other hosiery sold! Perhaps because women have had a voice in its perfecting, during these ten years that Realsilk Hosiery has been sold to them by Realsilk Representatives in their own homes. Their comments . . suggestions . . have helped to make Realsilk the favorite hosiery of *chic* women everywhere. Why not see these smart stockings, sponsored by a Fashion Committee of five famous women, in your own home, with your shoes and frocks? Realsilk Hosiery is sold only by Realsilk Representatives who call at your home. Branch offices in 250 cities in the United States and Canada. The Real Silk Hosiery Mills, Inc., Indianapolis, Indiana, U. S. A.

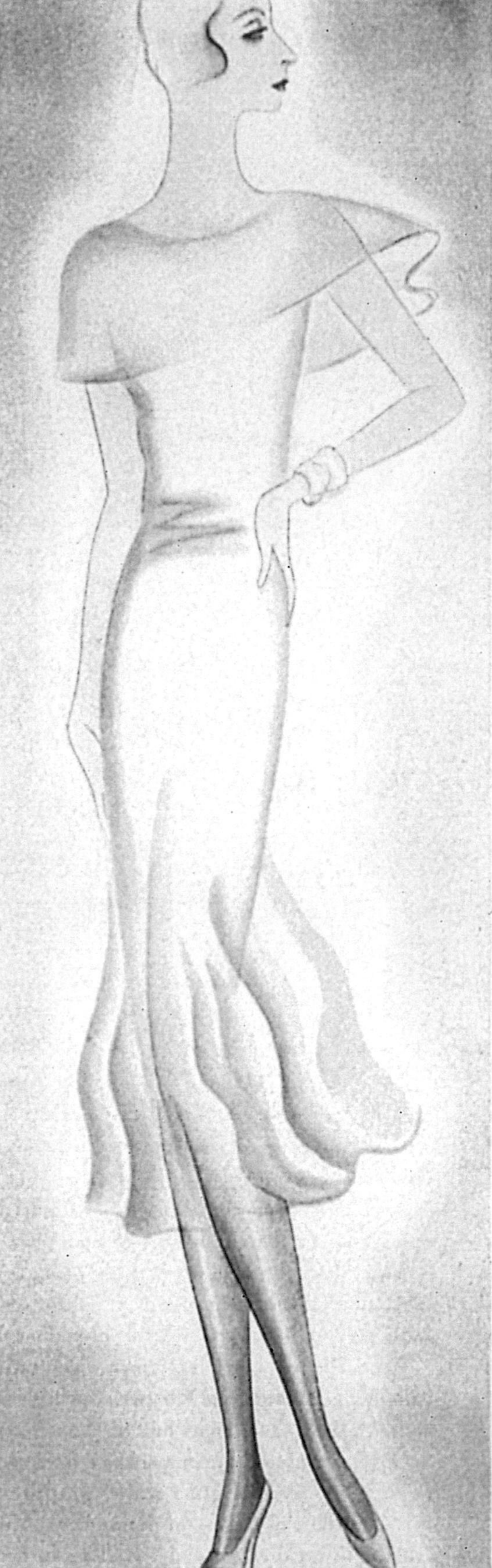

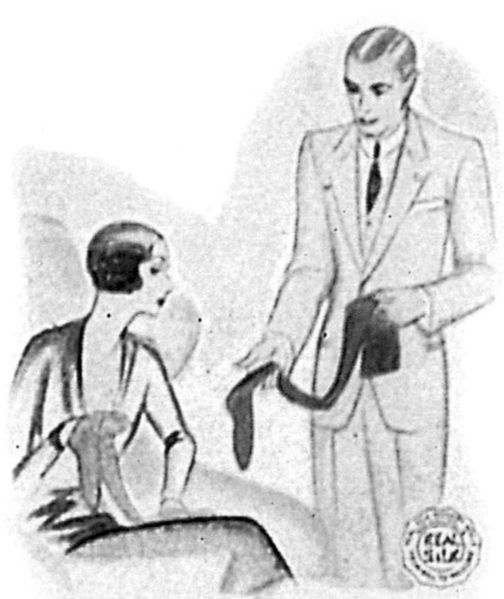

Lady Egerton
Neysa McMein
Lynn Fontanne
Elinor Patterson
Katherine Harford
the Realsilk Fashion Committee . .

Ask the Realsilk Representative to show you Realsilk's newest, sheerest stocking—style 100—*invisibly* reenforced for wear with low cut sandals. If he is not calling at your home regularly, 'phone your local Realsilk office.

the new REALSILK hosiery

Real Silk Hosiery, 1930

COLOR
PALM BEACH SUITS
It's very old fashioned to think that Palm Beach means a light color ● Palm Beach is the name of the most popular summer suit in the world: *The suit that lets your body breathe* ● You can have it in blue or brown or gray or white—in fact, a whole world of colors and patterns. ● The cloth is made by the famous GOODALL mills—by no one else—and is tailored by GOODALL experts into the smartest washable suits of the season ● You'll know you're getting the genuine when you see the trade marked label in the garment. Suits $17.75—Slacks $5.50—Dinner Formal $20.00. Goodall Company, Cincinnati, Ohio.
$17.75
TAILORED BY GOODALL
Palm Beach
FROM THE GENUINE CLOTH
HANS FLATO

Palm Beach Suits/Goodall Mills, 1938

"I had a problem
with ugly bulges
until I sent
the Spencer
coupon below"
Above: Note the bulging of the hips and abdomen in the ordinary corset. At right the same woman in her Spencer. Hips are slenderized and the abdominal bulge is gone.
Are your hips a problem? Are you troubled with a bulging abdomen or a "spare-tire" of flesh around the waist line? Then follow the example of the young woman in the photograph and find out what a Spencer can do for you.
Your Spencer corset and brassiere will effectively correct any figure fault because every section, every line is designed, cut and made to solve your figure problem and yours only. Spencers are light and flexible yet every Spencer is guaranteed to keep its lovely lines as long as it is worn!
Have a figure analysis—free
At any convenient time, a Spencer Corsetiere, trained in the Spencer designer's methods of figure analysis, will call at your home. A study of your figure will cost you nothing. Stop experimenting. Prices depend on materials selected. A wide range to suit every purse.
Send for interesting free booklet "Your Figure Problem"
Look in your telephone book under "Spencer Corsetiere" and call your nearest corsetiere or send us the coupon below for booklet. This will not obligate you in any way.
"I've lost inches in my Spencer"

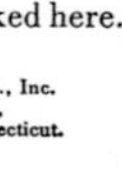

Copyright, 1939, Spencer Corset Co., Inc.
Write Anne Spencer
for personal advice FREE on figure faults checked here.
May 8, 1939
Anne Spencer, Spencer Corset Co., Inc. 133 Derby Avenue, New Haven, Connecticut.
Bulging hips
Bulging abdomen
Lordosis backline
Do You Want to Make Money?
Ambitious women may find business openings as corsetieres in every state. We train you. If interested, check here . . . . . ☐
Name
Address
Also made in Canada and England at Rock Island, Quebec, and 4 & 5 Old Bond St., London, W. I.
SPENCER INDIVIDUALLY DESIGNED CORSETS

Naughty Nautical
JANE WITHERS
has a wardrobe of three
CATALINAS!
all made figure-flattering with
CONTROLASTIC*
LEAVE it to Jane to do things enthusiastically . . . whether it's playing a lively, lovable role in her new 20th Century Fox film, "Boy Friend" . . . or finding the slickest swim suits ashore or afloat.
Smart juniors . . . here's your cue . . . it's Catalina, made with Firestone CONTROLastic, the new elastic yarn that whittles the sprouting teen-age figure to bathing beauty proportions.
CONTROLastic's unique construction (3 to 5 wrapped layers of pure rubber in each tiny strand) makes it extra resistant to sun, air and water . . . keeps your Catalina lively and figure-flattering all season long.
Jane Withers wears, reading from top: Zephyr Wool and Celanese rayon with CONTROLastic. Puckerette of Celanese rayon with CONTROLastic. Hand-blocked Sunflower Print on rayon with CONTROLastic. All in misses' sizes in beautiful beach colors . . . . . Each $4
Write for free autographed picture of Jane Withers in full color, to Pacific Knitting Mills, Los Angeles. See Catalina Swim Suits at better stores.
*Reg. U. S. Pat. Off.
STYLED FOR THE STARS OF HOLLYWOOD AND YOU!
Catalina
SWIM SUITS
WITH Controlastic
This label pledges Multi-ply elasticity and figure control
PACIFIC KNITTING MILLS, LOS ANGELES, CAL.

Catalina Swimwear, 1939

Catalina Swimwear was founded in 1907 as sweater and underwear manufacturer Bentz Knitting Mills. Under the name Pacific Knitting Mills, the company began producing knitted swimwear in 1912 and changed its name to Catalina Knitting Mills in 1928. The company was not the first swim brand to use the celebrity endorsement. Rival swimwear maker Jantzen landed Olympians Johnny Weissmueller and Duke Kahanamoku as spokesmen in 1924.

Catalina Swimmwear wurde 1907 als Hersteller von Pullovern und Unterwäsche unter dem Namen Bentz Knitting Mills gegründet. Als Pacific Knitting Mills begann das Unternehmen 1912 gestrickte Bademode zu produzieren und änderte seinen Namen 1928 schließlich in Catalina Knitting Mills. Die Firma nutzte als erster Bademodenhersteller die Empfehlung von Prominenten. Das Konkurrenzunternehmen Jantzen schaffte es 1924 die Olympioniken Johnny Weissmueller und Duke Kahanamoku als Fürsprecher zu verpflichten.

La marque Catalina Swimwear fut créée en 1907 par le fabricant de pulls et de sous-vêtements Bentz Knitting Mills. Sous le nom Pacific Knitting Mills, l'entreprise commença à produire des maillots de bain en maille dès 1912 avant d'être rebaptisée Catalina Knitting Mills en 1928. Elle ne fut pas la première à faire appel aux célébrités pour promouvoir ses produits, son concurrent Jantzen ayant choisi les champions olympiques Johnny Weissmueller et Duke Kahanamoku comme interprètes en 1924.

Spencer Corsets, 1939

► Montgomery Ward Department Store, 1930

The Princess Influence
ove Silk
B DANCE SET $2.98
C SILHOUETTE FITTED SLIP $3.98
D COMBINATION $1.98
E PURE DYE ALL SILK FLAT CREPE $3.95
HEAVY SILK CREPE DE CHINE REGULAR SIZES $2.95 EXTRA SIZES $3.98
F DANCE SET $1.98 STEP-IN $1.69
G LACE TRI $1.98 PLAIN TAILOR $1.98
Rayon Crepe Man
Creations in All Silk Crepe de Chine
L GOWN $2.98
M GOWN REGULAR SIZES $3.98 EXTRA SIZES $4.98
K CHEMISE $2.98
J SILK and RAYON TWILLED SATIN REGULAR SIZES $1.98 EXTRA SIZES $2.49 ALL RAYON TWILL REGULAR SIZES $1.49
lk and Rayon Satins
FINE QUALITY KNITTED RAYONS
N PANTIE $1.00 VEST 89¢ BLOOMER $1.00
CHARDONIZ
U BRASSIERE TOP COMBINATION $1.00
P HAND MADE GOWN $1.98
S VESTETTE 69¢ FANCY SHORTIE BLOOMER $1.00 PLAIN SHORTIE BLOOMER 79¢
T PAJAMA 1.98
R 3 PIECE ENSEMBLE $3.98 2 PIECE PAJAMA $1.98
O FAST COLOR PAJAMA $2.98
Z FAST COLO 3-PIECE ENSEMBL $1.98

Without Inbands

MEN'S CAPS
Newest Fabrics and Patterns

With Inbands

Soft Napped All Wool
Resembles Camel Hair
Dressy—Rich Looking $1.75

39 G 650—Medium gray. 39 G 651—Tan. SIZES: 6¾, 6⅞, 7, 7⅛, 7¼, 7⅜, 7½, 7⅝, 7¾. State size. Read How to Measure on Page 247. We Pay Postage. The featured style and material for 1931—promises popularity far excelling anything in recent years! All Wool. Just the Cap for early Fall wear. A perfect match for a camel hair coat. Hand shaped and hand blocked. Made in the popular 8-4 style. Silk-faced satin lining. Full leather sweatband. Unbreakable visor.

Adjustable Style $1.39

39 G 623—Fancy bluish-gray plaid. 39 G 625—Fancy tan plaid. SIZES: Adjustable from 6¼ to 7½. We Pay Postage. Will fit any head. Simply adjust buckle in front. Tailored of a swagger plaid material about two-thirds wool—very sturdy. Silk-faced satin lining. Genuine leather sweatband in front. Unbreakable visor.

Our Finest Cap $1.95

39 G 647—Gray. 39 G 649—Medium brown. SIZES: 6¾ to 7¼. State size. Read How to Measure on Page 247. We Pay Postage. Hand shaped of very fine All Wool material. Patterns perfectly matched. Lined with lustrous silk-faced satin. Unbreakable visor. Sanitary lined inband.

Leader Value—All Wool
Sateen Lined $1.39

39 G 606—Fancy medium brown plaid. 39 G 608—Fancy medium gray plaid. SIZES: 6¾, 6⅞, 7, 7⅛, 7¼, 7⅜, 7½, 7⅝, 7¾. State size. Read How to Measure on Page 247. We Pay Postage. Again we offer our Big Feature Cap value for men. Only $1.39—but the equal in quality, tailoring and style to most $2 caps. Hand shaped and hand blocked by one of the country's foremost cap makers. Fine All Wool top coating material. Stylish one-piece top with warm inband for cold weather. Sateen lined. Unbreakable visor.

Read How to Measure Page 247

All Wool Tweed $1.00

39 G 633—Medium gray. 39 G 634—Tan. SIZES: 6¾ to 7¾. Read How to Measure on Page 247. State size. We Pay Postage. A wonderful Cap for $1.00. Carefully made in 8-4 style of All Wool tweeds. Unbreakable visor. Leather sweatband in front. Full lined.

Peppy Collegiate $1.48

39 G 631—Light gray. 39 G 635—Tan. ALL SIZES: 6½ to 7½. State size. Postpaid. New Fall patterns and colors. Fashioned of fine fabrics, about two-thirds wool, in 8-4 style and fully lined with attractive rayon-faced material. Full leather sweatband; unbreakable visor.

Heavy Weight All Wool $1.29

39 G 617—Dark brown. 39 G 621—Dark gray. SIZES: 6¾, 6⅞, 7, 7⅛, 7¼, 7⅜, 7½, 7⅝, 7¾. Fine All Wool overcoating material, an extra heavy winter weight. Sateen lining. Warm inband. Unbreakable visor. State size. Postpaid.

Big Value! 89¢

39 G 609—Medium gray. 39 G 611—Brown. SIZES: 6¾, 6⅞, 7, 7⅛, 7¼, 7⅜, 7½. State size. We Pay Postage. Exceptional bargain! About two-thirds wool, balance silk. Warm inband to cover ears. Full cotton twill lined. Unbreakable visor.

Special Offer $1.00 Choice Each

Genuine Leather $1.49

39 G 721—Black. 39 G 723—Brown. SIZES: 6¾, 6⅞, 7, 7⅛, 7¼, 7⅜, 7½, 7⅝, 7¾. State size. Read How to Measure, Page 247. Postpaid. A genuine sheepskin leather Cap—built to stand rough wear. Great for every man, but particularly for men wearing leather coats. Made in the 8-4 style. Warm lined inband pulls down over ears. Full flannel lined. Unbreakable visor. Entire cap is strong, durable—sure to give several seasons' wear. Rushed to you by Ward's speedy service!

The Genuine "Scotch" Cap ←

39 G 729—Navy blue only... $1.00 SIZES: 6¾, 6⅞, 7, 7⅛, 7¼, 7⅜, 7½, 7⅝, 7¾. State size. We Pay Postage. A big bargain leader in a popular Cap. Heavy weight All Wool. The genuine original "Scotch" Cap—famous for complete protection against cold. Full flannel lined. Unbreakable visor. Warm inband that pulls well down over the ears in cold weather. Speedy Same Day shipping service.

Corduroy "Tie-Top" →

39 G 733—Tan. 39 G 734—Navy blue........ $1.00 SIZES: 6¾, 6⅞, 7, 7⅛, 7¼, 7⅜, 7½, 7⅝, 7¾. State size. Be sure to read How to Measure on Page 247. We Pay Postage. The ace of $1 Corduroy Cap values. Fur lined inband and tie top of double thickness to pull down over ears in cold weather. Full lined with chamois-like cloth. Extra quality at a money saving price.

Leather Judge Style $1.49

39 G 711—Black. 39 G 715—Brown. SIZES: 6¾, 6⅞, 7, 7⅛, 7¼, 7⅜, 7½, 7⅝, 7¾. State size. Be sure to read How to Measure, Page 247. We Pay Postage. Popular Judge style Cap of genuine sheepskin leather—tough, durable and pliable. Full flannel lined. Unbreakable visor. Warm inband to protect the ears in cold weather.

Leather Helmet
All Wool Lined

39 G 704—Black leather. 39 G 705—Brown leather. $1.00 SIZES: 6¾, 6⅞, 7, 7⅛, 7¼, 7⅜, 7½. State size. We Pay Postage. Big value! A genuine sheepskin leather Helmet far superior to most helmets priced near one dollar. Months of hard wear prove its real quality. The leather is soft and pliable, yet very durable. Full lined with thick warm All Wool flannel.

Mohawk Knit Wool

39 G 759—Navy blue. 39 G 761—Gray........ $1.00 SIZES: 6¾, 6⅞, 7, 7⅛, 7¼, 7⅜, 7½. State size. Postpaid. A new, warm Cap of All Wool Mohawk knit. All Wool lining. Unbreakable visor. Great for men who work outdoors. Outside pulldown to cover ears in cold weather.

Wool Judge Cap

39 G 725—Assorted colors...... $1.00 SIZES: 6¾, 6⅞, 7, 7⅛, 7¼, 7⅜, 7½. State size. Postpaid. Assorted fine heavy All Wool overcoating. Full lined with strong cotton twill. Lined inband. Unbreakable visor

Served With BYRD Expedition

Wonder Value 89¢

39 G 731—Dark blue Melton cloth. 39 G 732—Drab brown corduroy. 39 G 735—Dark blue corduroy. SIZES: 6¾ to 7¾. State size. Served at the North and South Pole! Warm and long wearing. Full lined with warm red flannel. Outside slide band. Unbreakable visor. Postpaid.

Silk Pile Plush $1.69

39 G 753—Black only. SIZES: 6¾, 6⅞, 7, 7⅛, 7¼, 7⅜, 7½, 7⅝, 7¾. State size. Read How to Measure on Page 247. We Pay Postage. Heavy Silk pile plush. Full sateen lined, hand blocked and has an unbreakable visor. Warm lined inside band. An unusually good quality Cap.
39 G 751—Same as above except medium weight plush...... $1.29

Bargain "Tie-Top" 69¢

39 G 703—Drab only. SIZES: 6¾, 6⅞, 7, 7⅛, 7¼, 7⅜, 7½. State size. Read How to Measure on Page 247. Postpaid. A low priced thick set corduroy Cap that wears well. Full lined with warm lining. Unbreakable visor.

Horsehide Helmet $1.49

39 G 755—Black. 39 G 757—Brown. SIZES: 6¾ to 7½. State size. Read How to Measure on Page 247. Postpaid. Men—match your leather coat with this durable genuine horsehide Helmet. You'll be a long, long time wearing it out too, because horsehide is the strongest leather used in clothing. Full lined with warm wool cloth. Adjustable snap fastens under chin. Keeps the entire head warm. Ventilation eyelets for ears. The workmanship is sturdy enough to last as long as the leather!

Wool Scotch Model 79¢

39 G 719—Navy blue only. SIZES: 6¾, 6⅞, 7, 7⅛, 7¼, 7⅜, 7½. State size. "Scotch" model of All Wool Melton, full lined with part wool felt. Warm inband. Unbreakable visor. Postpaid.

K

» » Ward's Complete Guarantee Applies to Everything In This Book « «

245

Montgomery Ward Department Store, 1930

The first few decades of the 20th century saw a proliferation of hat styles for men — and a gradual stratification of hat styles along class lines. Caps became the hat of choice of working-class men, and a popular choice for sporting and other outdoor activities.

In den ersten Jahrzehnten des 20. Jahrhunderts erlebte man eine deutliche Vermehrung der Hutmodelle für Herren – wie auch eine schrittweise Schichtenbildung der Hutvarianten entlang der Klassengrenzen. Kappen wurden zur Lieblingskopfbedeckung der Arbeiter, sowie beliebt beim Sport und anderen Aktivitäten im Freien.

Les premières décennies du 20ème siècle assistèrent à la prolifération des modèles de chapeaux pour homme, ainsi qu'à leur stratification progressive en fonction des classes sociales. La casquette devint le couvre-chef préféré des ouvriers, mais aussi un modèle prisé pour le sport et autres activités de plein air.

► Keds Athletic Shoes, 1937

reat doings in the grand stand. The lad about to present his date with
a personally fielded baseball admits he's smart to wear Keds
uban Welt oxfords. They equip him for emergencies
requiring athletic skill and are tops to wear with
's loud summer suits. Heavy duck uppers and
vulcanized crepe out-soles take merciless
unishment. Built on the Keds "Scientific
Last" with Keds "Shock-Proof"
soles. White or navy blue.
SCIENTIFIC LAST
Making an impression—easy for the fellow who has nifty chatter and wears clothes with an air. He thinks Keds Majestic oxfords are great for tennis and swell with his usual summer get-up. Striped bumper toe strip and narrow banding add color interest. The tile red suede finish of the crepe sole is a new reason for hoisting feet to porch rails. Keds "Flexible Arch Cushion" and "Flex-Weve Shock-Proof" insole Cushioned heel seat.
Keds
Headed for important business down at the
orner. Keeping up a reputation for speed requires
mething special in shoes. Bike Keds, with Keds
"Flexible Arch Cushion" and "Shock-Proof" insole,
the bill. The extension soles give solid anchorage for
oller skates. Stream-line-cut top prevents binding.
leavy brown tire duck with pigskin-finish trimming.
Outboard motors are the doggonest — worse than a girl, almost. His solace is in the substantial beauty of brilliant Keds Yeoman oxfords braced against the stern. Swell to know that the soft, porous duck in the uppers is the kind used in tires. A deep layer of ground cork makes the thick sole cool and featherweight. "Flex-Weve Shock-Proof" insole. Nottingham blue, Alan-a-Dale blue, Horn white, Will Scarlet red (illustrated), and Friar Tuck brown.
An engineering feat to be proud of — the cross
annels which give air-pump action to the new
Keds Ventilating Sole. A shoe that lets the
ot breathe through the sole as well as through
the upper is a natural for gym. White, non-
arking crepe type soles. Keds "Scientific Last"
and "Shock-Proof" insole. Black or brown.
Keds
SHOCK-PROOF INSOLE
REG. U. S. PAT. OFF.
Keds
They are not Keds unless the name Keds appears on the shoes.
$1.00 to $2.50
The Natural Shoe for America at Play
United States Rubber Company
United States Rubber Products, Inc., 1790 B'way, N. Y.
FLEXIBLE ARCH CUSHION

REGISTERED
MOVEO ET PROFICIO
KNOX
Exclusive
Interpretations of the
Ruling Fashion
KNOX
Semi-Sport Hats
FOR TOWN AND COUNTRY
KNOX THE HATTER
Fifth Avenue at 40th Street

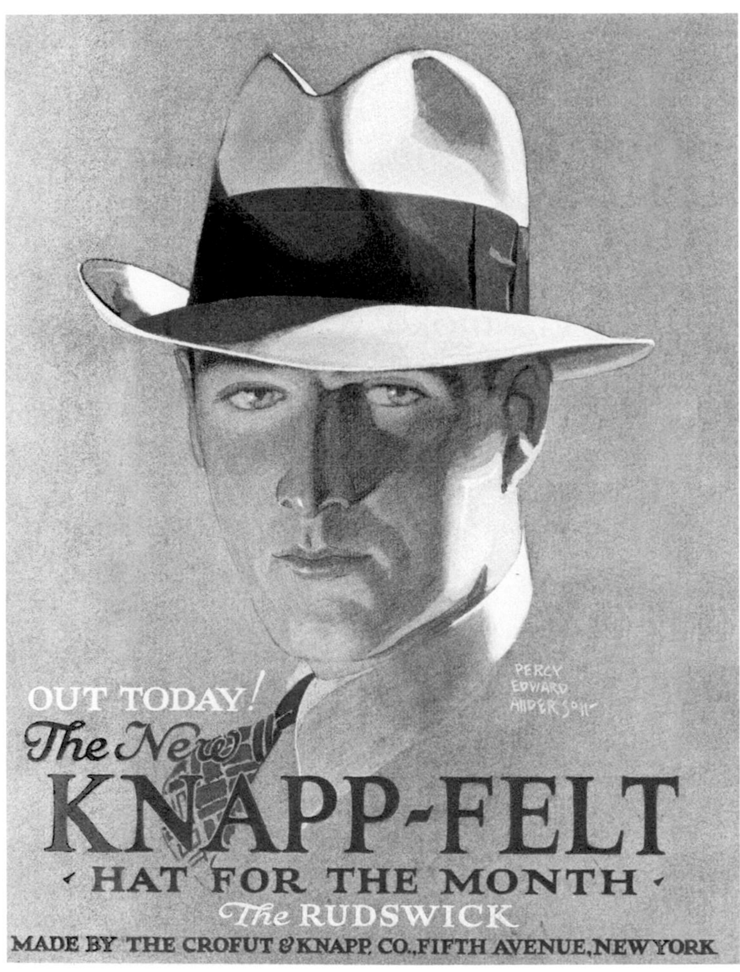

Knapp-Felt Hats, 1930

Knapp-Felt Hats, 1929

Knox Hats, 1939 ◂

Real Silk Hosiery, 1939

REAL SILK
HOSIERY

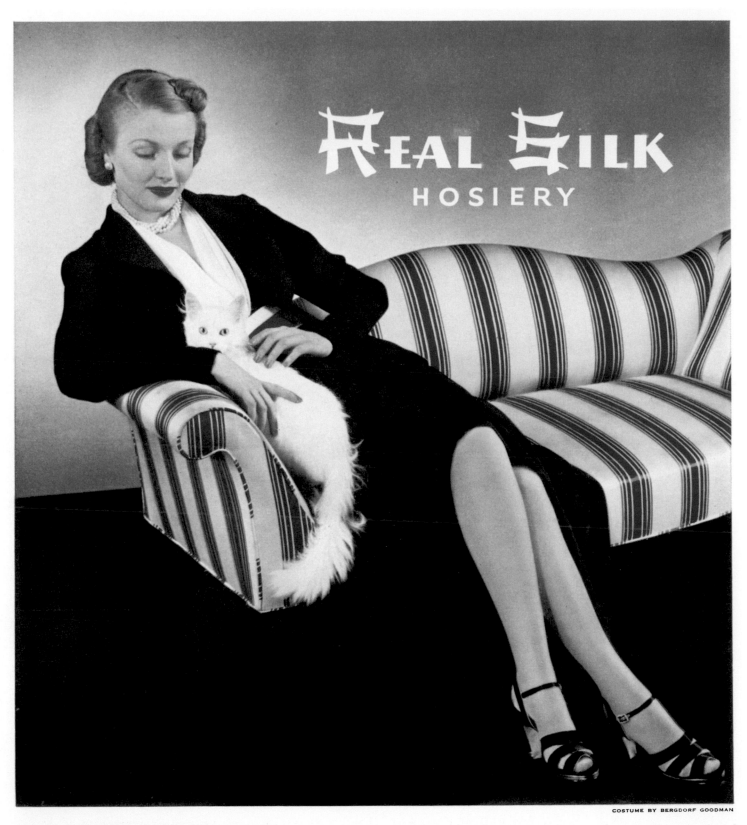

COSTUME BY BERGDORF GOODMAN

Our Shop-at-Home Service makes it easier for women to buy—Realsilk Representatives call on you—no shopping hurry—no parking worry . . . *Our Way* of manufacturing stockings makes them more economical for women to buy—pure, fresh silk—more snag-resistant twist—best and most permanent dyes . . . *These qualities* every time mean longer average wear.

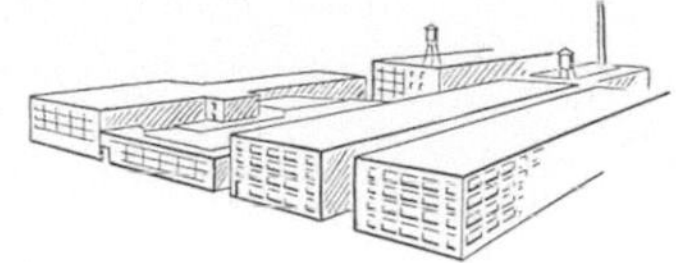

World's largest manufacturer of silk hosiery for men and women.
Real Silk Hosiery Mills, Inc.. Indianapolis, Ind. Branch Sales Offices in 200 Cities

Real Silk Hosiery, 1939

THIS WINTER'S SKI TRAILS will blaze with all the brilliant colors of next summer's race tracks . . . in especially designed ski clothes by Puritan, of Satin Ski Twill, in the colors of famous racing stables. Satin Ski Twill is a new textile triumph by Skinner . . . a Crown Tested Rayon fabric, check-tested and approved for color fastness, dry cleanability, moisture repellance, and general wearing qualities. See these clothes at your favorite store, or write to PURITAN KNITTING MILLS, Corp., 1270 Broadway, New York City.
Satin Ski Twill by SKINNER
PURITAN
hits the Ski Trail with
RACING COLORS
in a
CROWN TESTED
RAYON
FABRIC
Robert Goodman
SPORTSWEAR
by PURITAN
CROWN TESTED QUALITY FABRIC

Puritan Skiwear, 1939

Skiing has a long history in Scandinavian countries, but in the 1930s the sport was still relatively new in the U.S. Downhill and combined slalom events were first added to the Olympic Games in Garmisch-Partenkirchen, Germany, in 1936. Aimed at a burgeoning amateur ski market, this Puritan advertisement touts its skiwear's use of rayon, a fabric invented in the mid-19th century as an "artificial silk," which is not typically considered to be a cold-weather fabric.

Das Skifahren hat in den Ländern Skandinaviens lange Tradition, in den 1930er Jahren war es in den USA allerdings noch ein relativ junger Sport. Abfahrt und Kombinationsslalom standen erstmals bei dem Olympischen Spielen 1936 in Garmisch-Partenkirchen auf dem Programm. Der wachsenden Zielgruppe der Amateurskifahrer verkündet diese Werbung von Puritan, dass man für seine Skibekleidung Rayon verwendet. Der Stoff wurde Mitte des 19. Jahrhunderts als eine Form von „Kunstseide" erfunden und galt nicht gerade als prädestiniertes Material für kalte Temperaturen.

Pratiqué depuis longtemps dans les pays scandinaves, le ski était un sport relativement nouveau aux Etats-Unis dans les années 30. Les premières compétitions olympiques de descente et de slalom eurent lieu aux Jeux de Garmisch-Partenkirchen en Allemagne en 1936. Ciblant le marché émergent des amateurs de ski, cette publicité de Puritan promouvait ses vêtements de ski en rayonne, un tissu inventé au milieu du 19ème siècle comme une « soie artificielle » qui, pourtant, n'était généralement pas considéré comme adapté aux climats froids.

► Interwoven Socks, 1934

B. Shepherd

C. M. O. Toppers, ca. 1938

Designer Elsa Schiaparelli was one of several ex-pat European designers living and working in the United States. A friend of artists Salvador Dalí, Man Ray, and Jean Cocteau, Schiaparelli designed avant-garde apparel with details that had an uncanny knack for filtering into the mainstream. Among "Schiap's" inventions: the padded shoulder.

Die Designerin Elsa Schiaparelli war eine von vielen emigrierten europäischen Modeschöpfern, die in den Vereinigten Staaten lebten und arbeiteten. Als Freundin von Künstlern wie Salvador Dalí, Man Ray und Jean Cocteau entwarf Schiaparelli Avantgarde-Mode mit Details, die verblüffend oft ihren Weg in den Massengeschmack fanden. Eine von „Schiap's" Erfindungen: Schulterpolster.

Elsa Schiaparelli compta parmi les couturiers qui fuirent l'Europe pour venir vivre et travailler aux Etats-Unis. Amie des artistes Salvador Dalí, Man Ray et Jean Cocteau, elle conçut des vêtements avant-gardistes dont les détails réussirent à s'infiltrer dans la mode du quotidien. Parmi les inventions d'Elsa Schiaparelli : l'épaulette.

► Nettleton Shoes, 1936

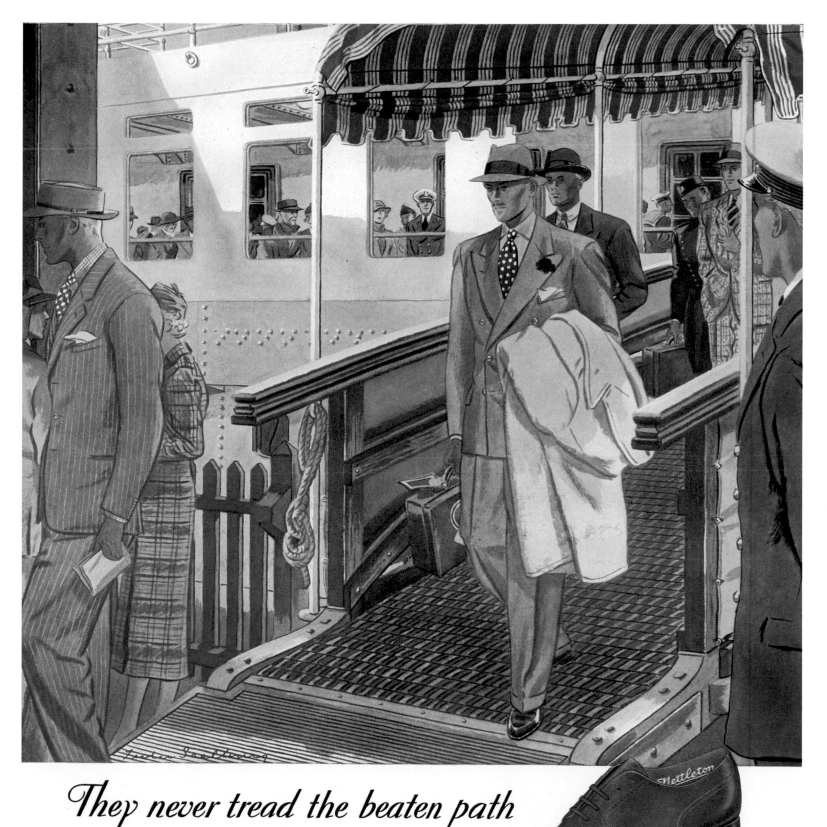

They never tread the beaten path

As mass manufacture reduces more and more things to a dead level of similarity, the product of individual craftsmanship stands out in sharp relief. Fine leather working is not a lost art in the making of Nettleton Shoes. They, like the men who wear them, reflect character which does not tread the beaten path. A. E. Nettleton Co., H. W. Cook, Pres., Syracuse, N.Y.

The ALGONQUIN
Hand-sewed vamp. Remarkably comfortable. An exclusive Nettleton Pattern.
Ten Dollars

Nettleton

GENTLEMEN'S FINE SHOES

PRICED TEN TO TWENTY DOLLARS

UNNECESSARY EMBARRASSMENT

Number 742

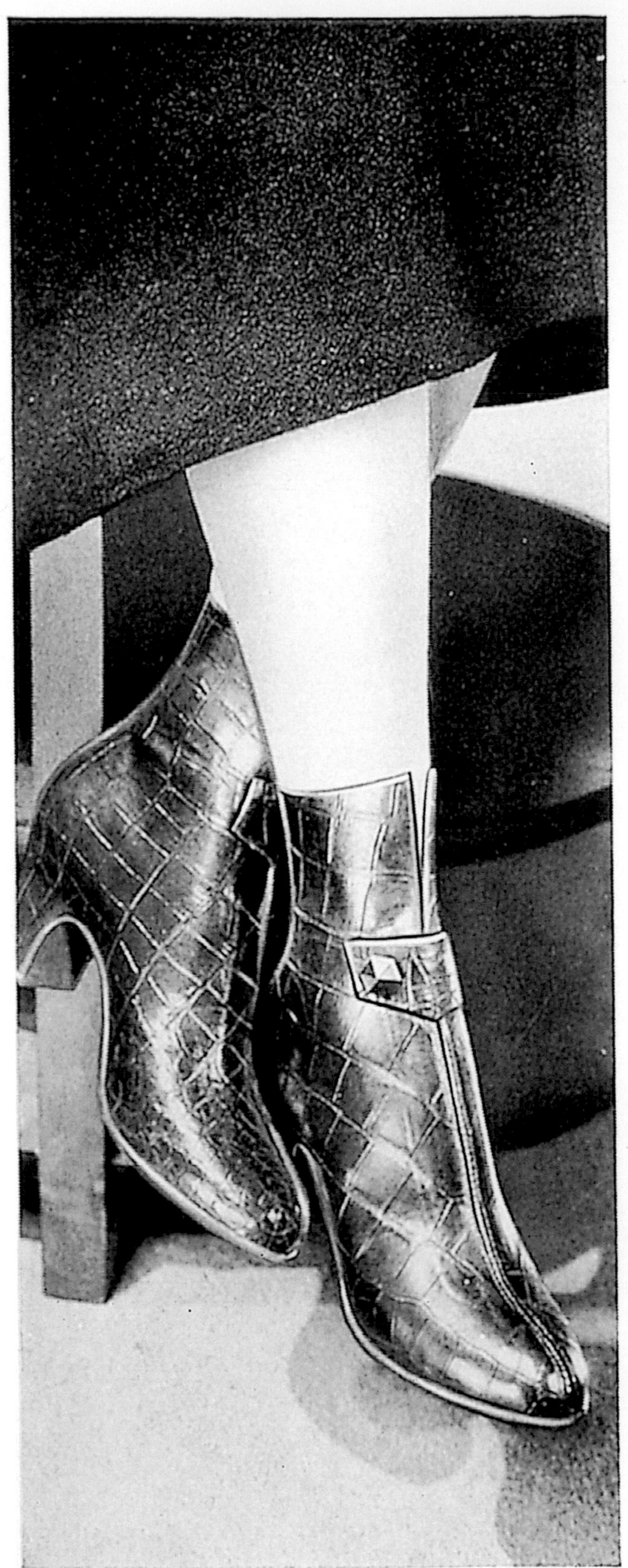

SHUGLOV—*Alligator Zipper Model—exact replica in light, supple rubber of the pattern and color of alligator! Genuine Talon Fastener.*

CAN you tell *galoshes* from *shoes*, when you see them? The answer to that of course, is "don't be silly."

But it's a hundred to one, the first time you see the new Shuglovs you'll think they are really *leather* shoes!

For they look like *leather* and they *fit* like shoes!

There's one model that's for all the world like fine *kid*; another you'll be sure is made of alligator skin, till you weigh its feather lightness in your hand. (These leather effects are obtained by the patented Textran process exclusive with Goodrich.)

This year it will be just as embarrassing to appear in the typical clumsy old "galosh" as it would be to wear your grandmother's poke bonnet with a smart fall suit!

One glimpse of Shuglovs and you'll *have* to have a pair. Maybe two!

. . . and you'll find them as trim and comfortable as they are smart. They slip over your shoes as smoothly as a kid glove slips over your hand.

Another surprise about Shuglovs! That unpleasant *rubber-smell* simply isn't there. It's gone, completely. In its place is just a hint of a pleasing delicate scent!

Choose your Shuglovs now — don't let the next rainstorm catch you without smart wet-weather footwear!

Shuglov

by **GOODRICH**

LIGHT AS AN EVENING SLIPPER
FITS LIKE A KID GLOVE

6 inches of snow on the day of Ann's tea! You dig out your old galoshes...

You'd forgotten how bulgy they were. Oh, well, galoshes don't matter...

You meet Janet. Can those slim things she's wearing be galoshes?

You meet Nancy. And discover her galoshes, too, have that slick, poured-in look. One of life's embarrassing moments you're NOT going to repeat!

Well, give your galoshes to the laundress and get a pair of Shuglovs!

THERE ARE MANY OTHER STYLES OF GOODRICH WATERPROOF FOOTWEAR
ZIPPERS • SHOWER BOOTS • LIGHT RUBBERS • FOR ALL THE FAMILY

This is a BOW TIE *year!*

IN HOLLYWOOD, Palm Beach and Broadway—the *bow* tie is unmistakably *the* tie style. And how fortunate for mankind that this week—and each succeeding week—you'll see a pronouncedly larger number of young men wearing smart bow ties.

In the first place, a bow tie is the most sensible tie any man can wear. It is truly correct. It is jaunty. A horizontal dash of tie-color is the dominant note of man's otherwise drab attire—and it relieves the monotony of vertical lines. It registers alertness. It breathes good grooming. It brings out the best in any man's face. It's on in a jiffy and amazingly comfortable with soft, semi-soft or starched collar.

The smartest bow ties are Spur Ties—the choice of millions. Tied by expert feminine fingers—they stay tied. And that secret of the phenomenal success of Spur Tie—the concealed, patented "Innerform"—permits you to adjust the wings to suit your *personal* fancy. You owe it to yourself to wear a Spur Tie the smartest tie that ever set tie style. Step into a young men's store today and see those wonderful new spring Spur Tie colors and patterns—the smartest and most sensible ties that ever adorned masculine necks.

JOHN BOLES

Star in the Universal Picture Triumph "La Marseillaise"

John Boles, "The Golden Tenor of the talking screen," caps his great successes in "The Desert Song" and "Rio Rita" with "La Marseillaise"—the story of the song that inflamed a nation to red revolt and triumph. Laura LaPlante is the co-star in this burning love story.

Insist that the Spur Tie red label shown above is on every tie and avoid inferior imitations. You can shape a Spur Tie in any way you like—fluffy or flat, severe or sportive—and the patented H-shaped Innerform holds it that way.

FREE

You'll enjoy this fascinating little book, "Off the Lot." Full of charming photographs. All about motion picture stars. For your copy write to Hewes & Potter, Inc., 65-SB Bedford Street, Boston, Massachusetts.

Spur Tie

50¢ 75¢ $1.00

TIED BY HAND · · · IT STAYS TIED

HEWES & POTTER, Inc., 65-SB Bedford Street, Boston, Mass. 200 Fifth Avenue, New York. 120 Battery Street, San Francisco. 426 South Spring Street, Los Angeles. 412 S. Wells Street, Chicago. 1604 Arapahoe Street, Denver. Made in Canada by Tooke Bros., Ltd., Montreal. In Australia: Wallace, Buck & Goodes, Pty., Ltd., Sydney.

LONDON STYLE...LUXURIOUS COMFORT

Sheer splendor . . . with deep regard for the proper thing! . . . that's the Coronation—the inspiration for the Hickok styles of the season. Correct color schemes of royal richness. Jewelry-like fittings . . . all incorporated with matchless *ActionBAK* comfort—exclusively Hickok.

Unhampered *action*—you move as you please and *ActionBAK* smoothly conforms. No nagging pull at hips or shoulders—no sagging trousers. This faultless service lasts, and *ActionBAK* style stays "like new"—because of Hickok long-life webbing, and extra-durable cable elastic cords. You will want more than just one pair of Hickok *ActionBAK* braces. HICKOK, Rochester, N.Y.

HICKOK

ActionBAK Braces

BELTS · BUCKLES · BRACES · GARTERS · JEWELRY

STYLE LEADERSHIP

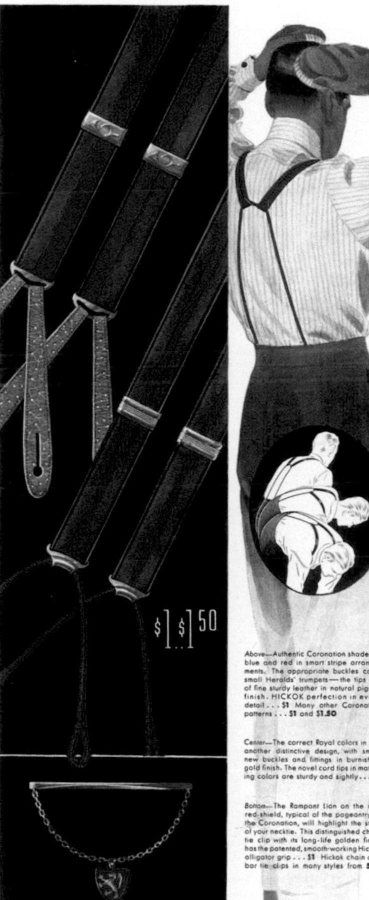

Above—Authentic Coronation shades of blue and red in smart stripe arrangements. The appropriate buckles carry small Heralds' trumpets—the tips are of fine sturdy leather in natural pigskin finish. HICKOK perfection in every detail . . . $1 Many other Coronation patterns . . . $1 and $1.50

Center—The correct Royal colors in still another distinctive design, with smart new buckles and fittings in burnished gold finish. The novel cord tips in matching colors are sturdy and sightly . . . $1

Bottom—The Rampant Lion on the rich red-shield, typical of the pageantry of the Coronation, will highlight the style of your necktie. This distinguished chain tie clip with its long-life golden finish has the patented, smooth-working Hickok alligator grip . . . $1 Hickok chain and bar tie clips in many styles from 50c

Spur Tie Bowties, 1930

Hickok Braces, 1937

Goodrich Footwear, 1932 ◂

178

1. Ribbed satin mule (with hard sole) in all the latest colors . . $4.00
2. The famous Comfy, in every shade of soft, long-wearing felt . $2.00
3. A leather Comfy in soft calf — in black and colors $3.00
4. A corduroy Comfy D'Orsay, trimmed with lamb's wool in pastel shades $3.00
5. A Christmas-y satin-and-fur mule (with hard sole) in all the fashionable colors $4.00
6. A new Comfy mule with all-over embroidery, daintily trimmed with marabou $3.00
7. The Comfy Loll, of crepe, in black and colors $3.00

Many other styles and materials at a variety of prices

DANIEL GREEN CO., DOLGEVILLE, N. Y.
LEISURE FOOTWEAR
"COMFYS" AND FORMALS

DANIEL GREENS make *Better* gifts

BECAUSE DANIEL GREEN MAKES BETTER SLIPPERS

When people find Daniel Green on the sole of a slipper they know you want them to have the best.

Everyone knows what the name Daniel Green means, not only because it has been famous for fifty years but because it guarantees that a slipper is the finest quality.

Nothing but the best goes into the making of a Daniel Green . . . and there is a smart style, a perfect fitting size, and a favorite color for every person on your list, man or woman, young or old.

Just to show how easy a Daniel Green dealer can make your shopping, a few of the most popular styles for Christmas gifts are shown and described here.

LOOK FOR THE NAME — NONE GENUINE WITHOUT IT

Daniel Greens Slippers, 1935

▸ Burdine's Department Store, 1934

5
6

AFTER THE WAR, PARIS DESIGNER CHRISTIAN DIOR WISELY CALCULATED THAT RETURNING VETERANS WOULD BE PICTURING AN IDEALIZED WOMAN WAITING BACK HOME – AND WOMEN, MANY OF WHOM HAD BEEN WORKING OR SERVING IN THE ARMED FORCES, WERE EAGER TO RETURN TO A MORE FEMININE LOOK.

NACH DEM KRIEG, SO HATTE DER PARISER DESIGNER CHRISTIAN DIOR WEISE VORHERGESEHEN, WÜRDEN DIE HEIMKEHRENDEN VETERANEN SICH EINE IDEALISIERTE FRAU AUSMALEN, DIE SIE ZU HAUSE ERWARTETE. UND DIE FRAUEN, VON DENEN VIELE BERUFSTÄTIG WAREN ODER BEI DEN STREITKRÄFTEN GEDIENT HATTEN, WAREN EBENFALLS BESTREBT, ZU EINEM FEMININEREN LOOK ZURÜCKZUKEHREN.

UNE FOIS LA PAIX RESTAURÉE, LE COUTURIER PARISIEN CHRISTIAN DIOR PRÉDIT AVEC SAGESSE QU'À LEUR RETOUR, LES SOLDATS AURONT ENVIE DE RETROUVER L'IMAGE D'UNE FEMME IDÉALISÉE À LA MAISON; QUANT AUX FEMMES, DONT UN GRAND NOMBRE A TRAVAILLÉ OU SERVI DANS LES FORCES ARMÉES, ELLES SONT IMPATIENTES DE REVENIR À UN LOOK PLUS FÉMININ.

1940

A WORLD WAR AND A NEW LOOK
DER ZWEITE WELTKRIEG UND DER NEW LOOK
SECONDE GUERRE MONDIALE ET NEW LOOK

-1949

Hart Schaffner & Marx Menswear, 1946 ◄◄

J. C. Penney Department Store, 1956 ◄

Red Goose Shoes, 1944

FORTIES FASHIONS WERE, BY AND LARGE, CONSTRAINED BY TURBULENT TIMES. War between England and Germany began in 1939, and, in 1942, Japan bombed Pearl Harbor, bringing the Japanese and Americans into the conflict. Until then, Paris had remained the undisputed center of fashion, but with the start of the war, many designers, including Chanel, closed shop. Mainbocher, the designer of the Duchess of Windsor's wedding dress, moved to New York, where he continued designing his own collection, as well as uniforms for the Girl Scouts, the Red Cross, and the WAVES (the U.S. Navy's women's volunteer corps).

Americans had plenty of local talent as well, including Hattie Carnegie, Norman Norell, and Claire McCardell, the inventor of American sportswear, whose introductions to the fashion lexicon include mix-and-match separates and the ballet-slipper flat.

Although the Oscar-winning film *Gone With the Wind* was ostensibly a period piece, fashions from the blockbuster film had made their way into fashions. Vivien Leigh's bonnets, trimmed in ribbons, feathers, and lace veils, were designed by John P. John under his label John-Frederics, and they provided inspiration for modern-day women, as did Leigh's rolled hairstyle and snoods.

If the emphasis in the 1920s was on the collegiate set, by the 1940s, the notion of the "youth market" was considerably younger. In the popular Andy Hardy movies, a teenage Mickey Rooney was winning fans — as his character won over co-stars Judy Garland, Lana Turner, and Ava Gardner. Crooner Frank Sinatra was drawing crowds of swooning fans dubbed "bobby soxers" because of their short socks and saddle shoes. *Seventeen* magazine was introduced in 1944 to cater to the teen market, and *Harper's Bazaar* launched its own teen magazine, called *Junior Bazaar*.

During the war, manufacturers were under strict materials-rationing guidelines, putting an end to dramatic but wasteful features such as hoods and shawls, full skirts, wide belts, and cuffed coat sleeves. The use of zippers and metal fasteners was also curtailed, which gave rise to new innovations, like the wraparound skirt. Rationing also led to the concept of "day-to-night" dressing. And the shortage of nylon for stockings inspired a short-lived leg-makeup trend — seams were drawn on with an eyebrow pencil. Indeed, the '40s was a great time for fads. For women, there were turbans, sailor hats, and adhesive "beauty marks" made from tiny bits of cut silk. For teens, there were army boots for boys and rolled blue jeans and oversize men's shirts for girls.

The mood of women's fashion in the war years reflected the mood of the country: sensible and austere. But after the war, Paris designer Christian Dior wisely calculated that returning veterans would be picturing an idealized woman waiting back home — and women, many of whom had been working or serving in the armed forces, were eager to return to a more feminine look. Dior's first postwar collection, in 1947, is the one he is best remembered for. The look was a radical departure, with longer, fuller skirts; soft-shouldered jackets that emphasized a padded bust; and a tiny, corseted wasp waist — all atop pointed-toe, spike-heel shoes. *Harper's Bazaar* editor Carmel Snow dubbed it the New Look.

1940

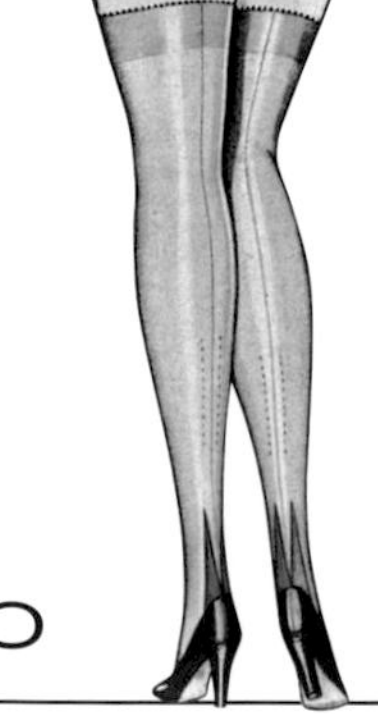

1940 Nylon stockings available to American women nationwide

Nylonstrümpfe gibt es für Frauen in ganz Amerika zu kaufen

On trouve désormais des bas en nylon à travers tous les Etats-Unis

1942 Humphrey Bogart dons de rigueur fedora in *Casablanca*

Humphrey Bogart trägt in *Casablanca* den unerlässlichen weichen Filzhut

Humphrey Bogart porte le fedora de rigueur dans *Casablanca*

1943 Frank Sinatra's teenage fans dubbed "bobby-soxers"

Frank Sinatras Teenager-Fans werden „bobby-soxers" genannt

Les adolescentes fans de Frank Sinatra sont surnommées les « bobby-soxers »

1943 Rosie the Riveter, symbol of six million American women in WWII-era workforce

Rosie the Riveter (dt. die Nieterin) war die Symbolfigur für sechs Millionen Amerikanerinnen, die während des zweiten Weltkriegs in der Rüstungsindustrie arbeiteten

Rosie la Riveteuse devient le symbole des six millions d'Américaines qui produisent le matériel de guerre pendant la Seconde Guerre mondiale

DIE MODE DER 1940ER JAHRE WAR IM GROSSEN UND GANZEN VON DEN HERRSCHENDEN SCHWEREN ZEITEN BESTIMMT. DER KRIEG ZWISCHEN ZWISCHEN ENGLAND UND DEUTSCHLAND BEGANN 1939; 1942 BOMBARDIERTE JAPAN PEARL HARBOR, was zum offenen Konflikt zwischen Japanern und Amerikanern führte. Bis dahin hatte Paris als unangefochtenes Zentrum der Mode gegolten. Mit Kriegsbeginn schlossen jedoch viele Designer, darunter auch Chanel, ihre Läden. Mainbocher, der das Hochzeitskleid der Herzogin von Windsor entworfen hatte, verlegte seinen Wohnsitz nach New York, wo er weiterhin seine eigene Kollektion kreierte, aber auch Uniformen für die Pfadfinderinnen, das Rote Kreuz und für WAVES (das weibliche Freiwilligenkorps der US-Marine) designte.

In Amerika gab es allerdings auch zahlreiche einheimische Talente wie Hattie Carnegie, Norman Norell und Claire McCardell, die Erfinderin der amerikanischen Sportswear, die sich unter anderem mit kombinierbaren Basics und den flachen Ballerinas einen Platz in den Modelexika sicherte.

Auch wenn der oscar-prämierte Blockbuster *Vom Winde verweht* offensichtlich ein Historienfilm war, schafften es einige modische Trends aus dem Kassenschlager in die aktuelle Mode. Vivien Leighs mit Bändern, Federn und Spitzenschleiern verzierte Hauben waren Entwürfe von John P. John für sein Label John-Frederics; sie dienten modernen Frauen ebenso als Inspiration wie Leighs Lockenfrisuren und Haarnetze.

Während sich die 1920er noch eher studentisch präsentierten, war das Verständnis des „jugendlichen Marktes" in den Vierzigern ein deutlich jüngeres. In den beliebten Filmen von Andy Hardy eroberte der Teenager Mickey Rooney die Herzen der Fans wie auch die seiner Co-Stars Judy Garland, Lana Turner und Ava Gardner. Der singende Frank Sinatra lockte massenhaft in Ohnmacht fallende Fans an, die man wegen ihrer kurzen Socken und Sattelschuhe „bobby soxers" nannte. 1944 kam speziell für das Teenager-Publikum die Zeitschrift *Seventeen* auf den Markt; und *Harper's Bazaar* lieferte mit *Junior Bazaar* sein eigenes Teenager-Magazin.

Während des Krieges waren die Hersteller strikten Rationierungsvorschriften unterworfen, die verschwenderischen Effekten mit dramatischer Wirkung wie Kapuzen und Schals, weiten Röcken, breiten Gürteln oder Ärmelaufschlägen ein Ende machten. Die Verwendung von Reißverschlüssen und metallenen Haken und Ösen war ebenfalls eingeschränkt, was Spielraum für Innovationen wie den Wickelrock bot. Die Rationierung förderte auch das Konzept einer Garderobe, die „von morgens bis abends" tragbar war. Der Mangel an Nylon für Strümpfe brachte einen kurzlebigen Make-up-Trend hervor – mit Augenbrauenstift auf die nackten Beine gemalte Strumpfnähte. In der Tat waren die 40er eine Zeit der Modetorheiten. Für Frauen gab es Turbane, Matrosenmützen und selbstklebende Schönheitspflaster aus winzigen Stückchen Seide. Teenagerjungs trugen Soldatenstiefel, Mädchen hochgerollte Bluejeans und übergroße Herrenhemden.

Die Stimmung in der Damenmode während der Kriegsjahre spiegelte in den USA die Atmosphäre im Land wider: vernünftig und von Entsagung geprägt. Nach dem Krieg jedoch, so hatte der Pariser Designer Christian Dior weise vorhergesehen, würden die heimkehrenden Veteranen sich eine idealisierte Frau ausmalen, die sie zu Hause erwartete. Und die Frauen, von denen viele berufstätig waren oder bei den Streitkräften gedient hatten, waren ebenfalls bestrebt, zu einem feminineren Look zurückzukehren. Diors erste Nachkriegskollektion von 1947 ist dabei am deutlichsten in Erinnerung geblieben. Der Look bedeutete eine radikale Abkehr von der aktuellen Mode, mit längeren, weiteren Röcken, Jacken mit weicher Schulterpartie, die die ausgepolsterte Büste noch betonten, und einer winzigen, geschnürten Wespentaille – dazu spitze Schuhe mit Pfennigabsätzen. Carmel Snow, die Herausgeberin von *Harper's Bazaar*, taufte das Ganze New Look.

1943

1943 Claire McCardell's American Look collection debuts at Lord & Taylor

Claire McCardell gibt mit ihrer Kollektion American Look ihr Debut bei Lord & Taylor

Lord & Taylor lance la collection American Look de Claire McCardell

1945 Wide postwar ties take on bold patterns, including Art Deco and Asian designs

Die breiten Krawatten der Nachkriegszeit zeigen kräftige Muster, darunter auch Art déco und asiatisch anmutende Motive

Les cravates larges de l'après-guerre arborent des motifs audacieux, notamment des dessins Art Déco et asiatiques

1945 "Victory Rolls" hairstyle celebrates Allies' victory in WWII

Die Frisur namens „Victory Rolls" feiert den Sieg der Alliierten im 2. Weltkrieg

La coiffure « Victory Rolls » célèbre la victoire des Alliés

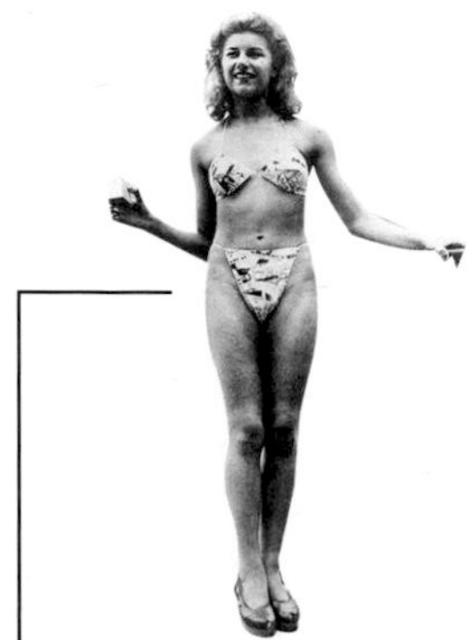

1946 Engineer Louis Réard scandalizes Paris with G-string bikini bathing suit

Der Ingenieur Louis Réard sorgt mit dem G-String-Bikini für einen Skandal in Paris

L'ingénieur Louis Réard scandalise Paris avec son bikini

es that live
rstmann
WOOLEN COMPANY
PASSAIC, N. J.

Forstmann Woolen Co., 1941 ◂◂

Hart Schaffner & Marx Menswear, 1946 ◂

▸▸ Color Affiliates, 1940

LA MODE DES ANNÉES 40 EST LARGEMENT DICTÉE PAR LES CONTRAINTES D'UNE PÉRIODE DE CONFLITS. LA GUERRE ENTRE L'ANGLETERRE ET L'ALLEMAGNE DÉBUTE EN 1939 ET, EN 1942, LE JAPON BOMBARDE PEARL HARBOR, entraînant les Japonais et les Américains dans la Seconde Guerre mondiale. Si Paris était restée la capitale incontestée de la mode, l'entrée en guerre voit de nombreux couturiers fermer boutique, dont Chanel. Le couturier Mainbocher, qui avait conçu la robe de mariée de la duchesse de Windsor, s'installe à New York où il continue à créer sa propre collection, ainsi que des uniformes pour les Girl Scouts, la Croix-Rouge et le WAVES (division de l'U.S. Navy uniquement composée de femmes volontaires).

Les Etats-Unis ne manquent pas non plus de talents: Hattie Carnegie, Norman Norell et Claire McCardell, l'inventrice du sportswear américain, dont les entrées au grand dictionnaire de la mode incluent les twinsets et les ballerines plates.

Bien qu'*Autant en emporte le vent* soit évidemment un film d'époque, les costumes de cet immense succès du cinéma aux multiples Oscars trouvent leur imitation dans la mode du moment. Ornés de rubans, de plumes et de voilettes en dentelle, les bonnets de Vivien Leigh conçus par John P. John sous sa marque John-Frederics inspirent les femmes, tout comme les chignons et les résilles à cheveux de l'actrice.

Alors que les années 20 avaient mis à l'honneur l'accoutrement des étudiants, la notion de « marché jeune » prend un vrai bain de jouvence dans les années 40. Dans la saga à succès des films Andy Hardy, un Mickey Rooney adolescent gagne de nombreux fans, son personnage donnant brillamment la réplique à Judy Garland, Lana Turner et Ava Gardner. Le crooner Frank Sinatra attire des foules d'admiratrices en délire surnommées les « bobby soxers » parce qu'elles portent des socquettes et des richelieus. Le magazine *Seventeen* est lancé en 1944 pour cibler marché des adolescents, ainsi que *Junior Bazaar*, la revue pour ados créée par *Harper's Bazaar*.

Pendant la guerre, l'industrie est soumise à des directives très strictes en raison du rationnement des matériaux, ce qui met un terme à la production des vêtements spectaculaires mais trop gourmands en tissu, par exemple les capuches et les châles, les jupes amples, les ceintures larges et les manches de manteau à revers. Comme on utilise moins de fermetures à zip et de boutons en métal, des innovations telles que la jupe portefeuille voient le jour. Le rationnement fait aussi émerger le concept de l'habillement adapté « du matin au soir ». Quant à la pénurie de nylon pour les bas, elle inspire la tendance éphémère du maquillage des jambes, les femmes se dessinant une fausse couture à l'aide d'un crayon à sourcils. Les années 40 voient en fait proliférer toutes sortes de folies. Les femmes se coiffent de turbans ou de casquettes de marin, et on trouve aussi des « grains de beauté » adhésifs coupés dans de minuscules morceaux de soie. Côté ados, les garçons portent des brodequins militaires, et les filles, des jeans roulés à l'ourlet avec des chemises d'homme trop grandes pour elles.

Pendant les années de guerre, l'humeur de la mode féminine reflète celle du pays: sensée et austère. Une fois la paix restaurée, le couturier parisien Christian Dior prédit avec sagesse qu'à leur retour les soldats auront envie de retrouver l'image d'une femme idéalisée à la maison; quant aux femmes, dont un grand nombre ont travaillé ou servi dans les forces armées, elles sont impatientes de revenir à un look plus féminin. En 1947, la première collection Dior d'après-guerre est celle qui le fera passer à la postérité. Il propose un look radicalement différent, avec des jupes plus longues et plus amples, des vestes aux épaules douces qui soulignent une poitrine rehaussée et une taille de guêpe corsetée, le tout porté avec des chaussures à bouts pointus et talons aiguilles. C'est Carmel Snow, la rédactrice en chef d'*Harper's Bazaar*, qui qualifie cette silhouette de « New Look ».

1947

1947 Sales of boxer shorts begin to outpace briefs

Die Verkaufszahlen für Boxershorts übersteigen erstmals die kurzer Herrenunterhosen

Les ventes de caleçons commencent à surpasser celles des slips

1948 Dior's feminine, nipped-waist New Look hits mass market

Diors femininer, taillenbetonter New Look erreicht den Massenmarkt

Le New Look féminin à taille de guêpe de Dior descend dans la rue

1948 Peep-toe heels reach peak popularity

Zehenfreie High-Heels erreichen den Gipfel ihrer Beliebtheit

Les chaussures à talon ouvertes sur les orteils atteignent des sommets de popularité

1949 Introduction of stitched, long-line cone (or "bullet") bra

Markteinführung des abgenähten, länglich konischen Spitz-BHs (engl. bullet bra)

Lancement du soutien-gorge à bonnets « en obus »

color matching. . . A PROBLEM

*R*emember when color matching of gloves, hat, shoes or bag to go with your new costume meant tramping-the-town . . . then wearily compromising on a "near match"?

COLOR AFFILIATES *have changed all that!*

Imagine the head of the great house of Stroock woolens . . . Koret, who makes the finest bags the world over . . . Mallinson's silk color experts . . Kislav gloves, style and color *right* for a generation . . . two top-flight shoe creators, Delman and Palter DeLiso . . . the head of the famous house of G. Howard Hodge hats . . . Elizabeth Arden . . . all getting together, pooling their resources, their talents, their capabilities . . . making available to you *now* for fall and winter wear, colors that are right from tip to toe!

That's great news... *important* news! So exciting, that leading fashion magazines write editorials about it! And *these* are the colors:

INDIAN SUMMER
rich, ripe russet

BARK BROWN
mellow, harvest brown

NIGHTFLIGHT BLUE
dark autumn navy

JUNIPER GREEN
autumn forest green

HUCKLEBERRY
frost-nipped purple

SCARECROW GREY
soft, flattering grey

DELMAN

Match them! Mix them! They're *planned, dyed, fashioned* for wear with each other. And to *complete* this symphony of color, wear Elizabeth Arden's new fall make-up, Cinnabar, created *for* Color Affiliates colors!

for that "custom" look, just follow Color Affiliates!

COLOR AFFILIATES

COLOR *affiliates*

G. HOWARD HODGE
KISLAV
KORET
STROOCK fabrics
PALTER DeLISO
Elizabeth Arden
ELIZABETH ARDEN
MALLINSON fabrics

► Connie Casuals Shoes, 1945

In Europe, rationing regulations affected consumers and manufacturers alike. In the United States, rationing was less severe, but manufacturers were under strict materials-rationing guidelines, particularly regarding such materials as rubber and metal. By advertising their shoes as "ration free," this company tapped into consumers' desire to "do their part" for the war.

In Europa trafen Rationierungsmaßnahmen Konsumenten und Hersteller gleichermaßen. In den USA war die Verknappung weniger schlimm, doch unterlagen die Produzenten strikten Vorschriften, insbesondere was die Verwendung von Materialien wie Gummi und Metall betraf. Mit dem Vermerk „ration free" beworbene Schuhe entsprachen dem Wunsch der Kundschaft, „ihren Beitrag" zum Krieg zu leisten.

En Europe, les consommateurs comme les industriels subirent les contraintes du rationnement. Aux Etats-Unis, en dépit de mesures moins sévères, les fabricants étaient soumis à des directives de rationnement très strictes sur les matériaux, particulièrement pour le caoutchouc et le métal. En proclamant que ses chaussures étaient fabriquées « sans matériaux rationnés », la marque Connie Casuals Shoes misait sur le désir des consommateurs de participer à l'effort de guerre.

Naturalizer Shoes, 1943

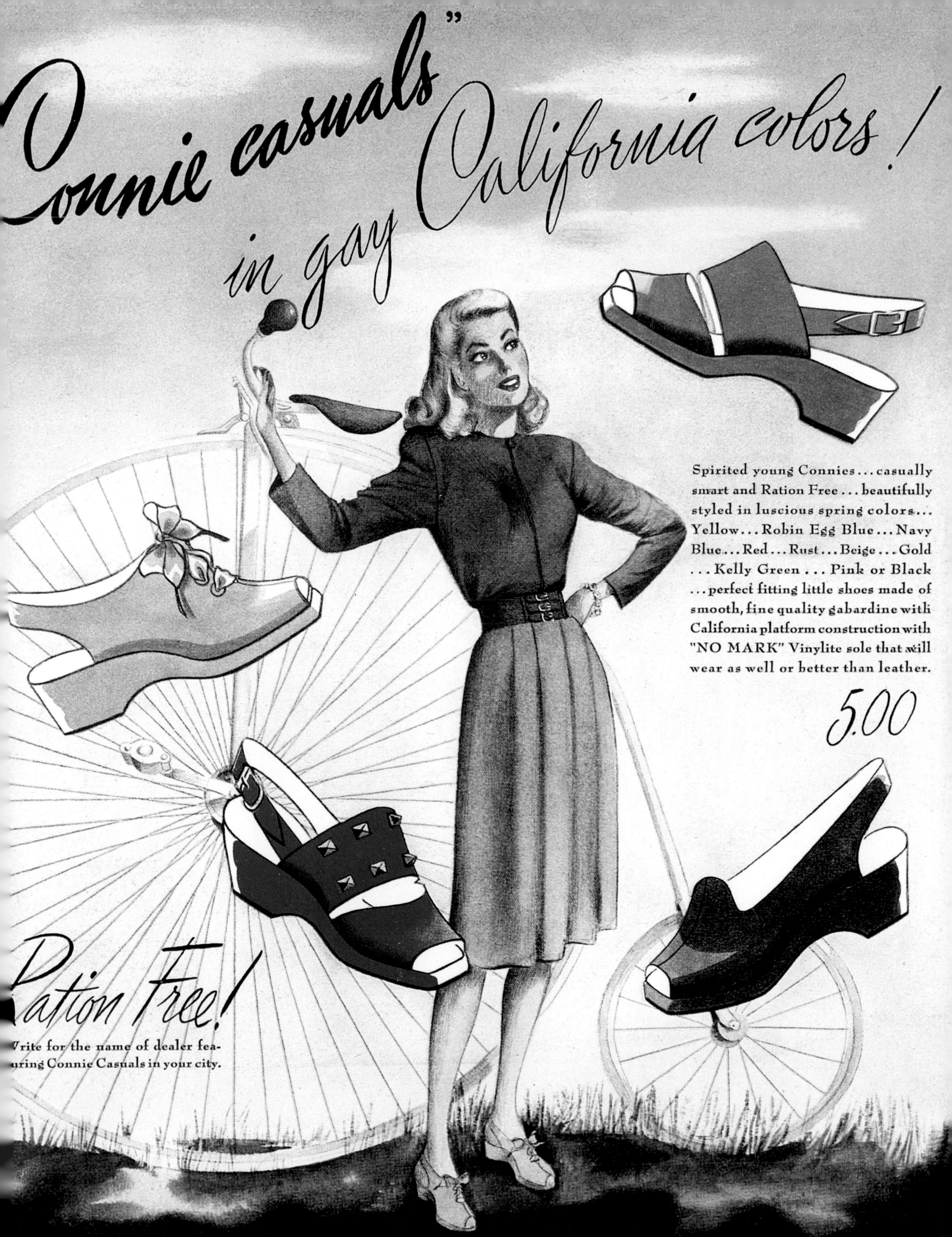

"Connie casuals" in gay California colors!
Spirited young Connies . . . casually smart and Ration Free . . . beautifully styled in luscious spring colors . . . Yellow . . . Robin Egg Blue . . . Navy Blue . . . Red . . . Rust . . . Beige . . . Gold . . . Kelly Green . . . Pink or Black . . . perfect fitting little shoes made of smooth, fine quality gabardine with California platform construction with "NO MARK" Vinylite sole that will wear as well or better than leather.
5.00
Ration Free!
Write for the name of dealer featuring Connie Casuals in your city.

DAKS
REGD
The famous British comfort-in-action trousers
$29.50
Manufactured by S. SIMPSON LTD. London, England
Brooks Brothers,
NEW YORK — BOSTON
CARSON PIRIE SCOTT & CO.
CHICAGO
The Halle Bros. Co
CLEVELAND
John Jarrell INC.
ATLANTA — NEW YORK
McFARLIN CLOTHING Co
ROCHESTER
Roos Bros
CALIFORNIA
Jerry Rothschild
BEVERLY HILLS
F.R. TRIPLER & CO.
NEW YORK
Simpson Imports, Inc. • 9 E. 38th Street • New York 16, N. Y.

BLACK
STANDS OUT
Naturalizer
the shoe with the
beautiful fit $6.95
$7.45 WEST
OF ROCKIES
Subject to O.P.A. price increase
NATURALIZER DIVISION
BROWN SHOE COMPANY, ST LOUIS

Naturalizer Shoes, 1946

Daks Trousers, 1948 ◄

Loveliness steps out!
Like a fresh burst of June sunshine, colorful things of VINYLITE Plastics are here in swift profusion!
In the vanguard march VINYLITE Plastic shoe soles. Brilliant or basic shades to harmonize with your costumes . . . tough but resilient and light . . . virtually slip-proof on wet pavements!
In the man's domain, belts and suspenders of VINYLITE Plastic head the list for smartness combined with genuine utility. Men like their good looks—but they brag about the way they wear and wear!
Handbags in special finishes come in for compliments, too—from discriminating women and from leading designers who have enthusiastically welcomed rich, handsome VINYLITE Plastic materials for the best expression of their art.
While on the subject of durability—have you seen the new upholstery of VINYLITE Plastic? Stainproof, scuffproof, it's the modern-day material for colorful play room, rumpus room, porch, and so on! And for sound practicality, nothing matches zippered garment bags of VINYLITE Plastic . . . bags that won't tear . . . bags that defy dust.
Wherever you shop today you're bound to spy new things of VINYLITE Plastics . . . things that will help to make you a more attractive person . . . your family a happier group . . . your home a more exciting place in which to live! Look for them!
You know it's right if it's
Vinylite
PLASTICS
BAKELITE CORPORATION
Unit of Union Carbide and Carbon Corporation UCC
30 East 42nd Street, New York 17, N. Y.

Vinylite Plastics Shoes, 1946

▸ Vinylite Plastics Raingear, 1946

Life is Bright

with Vinylite plastics
TRADE-MARK

Every time you turn around you find something made of VINYLITE Plastics . . . something bright and colorful . . . something rich and handsome . . . something to protect you . . . something to make your home happier.

Among them are VINYLITE Plastic *raincoats* that wear well, keep you *desert-dry* . . . high-gloss *shoes* that start smart and end smart, holding their beauty of line and brilliant luster without cracking and without scuffing.

The sleek richness of those glistening new *handbags* made of VINYLITE Plastics is something new, too. Their weather-wise quality outlives their style!

And in your bathroom a *shower curtain* that keeps its youth...its enduring beauty! Completely waterproof shower curtains made of VINYLITE Plastics don't crack or stiffen . . . will not mildew!

Almost beyond belief are the new non-shatterable VINYLITE Plastic phonograph *records*. They give matchless high-fidelity tones because needle noise is almost completely eliminated.

And now you're familiar with just a few of the wonderful things made with and from VINYLITE Plastics. But don't stop here. Look for the trademark "VINYLITE" wherever you go shopping. You'll find it on more and more outstanding articles made of this superior brand of plastic.

BAKELITE CORPORATION
UCC *Unit of Union Carbide and Carbon Corporation*
30 East 42nd Street, New York 17, N. Y.

You know it's right if it's

It's no secret why more smart women wear Gold Cross Shoes than any other brand of fine footwear in the world. For it's smart to be young. And every finely crafted, lovely young style in Gold Cross Shoes is Fit-Tested* to keep the swing of Youth in your step
Forsberg
A
B
C
GOLD
RED CROSS SHOES
AMERICA'S UNCHALLENGED SHOE VALUE
Illustrated: A. The Serena, B. Country Club, C. The Parkview.
*Before any new Gold Cross style is released, handmade originals are worn, walked in for weeks . . . checked . . . tested . . . fit-perfected. Look in your local newspaper and dealer's window for special "Advertised in LIFE" showing of Gold Cross Shoes, this week.
*COPYRIGHTED 1945, BY THE UNITED STATES SHOE CORP., CINCINNATI 7, OHIO. GOLD CROSS SHOES ARE MANUFACTURED AND DISTRIBUTED IN ENGLAND BY SOMERVELL BROS., LTD., IN AUSTRALIA BY "GOLD CROSS SHOES,"

Yes, Plateau is a modern day wonder fabric loomed by Pacific with a new comfort feature that makes you hardly conscious of wearing a suit! Through prelaxed flexibility all tension has been relieved. The weight is evenly distributed over your shoulders for full body freedom. Plateau actually feels lighter, though standard in weight. It's the suit with the weightless feel!
"You scarcely feel it!"
Prelaxed flexibility allows a softer drape, enhancing the beauty of the fabric. Plateau has been so woven of firm, resilient worsted yarns as to produce a soft, radiant bloom sheen . . . a texture caressingly smooth to the touch. Exclusively made by Timely Clothes, whose *Balanced Tailoring makes Plateau a suit of striking appeal . . . a moderately priced, distinctive addition to your wardrobe. Pacific Mills, Worsted Division, 261 Fifth Avenue, New York 16.
*REG. U. S. PAT. OFF.
Pacific
Worsteds Woolens
PLATEAU SUITS and slacks are now available in limited but growing quantities at leading stores, the country over. For further information write to Timely Clothes, Rochester 2, New York; or Pacific Mills, Worsted Division, Retail Service Bureau, 200 Fifth Avenue, New York 10.
TIMELY CLOTHES
PLATEAU
LOOK TO THE Fabric FIRST—BUY PACIFIC

Plateau Suits/Pacific Mills, 1946

Gold Cross Shoes, 1947 ◂

Ever try translating baby talk
into a French hat?
She tried on a mad hat from Paris, then turned to our saleswoman and said, "I'll take it if you'll make one just like it for my doll! Twenty years ago this Christmas I promised my first doll that someday I'd buy her the loveliest hat in Marshall Field & Company. You see, I want that old doll of mine—with her pretty new hat—to be my own little girl's first Christmas doll!"
The doll and her doll house had both come from Marshall Field & Company, of course—first of the many things that were to be such memorable milestones in a young woman's life. Tricycle, prom dress, diamond, trousseau, wedding gifts—then layette and nursery furniture. Hers could be the story of generations of Chicagoans—and out-of-towners, too—who've almost literally grown up in Marshall Field & Company. This being an inseparable part of the lives of so many people is our proudest possession, our reason for being. We like to think our store is a place where your dreams will turn into the things you want most—and perhaps can't find anywhere else. A fabulous place where you'll always discover something new you'll enjoy, even if it's just an idea. Won't you come see what we have, what we're doing, the next time you're in Chicago?
Marshall Field & Company
CHICAGO

Marshall Field & Co. Department Store, 1946

John P. John and Frederic Hirst, the design team behind millinery label John-Frederics, created Vivien Leigh's hats for the Academy Award–winning film *Gone With the Wind*. Though a period piece, the 1939 film inspired hat and hair trends for most of the 1940s, including ribbon-trimmed bonnets and snoods.

John P. John und Frederic Hirst, das Designerteam hinter dem Modelabel John-Frederics entwarf Vivien Leighs Hüte für den oscarprämierten Streifen *Vom Winde verweht*. Und obwohl es sich um einen Historienschinken handelte, lieferte der Film von 1939 die meisten Hut- und Frisurentrends der 1940er Jahre, etwa die bändergeschmückten Hauben und Haarnetze.

John P. John et Frederic Hirst, le duo de concepteurs travaillant pour la marque de chapeaux John-Frederics, créèrent les modèles portés par Vivien Leigh dans le film multi-oscarisé *Autant en emporte le vent*. Sorti en 1939, ce film en costumes d'époque inspira pourtant les tendances de coiffures et de chapeaux pendant la majeure partie des années 40, y compris les bonnets passepoilés de ruban et les résilles pour cheveux.

► Lilly Daché Hair Nets, 1944

202

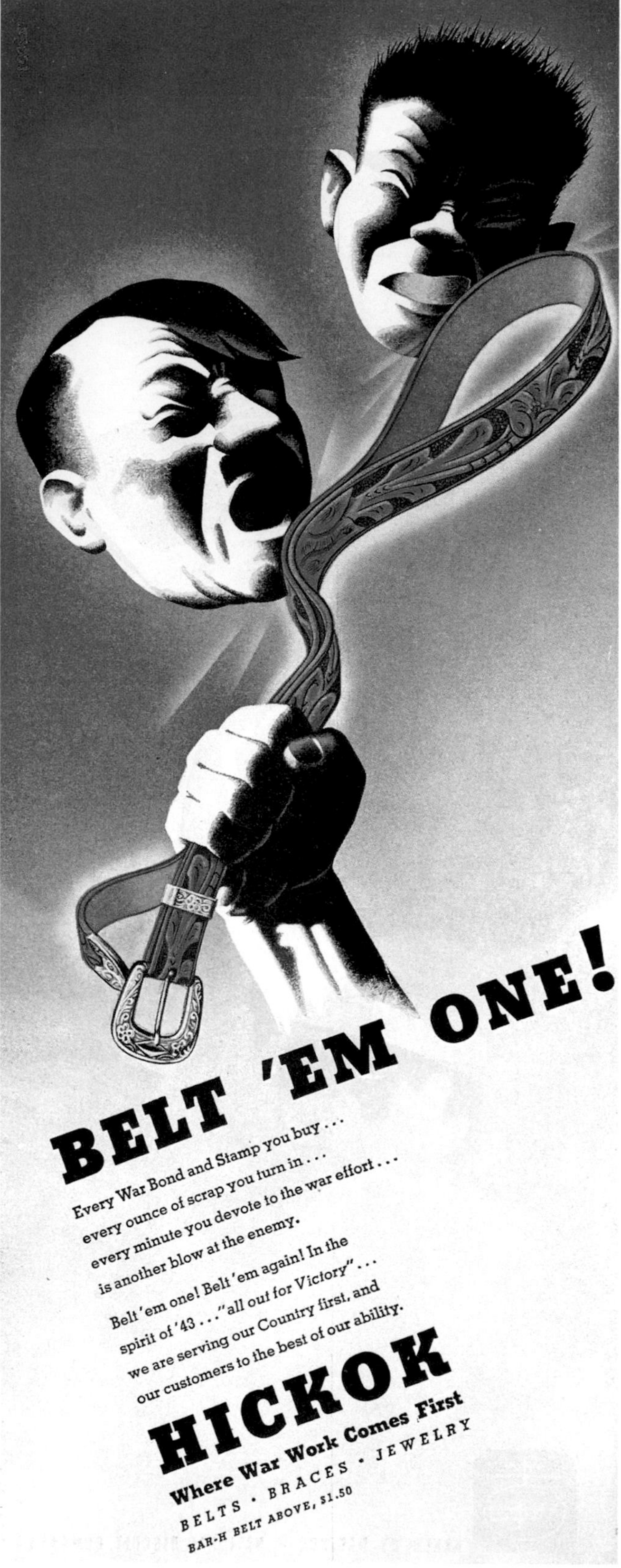

Fashion Frocks, 1943

Hickok Belts, 1943

By 1943, Hollywood was releasing pro-America propaganda films designed to boost morale at home during the war. Fashion manufacturers got into the act with ads crafted to appeal to consumers' patriotism as well as their pocket books.

Ab 1943 brachte Hollywood patriotische Propagandafilme heraus, die dazu gedacht waren, während des Krieges die Moral im eigenen Land zu stärken. Die Modehersteller schlossen sich mit Anzeigen an, die darauf abzielten, an den Patriotismus der Konsumenten zu appellieren, aber auch deren Geldbörsen im Visier hatten.

En 1943, Hollywood sortit des films de propagande pro-américaine conçus pour remonter le moral de la nation pendant la guerre. Les fabricants de vêtements y participèrent avec des publicités misant sur le patriotisme des consommateurs et leur besoin de faire des économies.

► Lee Workwear, 1943

You'll wake up some morning with the last belligerent Jap gone the way of his ignoble ancestors. The shout of "Heil Hitler" will no longer threaten slavery and death for free people.

To hasten that day you accepted rationing of the miles you drive, the very food on your table, the fuel to heat your home in winter. *This, is America at war!*

From time to time, you may have found your Lee Dealer temporarily short of your favorite Lee Work Clothes. But you have been patient because you knew that somehow, the materials for the particular Lee you wanted at the moment had gone to clothe a soldier.

Until "The Great Day" comes, Lee Work Clothes will continue to fight on many fronts. In the meantime your Lee Dealer is receiving new shipments of Lee Work Clothes as often and in whatever quantities available after military needs have been met. 203

Now, as always, you'll find LEE is your best buy in work clothes. If your Lee Dealer doesn't have exactly the garment you want, he may have a different one suitable for your purpose. If you should happen to hit one of those rare times when he can't supply you at all, you'll be glad you waited a few days for the garment with this unconditional guarantee, "Your Lee garment must *look better, fit better, wear longer* than any garment you've ever worn . . . or you get a new one free or your money back."

Highest Quality
UNION MADE
Lee
Work Clothes and
Industrial Uniforms

JELT DENIM OVERALLS • UNION-ALLS • MATCHED SHIRTS AND PANTS • WHIPCORDS • DUNGAREES COWBOY PANTS • INDUSTRIAL UNIFORMS

Copr. 1943, The H. D. Lee Company, Inc., Kansas City, Mo. • Trenton N. J. South Bend, Ind. • Minneapolis, Minn. • San Francisco, Calif. • Salina, Kans.

IN PEACE OR WAR—THE LARGEST SELLING LINE OF ITS KIND IN AMERICA

"Stepping Out" with

IF YOU CAN'T ALWAYS GET JUST THE INTER WOVEN SOCKS YOU WANT...PLEASE BEAR IN MIND... INTER-WOVEN WAS CALLED UPON TO SUPPLY MILLIONS OF PAIRS OF SOCKS TO THE ARMED FORCES.

*Inter Woven

FELL

It's Lee 6 to 1

THE H. D. LEE COMPANY

Kansas City, Mo. • South Bend, Ind. • Trenton, N. J.
Minneapolis, Minn. • San Francisco, Calif. • Salina, Kansas

In a nationwide survey* among thousands of men doing all types of work, the question was asked . . . "What brand of overalls do *you* prefer?" Lee Jelt Denim Overalls led the next brand by a margin of *6 to 1.*

Why is Lee the choice of common-sense, money-wise workingmen? Because they *know* bedrock work clothes value! They know Lee's exclusive fabrics wear longer and wash better. They know Lee "Tailored Sizes" mean perfect fit, lasting comfort and better appearance.

Buy Lee Work Clothes . . . at leading stores coast-to-coast.

* * *

THERE'S A LEE FOR EVERY JOB!

JELT DENIM OVERALLS • UNION-ALLS • MATCHED SHIRTS AND PANTS • DUNGAREES • COWBOY PANTS

**Survey made by a prominent publishing company.*

WORLD'S LARGEST MANUFACTURERS OF UNION-MADE WORK CLOTHES

Lee Workwear, 1946

Interwoven Socks, 1945 ◄

America's Largest Selling Caps

W71F—All wool reprocessed. Swivel earmuffs. Vinylite windshield. All colors. $1.50 and $1.95
223L — Cape helmet. Full alpaca lining. Plastic goggles. Very warm. $2.95

W105J — Water repellent heavy poplin. Alpaca lapels. Adjustable strap. Vinylite windshield. All colors. $1.95

W50FJ—All wool two-tone effect. Swivel earmuffs. All colors. $1.50 and $1.95

WITH WINTER MONTHS not far away, millions of American lads will again wear HUGGER CAPS. Guard your boy against winter head colds. Keep his head warm with a HUGGER CAP. America's best values . . . $1.00 to $2.95.

206

W49F—All wool window pane plaids. Swivel earmuffs. Vinylite windshield. All colors. $1.95 and $2.50

3SE — All wool covert Eton cap. Warm inband. All colors. $1.50

See these HUGGER CAPS at your dealer today or write

HUGGER CAPS

A DIVISION OF PORTIS STYLE INDUSTRIES, INC.
320 W. Ohio Street, Chicago, 10, Ill. • New York Office: 1199 Broadway

HUGGER
U. S. PATENT 2159609 TRADEMARK REG.
America's Largest Selling Caps
W20S—All wool Window Pane Plaids. Warm inband. Vinylite windshield. All colors. $1.95
W2—Perfect Ski Cap. "COLD-FIRE" fabric. Fluorescent water-repellent. Vinylite green glare shade. Alpaca inband. Brilliant colors. $2.50
COME WINTER . . . and millions of men, young and old, will be wearing HUGGER CAPS. Finest all-around cap for all out-of-door work and sports . . . Ideal for hunting, skating, skiing. Quality fabrics and workmanship. America's best values . . . $1.00 to $2.95
W202 — Heavy Cavalry Twill with Dakota* Alpaca inband. Protects forehead. Water-repellent. All colors. $1.95
TESTED AND COMMENDED BY PARENTS' MAGAZINE CONSUMER SERVICE BUREAU
Guaranteed by Good Housekeeping
W166 — Heavy gabardine. Water-repellent. Warm inband. All colors. $1.00
S18 — All wool Buffalo checks. Warm inband. All colors. $1.50
"COLDFIRE" R — Tan reversible Corduroy and Fire Orange "COLD-FIRE" fabric. (Invisible to deer). Fluorescent, water-repellent. Alpaca inband. $2.50
*Pat. appl. for
Allen

See these HUGGER CAPS at your dealer today or write

HUGGER CAPS

A DIVISION OF PORTIS STYLE INDUSTRIES, INC.
320 W. Ohio Street, Chicago 10, Ill. • New York Office: 1199 Broadway

Hugger Caps, 1949

Hugger Caps, 1949

▸ Keds Athletic Shoes, 1941

BIG DEEDS ARE OFTEN BORN IN DREAMS

ars ago a young football coach came into our office. were so impressed with his character and intelligence, ced him to become head of our Keds Sports Depart- hat position he still holds—to such extent as his coach- onsibilities permit. You know Frank Leahy as coach Seven Blocks of Granite," as coach of the winning the latest Sugar Bowl contest. We know him as an devoted pupil of Knute Rockne; as the man who, working with Stephen Epler, produced the Epler six-man football shoe; as the expert coach who developed a brand new last for Keds basketball shoes. To the boys of America, we give "Frank Leahy." And for 1941, we give you a booklet on football that Frank Leahy is now preparing. If you wish us to reserve a copy for you, or if you would like a copy of the above illustration, suitable for framing, just send your name and address to Keds Sports Department. Both are free.

United States Rubber Company · Rockefeller Center, New York, N. Y.

The Shoe of Champions

KNOX

Foxhound

208

Latest style expression of this famous Knox-exclusive snap-brim, in fine felt finished to a new silky softness. Illustrated, in "Citron," and in "Hickory." $10.00 and $12.50

Knox the Hatter, 452 Fifth Avenue, New York

Now being shown by your Knox dealer.

KNOX

"Hats made so fine that all others must be compared to them."

Charles Knox 1838

Stetson Hats, 1949

British-born Hollywood actor David Niven was known for his cool demeanor and suave sophistication. By teaming with Niven, Texas company Stetson – manufacturer of the "hat of the West" – hoped to capture some of the actor's panache.

Der in Großbritannien geborene Hollywood-Schauspieler David Niven war berühmt für sein abgeklärtes Auftreten und seine weltmännische Eleganz. Indem man sich mit ihm zusammentat, erhoffte sich die texanische Firma Stetson – Hersteller des „Hat of the West" –, etwas von der Extravaganz des Schauspielers auszustrahlen.

D'origine britannique, l'acteur hollywoodien David Niven était connu pour son flegme et son raffinement. En s'associant avec lui, l'entreprise texane Stetson, fabricant du « chapeau de l'Ouest », espérait s'approprier un peu de son panache.

Knox Hats, 1947 ◄

DAVID NIVEN, STARRING IN SAMUEL GOLDWYN'S "THE ELUSIVE PIMPERNEL"

The Stetson is part of the man

David Niven wouldn't consider himself well dressed if he went out without his Stetson. Famous Stetson quality gives him that important "well-dressed feeling." With faultless Stetson styling, he *knows* he looks his best. See what this smartly formal *Squire* in *Sky Grey* does for David? See what it can do for you!

The Squire by STETSON *in Sky Grey $15*

Keep your money

in the fight

Let's not get overconfident. The war isn't won yet.
G. I. Joe is still over there fighting with your dollars . . .
and *he* isn't putting down his rifle till V-Day.
Could you look him in the eye and consider
cashing in your Bonds . . . debate about
buying more? Right, you couldn't.
Buy all the Bonds you can afford.
Buy the Bonds you *can't* afford.
And hang on to them. *Keep your money in the fight.*

What is the "Hart Schaffner & Marx touch"
. . . subtle tailoring . . . sensible design?
Whatever it is, it's made Hart Schaffner & Marx
the best-known clothing name in the world.

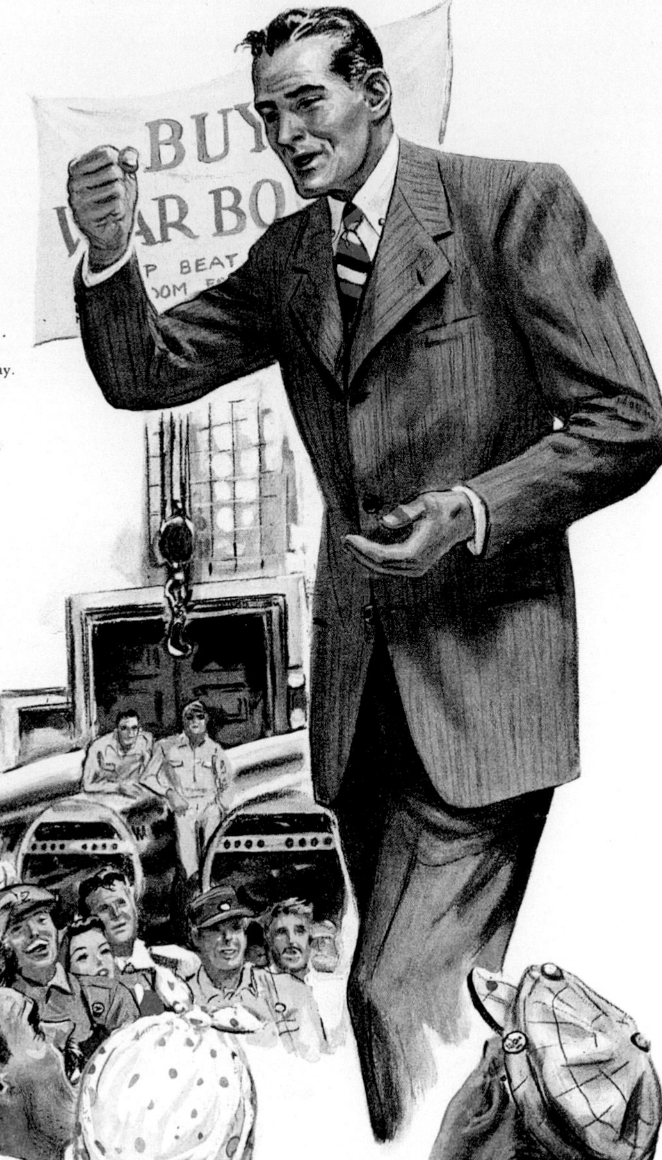

HART SCHAFFNER & MARX

The Trumpeter Label . . a small thing to look for . . a big thing to find

Hart Schaffner & Marx Menswear, 1944

Hart Schaffner & Marx was one of many U.S. companies producing patriotic ads during the Second World War. The Chicago suitmaker's approach was curious: It appears to be telling the consumer not to buy its product, but to buy war bonds instead.

Hart Schaffner & Marx war eine der vielen US-Firmen, die während des Zweiten Weltkriegs patriotische Annoncen schalteten. Der Anzughersteller aus Chicago wählte einen kuriosen Ansatz: Er scheint der Kundschaft zu raten, nicht seine Produkte zu kaufen, sondern stattdessen Kriegsanleihen zu erwerben.

Hart Schaffner & Marx, tailleur pour homme à Chicago, fut l'une des nombreuses entreprises américaines à produire des publicités patriotiques pendant la Seconde Guerre mondiale. Son approche était étrange : elle semble inciter le consommateur à acheter des bons de guerre plutôt que ses produits.

▸ Worumbo Fabric/Eagle Clothes/Lo Balbo Coats, 1949

COOL AIRTONES

BARATHEA WHITES

SOLIDS AND STRIPES

COMMUTER TONES

HARRY BECKHOFF

The only duplicate of a Palm Beach Suit is another

PALM BEACH SUIT

AND HAVING TWO isn't a bad idea—for then there's one for town and one for country—and a welcome third or fourth can be made in a twinkling, (by mixing the coat of one with the trousers of the other). Two suits offer you four changes—

And that's quite a wardrobe, quite an economy—for the price of the new Palm Beach is just **$17.75**

You'll know it by the "open-windowed" weave that lets your body breathe—by the wealth of colors for all occasions—by its perfect washability and splendid fit: But still easier—you'll know it by the label—sewn in every real Palm Beach garment.

See it at your clothier's in the softer, lighter Airtones for Sports—in Commuter tones for town. And the new smart Whites.

Palm Beach slacks $5.50 • *Sport coats* $13.50 • *Evening Formals* $20.00 • *Students' suits (sizes 16 to 22)* $16.50

$3250 IN PRIZES
Enter the Palm Beach contest. First prize, $1000. Second prize, $500. 235 other cash awards. Your clothier has Entry Blank and complete details.

TAILORED BY GOODALL
Palm Beach
FROM THE GENUINE CLOTH

Goodall Co. • Cincinnati

A GREAT GIFT FOR DAD

NEW DISCOVERIES
See the tropical worsted discoveries of 1941: Goodall Tropic Weight at $25. Tropic Weight De Luxe at $32.50. At your clothier's—today.

Springs Mills Fabrics, 1948

Throughout the late 1940s and '50s, textile maker Springs Mills ran a risqué campaign conceived and written by company owner Elliot Springs. Springs had some difficulty convincing his ad agency of the value of the concept, explaining in a 1947 letter, "A lot of dumb bunnies will ... write in and bawl us out for being vulgar and stupid. Then some people will take a second look and catch the burlesque, and be very proud that they're so smart. They'll think they are the only one to get it, and write to tell us about it."

In den späten 1940ern und den 50ern fuhr der Textilhersteller Springs Mills eine riskante Kampagne, die der Besitzer des Unternehmens Elliot Springs selbst konzipiert und geschrieben hatte. Springs hatte einige Mühe, seine Werbeagentur vom Wert des Konzepts zu überzeugen und führte in einem Brief von 1947 aus: „Eine Menge dummer Gänse wird ... uns anschreiben und uns als vulgär und blöd niedermachen. Dann werden einige Leute einen zweiten Blick riskieren und die Posse durchschauen und sehr stolz darauf sein, dass sie so clever sind. Sie werden denken, dass sie die einzige sind, die es kapiert haben, und uns schreiben, um uns eben dies zu vermelden."

A la fin des années 40 et tout au long des années 50, le fabricant textile Springs Mills utilisa une audacieuse campagne conçue et rédigée par le propriétaire de l'entreprise, Elliot Springs. Ce dernier eut du mal à convaincre son agence publicitaire de la valeur de son concept, comme il l'expliqua dans une lettre de 1947 : « Des tas de crétins vont... se plaindre et nous hurler dessus en nous accusant d'être bêtes et vulgaires. Puis, certaines personnes y réfléchiront à deux fois, saisiront l'aspect burlesque et se féliciteront d'être aussi intelligentes. Elles penseront être les seules à nous comprendre et nous écrirons pour nous le faire savoir. »

Palm Beach Suits/Goodall Mills, 1941 ◄

SPRINGMAID
FABRICS
THE SPRINGS COTTON MILLS
Perfume and Parabolics

During the war, The Springs Cotton Mills was called upon to develop a special fabric for camouflage. It was used in the Pacific to conceal ammunition dumps and gun emplacements, but the Japanese learned to detect it because of its lack of jungle smells. To overcome this, when the fabric was dyed, it was also impregnated with a permanent odor of hibiscus, hydrangea, and old rubber boots. The deception was so successful that when Tokyo fell, the victorious invaders hung a piece of this fabric on a Japanese flagpole.

This process has been patented, and the fabric is now available to the false bottom and bust bucket business as SPRINGMAID *PERKER,* made of combed yarns, 37″ wide, 152 x 68 approximate count, weight about 3.30, the white with gardenia, the pink with camellia, the blush with jasmine, and the nude dusty.

If you want to achieve that careless look and avoid skater's steam, kill two birds with one stone by getting a camouflaged callipygian camisole with the SPRINGMAID label on the bottom of your trademark.

SPRINGS MILLS

200 CHURCH STREET • NEW YORK 13, NEW YORK

CHICAGO DALLAS LOS ANGELES

Coming soon . . . SPRINGMAID *sheets, pillowcases, diapers, broadcloth, poplins, and tubings.*

The "Petty Girl" suit of 1940

BY JANTZEN

A great artist turns to swim suit design! With the same master strokes in simplicity of line that have made him so famous with brush and canvas. Here's George Petty's conception of the Suit of Youth, classic in design with slenderizing princess lines.

Tailored by Jantzen in a perfectly amazing new fabric, *Sea Ripple.* A swim suit that actually stretches all ways! A swim suit with real foundation garment control! It fits as you have never known a swim suit could fit. See it—feel it—try it on. Lastex* yarn has been knitted-in for perfect figure-molding. There's a new experience in beauty of line and perfection of fit awaiting you. In the new fashionable colors—$6.95 in U.S.A. For illustrated style folder, men's or women's, address Dept. 311.

A reproduction of this Petty Painting without advertising copy will be sent on receipt of 10c in stamps or coin.

JANTZEN KNITTING MILLS, PORTLAND, OREGON; VANCOUVER, CANADA

*Reg. U.S. Pat. Off.

- IF YOU LIKE SMOOTH CURVES YOU'LL LOVE THIS SUIT -

George PETTY

Jantzen

SWIM SUITS *AND SUN CLOTHES*

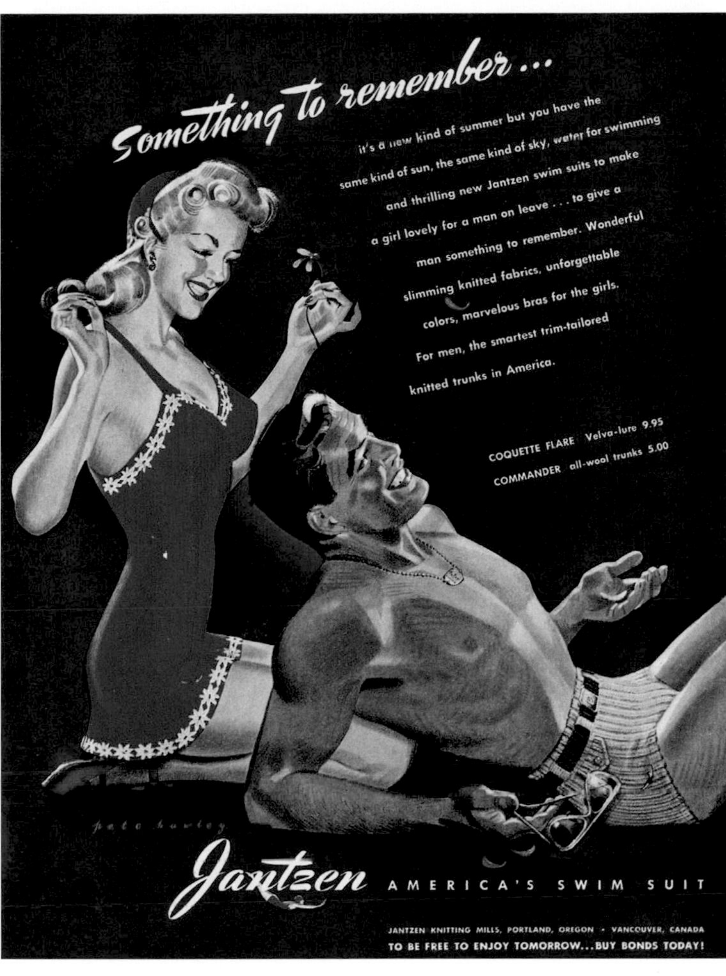

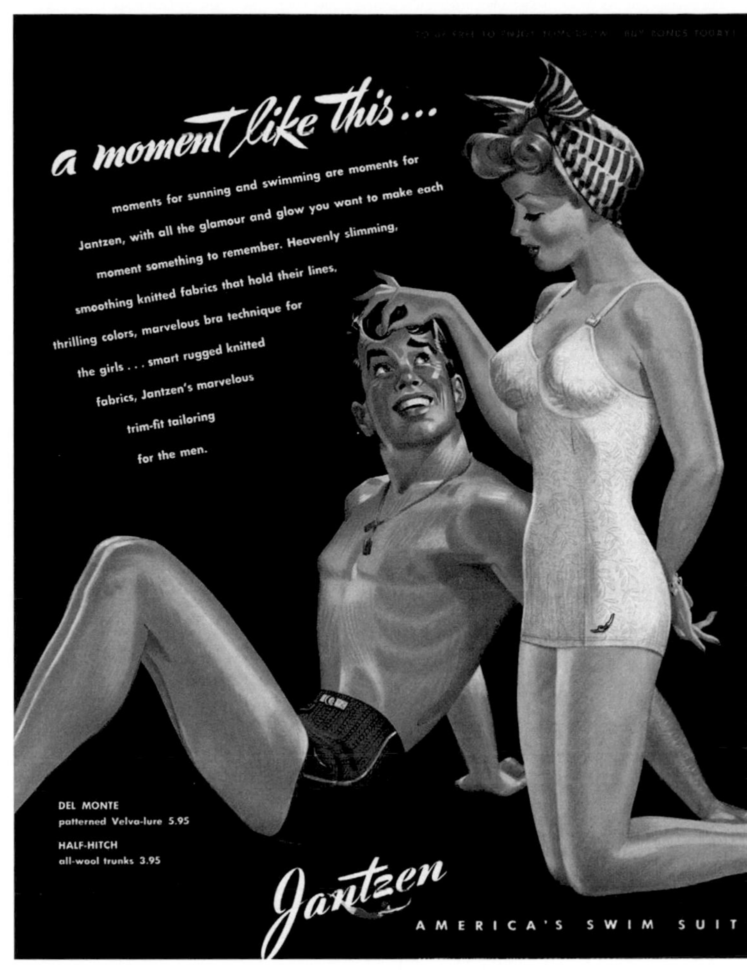

Jantzen Swimwear, 1940 ◄

Popular pinup artist George Petty created the red diving girl in the Jantzen logo, as well as illustrations for many of the company's ads in the 1940s. His style was so ubiquitous that Jantzen commissioned him to design this "Suit of Youth" swimsuit. The popular ad ran in major American magazines for months.

Der bekannte Pin-up-Künstler George Petty entwarf das rote tauchende Mädchen des Jantzen-Logos sowie Illustrationen für viele Anzeigen der Firma in den 1940er Jahren. Sein Stil war so allgegenwärtig, dass Jantzen ihn beauftragte, diesen „Suit of Youth"-Badeanzug zu entwerfen. Die beliebte Anzeige wurde in den großen amerikanischen Zeitschriften monatelang geschaltet.

Le célèbre dessinateur de pin-up George Petty créa la plongeuse en maillot rouge du logo Jantzen, ainsi que des illustrations pour de nombreuses publicités de l'entreprise dans les années 40. Son style était si universel que Jantzen lui demanda de concevoir ce maillot de bain « Suit of Youth ». Ce célèbre visuel fut publié dans les plus grands magazines américains pendant des mois.

Jantzen Swimwear, 1943

Jantzen Swimwear, 1943

Little Boy Blue
Little Boy Blue,
Awake from your sleep;
The girl of your dreams
Is bewitching your sheep.
How does she do it?
That's plain to see;
It's the glamour she gets
From her Life Bras three.
From morn, 'til night,
At work, at play,
Be a dream girl too
The Formfit way.
Life BY Formfit
LOOK FOR THIS LABEL
KEEP A BRA WARDROBE
Day Life—Sports Life—Night Life
$1.25—$1.75—$2.50—$3.50
FLAT CHESTED? WRITE FOR INFORMATION ABOUT INFLATION
—THE BRASSIERE FOR FLAT CHESTED WOMEN
MADE BY THE FORMFIT COMPANY • • CHICAGO • • NEW YOR

Formfit Brassieres, 1942 ◂

The silhouette of the 1940s was a marked departure from the '30s long-and-lean-look. Clothing was more structured, with strong shoulders and a full bust. Where undergarments of the previous decade emphasized a smooth line and flat stomach, in the 1940s lingerie began to provide more support for the bust.

Die Silhouette der 1940er war eine klare Abkehr von dem Lang-und-dünn-Look der Dreißigerjahre. Die Kleidung war stärker strukturiert, kräftige Schultern und üppige Oberweite wurden betont. Während die Unterkleider des vorangegangenen Jahrzehnts eine weiche Linie und einen flachen Bauch betonten, dienten die Dessous der 40er Jahre eher dem Halt der Brust.

La silhouette des années 40 se démarque nettement du look long et frêle des années 30. Les vêtements étaient plus structurés, renforçant les épaules et la poitrine. Alors que les sous-vêtements de la décade précédente soulignaient une ligne lisse et un torse plat, la lingerie commença, au cours des années 40, à accentuer davantage le soutien du buste.

Jantzen Swimwear, 1946

Summer is for this
OURS
Summer is certainly for Jantzen . . . because summer is for swimming and sunning and loving and living . . . and two-somes like this and swim suits like these to inspire two-somes like this. Jantzen practically invented summer years ago by dreaming up swim suits to make you look wonderful, feel wonderful while swimming and sunning. This year's Jantzens have marvelous in-and-out-of-water glamour, plus freedom of action, thrilling new lines, new fabrics, new colors. For the girls 5.95 to 9.95. For men 2.95 to 5.95 . . . at most stores.
*Reg. U. S. Pat. Off.
TAN WITH JAN . . . Jantzen's marvelous sun-cream lotion for a smooth soft skin-tan
*Jantzen
SWIM SUITS • SUN CLOTHES

B.V.D.
Slim Trim
gives you a brand new figure
B.V.D.'s new SLIM-TRIM construction makes your last year's trunks as back-numbered as Model T.
These 1941 streamlined slimmers have an exclusive figure-form control that not only does something *to* you, but *for* you. A new, trimmer figure—yes. But more. The amazing SLIM-TRIM construction actually helps support your muscles, giving greater energy, new pep and vim. Before you go near the water, step into a pair . . . and step out with the best. You'll find them at all good stores.
MADE FOR THE B.V.D. BEST RETAIL TRADE
New B.V.D. Swim Suits
PICK THE FIGURE-TYPE DESIGNED TO HELP YOU!
LIEUTENANT
Slim, young and full of vim and vigor. Go out and mow down the lifeguard in your new B.V.D. trunks.
CAPTAIN
Slightly paunchy? B.V.D.'s ingenious SLIM-TRIM construction pulls you in; gives you gentle support.
COLONEL
The picture of virility. B.V.D.'s special figure-type trunks add new interest to the prime of life.
FIGURE-TYPE SWIM SUITS . . $1.95 . . $2.95 . . $3.95
"Next to myself I like B.V.D. best"
The B.V.D. Corporation, Empire State Building, N. Y. C. In Canada: The B.V.D. Company, Ltd., Montreal
39

YOU FLOAT

with Float-ees*

the swim trunks with

built-in "FLOATING POWER"

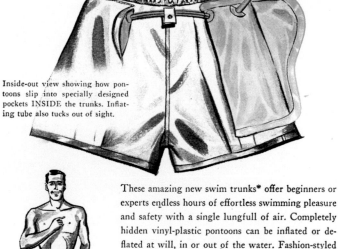

Inside-out view showing how pontoons slip into specially designed pockets INSIDE the trunks. Inflating tube also tucks out of sight.

These amazing new swim trunks* offer beginners or experts endless hours of effortless swimming pleasure and safety with a single lungfull of air. Completely hidden vinyl-plastic pontoons can be inflated or deflated at will, in or out of the water. Fashion-styled boxer trunks, Zelan treated, in prints and solid colors. Men's sizes (30-46) $7.50 . . . Boys' (6-16) $6.50 at stores everywhere or write.

Endorsed by leading coaches and swimmers. Send for *Free* illustrated Booklet "A" with swimming lesson by Adolph Kiefer, Olympic Champion.

SWIM SUITS *Pat.applied for.

FLOAT-EES CORPORATION • 1745 BROADWAY, NEW YORK 19, N. Y.

B. V. D. Swimwear, 1941

Although this is a far cry from Ocean Pacific, Quiksilver, or even the Beach Party films of the 1960s, surfing was already on the radar of savvy marketers. By the release of *Gidget* in 1959, surf culture had captured the nation.

Auch wenn man damals von Ocean Pacific, Quicksilver oder selbst den Beach-Party-Filmen der 1960er noch weit entfernt war, befand sich das Surfen schon auf dem Radar cleverer Werbestrategen. Als *Gidget* (dt. *April entdeckt die Männer*) 1959 in die Kinos kam, begeisterte sich die ganze Nation dafür.

Bien qu'on soit encore loin des marques telles Ocean Pacific et Quiksilver, ou même des films de plage prisés dans les années 60, les publicitaires les plus visionnaires exploitaient déjà l'image du surf. Lors de la sortie du film *Un Amour de vacances* en 1959, la culture surf déferlera pour de bon sur les Etats-Unis.

Float-ees Swimwear, 1947

▸ Jantzen Swimwear, 1941

▸▸ Jantzen Swimwear, 1949

This way to the Beach
Go to the beach in a Jantzen!
Play in the sun, ride the waves,
swim with the tide, looking your best ...
young, gay, alive and thrilled to be alive.
Jantzen does this for all the girls
with exciting new "Lastex" knitted
swim suit fabrics; rib-trimming,
hip-slimming foundation control; a marvelous
new Beauty-Lift Bra; glamorous, glorious colors.
And for all the men ... the famous Jantzen fit in
trunks and toppers, athletic-tailored the Jantzen way.
Start now ... stop at your favorite store to get your Jantzen
... go on from there to a wonderful summer.
LITTLE ADMIRAL, Jantzen's sea-going glamorizer in Velva-Lure 7.95.
THE SPEEDSTER, Jantzen's stunning Brittany-knit worsted and "Lastex" trunks 3.95.
Other Jantzens for women, 4.95 to 10.95. Men's Trunks, 2.95 to 4.95.
At leading stores, or write for illustrated style folder.
A. Varga
Jantzen
JANTZEN KNITTING MILLS....PORTLAND, OREGON; VANCOUVER, CANADA

Jantzen

thoroughly man-tailored

sunclothes

come on you sunners...line up for the best looks of your life! Jantzen has everything you need...the smartest, best-fitting, best-performing man-tailored sun classics... finest quality washable fabrics...special-for-Jantzen wonderful-looking fast colors. Jantzen is famous for girls' shorts...fly-front shorts of Crompton finest cotton corduroy as in "Romper", left, 5.95...other shorts, 2.95 to 9.95. Jantzen is famous for tee shirts of finest quality combed cotton, as the striped shirt, for men, too, 2.95...the shirt-collared tee shirt, for girls as well, 3.95. Jantzen is famous for men's shorts, perfect boxers like "Amphibian", in cool Celanese rayon "Sunyana" 4.95 ...and many others 3.95 to 9.95...at leading stores.

• WRITE FOR FREE STYLE FOLDER
...showing other marvelous Jantzens

JANTZEN KNITTING MILLS, INC., Dept. M, PORTLAND 14, ORE.

from Jantzen
"WATER BOY"
"ECLIPSE"
"HI-DIVER"
come on you swimmers...Jantzen has for you the world's finest swim suits and swim trunks... marvelous new exclusive Lastex-powered fabrics... famous Jantzen girdle control and uplifting bras for girls...flawless-fit, trim athletic lines for men. "Eclipse", in light-as-air Cordo-Lastex, with detachable shoulder straps is 9.95..."Ecstasy" (opposite page) finest quality satin Lastex with terrific new Jantzen Stay-Bra 15.95 ...one-piece like it 17.95...others 8.95 to 17.95. Jantzen has for men the smoothest brief trunks like "Water Boy" left, in Jantzen special Cordo-Lastex 3.95. "Hi-Diver", right, in finest satin Lastex 5.95 ...others 3.95 to 6.95...at leading stores.
Jantzen
Lastex-powered figure-control
swim suits
TAN with JAN . . . for a glorious copper tan use Jan Sun Oil, for protection use Jan Sun Lotion.

AMERICAN VETERANS BACK FROM FIGHTING IN THE PACIFIC HAD BROUGHT HAWAIIAN SHIRTS AND SURF CULTURE TO THE MAINLAND, BUT IT WAS TEEN SURFER-GIRL KATHY "GIDGET" KOHNER'S INNOCENT EXPLOITS AT MALIBU BEACH THAT CEMENTED CALIFORNIA'S REPUTATION AS A FOUNTAINHEAD OF YOUTH CULTURE.

AMERIKAS VETERANEN AUS DEM PAZIFIK HATTEN HAWAIIHEMDEN UND SURFER-ATMOSPHÄRE MIT ANS FESTLAND GEBRACHT, ABER EIGENTLICH WAREN ES ERST DIE UNSCHULDIGEN HELDENTATEN DES TEENY-SURFER-GIRLS KATHY „GIDGET" KOHNER AM STRAND VON MALIBU, DIE KALIFORNIENS RUF ALS URQUELL DER JUGENDKULTUR UNTERMAUERTEN.

APRÈS AVOIR COMBATTU DANS LE PACIFIQUE, LES VÉTÉRANS AMÉRICAINS RAPPORTENT LES CHEMISES HAWAÏENNES ET LA MODE DU SURF SUR LE CONTINENT, MAIS C'ÉTAIT LA JEUNE SURFEUSE KATHY «GIDGET» KOHNER SUR LA PLAGE DE MALIBU ... QUI CIMENTE LA RÉPUTATION DE LA CALIFORNIE EN TANT QUE BERCEAU DE LA CULTURE JEUNE.

WILD ONES AND WOMANLY WILES
HALBSTARKE UND WEIBLICHE RAFFINESSE
JEUNES REBELLES ET CHARMES FÉMININS

-1959

Jantzen Swimwear, 1950 ◂

American Optical Company, 1959

WITH STRIKING RED HAIR, HIGH CHEEKBONES AND ARCHED EYEBROWS, MODEL SUZY PARKER WAS THE FACE OF THE 1950s, appearing on more than 60 magazine covers of the decade. She became Chanel's model of choice, and was photographed by Richard Avedon in Dior, whose New Look dominated women's fashions for a generation. The silhouette made its way to the big and small screens: Elizabeth Taylor's white, strapless, cinch-waist gown for the 1951 film *A Place in the Sun* became one of the most copied prom dresses of the era. Full skirts were key to Lucille Ball's wardrobe when *I Love Lucy* debuted on that new medium, television, in 1952.

By 1954, television sales had surpassed radio, as millions of families tuned in to watch situation comedies like *Father Knows Best* and *Leave It to Beaver*; game shows like *What's My Line?* and *Twenty One*; and variety shows like *Sid Caesar's Your Show of Shows*. Television proved to be a successful advertising vehicle, but for fashion, print remained the dominant medium. New magazines like *Playboy*, *Jet*, *Sports Illustrated*, *TV Guide*, and *Confidential* were launched, targeting new demographics.

Still, there were early examples of "as-seen-on TV" trends. Disney's Davy Crockett's popularity sent millions of children to the store to buy everything from coonskin caps to licensed Davy Crockett pajamas and lunchboxes. *American Bandstand* host Dick Clark showcased pop musicians and the latest dance trends, which helped define the "American teen."

American veterans back from fighting in the Pacific had brought Hawaiian shirts and surf culture to the mainland, but it was teen surfer-girl Kathy "Gidget" Kohner's innocent exploits at Malibu beach in *Gidget* that cemented California's reputation as a fountainhead of youth culture. James Dean and Natalie Wood offered another example of American teen life in 1955's *Rebel Without a Cause*, and, by 1956, Elvis Presley released *Heartbreak Hotel*, bringing rock 'n' roll to the fore. The rebel look worn by Dean and Presley — not to mention Marlon Brando, in 1953's *The Wild One* — was blue jeans, a white T-shirt, and a leather jacket. All were a stark contrast to the professional look of the day, slim and somber suits worn with a skinny tie and topped with a fedora.

In addition to Dior's full-skirt silhouette, '50s womenswear included pencil skirts, tailored suits, and dresses with demure ballet necklines or sexy, off-the-shoulder or strapless styles for evening. In 1954, Coco Chanel reopened for business. Her line of suits with boxy jackets trimmed with gold braid and accessorized with a pile of pearls became the hallmark of the design house.

While the decade's fashions were predominantly conservative, signs of change were already forming. In 1947, a French civil engineer, Louis Réard, introduced the bikini at a Paris fashion show. The following year, Italian designer Emilio Pucci created his first American collection for Lord & Taylor stores. In 1951, Finnish designer Armi Ratia launched the company that eventually became print-powerhouse Marimekko. Cristobal Balenciaga introduced balloon jackets, the cocoon coat, the sack dress, and the chemise; and Pierre Cardin created the bubble dress. The '60s were right around the corner.

1950

1950 Men's desert boot introduced; will become counterculture favorite by '60s

Der Desert Boot kommt auf den Markt und wird in den 60ern zum Lieblingsschuh der Protestbewegung

Lancement du bottillon en daim pour homme, un modèle qui sera privilégié par la contre-culture des années 60

1950 Original supermodel Suzy Parker arrives in Paris

Mit Suzy Parker trifft ein echtes Supermodel in Paris ein

Suzy Parker, la première top-modèle, débarque à Paris

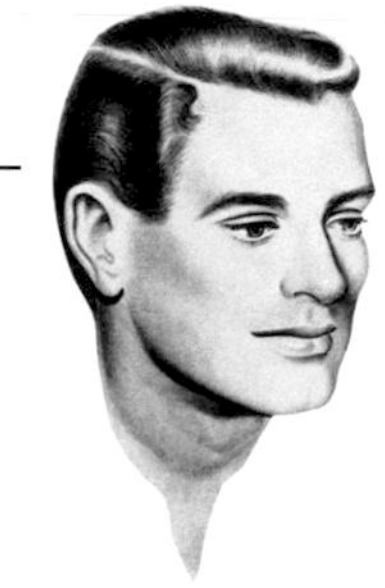

1950 Pomade-slicked hairstyles popular with teen boys throughout decade

Glatte Pomadefrisuren sind das Jahrzehnt hindurch bei Teenager-Jungs beliebt

Les adolescents adoptent les coiffures lissées à la brillantine pendant toute la décennie

1951 Elizabeth Taylor's strapless gown in *A Place in the Sun* most copied prom dress

Elizabeth Taylors schulterfreies Abendkleid aus *Ein Platz an der Sonne* avanciert zum meistkopierten Ballkleid

La robe bustier d'Elizabeth Taylor dans *Une Place au soleil* devient la robe de bal de promo la plus copiée de l'histoire

MIT FLAMMEND ROTEM HAAR, HOHEN WANGENKNOCHEN UND GESCHWUNGENEN AUGENBRAUEN WAR DAS FOTOMODELL SUZY PARKER DAS GESICHT DER 50ER, das im Laufe des Jahrzehnts mehr als sechzigmal die Titelseiten diverser Magazine schmückte. Sie avancierte zu Chanels Lieblingsmodell und wurde von Richard Avedon in Dior fotografiert, dessen New Look die Damenmode eine ganze Generation lang dominieren sollte. Die Silhouette beherrschte die große wie die kleine Leinwand: Elizabeth Taylors weißes, schulterfreies, tailliertes Abendkeid aus dem Film *Ein Platz an der Sonne* von 1951 war eines der meistkopierten Ballkleider jener Ära. Weite Röcke waren auch das Markenzeichen der Garderobe von Lucille Ball, als *I Love Lucy* 1952 im damals neuen Medium Fernsehen startete.

1954 hatten die Verkaufszahlen für Fernseher jene für Radios überholt, und Millionen von Familien verfolgten Sit-Coms wie *Vater ist der Beste* und *Erwachsen müßte man sein*, Spielshows wie *What's My Line?* und *Twenty One* sowie Unterhaltungssendungen wie Sid Caesars *Your Show of Shows*. Das Fernsehen erwies sich als erfolgreiches Werbemedium, doch für die Modebranche blieb der Printbereich am wichtigsten. Neue Magazine wie *Playboy*, *Mad*, *Jet*, *Sports Illustrated*, *TV Guide* und *Confidential* kamen auf den Markt und nahmen neue Zielgruppen ins Visier.

Es gab allerdings auch schon frühe Beispiele von „wie aus dem TV bekannt". So sorgte etwa die Beliebtheit von Disneys *Davy Crockett* dafür, dass Millionen amerikanischer Kinder die Geschäfte stürmten, um von Waschbärfellmützen bis hin zu lizensierten Pyjamas und Brotdosen einfach alles von Davy Crockett zu kaufen. Dick Clark, Gastgeber bei American Bandstand, präsentierte Popmusiker und die neuesten Modetänze und trug damit dazu bei, den typisch amerikanischen Teenager zu definieren.

Amerikas Veteranen aus dem Pazifik hatten Hawaiihemden und Surfer-Atmosphäre mit ans Festland gebracht, aber eigentlich waren es erst die unschuldigen Heldentaten des Teeny-Surfer-Girls Kathy „Gidget" Kohner am Strand von Malibu, die Kaliforniens Ruf als Urquell der Jugendkultur untermauerten. James Dean und Natalie Wood gaben in *Denn sie wissen nicht, was sie tun* von 1955 ein anderes Beispiel für ein amerikanisches Teenagerleben, und mit der Veröffentlichung von *Heartbreak Hotel* 1956 brachte Elvis Presley den Rock'n'Roll entscheidend nach vorn. Der Rebellen-Look von Dean und Presley – gar nicht zu reden von Marlon Brando in *Der Wilde* von 1953 – bestand aus Bluejeans, weißem T-Shirt und Lederjacke. Das war der denkbar größte Kontrast zum damaligen Business-Outfit, bestehend aus einem eng geschnittenen Anzug in gedeckter Farbe, schmaler Krawatten und Filzhut.

Neben Diors weitschwingenden Röcken gab es in der Damenmode der 50er auch Bleistiftröcke, figurnahe Kostüme und Kleider mit sittsamem Rundhalsausschnitt sowie sexy schulterfreie oder trägerlose Teile für den Abend. 1954 kehrte Coco Chanel ins Geschäft zurück. Ihre Kollektion aus Kostümen mit kastenförmigen Jacken, die mit Goldborten verziert waren und mit haufenweise Perlen getragen wurden, avancierte zum Markenzeichen ihres Modehauses.

Auch wenn die Trends des Jahrzehnts vornehmlich konservativ waren, so konnte man doch schon Anzeichen eines Wandels erkennen. 1947 ließ der französische Maschinenbauingenieur Louis Réard bei einer Pariser Modenschau erstmals einen Bikini vorführen. Im Jahr darauf entwarf der italienische Designer Emilio Pucci seine erste amerikanische Kollektion für die Kette Lord & Taylor.

1951 gründete die finnische Designerin Armi Ratia die Firma, die schließlich zu Marimekko, dem Spezialisten für Stoffdruck, wurde. Cristobal Balenciaga führte Ballonjacken, den Kokonmantel, das Sackkleid sowie das Hemdblusenkleid ein. Pierre Cardin erfand das Ballonkleid. Und die Sixties warteten schon um die Ecke.

1953

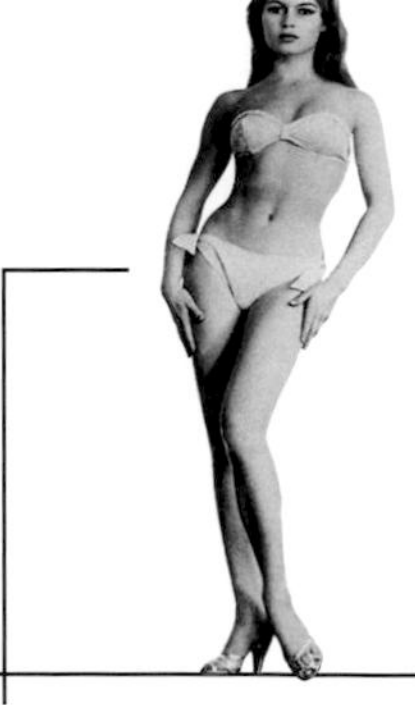

1953 Motorcycle jackets and T-shirts define Marlon Brando's rebel look in *The Wild One*

Motorradjacken und T-Shirts bestimmen Marlon Brandos Rebellen-Look in *Der Wilde*

Dans *L'Equipée Sauvage*, Marlon Brando donne vie au look rebelle en T-shirt et blouson de motard

1953 Ray-Ban patents Wayfarers; best-selling sunglass design of all time

Ray-Ban lässt sich die Wayfarers patentieren; das meistverkaufte Sonnenbrillenmodell aller Zeiten

Ray-Ban fait breveter les Wayfarers, les lunettes de soleil les plus vendues de l'histoire

1954 Pierre Cardin introduces bubble dress

Pierre Cardin präsentiert das Ballonkleid

Pierre Cardin lance la robe bulle

1956 Brigitte Bardot's appearance in *And God Created Woman* popularizes bikini

Brigitte Bardots Darstellung in *Und ewig lockt das Weib* macht den Bikini populär

Brigitte Bardot démocratise le bikini dans *Et Dieu créa la femme*

The PLAYBILL
The PLAYBILL
PLAYBILL

NORTHWEST
AIRLINES
208

Plateau Suits/Pacific Mills, 1950 ◂◂

Sarong Girdles, 1956 ◂

▸▸ Van Heusen Shirts, 1950

AVEC SES CHEVEUX ROUGE FEU, SES POMMETTES SAILLANTES ET SES SOURCILS ARQUÉS, LE MANNEQUIN SUZY PARKER EST LE VISAGE DES ANNÉES 50 qui fera plus de soixante couvertures de magazines au cours de la décennie. Elle devient le mannequin de prédilection de Chanel et se fait photographier par Richard Avedon habillée de Dior, dont le New Look domine la mode féminine pendant toute une génération. Cette silhouette fait son chemin jusqu'aux petit et au grand écrans : la robe bustier blanche cintrée à la taille portée par Elizabeth Taylor en 1951 dans le film *Une Place au soleil* devient l'un des modèles les plus copiés dans l'histoire des robes de bal de promo. En 1952, les jupes amples s'imposent comme un basique de la garde-robe de Lucille Ball dès les débuts de la série *L'Extravagante Lucie* sur ce nouveau média qu'est la télévision.

En 1954, les ventes de téléviseurs surpassent celles des radios alors que des millions de familles s'équipent pour regarder des feuilletons humoristiques tels *Papa a raison* et *Leave It to Beaver*, des jeux télévisés comme *What's My Line?* et *Twenty One* et des émissions de variétés, notamment *Your Show of Shows* animée par Sid Caesar. La télévision s'avère un formidable support publicitaire, mais la presse reste le média dominant pour la mode. De nouveaux magazines comme *Playboy*, *Mad*, *Jet*, *Sports Illustrated*, *TV Guide* et *Confidential* sont lancés à l'attention de nouvelles tranches démographiques.

On voit cependant apparaître les premiers exemples de modes « vues à la télé ». Face à la popularité du *Davy Crockett* de Disney, des millions d'enfants fréquentent les magasins pour acheter toutes sortes de choses, des casquettes en raton laveur aux pyjamas et cantines sous licence Davy Crockett. Dick Clark, l'animateur d'*American Bandstand*, présente des groupes de pop et les dernières danses à la mode, contribuant ainsi à définir le « teenager américain ».

Après avoir combattu dans le Pacifique, les vétérans américains rapportent les chemises hawaïennes et la mode du surf sur le continent, mais ce sont les exploits innocents de la jeune surfeuse Kathy « Gidget » Kohner sur la plage de Malibu dans le film *Un Amour de vacances* qui cimentent la réputation de la Californie en tant que berceau de la culture jeune. James Dean et Natalie Wood offrent un autre exemple de la vie des adolescents d'Amérique dans *La Fureur de vivre* en 1955, tandis qu'en 1956, Elvis Presley popularise le rock'n'roll en sortant *Heartbreak Hotel*. Le look de rebelle arboré par Dean et Presley – sans oublier Marlon Brando dans *L'Equipée sauvage* en 1953 – se compose d'un blue jean, d'un T-shirt blanc et d'un blouson de cuir. Leur allure contraste radicalement avec le look professionnel de l'époque, la plupart des hommes portant des costumes de couleur sombre et près du corps avec une étroite cravate et un fedora.

Outre la silhouette à jupe ample de Dior, la mode féminine des années 50 inclut des jupes droites, des tailleurs et des robes au modeste décolleté de danseuse, ou des modèles sexy, à bustier ou bretelle asymétrique pour le soir. En 1954, Coco Chanel reprend du service. Sa collection de tailleurs aux vestes carrées, gansés d'un galon doré et accessoirisés de plusieurs rangs de perles, devient la signature de sa maison de haute couture.

Si les tendances de l'époque sont majoritairement conservatrices, des signes de changement apparaissent déjà. En 1947, l'ingénieur civil français Louis Réard présente le bikini lors d'un défilé de mode parisien. L'année suivante, le couturier italien Emilio Pucci crée sa première collection américaine pour les magasins Lord & Taylor. En 1951, la créatrice finlandaise Armi Ratia fonde une entreprise destinée à devenir le géant des imprimés textiles Marimekko. Cristobal Balenciaga invente les vestes ballon, le manteau cocon, la robe sac et la robe-chemise, et Pierre Cardin, la robe bulle. Les années 60 pointent leur nez à l'horizon.

1956

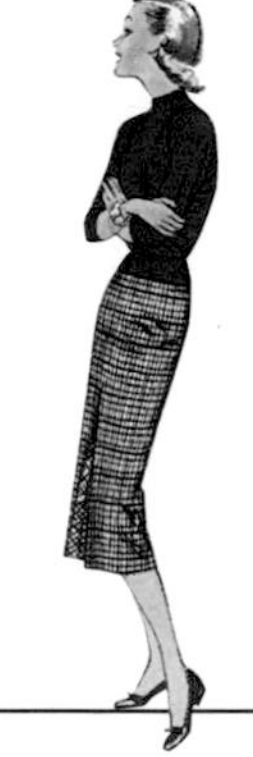

1956 Pencil skirts offer narrow alternative to New Look

Bleistiftröcke sind die schmale Alternative zum New Look

Les jupes droites offrent une alternative au New Look

1957 Pantyhose invented

Erfindung der Strumpfhose

Invention du collant

1958 Tai and Rosita Missoni present first Missoni collection in Milan

Tai und Rosita Missoni präsentieren in Mailand die erste Missoni-Kollektion

Tai et Rosita Missoni présentent la première collection Missoni à Milan

1958 Hairdresser Margaret Vinci Heldt creates "B-52" or beehive hairstyle

Die Friseurin Margaret Vinci Heldt erfindet „B-52", den Bienenkorb

La coiffeuse Margaret Vinci Heldt lance la mode des coiffures « en choucroute »

c'mon in ... the wearing's fine

Completely washable! They take to water like a mermaid. We're talking about the new—and we mean *new!*—Van Gab sport shirts. *Gabardine* ... like you've never seen! *Silky-smooth gabardine* ... with a new luxurious softness! *Finer-woven gabardin* ... that wears and wears and wears! We've tailored this fine fabric with famous Van Heusen magic sewmanship. Full-cut for action ... figure-tapered for look Shown here is famous California Lo-No model with exclusive two-way collar ... smart with or without a tie. Completely washable, stays size-right, color-fast. **$4.9** See Van Gab gabardine in other smart models—$2.95 to $5.95

The ties: Van Heusen Washable Poplin in 100% Nylon, 18 solid-color Sportones ... $1.50 each.
Phillips-Jones Corp., New York 1. Makers of Van Heusen Shirts • Ties • Pajamas • Collars • Sport Shirts

Look at those collars again! California Lo-No with "Fadeaway Collarband". Looks, fits right . . . with or without tie.

Season's biggest splash of color with 21 bright, new washable "Aquashades".

Sunset Red · Sea Clay · Shell Pink · Mermaid Mauve · Mist Grey · Tropi-Tan · Dune Tan · Ocean Blue · Sky Blue · Billow Blue · Pirate Gold · Sand Tan · Beach Beige · Deep Green · Briny Green · Gulf Green · Spray Green · Turtle Green · Sunglow Yellow · Oyster · Foam White

Van Heusen

REG. T. M.

new Van Gab Sport Shirts . . . *Completely washable* . . . $4.95

HATS—As healthy as they're handsome

THE "TEN GALLON"—The traditional hat of the Western plains has many functions. Its broad brim keeps glare out of the wearer's eyes and the high crown protects his head from the burning sun. It has been used as pillow, fire-fanner, and drinking cup!

WHETHER YOU PUNCH COWS or punch a clock, never forget the primary purpose of a hat—to *protect* you. A hat shades your eyes from aching glare, keeps sun and city soot off your hair, and guards your head against icy blasts. That's why when you go bare-headed you're just asking for trouble. It's foolish—especially when there is a handsome, well-styled hat just waiting to improve your appearance. Look in your dealer's window—he has a hat designed *right* for any occasion, wherever you go, or play, or work.

"Wear a Hat—It's as Healthy as It's Handsome!"

These fine hat labels have published this advertisement in the interests of good grooming and good health of American men.

DOBBS CAVANAGH KNOX
BERG BYRON C&K DUNLAP

Divisions of the Hat Corporation of America—Makers of Fine Hats for Men and Women

HATS—As healthy as they're handsome

THE HAVELOCK—The invention of Sir Henry Havelock of the British Army in India about 1850. Also known as the "kepi" and "forage cap" in other armies. The havelock shown here is worn by a French legionnaire. It's a handsome hat whose primary purpose is protection, to protect the back of the wearer's head and neck from the dangerous direct rays of the tropical sun.

NO MATTER WHERE YOU LIVE—in New York or New Caledonia—the purpose of your hat is to protect your eyes from glare, your hair from sun and soot, your head from icy blasts. That's the *primary* purpose of a hat. Don't go bareheaded—it simply isn't a very wise thing to do.
It's unkind to your sinuses, and definitely unkind to the hair on your head. There's a handsome hat waiting to improve your appearance—and to protect your head. Styled in shape and color to the moment, there's a *right* hat for the occasion wherever you go, or play, or work.

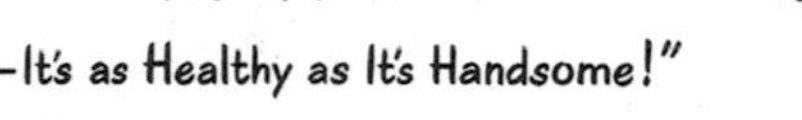

HATS—As healthy as they're handsome

THE SOLA TOPEE—The Indian sun helmet was first developed by the British Army in the early 19th Century. One of the world's most distinguished looking hats, it is white on the outside to reflect the sun, green-lined to help rest the eyes, and is filled with the light, porous pith of the Indian spongewood tree, to insulate against the heat rays of the sun.

YOUR HAT, too, is meant to protect you. It protects your hair from sun and soot, guards your eyes from painful glare, wards off the cold that can chill your head as well as your feet. Just as a practical matter—*it's wise to wear a hat.* It is rewarding, too. There's a healthy, appearance-improving hat waiting for you right now. In color and styling, it's *right* for the occasion—wherever you go, or play, or work.

"Wear a Hat—It's as Healthy as It's Handsome!"

Hat Corporation of America, 1952 ◄

Perhaps hat manufacturers saw their products' future as novelty accessories for a small niche market. In 1952, hatmakers banded together to extol the virtues – both practical and sartorial – of hats.

Vielleicht betrachteten die Hutmacher eine kleine Marktnische für neueste Accesoires als Zukunft für ihre Produkte. 1952 taten sich die Hutfabriken jedenfalls zusammen, um die praktischen wie eleganten Vorzüge von Hüten zu rühmen.

Les fabricants de chapeaux pensaient peut-être que l'avenir de leurs produits se trouvait dans le petit segment de marché des accessoires fantaisie. En 1952, ils s'unirent pour prôner les vertus tant pratiques que vestimentaires des chapeaux.

Hat Corporation of America, 1952

Hat Corporation of America, 1952

Quality at your feet
BROWN
SHOE COMPANY
you can't tell
the mothers from
the daughters in
mother-daughter
classics
Because everybody looks young
and has fun in these easy-living
casuals. And this year we've
given them a sophisticated new
slenderness that mothers and
daughters will both look smart in! Why
not try them on together?
Shoes Illustrated
6.95
Other styles, 6.95 to 10.95
Higher Denver West
westports by life stride
Life Stride Division, Brown Shoe Company, St. Louis

Life Stride Shoes, 1951

▸ Arrow Shirts, 1951

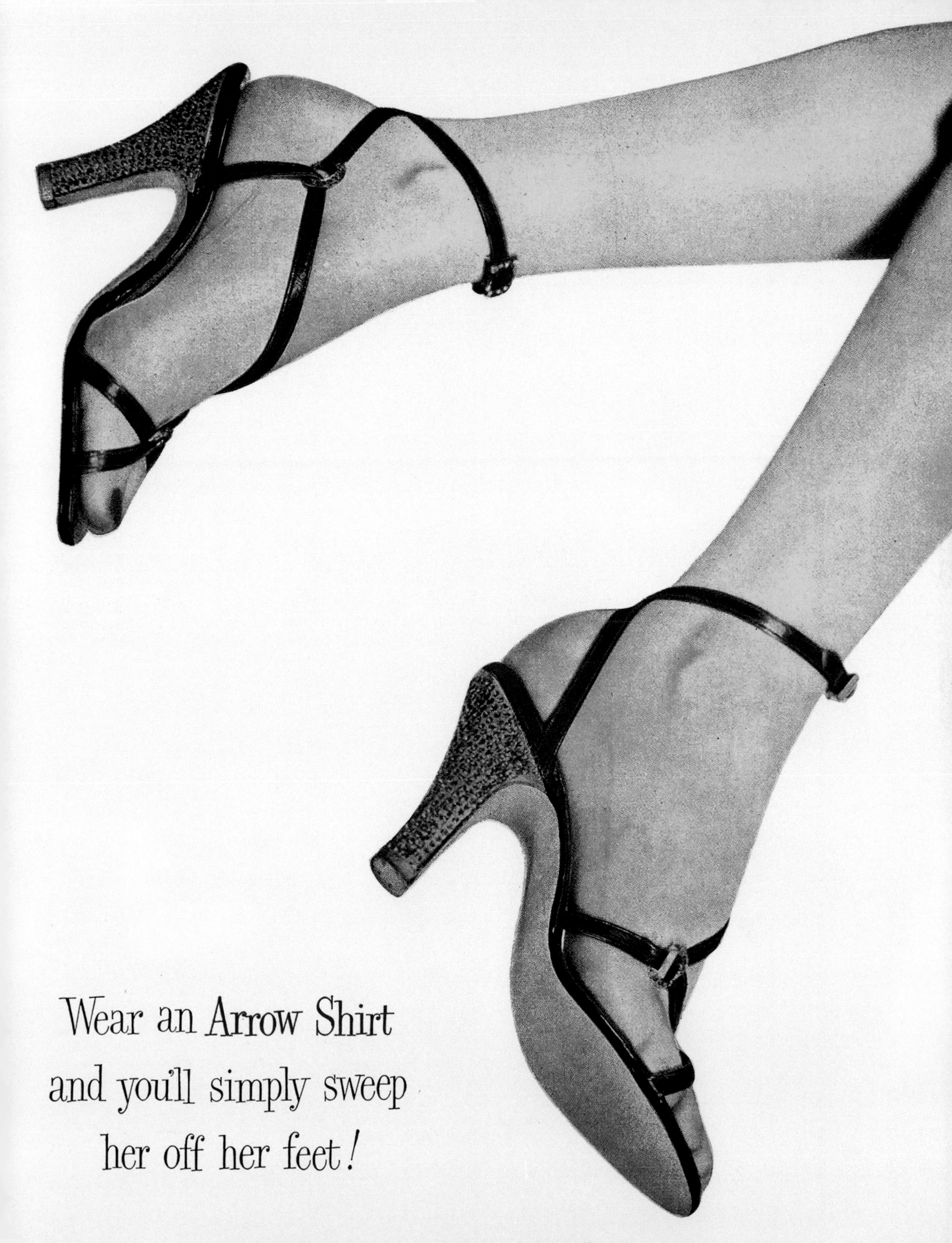
Wear an Arrow Shirt
and you'll simply sweep
her off her feet!

INTERNATIONAL NEWS
the next time you see Paris!
this is what you'll see
...this wonderful sight... this most thrilling new Jantzen Parisian swim suit, the "Dinard"... beautiful from every angle... and dramatic from every viewpoint... unquestionably the swim suit of the year. The Jantzen-Paris studio plotted it in Warshfast glamorous Lastex®-powered figure-controlling faille... and added fabulous Jantzen shaping magic deliberately to make a body wonderful-looking... in or out of water. Black and white, blue and mauve, brown and pink 19.95... from the fabulous Jantzen "international set" collection ... at leading stores.
(prices in U.S.A.)
Jantzen®
makes all girls gorgeous

for romancin'...
and entrancin'
...there's nothing like a Jantzen!
for that matter there's nothing like a Jantzen for swimming and slimming... nothing like the way a Jantzen fits, feels and looks... nothing like the wonderful figure-making job a Jantzen does... nothing like the marvelous Jantzen swim suit fabrics... in particular, Jantzen Nylastic, the magic-moulding fast-drying special Jantzen blend of nylon and laton, the finest swim suit fabric ever made. Girl's suit, detailed for romance, with marvelous Jantzen mouldable Stay-Bra 15.95... man's speed-cut racers 5.95... terrific colors for everybody... at most stores.
Jantzen
Nylastic
nylon-with-laton
swim suits
Matching Jantzen swim caps and Jandals in stunning pastels

Sweethearts in Swimsuits
For you...
and the one who
makes your
temperature rise...
Catalina look-alike
swimsuits!
Shown here—
a fabulous
Signature Fabric
from the land of
the Pharaohs.
See Catalina
Sweetheart Sets
also in Clansman's Plaid,
Dalmatian and
other fascinating
patterns.
Ladies' swimsuit:
Pharaoh's Darling—$10.95.
Men's sport set:
Sudan shirt—$6.95;
Sudan 3-row boxer—$4.95.
For name of nearest store, write: Sweethearts, Catalina, Inc., 443 So. San Pedro Los Angeles 13
© Catalina, Inc., a division of Julius KAYSER & Company hosiery • lingerie • gloves
Catalina
Tan with Tartan

Jantzen Swimwear, 1956 ◂

In the late '40s and early '50s, postwar couturiers and designers opened for business in Paris, re-establishing the city as a center for fashion. In this ad, Jantzen, known for its pinup- and sports-themed ads, took a different approach by emphasizing Parisian design and high-fashion sense.

In den späten 40ern und frühen 50ern eröffneten die Couturiers und Designer der Nachkriegsära Läden in Paris und machten die Stadt wieder zu einem Zentrum der Mode. In dieser Anzeige schlägt der für seine von Pin-ups und Sportthemen bekannte Hersteller Jantzen ungewohnte Töne an und betont das Pariser Design und hochmodische Eleganz.

A la fin des années 40 et au début des années 50, les couturiers et les créateurs de l'après-guerre s'installèrent à Paris, redorant le blason de la ville en tant que capitale de la mode. Dans cette publicité, la marque Jantzen, réputée pour ses visuels à pin-up ou thèmes sportifs, adopta une approche différente mettant en avant la création parisienne et le style haute couture.

Jantzen Swimwear, 1951

Catalina Swimwear, 1955

▸ Rose Marie Reid Swimwear, 1958

After the utilitarian ads of the war years, companies like Rose Marie Reid returned to presenting their products with an emphasis on the art of the ad and the beauty of the design.

Nach den nutzenorientierten Anzeigen der Kriegsjahre kehrten Firmen wie Rose Marie Reid dazu zurück, ihre Produkte wieder kunstvoll und mit Betonung auf das Design zu präsentieren.

Après les publicités utilitaires des années de guerre, des entreprises comme Rose Marie Reid revinrent au côté artistique et à la beauté graphique pour présenter leurs produits.

Catalina Swimwear, 1958

CROWN JEWELS OF THE SEA
Deliberately more than elegant, deliberately less than exotic... the damask-like, dress-like beauty of elasticized brocade in this dress sheath, Cameo. 25.00
Rose Marie Reid
LIMITED EDITIONS

Warm & Sunny
When It's Icy Cold

Maidenform Bras, 1956

Maidenform first dreamed up its "I dreamed" campaign in 1949. This 1956 ad recalls the 1943 Howard Hughes film *The Outlaw*, famous as much for Jane Russell's breakout performance as for the bra Hughes had his engineers design for the actress. Russell never wore the bra and the film was repeatedly banned until 1947.

Maidenform hatte sich die „I dreamed"-Kampagne schon 1949 ausgedacht. Diese Anzeige von 1956 erinnert an Howard Hughes Film *Geächtet* von 1943, der für Jane Russells Durchbruch ebenso verantwortlich war wie für den BH, den Hughes für die Schauspielerin hatte konstruieren lassen. Russell hat den BH niemals getragen und der Film wurde bis 1947 mehrmals verboten.

Maidenform inventa sa campagne « I dreamed » en 1949. Cette publicité de 1956 rappelle *Le Banni*, film d'Howard Hughes sorti en 1943, aussi célèbre pour avoir révélé Jane Russell que pour le fameux soutien-gorge conçu par les ingénieurs à la demande de Hughes. Jane Russell ne le porta jamais et le film subit plusieurs interdictions en salles avant sa sortie en 1947.

Borgana Furs, 1951 ◂

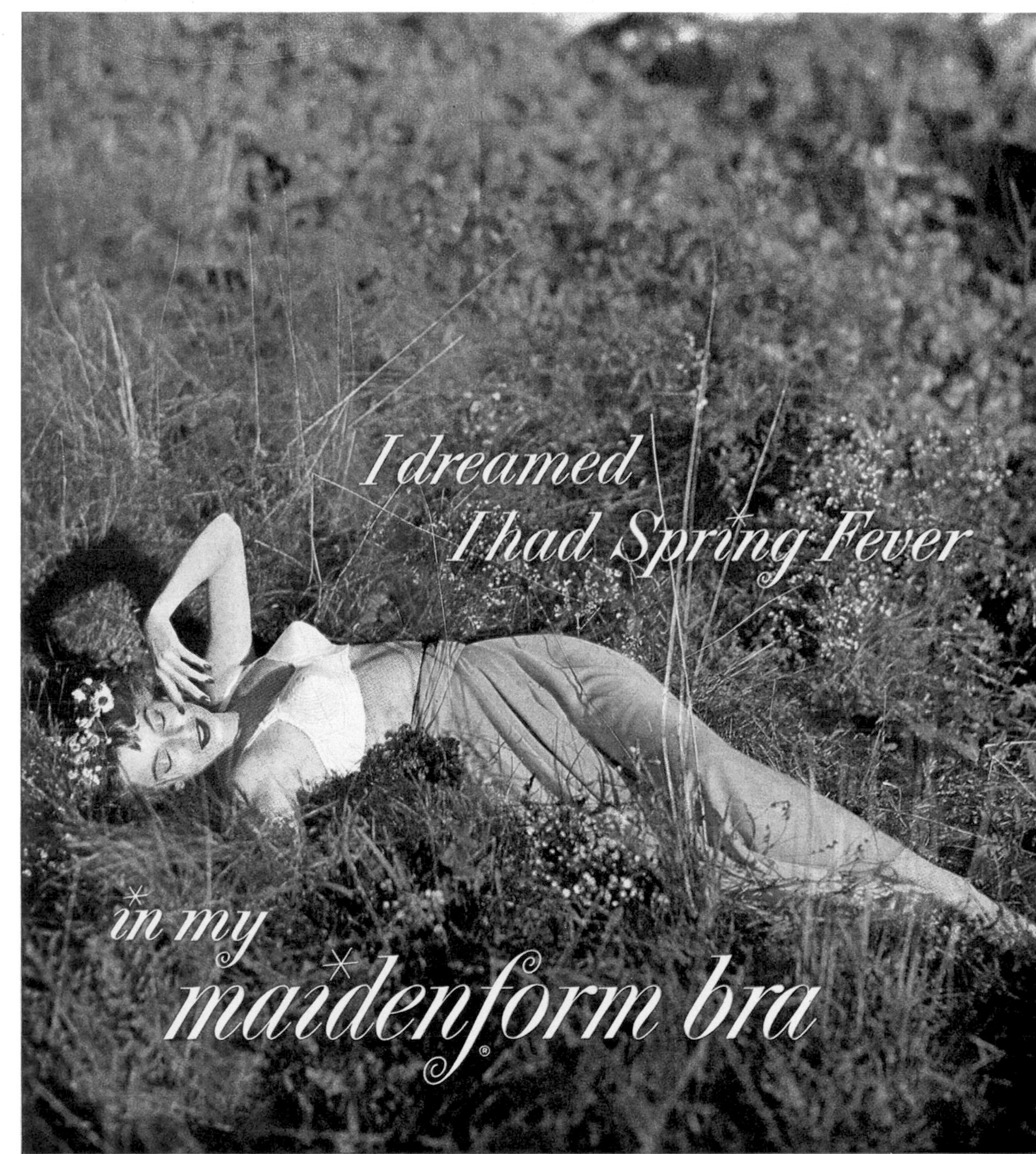

For the figure of your fondest day-dreams—Maidenform's lovely new Concerto* gives you curves that are more curvaceous, brings an exciting line to your outline! And it's all accomplished with row upon row of tiny, interlocked stitches! Each stitch catches up an inner cup-lining, pre-shapes this bra *just* enough to mould a fabulous form! In white stitched broadcloth, lace-margined. AA, A, B and C sizes...2.00

*REG. U.S. PAT. OFF. ©1956 MAIDEN FORM BRASSIERE CO., INC.

JULIUS GARFINCKEL & CO.

IN THE NATION'S CAPITAL

JO COPELAND OF PATTULLO DRAMATIZES THE IRREGULAR-PEPLUM SHEATH WITH BAS-RELIEF OF JET EMBROIDERY. BRONZE GREEN SILK SATIN.

ALSO AT DE PINNA, N. Y

Julius Garfinckel & Co. Department Store/Pattullo-Jo Copeland, 1954

► Maidenform Bras, 1956

I dreamed I was a Work of Art in my *maidenform* bra®*

PORTRAIT OF A LADY in a Maidenform masterpiece: the new Pre-Lude Once-Over Six-Way. Lifts your curves, snugs in your waist, moulds a fabulous figure! With "quick-change" six-way straps, to move or remove for every fashionable neckline. White cotton broadcloth, A, B and C cups...8.95

PRE-LUDE, ONCE-OVER AND SIX-WAY ALL ARE REGISTERED TRADEMARKS © MAIDEN FORM BRASSIERE CO., INC., NEW YORK 16

Flip yourself into a Jantzen Reversible!

this
becomes
this

Two swim trunks for the price of one—all you have to do is flip these remarkable reversibles inside out, and you have a brand new pattern!
One side features a smart checked cotton, the other side a solid color. If you like tartans (and who doesn't?), the authentic imported clan patterns are great. Of course they, too, are solid color when flipped inside out.
Many wonderful color combinations. All in sizes 28 to 36. Just $5.95.
Jantzen
Jantzen Inc., Portland, Oregon

Jantzen Swimwear, 1956

▸ Jantzen Swimwear, 1955

torso-oh!
thanks
to Jantzen
"shapemakery"
"torso-oh" is any girl's torso under the influence of Jantzen "shapemakery", wonderful new figuremaking technique that transforms any girl into a bathing beauty complete with the new higher bustline, the new long-body look, the always glamorous slim waist and exciting curves. "Shapemakery" is an exclusive Jantzen feature, combines the best swim suit bras with the best torso control, on the job all the time. "On the dot" left and "fine line" right have marvelous Jantzen "stay-bras", come in ®Lastex-powered faille with ®Celaperm dots, dream colors 16.95.
®Jantzen
most beautiful
most beautifying
swim suits in the world
Jantzen swim caps in heavenly Jantzen swim suit colors 1.50

Manhattan Ties, 1953

Postwar tie motifs ranged from the whimsical – Western imagery, pinup girls, tropical beaches – to the art-inspired. Geometric patterns inspired by Art Deco became popular, as did ties featuring the work of famous artists such as Salvador Dalí.

Die Krawattenmotive der Nachkriegszeit reichten von skurril – Westernszenen, Pin-up-Girls und tropische Strände – bis hin zu künstlerisch. Geometrische Muster im Stil des Art Déco waren ebenso beliebt wie die Werke berühmter Künstler wie Salvador Dalí.

Après la guerre, les motifs de cravate allaient des plus fantaisistes – imagerie western, pin-up, plages tropicales – aux plus artistiques. La mode était aux motifs géométriques d'inspiration Art Déco, ainsi qu'aux cravates reproduisant les œuvres d'artistes célèbres comme Salvador Dalí.

Arrow Shirts and Ties, 1950 ◂

new school of design in ties

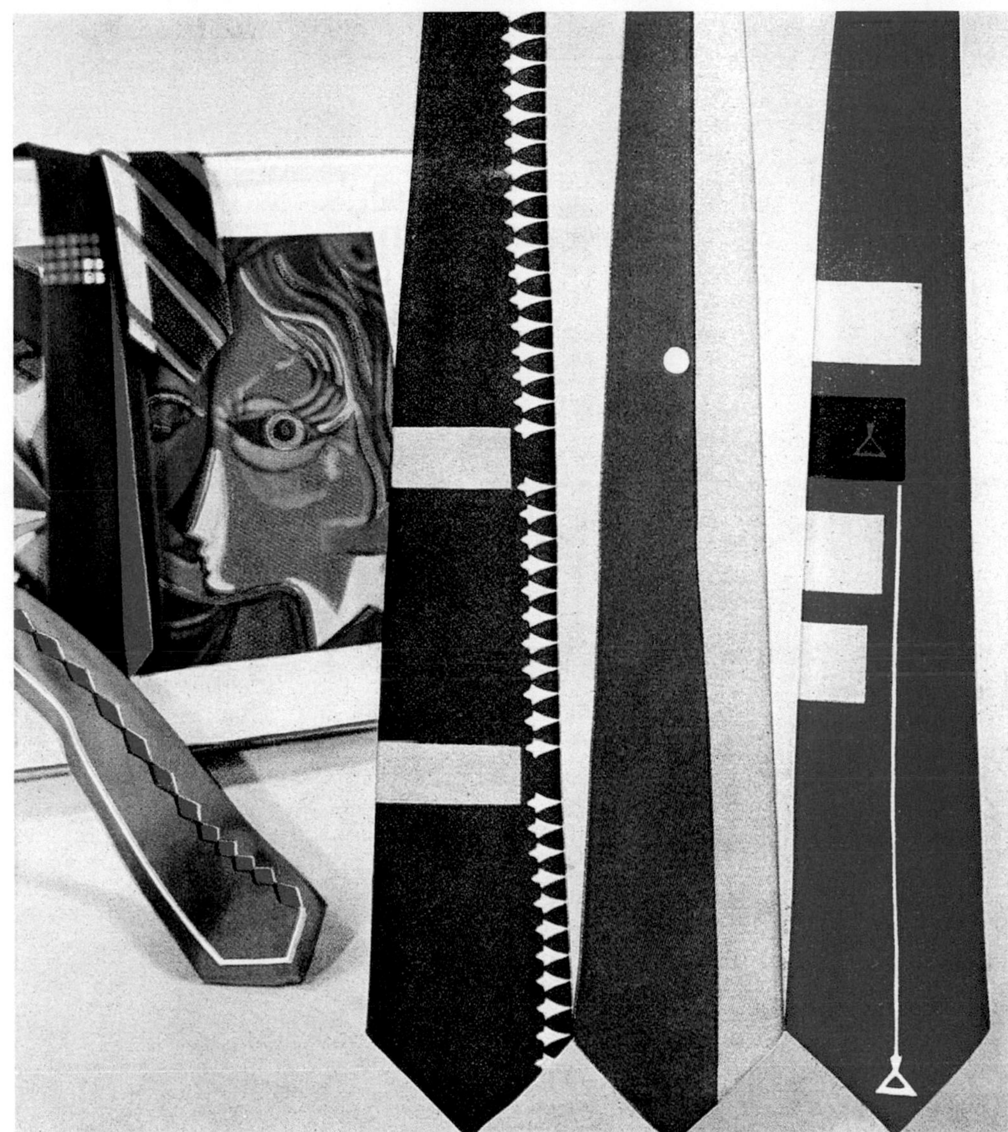

"side glances"

Manhattan combines the conservative and the unusual in a refreshing new note in printed acetate foulard neckwear. These new "Side Glance" ties offer distinctive designs—with the focus of interest on one side of the tie! In a wide array of color combinations—from bright to subdued.

styled by

SIDE GLANCES NECKWEAR, $1.50
OTHERS TO $3.50

©1953, THE MANHATTAN SHIRT CO., 444 MADISON AVENUE, NEW YORK, N. Y.

Uncanny—the way you can almost pick these life-like spring designs right off the fabric. Your whole outlook will brighten when you add a touch of spring to *your* wardrobe with any of these striking, *exclusive* Spring Shadow ties—by *Manhattan*. Eight unique designs—right from nature—in printed foulards. Your choice of a broad range of pastel colors.
Manhattan ®
Spring Shadows Neckwear, $1.50
© 1953, THE MANHATTAN SHIRT CO., 444 MADISON AVENUE, NEW YORK, N.Y.

WESTMINSTER SOCKS
SCORE WITH MEN

Sure they do! Westminster puts everything a man desires in their socks...

● QUALITY—the finest of yarns... expertly manufactured!

● STYLE—Striking patterns adapted to the fashions.

● COLOR—Assorted shades so popular for the fall season.

● PRICE—Just right for discriminating men —55¢ to $2.95.

WESTMINSTER, LTD.

EMPIRE STATE BUILDING · NEW YORK 1, N. Y.

SAN FRANCISCO 3
86 THIRD STREET
LOS ANGELES 14
629 SOUTH HILL STREET

CHICAGO 7
855 MERCHANDISE MART
BOSTON 11
38 CHAUNCY STREET

Westminster
FAMOUS AMERICAN SOCKS

for
closer
harmony

Hit a new high note with lustrous "Symphony-in-Satin" ties—music-making patterns in concert with your wardrobe . . . with your mood. If it's brass you need . . . on with the trumpets. Or for heartstring stuff . . . bring up the violins. Composed with Van Heusen skill . . . in fine fabrics that stay knotable . . . stay in shape. Makes sweet Christmas music, too, **$1.50**

Other Van Heusen ties, $1 to $2.50

Van Heusen REG. T. M.
symphony-in-satin ties

Phillips-Jones Corp., New York 1, N. Y., Makers of Van Heusen Shirts • Sport Shirts • Ties • Pajamas • Collars

Center-stitched with Nylon thread for utmost resiliency

Westminster Socks, 1950

Van Heusen Ties, 1950

Manhattan Ties, 1950 ◂

there is only one
Pendleton Sportswear
always virgin wool
Gather your new Pendleton Skirts
For you . . . four distinctive virgin wool fabrics colorful as autumn's leaves . . . four branch-slim skirts tailored in the simple, flattering lines of good fashion that smart women always admire in a genuine Pendleton! Plan to gather this whole new skirt wardrobe soon, each but $12.95 . . . with full-fashioned Pendleton sweaters in companion colors, from $8.95.
Ted Rand

For descriptive literature, in full color, on Pendleton Sportswear, write Dept. D-6, Pendleton Woolen Mills • Portland, Oregon

Pendleton Sportswear, 1956

Dior's New Look dominated women's silhouettes in the 1950s, but it was not women's only fashion option. Pencil skirts and figure-hugging sweaters were also in vogue. Pendleton got its start in the 19th century as a wool mill based in the United States' Pacific Northwest. The company branched into women's apparel in 1949 and saw instant success with its "49er" jacket

Diors New Look dominierte die Silhouetten der Damen in den 1950ern, aber er war nicht die einzige modische Option für die Frauen damals. Bleistiftröcke und figurnahe Pullover waren ebenso en vogue. Pendleton hatte im 19. Jahrhundert als Wollspinnerei mit Sitz im Nordwesten der USA begonnen. Das Unternehmen begann 1949 mit Damenbekleidung und erzielte mit seiner Jacke „49er" auch sofort einen Erfolg.

Le New Look de Dior domina la mode féminine dans les années 50, mais les femmes disposaient aussi d'autres options. Les jupes droites et les pulls moulants étaient également en vogue. Après des débuts au 19ème siècle en tant qu'usine de laine au nord de la côte ouest des Etats-Unis, la société Pendleton se diversifia dans la mode pour femme en 1949 et remporta un succès immédiat avec sa veste « 49er ».

► Hart Schaffner & Marx Menswear, 1950

The suit that *looks* right and *feels* right
when you first try it on is most likely the
one that will be best for you. A suit that fits
will conform to your figure without any strain
anywhere, whether you're sitting, standing or
stretching. How can you find such a suit? Go to
the dealer who sells Hart Schaffner & Marx clothes.
He not only wants to find the right suit for you . . . he
is best able to do so. He is able to select from the 253
different combinations of sizes and shapes that we make.
This is the famous Pan American suit in the three-button, patch-pocket model. There are, of course, other models, patterns and colors.
HART SCHAFFNER & MARX®

Don't Settle for Less!
Feel like a million!
Why accept less when you can be sure of complete comfort with Jockey Underwear! It fits snug as your skin, moves as you move, gives you positive masculine support. Look for the mark, "Y-Front," on the garment—it's your assurance that you're getting the famous Coopers product—and one of many reasons why Jockey gives you a real lift. See your dealer soon—be "Hip-Taped" for perfect fit—then do as millions do—feel like a million in Jockey brand Underwear!
Comfort for Your Every Need—for Every Occasion
Jockey Shorts for active sports
Jockey Midway for everyday wear
Jockey Over-Knee for upper-leg protection
Jockey Longs for full-leg protection
Jockey Bellin for dress-up wear
WEAR
Jockey*
Underwear made ONLY by
Coopers*
The Famous Brand of Knit Support Underwear
Licensees: Canada, J. R. Moodie; Australia, Speedo Knitting Mills; Scotland, Lyle & Scott; New Zealand, Lane, Walker, Rudkin; Switzerland, Vollmoeller; France, Verdier; Colombia, Textiles Ego; Italy, Sacit; Austria, Poeschl; Denmark, Taco; South Africa, Ninian & Lester.
*®Coopers, Inc., Kenosha, Wis.
JOCKEY Y FRONT

Munsingwear Boxer Shorts, 1951

Munsingwear Boxer Shorts, 1951

Jockey Underwear, 1950 ◂

SATEEN STRIPE
SEERSUCKER PLAID
SANDBAR DENIM
MIGNONNE CHAMBRAY
MIGNONNE CHAMBRAY
Serbin
OF FLORIDA
designs this sweater dress in Avondale Plaid: grey, blue or coral; 8-18, about $25. At stores listed on opposite page.
DUBLIN BRIGHT
BRITEWEAVE
SANDBAR DENIM
The liveliest colors in cottons
AVONDALE
PERMA-PRESSED® COTTONS—Little or no ironing
A joy to see, to wear . . . Avondale Cottons in Companion Colors to mix and match to your heart's content. And these lively colors stay fresh and bright through suds and sun. Upkeep is easy, Avondale Cottons are Perma-Pressed for wash and wear with little or no ironing. So look for the Avondale tag on the smartest clothes . . . like this Serbin fashion, for instance. By-the-yard, too, at popular prices. At fine stores.
Sew your own with McCall Pattern No. 3289. Avondale Cottons are guaranteed to be as represented. If for any reason you are not satisfied, we will replace fabric or refund purchase price. Avondale Mills, Comer Building, Birmingham, Alabama.

Avondale Cottons/Serbin of Florida, 1959

▸ Ship 'n Shore Blouses, 1953

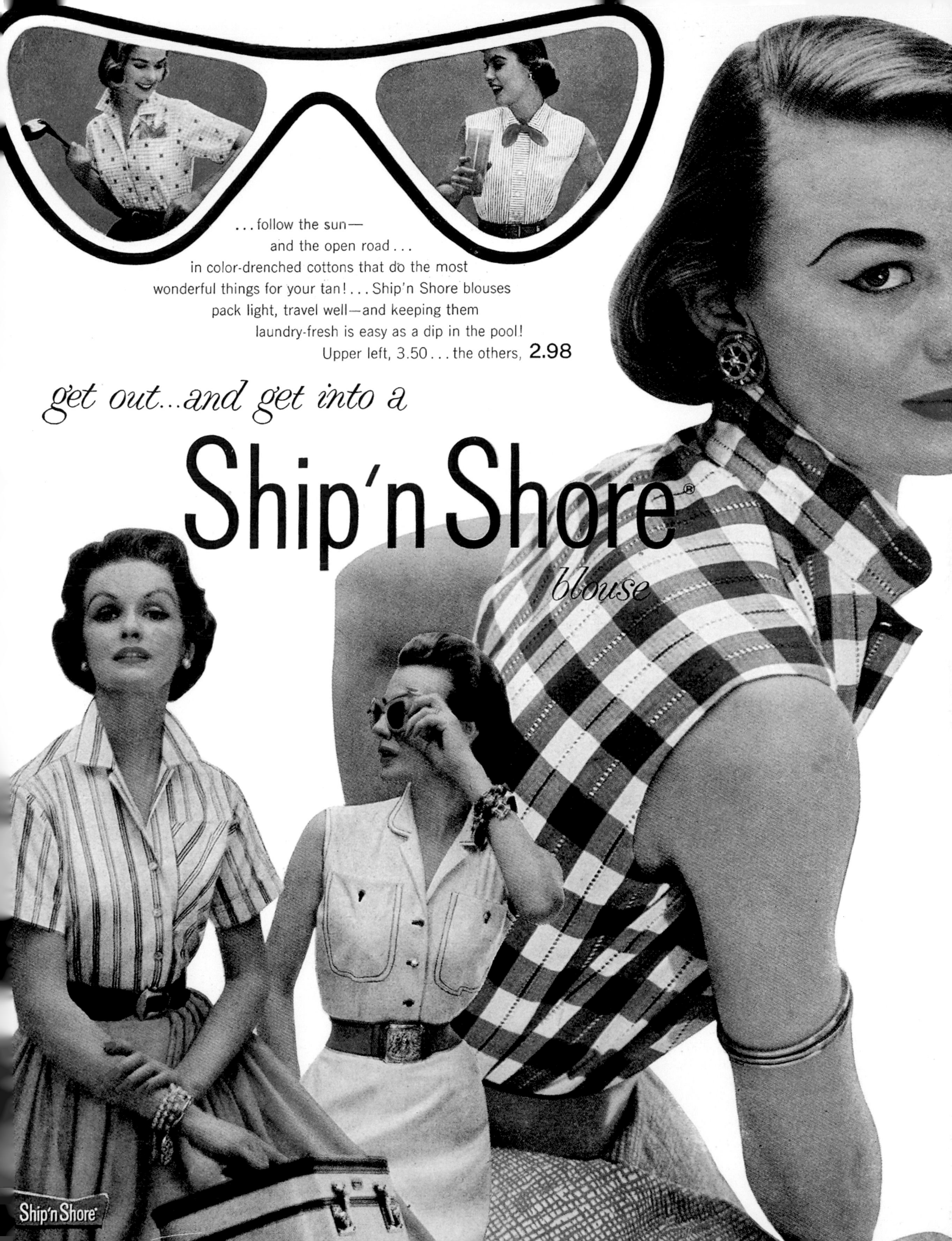
. . . follow the sun—
and the open road . . .
in color-drenched cottons that do the most
wonderful things for your tan! . . . Ship'n Shore blouses
pack light, travel well—and keeping them
laundry-fresh is easy as a dip in the pool!
Upper left, 3.50 . . . the others, 2.98
get out...and get into a
Ship'n Shore®
blouse
Ship'n Shore

SEE HOW LITTLE TRED-LITES COST FOR THE ENTIRE FAMILY

Surprisingly less than you'd expect! The whole family can step out together and stay within the budget . . . in these carefree casuals that put a soft, deep-yielding cushion between your foot and the ground. In many styles and many colors . . . for work and play . . . shoes that wear a long, long time and cost so very little.

Prices slightly higher Denver West

Tred-Lite®

by Cambridge

CAMBRIDGE RUBBER COMPANY, CAMBRIDGE, MASS.

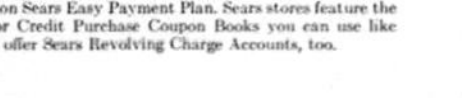

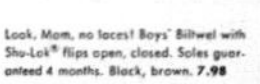

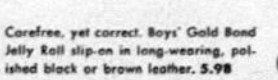

Sears, Roebuck and Co. Department Store, 1951

In the years following World War II, America saw a surge in births, known as the baby boom. Savvy retailers and manufacturers saw the soaring birthrate as a sign to start catering to families by adding more kid-focused products to their mix.

In den Jahren nach dem Zweiten Weltkrieg erlebte Amerika eine steigende Geburtenrate, den sogenannten Babyboom. Kluge Einzelhändler und Produzenten nahmen den Trend als Startsignal, um sich Familien anzudienen, indem sie mehr kindgerechte Produkte in ihr Sortiment aufnahmen.

Pendant l'après-guerre, les Etats-Unis connurent une recrudescence des naissances, le fameux baby-boom. Les détaillants et les fabricants les plus avisés virent dans cette explosion du taux de natalité un signe afin d'élarger leur collection d'articles pour enfant.

Tred-Lite Shoes, 1954 ◂

1
2
3
4

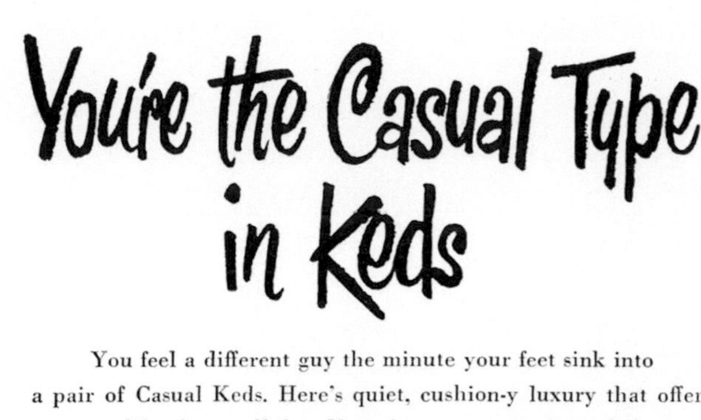

You're the Casual Type
in Keds

You feel a different guy the minute your feet sink into
a pair of Casual Keds. Here's quiet, cushion-y luxury that offers
a life of ease all day. Your feet are on an air-cooled
vacation in these summery shoes that breathe when you walk.
And they come in so many handsome styles and colors—
all washable—you can wear Keds everywhere!

BOOSTERS
Brown, Blue, Natural,
Faded Blue Denim, Maine Brown,
Maize, Green, Claret.
BAREFOOT SANDALS
Team these with shorts, or slacks.
Instep straps woven with
Lastex. Maize, Claret.
DENIM SLIP-ONS
Instep gores made with Lastex
cling yet never bind.
Brown or Faded Blue Denim.
LOOP-TIES
Town smoothies, are right at home
in the country, too.
Maine Brown, Blue, Green.

CLEAT-TRED OXFORDS
Slipproof soles for campus or golf.
Maine Brown, Sand.
U.S. Keds®
The Shoes of Champions–They Wash
GORE CASUALS
Just slip them on—
they're eased with Lastex.
Maine Brown or Blue.
UNITED STATES RUBBER COMPANY
Rockefeller Center, New York

Keds Shoes, 1951

Mansfield Shoes, 1957 ◄

Perma-Lift Brassieres, 1957

Christian Dior, creator of the New Look, once said, "Without foundation, there can be no fashion." Although Dior's look was most often associated with the wasp waist, most women wore some sort of foundation garment, such as long-leg panty girdles. At the time of this ad, two new developments were just a few years off: pantyhose and Lycra, both introduced in 1959.

Christian Dior, der Erfinder des New Look, sagte einmal: „Keine Mode ohne Mieder." Obwohl man mit Diors Look am häufigsten die Wespentaille assoziiert, trugen die meisten Frauen eine Art Basiskleidung darunter, ein Miederhöschen mit langem Bein. Zum Zeitpunkt dieser Anzeige waren zwei Neuentwicklungen nur noch wenige Jahre entfernt: die Strumpfhose und Lycra, die beide 1959 auf den Markt kamen.

« Sans sous-vêtements, il n'y a pas de mode », dit un jour Christian Dior, le créateur du New Look. Bien que sa silhouette fût plus souvent associée à la taille de guêpe, la plupart des femmes portaient des sous-vêtements de soutien sous une forme ou une autre, tels que les gaines longues. Cette publicité précéda de quelques années deux nouvelles inventions : le collant et le Lycra, tous deux lancés en 1959.

► Peter Pan Brassieres, 1954

NO HELP NEEDED

Your New PERMA·LIFT BARE-BACK Bra hooks in front—so quick—so easy

Lucky girl—you can forget all about those exasperating struggles with elusive back fastenings, for darling, those days of twisting, turning, reaching are all behind you. This chic new "Perma·lift"* Bare-Back Bra hooks in front—quickly, easily—without fuss or nonsense. And the clever, little hooks will never show—even through your clingiest, slinkiest dress. Be comfortably fitted today.

Style No. 88—Exclusive Criss-Cross** design keeps your Bare-Back Bra comfortably in place always. And Magic Insets in the cups support you from below In Dacron, only $8.95. In "D" cup—$10.00.

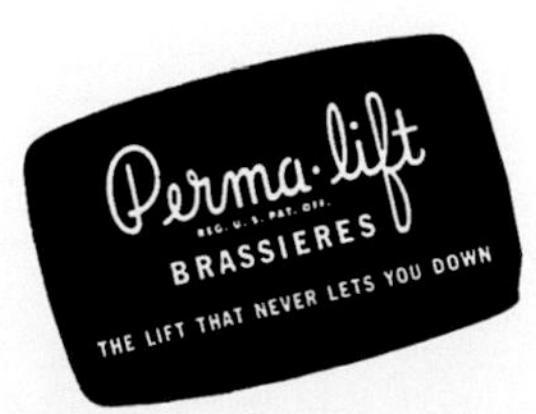

**Reg. U. S. Pat. Off. · **Pat. Applied For · A product of A. Stein & Company · Chicago—New York—Los Angeles* *Prices may be slightly higher west of the Rockies*

7

the genius of Peter Pan shapes a beautiful

None
So
Cool

These are the panties that never get clingy, never feel clammy—even on the warmest days. Cool in Summer, comfortable always, because they're naturally absorbent!

the **KNIT** with the **FIT** where you **SIT**

They g-i-v-e with every motion, really fit your figure—they're made for an active life. Easy to care for, they wash and dry quickly, need no ironing. All panty styles.

PANTIES OF
Spun-lo
RAYON FABRIC
ONLY ABOUT 69¢

NDUSTRIAL RAYON CORPORATION,

Frederick's of Hollywood Lingerie, 1951

Frederick's of Hollywood was founded in 1946 by Frederick Mellinger. The company nurtured its racy image for many years in advertisements, catalogs, and stores. Only recently has the lingerie maker scaled back its provocative ads to compete with much-larger rival Victoria's Secret.

Frederick's of Hollywood wurde 1946 von Frederick Mellinger gegründet. Jahrelang förderte die Firma ihr gewagtes Image mit Anzeigen, Katalogen und in ihren Läden. Erst kürzlich hat der Dessous-Hersteller seine provokativen Anzeigen zurückgefahren, um mit dem viel größeren Konkurrenten Victoria's Secret mithalten zu können.

Frederick Mellinger fonda l'entreprise Frederick's of Hollywood en 1946. Pendant de nombreuses années, elle se distingua par son image pleine de verve à travers ses publicités, ses catalogues et ses points de vente. Face à la concurrence de son imposant rival Victoria's Secret, le fabricant de lingerie a récemment décidé d'atténuer son image provocante.

Spun-Lo Underwear, 1954

► Warner's Lingerie, 1956

#952-953, with strong leno elastic sides, a down-stretching satin elastic back. White or Pink, $16.50. The bra—#1045 at $3.95.

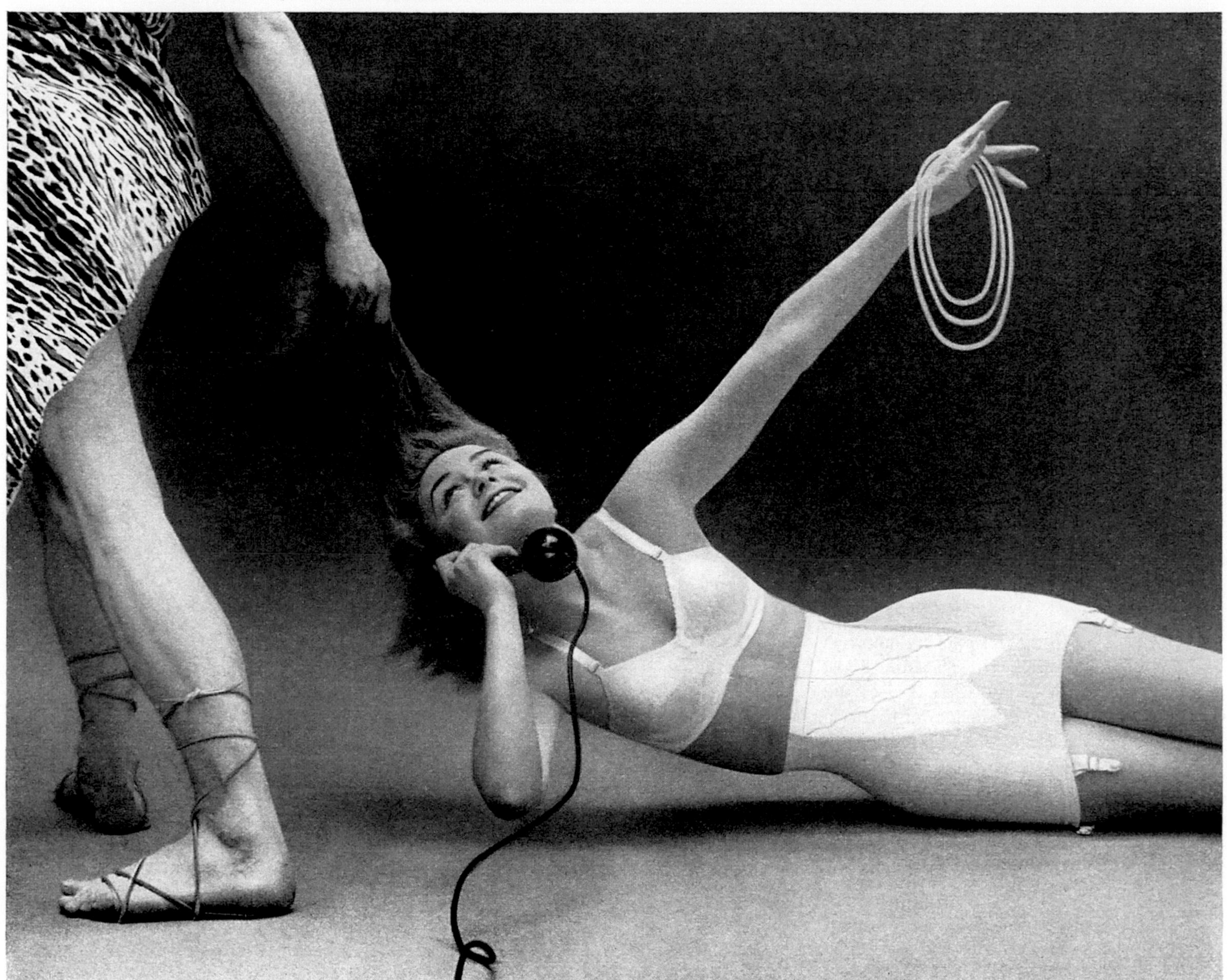

263

Come out of the bone age, darling...

Warner's exclusive new STA-FLAT replaces pokey bones with circular springlets

WARNER'S takes the cave-man manners out of old-fashioned girdles (poke, shove, groan), removes those long front bones that dug into your midriff. Now control's achieved with light springlets pocketed in the girdle's front panel. They're light and flexible—modern as your way of life, sensible as vitamins.

Far better control, too — STA-FLAT gives not just pinpoint support, like old-fashioned bones, but firms a greater area with lively comfort. Bend, breathe, sit . . . STA-FLAT™ moves through the day with you, responds to every movement of your body . . . all with unbelievable lightness. And at the same time, it gives you extra support where you need it most (midriff, waist, tummy).

You don't need to wear armor to be a charmer. Warner's is happy to give the dinosaur his due—but not on you. Come out beautifully, into the light, free whirl of today! At your nicest stores, here and in Canada.

WARNER'S®

Bras • Girdles • Corselettes

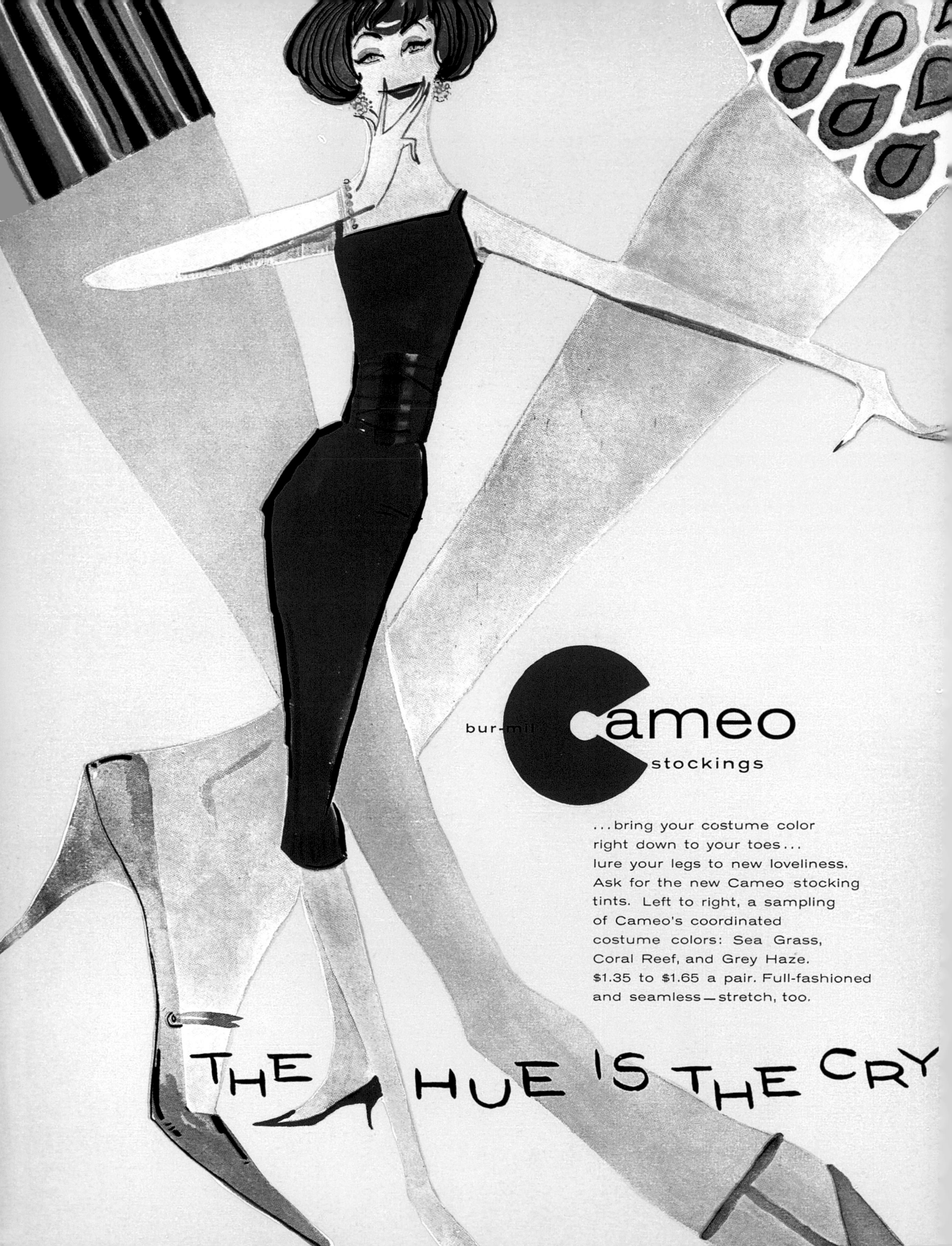
bur-mil Cameo stockings
...bring your costume color right down to your toes... lure your legs to new loveliness. Ask for the new Cameo stocking tints. Left to right, a sampling of Cameo's coordinated costume colors: Sea Grass, Coral Reef, and Grey Haze. $1.35 to $1.65 a pair. Full-fashioned and seamless—stretch, too.
THE HUE IS THE CRY

Galey & Lord Cottons, 1958

The end of the 1950s saw the innovative creations of Cristobal Balenciaga (the baby-doll dress, the cocoon coat, the balloon skirt, and the sack dress), and Pierre Cardin (the bubble dress). Even textile company Galey & Lord, best known for its khaki and denim products, created an unexpected juxtaposition with its more fashion-forward looks.

Am Ende der 1950er standen innovative Kreationen von Pierre Cardin (das Ballonkleid) und Cristobal Balenciaga (das Babydoll-Kleid, der Kokonmantel, der Ballonrock und das Sackkleid). Selbst das Textilunternehmen Galey & Lord, das vor allem für seine Khaki- und Jeansprodukte bekannt war, schuf mit seinen stärker modeorientierten Looks ein überraschendes Nebeneinander.

La fin des années 50 fut le témoin des créations innovantes de Pierre Cardin (la robe bulle) et de Cristobal Balenciaga (la robe baby-doll, le manteau cocon, la jupe boule et la robe sac). Même le fabricant textile Galey & Lord, surtout connu pour ses produits en toile et en denim, créa la surprise en proposant des looks plus tendance.

Cameo Stockings, 1958 ◄

blazing
cottons
Galey & Lord
GALEY and LORD, A MEMBER OF BURLINGTON INDUSTRIES
Burlington

266

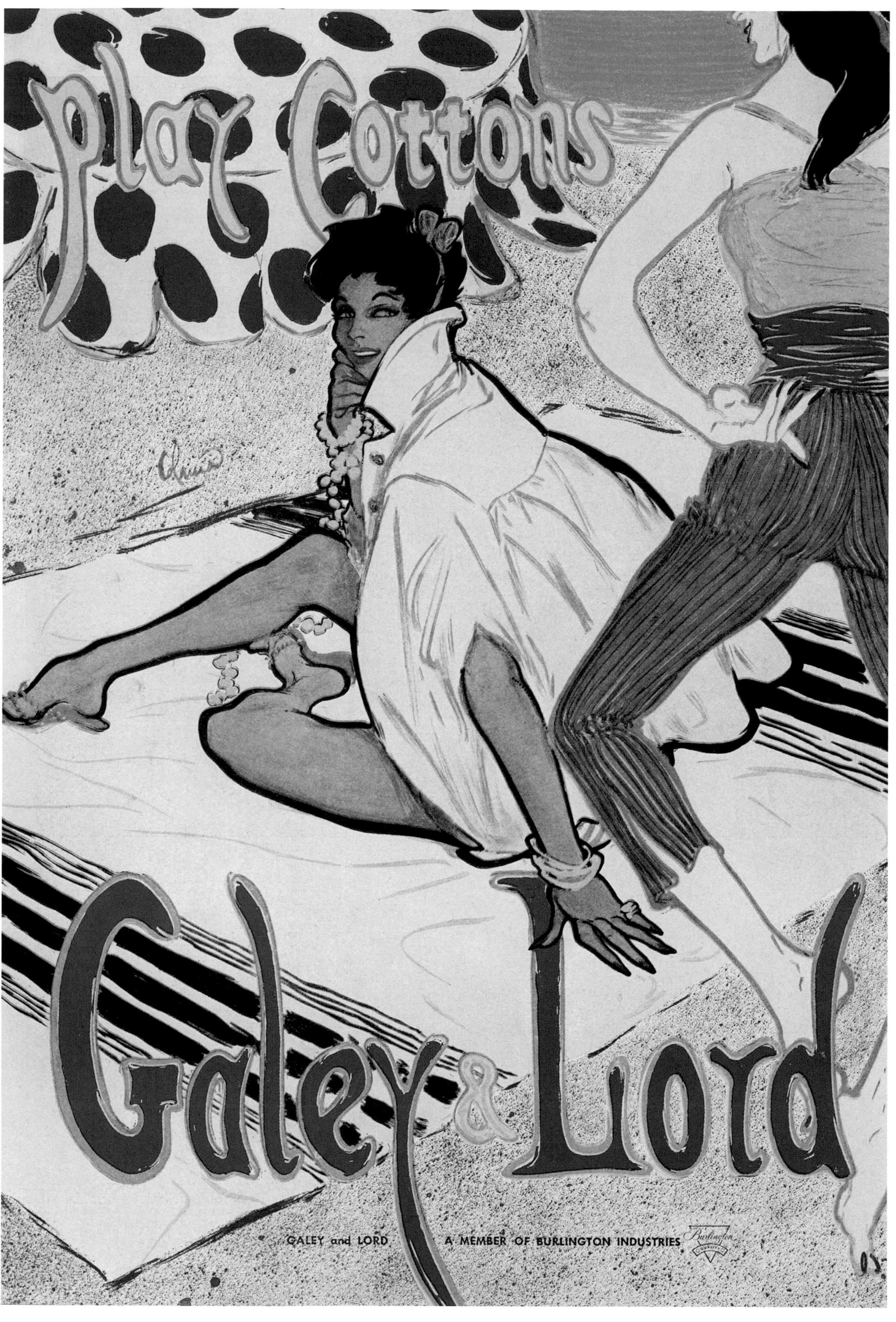

Galey & Lord Cottons, 1956

▸ Tussy Medicare, 1959

Morrow

Put some romance in your "loaf life"!

ARROW

Bali Cay

Whether you're taking a cruise to the Caribbean or just a week-end jaunt to the beach, do it with a splash! Add some *color* to the landscape; pick up an armful of Arrow *Bali Cays!*

These beauties are as colorful as a coral reef… and just as washable! They come in big, splashy patterns and small, neat designs in both cotton and rayon fabrics. In short or long sleeves. And all have the amazing Arafold Collar. Prices about $4.50 and up. (Subject to government regulation.) See *Bali Cay* at your Arrow dealer's now!

Cluett, Peabody & Co., Inc., Arrow Shirts • Sports Shirts • Ties • Handkerchiefs • Underwear.

Arrow Shirts, 1952

Hawaiian shirts had a history dating back to the 1930s, but the '50s interest in kitsch – plus the thousands of U.S. veterans' experiences while stationed in Polynesia – helped popularize the Aloha shirt back on the mainland.

Die Geschichte der Hawaiihemden reichte bis in die 1930er Jahre zurück, doch die Begeisterung der 50er für Kitsch – plus die Erinnerungen Tausender US-Veteranen, die in Polynesien stationiert gewesen waren – verhalfen dem Aloha-Shirt zu neuer Beliebtheit auf dem amerikanischen Festland.

L'histoire de la chemise hawaïenne remonte aux années 30, mais l'intérêt des années 50 pour le kitsch – et le retour de milliers de vétérans américains de Polynésie – contribua au renouveau de la chemise Aloha sur le continent.

► Van Heusen Shirts, 1951

►► McGregor Sportswear, 1959

a feast for the eyes!
What more could a man ask for! Just one touch of new, soft, smooth, Vanuana Sport Shirts and you'll be humming "Sweet Leilani" all season long. As luxurious and rich-looking as a tropical paradise . . . as cool and exciting as a night in Waikiki. Sixteen bright, solid, South Sea colors that dance before your eyes. Short sleeves. $3.65 or long sleeves. $4.50.
Phillips-Jones Corp., N. Y. 1, N. Y., Makers of Van Heusen Shirts • Sport Shirts • Ties • Pajamas • Handkerchiefs • Collars
Van Heusen
REG. T. M.
Vanuana sport shirts
VAN HEUSEN
VAN HEUSEN
Fashion Academy Award 1951

Nylon Fleece by
PRINCETON-Knit
WARM, LIGHTWEIGHT, WASHABLE!
Rich colors from the Land of the Midnight Sun . . . Arctic-tested fabrics . . . luxurious linings that seal in body heat—snug out Winter's worst. FABULOUS NEW FASHIONS—masculine, brawny coats for feather-weight warmth—action-free comfort—wash 'n' wear easy care and economy.
Nylfleece Icelander—warmest nylon fleece, knit collar and cuffs. Lining of quilted nylon. $29.95. Washable Polon Bardu Cru-neck Sweater. $10.95.
Mt. Washington Coat—silky-soft nylon fleece reversing to nylon taffeta. Self hood—thick-ribbed, bulk-knit cuffs—Conmatic zipper front. $35.00.
International Ice Bird—richest nylon fleece with bulky-knit attached hood. Rib-knit cuffs, rib-knit insert at waistband ward off winds. $20.00.
Nylon Sea Turtle—elegantly striped nylon fleece reverses to nylon taffeta. Unique zipper goes all the way up—forms true turtleneck. $25.00.
McGREGOR* GOES TO THE ENDS OF TH
McGREGOR Sportswear Also boy-sized, boy-priced. McGregor-Doniger Inc., 303 5th Ave., New York 16, N.Y. *T.M.

SABENA

BELGIAN *World* AIRLINES

McGregor . . . a new adventure in sportswear. Sabena . . . a new adventure in flying! Daily DC-7C's non-stop to Europe plus helicopter service to the "Heart-of-Paris."

ARTH FOR NEW CLIMATE CONTROL OUTERCOATS...

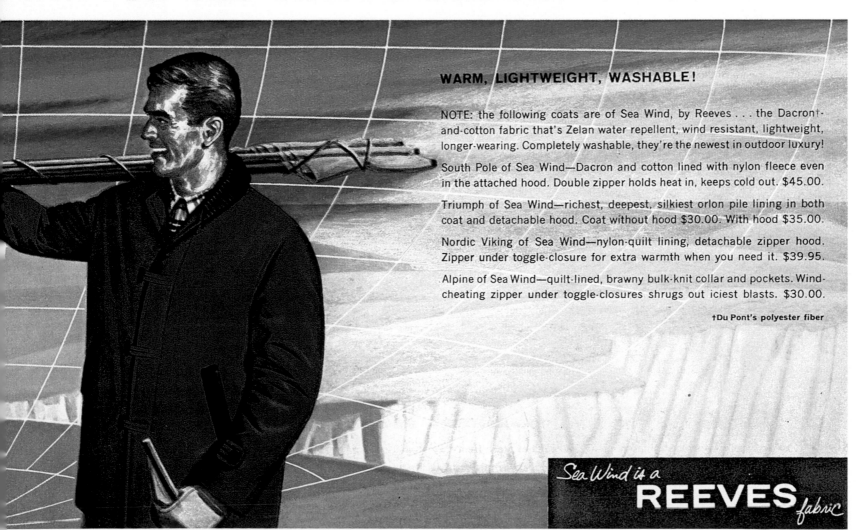

WARM, LIGHTWEIGHT, WASHABLE!

NOTE: the following coats are of Sea Wind, by Reeves . . . the Dacron†-and-cotton fabric that's Zelan water repellent, wind resistant, lightweight, longer-wearing. Completely washable, they're the newest in outdoor luxury!

South Pole of Sea Wind—Dacron and cotton lined with nylon fleece even in the attached hood. Double zipper holds heat in, keeps cold out. $45.00.

Triumph of Sea Wind—richest, deepest, silkiest orlon pile lining in both coat and detachable hood. Coat without hood $30.00. With hood $35.00.

Nordic Viking of Sea Wind—nylon-quilt lining, detachable zipper hood. Zipper under toggle-closure for extra warmth when you need it. $39.95.

Alpine of Sea Wind—quilt-lined, brawny bulk-knit collar and pockets. Wind-cheating zipper under toggle-closures shrugs out iciest blasts. $30.00.

†Du Pont's polyester fiber

Sea Wind is a **REEVES** *fabric*

BY THE MID-'60s, NEW SILHOUETTES PIONEERED BY CARDIN AND BALENCIAGA WERE MODERNIZING WOMEN'S FASHION. ANDRÉ COURRÈGES LAUNCHED AN ULTRA-MODERN SPACE-THEMED COLLECTION, AND RUDI GERNREICH WAS SOON DEFINING MOD FASHION...

AB MITTE DER SECHZIGER MODERNISIERTEN JEDOCH NEUE SILHOUETTEN, WIE CARDIN UND BALENCIAGA SIE EINGEFÜHRT HATTEN, DIE DAMENMODE. ANDRÉ COURRÈGES PRÄSENTIERTE EINE ULTRAMODERNE KOLLEKTION ZUM THEMA WELTRAUM, WÄHREND RUDI GERNREICH ALSBALD DEN MOD-LOOK DEFINIERTE ...

LES NOUVELLES SILHOUETTES INVENTÉES PAR CARDIN ET BALENCIAGA MODERNISENT LA MODE FÉMININE VERS LE MILIEU DES ANNÉES 60. ANDRÉ COURRÈGES LANCE UNE COLLECTION ULTRAMODERNE À THÈME SPATIAL, ET RUDI GERNREICH JETTE LES BASES DE LA TENDANCE MOD...

FROM CAMELOT TO THE SPACE AGE

VON CAMELOT INS WELTRAUMZEITALTER

DE L'ÂGE D'OR AU SPACE AGE

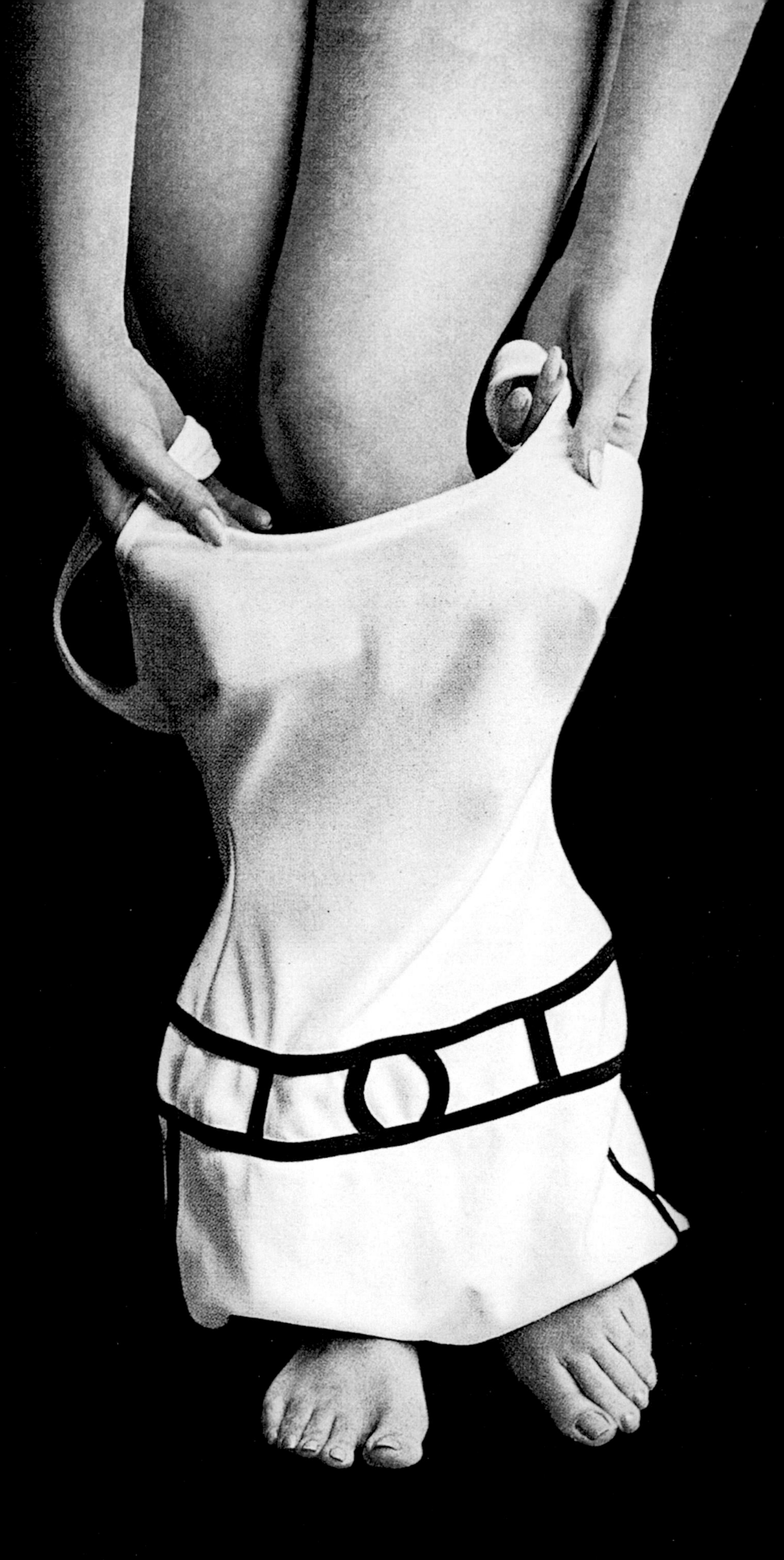

Oleg Cassini for Peter Pan Swimwear, 1967 ◂◂

Pond's Fresh-Start Cleanser, 1966 ◂

Catalina Swimwear, 1961

JACQUELINE KENNEDY WAS THE STYLISH IDEAL OF THE OPENING YEARS OF THE DECADE. The worldly Jackie was a connoisseur of European couture, but, as America's first lady, she selected an American, Oleg Cassini, to design her wardrobe. Together they became known for simple suits, sheath dresses, pillbox hats, and understated but elegant evening gowns.

At the same time, Audrey Hepburn was both youthful and sophisticated wearing Hubert de Givenchy as Holly Golightly in *Breakfast at Tiffany's*. The "little black dress" had been introduced by Chanel in 1926, but Givenchy's glamorous version inspired the cocktail-party uniform for generations of women.

While the full-skirted look of the 1950s remained fashionable, by the mid-'60s, new silhouettes pioneered by Cardin and Balenciaga were modernizing women's fashion. André Courrèges launched an ultramodern space-themed collection, and Rudi Gernreich was soon defining Mod fashion—notably with his shocking topless swimsuit, the "monokini." Ursula Andress, wearing a white bikini, and Sean Connery, wearing slim suits, set the stylish tone for the first James Bond film, *Dr. No*, released in 1962.

In Europe, Barbara Hulanicki launched Biba's postal boutique catalog, precursor to the iconic London boutique; and Americans got a glimpse of the future of pop music when the Beatles performed on *The Ed Sullivan Show* in 1964.

The decade's fashions—and politics—dramatically changed course in 1965. Model Jean Shrimpton shocked crowds at the Victoria Derby in Melbourne, Australia, by wearing a short skirt and no gloves. Venerable but struggling women's magazine *Cosmopolitan* dramatically and successfully changed its focus when it hired *Sex and the Single Girl* author Helen Gurley Brown as editor-in-chief. And 3,500 U.S. marines arrived in Vietnam, signaling an official start to an ongoing conflict that would soon divide the nation.

Within the year, the National Organization for Women was founded, and counterculture musical *Hair* opened on Broadway. Twiggy, with her slim frame and trademark androgynous haircut, began her modeling career in London as the face of the "Swinging Look," and British designer Mary Quant, inspired

by Courrèges, introduced skirts cut six to seven inches above the knee in her London boutique, Bazaar.

The 1965 film *Dr. Zhivago* sparked a Russian fashion trend, as women donned mid-calf great coats, fur hats, and military boots, which segued seamlessly into Renaissance and Gypsy trends. Women's carefully molded bouffant and flip hairstyles gave way to longer, more natural looks. And younger men opted for longer hair and facial hair. African Americans began to embrace African culture, launching a trend for printed dashiki tunics and natural hairstyles.

And while the second half of the decade was dominated by the youth market and street-inspired fashions, high-end designers continued to redefine the luxury market. Roy Halston Frowick, a former hatmaker, launched his first ready-to-wear collection under the label Halston. Geoffrey Beene, who had launched his women's collection in the early '60s, added menswear to the mix. And, in 1966, Yves Saint Laurent—protégé and successor to Christian Dior—introduced "Le Smoking," his tuxedo cut for women, soon to be followed by his safari collection. His popular suits arrived with women's liberation—women were wearing the pants, and they liked it.

1960

1960 Sales boom for DuPont's Orlon fiber

DuPonts Kunstfaser Orlon verkauft sich sensationell

Les ventes de la fibre Orlon de DuPont explosent

1962 K-mart opens

Eröffnung von K-mart

Ouverture de K-mart

1962 Yves Saint Laurent opens eponymous fashion house

Yves Saint Laurent eröffnet das nach ihm benannte Modehaus

Yves Saint Laurent ouvre sa maison de haute couture éponyme

1963 Audrey Hepburn dons trendsetting little black dress in *Breakfast at Tiffany's*

Audrey Hepburn trägt in *Frühstück bei Tiffany* ein kleines Schwarzes, das einen Trend begründet

Audrey Hepburn lance la mode de la petite robe noire dans *Diamants sur canapé*

JACQUELINE KENNEDY WAR DIE STILIKONE DER ERSTEN JAHRE DIESER DEKADE. Die weltgewandte Jackie war eine Kennerin der europäischen Couture, doch als Amerikas First Lady erwählte sie den Amerikaner Oleg Cassini zum Designer ihrer Garderobe. Gemeinsam wurden sie berühmt für schlichte Kostüme, Etuikleider, Pillbox-Hüte und dezente, aber überaus elegante Abendkleider.

Gleichzeitig trug die jugendliche und zugleich anspruchsvolle Audrey Hepburn als Holly Golightly in *Frühstück bei Tiffany* Hubert de Givenchy. Das „kleine Schwarze" war 1926 von Chanel erfunden worden, doch erst Givenchys glamouröse Version machte es für Generationen von Frauen zur Einheitsgarderobe auf Cocktailpartys.

Der Look der 1950er mit seinen weiten Röcken blieb noch eine Weile in Mode, ab Mitte der Sechziger modernisierten jedoch neue Silhouetten, wie Cardin und Balenciaga sie eingeführt hatten, die Damenmode. André Courrèges präsentierte eine ultramoderne Kollektion zum Thema Weltraum, während Rudi Gernreich alsbald den Mod-Look definierte – insbesondere mit seinem schockierenden Oben-ohne-Badeanzug, dem „Monokini". Ursula Andress im weißen Bikini und Sean Connery in figurnahen Anzügen gaben modisch den Ton im ersten James-Bond-Film *Dr. No* an, der 1962 in die Kinos kam.

In Europa startete Barbara Hulanicki das Versandhaus Biba, Vorläufer der gleichnamigen legendären Londoner Boutique. Gleichzeitig bekamen die Amerikaner eine Ahnung von der Zukunft der Popmusik, als die Beatles 1964 in der *Ed Sullivan Show* auftraten.

In modischer – und auch in politischer – Hinsicht änderte sich der Kurs dieses Jahrzehnts 1965 auf dramatische Weise. Das Fotomodell Jean Shrimpton schockierte das Publikum des Victoria Derby im australischen Melbourne, als sie im kurzen Rock und ohne Handschuhe erschien. Das ehrwürdige, aber um seine Existenz ringende Frauenmagazin *Cosmopolitan* änderte seine Ausrichtung auf ebenso dramatische wie erfolgreiche Weise, als es die Autorin von *Sex and the Single Girl* (dt. – und ledige Mädchen), Helen Gurley Brown, als Chefredakteurin engagierte. Zur selben Zeit trafen 3.500 U. S. Marines in Vietnam ein, was quasi den offiziellen Beginn eines anhaltenden Konflikts bedeutete, der bald die gesamte amerikanische Nation spalten sollte.

Im gleichen Jahr wurde auch die National Organization for Women gegründet, und das Protest-Musical *Hair* hatte am Broadway Premiere. Die superschlanke Twiggy mit ihrem unverwechselbaren androgynen Haarschnitt begann ihre Modelkarriere in London als das Gesicht des „Swinging Look". Die britische Designerin Mary Quant bot, inspiriert von Courrèges, in ihrer Londoner Boutique Bazaar erstmals Röcke an, die eine Handbreit über dem Knie endeten.

Der Film *Dr. Schiwago* von 1965 löste einen Trend zu russischer Mode aus: Frauen kleideten sich in wadenlange üppige Mäntel, trugen Pelzmützen und Militärstiefel. Der Übergang zu Renaissance- und Zigeunerstil war nahtlos.

Die sorgsam gestalteten Turmfrisuren und komplizierten Haarmoden machten längeren, natürlicheren Looks Platz. Auch jüngere Männer ließen sich die Haare länger und Bärte wachsen. Afroamerikaner besannen sich auf die afrikanische Kultur und lösten einen Trend zu bedruckten Dashiki-Tuniken und naturbelassenen Frisuren aus.

Und während die zweite Hälfte des Jahrzehnts von jugendlichen Käufern und modischen Alltagstrends bestimmt wurde, fuhren die Nobeldesigner fort, den Luxusmarkt neu zu definieren. Der ehemalige Modist Roy Halston Frowick präsentierte seine erste Prêt-à-porter-Kollektion unter dem Label Halston. Geoffrey Beene, der Anfang der Sechziger seine erste Damenkollektion herausgebracht hatte, ergänzte seine Palette durch Herrenmode. Und 1966 stellte Yves Saint Laurent – Protégé and Nachfolger von Christian Dior – „Le Smoking" für Damen vor und bald darauf seine Safarikollektion. Seine beliebten Hosenanzüge fielen zeitlich mit dem Erstarken der Frauenbewegung zusammen. Frauen hatten die Hosen an – und fanden Gefallen daran.

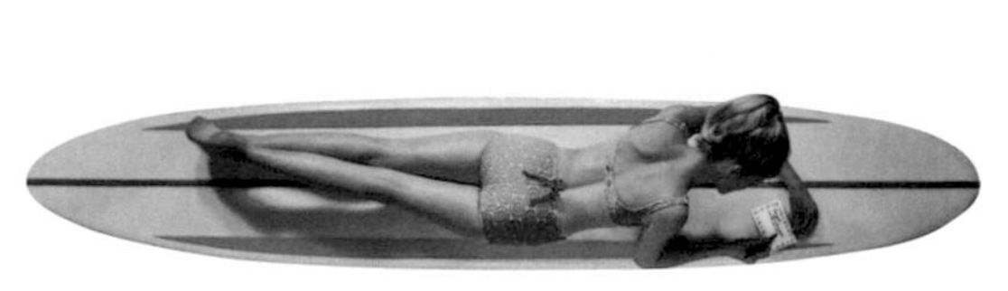

1964

1964 Beatles arrival in America starts skinny-tie trend

Die Ankunft der Beatles in Amerika bereitet der schmalen Krawatte den Weg

La venue des Beatles aux Etats-Unis déclenche la mode des cravates fines

1965 Miniskirts and go-go boots define future look of André Courrèges

Miniskirts und Go-go-Stiefel prägen den futuristischen Look von André Courrèges

La minijupe et les cuissardes définissent le futur look d'André Courrèges

1965 Surfer girl Gidget leaps from book and film to small screen

Das Surfergirl Gidget springt aus Buch und Kinofilm auf die Fernsehschirme

Le personnage de la surfeuse Gidget passe du roman et du cinéma et à la télévision

1966 Twiggy's urchin hairstyle captures Mary Quant's "Chelsea Look"

Twiggys jungenhafte Frisur entspricht Mary Quants „Chelsea Look"

La coupe au bol effilée de Twiggy incarne le « Chelsea Look » de Mary Quant

Plaza 8/Perma-Lift Undergarments, 1966 ◂◂

NFL Sportswear, 1969 ◂

▸▸ Dan River Wash & Wear Cottons, 1962

AU DÉBUT DES ANNÉES 60, JACQUELINE KENNEDY INCARNE LA FIGURE DE MODE PAR EXCELLENCE. La mondaine Jackie est une experte de la haute couture européenne, mais en tant que première dame des Etats-Unis, c'est au créateur américain Oleg Cassini qu'elle commande sa garde-robe. Tous deux se font une renommèe grâce à leurs tailleurs simples, leurs robes fourreau, leurs petits chapeaux ronds sans bord et leurs robes du soir sobres mais élégantes.

Au même moment, Audrey Hepburn resplendit de jeunesse et de raffinement en Hubert de Givenchy dans son personnage d'Holly Golightly pour *Diamants sur canapé*. Givenchy revisite la « petite robe noire » introduite par Chanel en 1926 sous une version glamour qui deviendra l'uniforme de cocktail de plusieurs générations de femmes.

Alors que les jupes amples des années 50 restent à la mode, les nouvelles silhouettes inventées par Cardin et Balenciaga modernisent la mode féminine vers le milieu des années 60. André Courrèges lance une collection ultra-moderne à thème spatial, et Rudi Gernreich jette les bases de la tendance Mod, notamment avec son scandaleux maillot de bain « topless », le monokini. Ursula Andress en bikini blanc et Sean Connery dans ses costumes ajustés donnent le ton de la mode dans *James Bond 007 contre Dr. No*, premier opus de la saga initiée en 1962.

En Europe, Barbara Hulanicki lance le catalogue de vente par correspondance de Biba, précurseur de l'incontournable boutique de Londres; en 1964, les Américains se font une idée de l'avenir de la pop music lors du passage des Beatles au *Ed Sullivan Show*.

A l'instar de la politique, la mode de la décennie connaît un revirement spectaculaire en 1965. Au Derby Victoria de Melbourne en Australie, le mannequin Jean Shrimpton choque la foule en apparaissant sans gants et en jupe courte. En grande difficulté, le vénérable magazine féminin *Cosmopolitan* change radicalement de ton en embauchant Helen Gurley Brown, l'auteur d'*Une Vierge sur canapé*, au poste de rédactrice en chef. 3 500 Marines américains débarquent au Vietnam, officialisant le début d'un interminable conflit qui n'allait pas tarder à diviser les Etats-Unis.

Cette année voit également la création de mouvements d'émancipation féminine et la première de la comédie musicale alternative *Hair* à Broadway. Avec sa silhouette menue et sa coupe de cheveux androgyne, Twiggy entame sa carrière de mannequin à Londres en tant que visage du « Swinging London », tandis que la créatrice britannique Mary Quant, inspirée par Courrèges, lance des jupes s'arrêtant quinze à dix-huit centimètres au-dessus du genou chez Bazaar, sa boutique londonienne.

En 1965, *Le Docteur Jivago* lance la tendance russe, les femmes arborant de sublimes manteaux tombant à mi-mollet, des chapeaux en fourrure et des brodequins militaires qui s'intègrent facilement aux tendances Renaissance et gitane. Les coiffures soigneusement crêpées et les brushings à la Nana Mouskouri cèdent la place à des coupes plus longues, plus naturelles. Quant aux jeunes gens, ils optent aussi pour les cheveux longs et se laissent pousser la barbe. Les Afro-américains se tournent vers la culture africaine et lancent la mode des tuniques Dashiki imprimées et des coupes afro.

Alors que la seconde partie des années 60 est dominée par le marché des jeunes et la mode inspirée de la rue, les couturiers haut de gamme continuent à redéfinir l'industrie du luxe. Roy Halston Frowick, un ancien chapelier, lance sa première collection de prêt-à-porter sous la griffe Halston. Geoffrey Beene, qui proposait une collection pour femme depuis le début des années 60, se diversifie dans la mode masculine. Et en 1966, Yves Saint Laurent – le protégé et successeur de Christian Dior – introduit « Le Smoking » pour femme, rapidement suivi par sa collection safari. Ses tailleurs-pantalons à succès coïncident avec l'émancipation féminine: les femmes portent des pantalons et elles aiment ça.

1967 Summer of Love

Summer of Love

Les Américains vivent leur « Summer of Love »

1967 Afro hairstyle symbolic of Black Is Beautiful movement in U.S.

Afrofrisuren symbolisieren die Bewegung „Black Is Beautiful" in den USA

Aux Etats-Unis, les coupes afro symbolisent le mouvement « Black Is Beautiful »

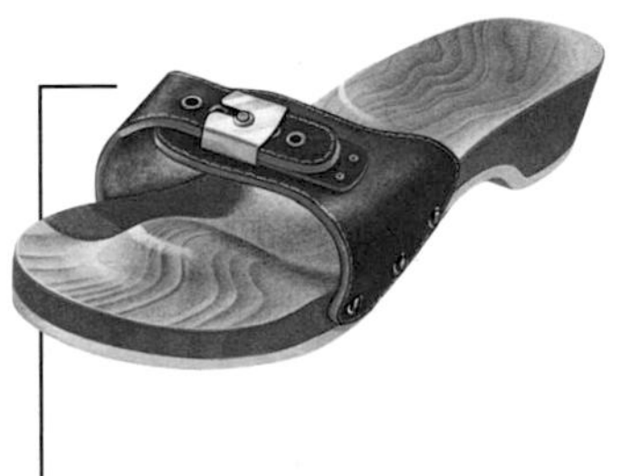

1968 Dr. Scholl's exercise sandal introduced; one million pairs sold by end of 1972

Dr. Scholls Gymnastiksandale kommt auf den Markt; bis Ende 1972 verkauft sie sich eine Million mal

Lancement des sandales Exercise du Dr. Scholl; un million de paires vendues fin 1972

1969 The Gap founded

Gründung von The Gap

Fondation de The Gap

Post-haste Prose by Montag
In the swim of this fast-moving modern world, a gal has to make every minute count . . . so post-haste she pens a bit of hot news or cool chit-chat to a friend on Post-A-Cards or French Notes. There's a choice of designs and colors and papers . . . all dashing. Post-A-Cards are a mere 59c and 69c for a pad or a box and French Notes just a little ole dollar.
At Stores Where You'd Expect to Find the Newest Ideas in Notes.
Montag
Atlanta–New York–Dallas

but your hairdo isn't!

You're the belle of the beach! Sava-Wave inner rim in Kleinert's fashion swim caps "seals out" water, keeps your hair dry and beautiful. Ondine (shown) hugs head in a cascade of face-flattering petals. New ombré color effect in pink, green, blue, gold, black and orange. Price $6. Other Sava-Wave caps from $1.25.

Who would have thought of it but Kleinert's.

485 FIFTH AVE., N. Y., N. Y. · TORONTO, CANADA · LONDON, ENGLAND

Kleinert's SWIM CAPS

Kleinert's Swim Caps, 1962

Montag Post-A-Cards, 1966 ◂

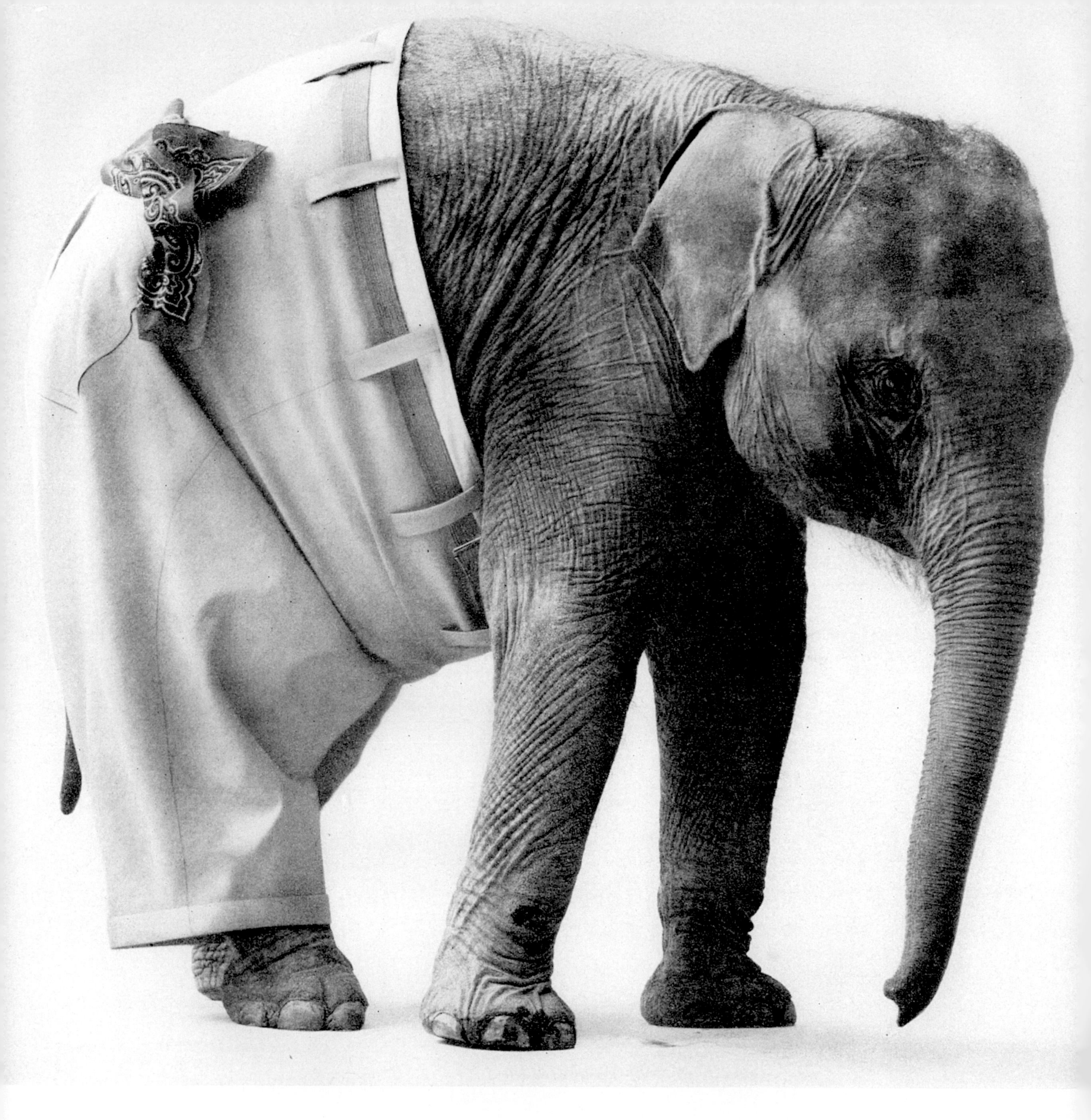

(A little reminder)

This is an elephant. Wearing a pair of pants.

The elephant is loxodonta africana. The pants are "Sanforized-Plus". The elephant is wrinkled. It's not his fault. He was made that way. The pants are never wrinkled. They were made that way, too.

They were made to be labeled, "Sanforized-Plus". Repeat. "Sanforized-Plus". The tag that lets you trust in wash-and-wear. Just as "Sanforized" protects you against shrinkage in cottons, so "Sanforized-Plus" assures you of wash-and-wear that really works. There's no more "wash-and-wonder." If you see it is marked "Sanforized-Plus", you can be sure:

It won't wrinkle from washing. It'll stay smooth while worn. It'll survive wash after wash. It won't shrink out of fit.

In other words, "Sanforized-Plus" means wash-and-wear that really works. So always be sure to look for our label. Our model never forgets. Don't you!

•SANFORIZED•
TRADE ® MARK
says it won't shrink out of fit

says it's tested wash-and-wear

CLUETT, PEABODY & CO., INC., PERMITS USE OF ITS TRADEMARK "SANFORIZED-PLUS" ONLY ON FABRICS WHICH MEET ITS ESTABLISHED TEST REQUIREMENTS FOR SHRINKAGE, SMOOTHNESS AFTER WASHING, CREASE RECOVERY, TENSILE STRENGTH AND TEAR STRENGTH. FABRICS BEARING THE TRADEMARKS "SANFORIZED" OR "SANFORIZED-PLUS" WILL NOT SHRINK MORE THAN 1% BY THE GOVERNMENT'S STANDARD TEST.

Sanforized Menswear, 1963 ◄

Sanford L. Cluett, a nephew of the founders of Cluett collars who joined his uncles' company in 1919, invented the Sanforized process, which controls shrinkage and wrinkling for cotton and cotton-blend fabrics. These ads follow in the tongue-in-cheek tradition of adman Bill Bernbach, whose company, Doyle Dane Bernbach, created the Volkswagen "Think Small" campaign.

Sanford L. Cluett, ein Neffe des Gründers der Kragenfabrik Cluett, der 1919 in das Unternehmen seines Onkels eintrat, erfand das Sanforized-Verfahren. Dies verhindert das Einlaufen und Knittern von Baumwollstoff und Baumwollmischgewebe. Diese Anzeigen folgen der ironischen Tradition des Werbemachers Bill Bernbach, dessen Agentur Doyle Dane Bernbach die Volkswagen-Kampagne „Think Small" kreierte.

Sanford L. Cluett, neveu des fondateurs des cols Cluett, rejoignit l'entreprise de ses oncles en 1919 et inventa le procédé de sanforisage anti-rétrécissement et anti-plis pour le coton et les tissus en mélange de coton. Ces visuels s'inscrivent dans la tradition d'humour décalé du publicitaire Bill Bernbach, dont l'agence Doyle Dane Bernbach créa la campagne « Think Small » de Volkswagen.

Bill Blass for Maurice Rentner Womenswear, 1966

Sears has it. The first inside-outside Actionwear* outfit for juniors. Including the new Actionwear bra and panty girdle. The Actionwear underwear is made with Chemstrand Blue "C"® spandex. This means you get great comfort plus control. Smoothline seam-free cup bra with stretchy straps, sizes A and B, 32 to 36. About $5. Design-in-Motion® panty Girdle, with mesh inserts in back for extra give, 5-15 (junior sizes). About $6. Now you're ready for Actionwear pants (100% stretch B "C"® nylon) and Actionwear top (50% polyester/50% stretch Blue "C nylon). Top, S-M-L (junior sizes) about $5. Pants 5-13, about $9. Also in lo and pale blue. And all tagged Actionwear, the very best in stretch clothes. Tes and approved by Chemstrand. So run right now to Sears, Roebuck and That's where the Action is for juniors.

Actionwear
The very best in stretch clot

NYLON & SPANDEX
CHEMSTRAND

CHEMSTRAND, N.Y. 10001, A DIVISION OF Monsanto

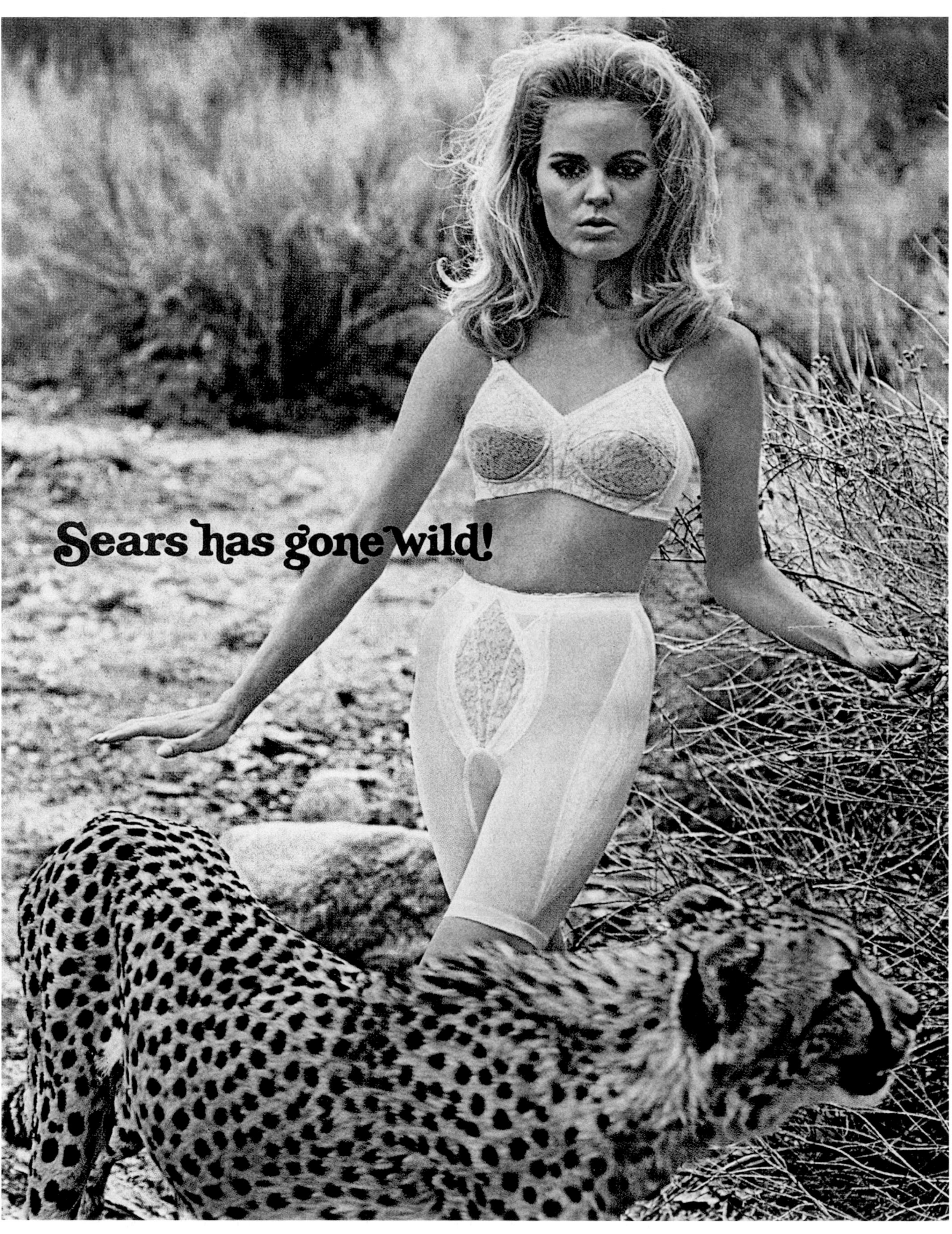

Sears Adventuress Undergarments, 1969

Actionwear Clothing/Sears, Roebuck and Co. Department Store, 1966 ◂

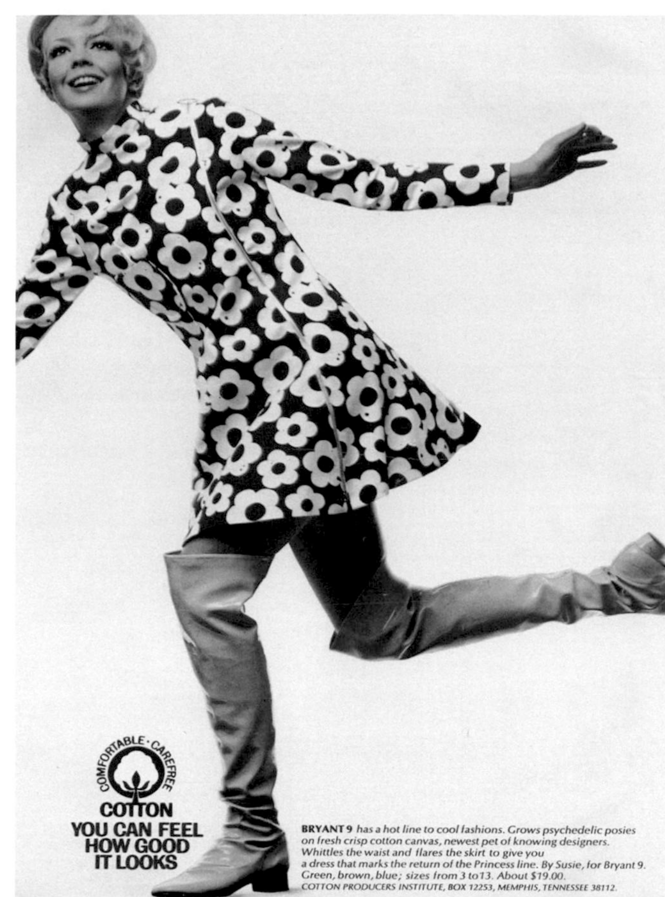

COMFORTABLE · CAREFREE
COTTON
YOU CAN FEEL
HOW GOOD
IT LOOKS
BRYANT 9 has a hot line to cool fashions. Grows psychedelic posies on fresh crisp cotton canvas, newest pet of knowing designers. Whittles the waist and flares the skirt to give you a dress that marks the return of the Princess line. By Susie, for Bryant 9. Green, brown, blue; sizes from 3 to 13. About $19.00.
COTTON PRODUCERS INSTITUTE, BOX 12253, MEMPHIS, TENNESSEE 38112.

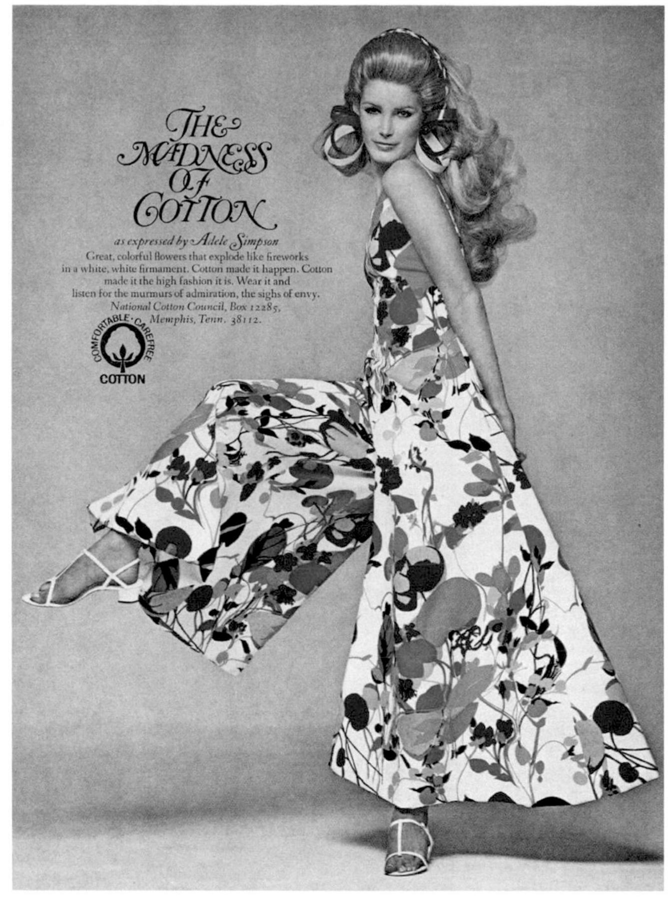

THE MADNESS OF COTTON
as expressed by Adele Simpson
Great, colorful flowers that explode like fireworks in a white, white firmament. Cotton made it happen. Cotton made it the high fashion it is. Wear it and listen for the murmurs of admiration, the sighs of envy.
National Cotton Council, Box 12285, Memphis, Tenn. 38112.
COMFORTABLE · CAREFREE
COTTON

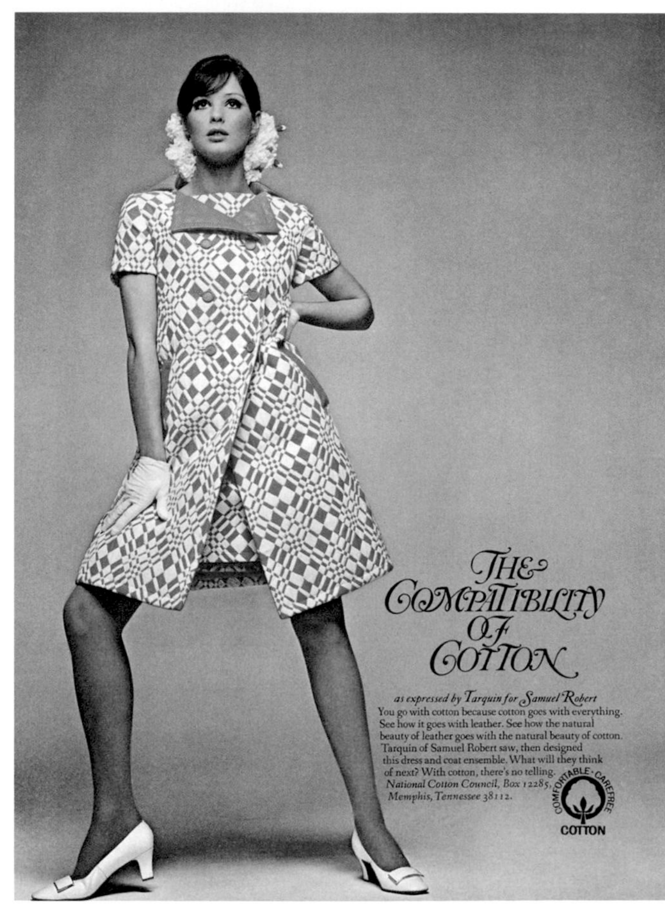

THE COMPATIBILITY OF COTTON
as expressed by Tarquin for Samuel Robert
You go with cotton because cotton goes with everything. See how it goes with leather. See how the natural beauty of leather goes with the natural beauty of cotton. Tarquin of Samuel Robert saw, then designed this dress and coat ensemble. What will they think of next? With cotton, there's no telling.
National Cotton Council, Box 12285, Memphis, Tennessee 38112.
COMFORTABLE · CAREFREE
COTTON

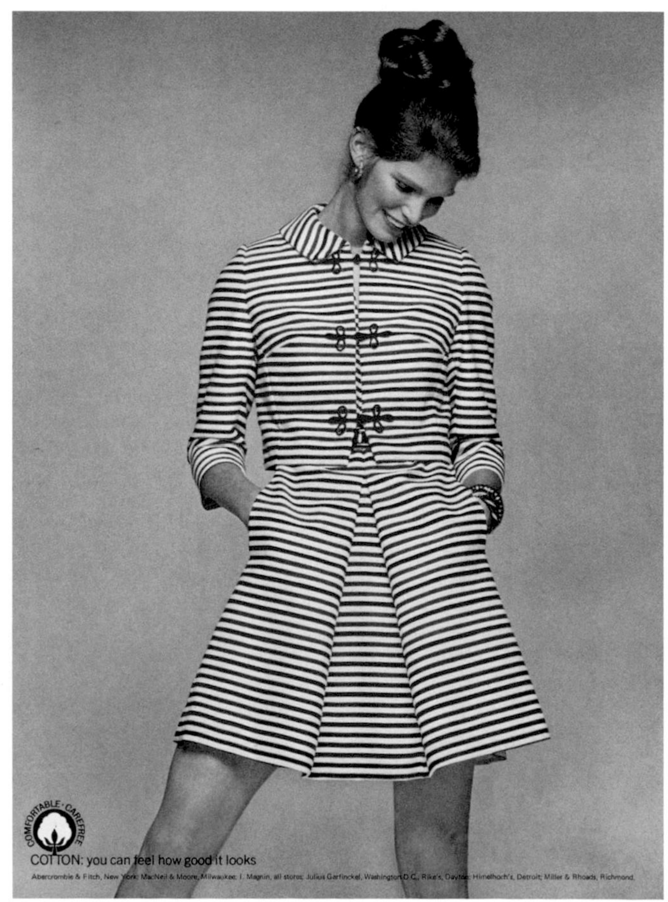

COMFORTABLE · CAREFREE
COTTON: you can feel how good it looks

Cotton Producers Institute/Bryant 9 Womenswear, 1968 National Cotton Council/Adele Simpson Womenswear, 1967

National Cotton Council/Tarquin for Samuel Robert Womenswear, 1967 Cotton Producers Institute/Custom Casuals by Tom Mallo, 1969

► DuPont Dacron/Junior Accent Womenswear, 1961

Dacron.® It ought to be a law.

JUNIOR ACCENT thinks 'twould be a crime for pure pizzaz not to have the lasting shape of "Dacron". Thus, this sonic knit that has—a print so bold you can almost hear it. And a fresh so great it goes on forever. And why? Because it's 100% Dacron* polyester. In red/white/navy, yellow/white/black. Sizes 6-16. About $46. Available at Franklin Simon, New York and branches; Town and Country, Des Moines; Joseph Horne Co., Pittsburgh; Frederick & Nelson, Seattle.

*DU PONT'S REGISTERED TRADEMARK. DU PONT MAKES FIBERS, NOT FABRICS OR FASHIONS. EARRINGS BY HATTIE CARNEGIE.

Better Things for Better Living . . . *through Chemistry*

THE LEESURE LOOK: Lee Slim 'n Trim tapered slacks!

These tapered slacks can take all the bounce a Trampoline® can dish out—or show up for a party! Lee tailors all the things you like into these slacks ... makes 'em sharp enough for practically any occasion. Here's classic styling—in high-sheen, Narrow Wale Cord (Loden Green) and Super Polished Cotton (Sand). Also featured above are new "Lee Trims," slim beltless slacks in new Textured Weave Polished Cotton (Cactus Green). "Sanforized-Plus" for easy care. Priced from only $4.95! And look at those great Lee sport shirts. Unlimited selection from just $3.98!

Leesures® by Lee

© 1961, H. D. Lee Company, Kansas City, Mo.

THE LEESURE LOOK: Lee High-Sheen tapered slacks!

Once you pull on these tapered slacks you'll practically live in them. They're that sharp. They're that comfortable. Made of exclusive "Lee Lustre" smooth polished cotton and twill, they're the latest thing for casual wear. And these slacks keep their sheen. It's woven in to last the life of the fabric. "Sanforized-Plus" for easy care, permanent fit. Classic tailoring with latest style details—in Tawn, Sand and shades of green. Only $5.95. Team 'em up with smart Lee sport shirts and you're really swinging!

Leesures® by Lee

© 1961, H. D. Lee Company, Kansas City, Mo.

Lee Leesures Slacks, 1961

Lee Leesures Slacks, 1961

▸ Creslan Acrylic Fiber/Catalina Sportswear, 1960

THE CATALINA® MAN discovers Creslan®
ACRYLIC FIBER
For the golfer who takes his sports and sportshirts seriously, this handsome lightweight shirt is knit to fit in 70% Creslan acrylic fiber, 30% nylon. It lets a man swing with comfort. It dries into perfect shape after laundering. In sporting colors, about $12.95. Cyanamid makes the Creslan acrylic fiber; Catalina makes the garments. American Cyanamid Company, New York.
Color co-ordinated hosiery available from Esquire Socks.
CYANAMID

Hathaway Shirts, 1968

An update of David Ogilvy's famous "Man in the Hathaway Shirt" campaign featured a debonair man in an eye patch. Running from 1951 into the late '80s, the ads showed the Hathaway man engaging in activities from the ordinary to the exotic – but always in a crisp Hathaway shirt and a mysterious eye patch.

Eine Neuauflage der berühmten Kampagne „Man in the Hathaway Shirt" von David Ogilvy zeigte einen charmanten Mann mit Augenklappe. Die von 1951 bis in die späten 80er geschalteten Anzeigen zeigten den Hathaway-Mann bei den unterschiedlichsten Aktivitäten – von konventionell bis exotisch, aber stets in einem gestärkten Hathaway-Hemd und mit der geheimnisvollen Augenklappe.

Une version moderne de la célèbre campagne « Man in the Hathaway Shirt » de David Ogilvy présentait un homme jovial doté d'un couvre-œil. De 1951 à la fin des années 80, ces publicités montrèrent l'homme Hathaway engagé dans des activités ordinaires ou originales, mais toujours vêtu d'une impeccable chemise Hathaway et de son mystérieux couvre-œil.

Mavest Menswear, 1968 ◂

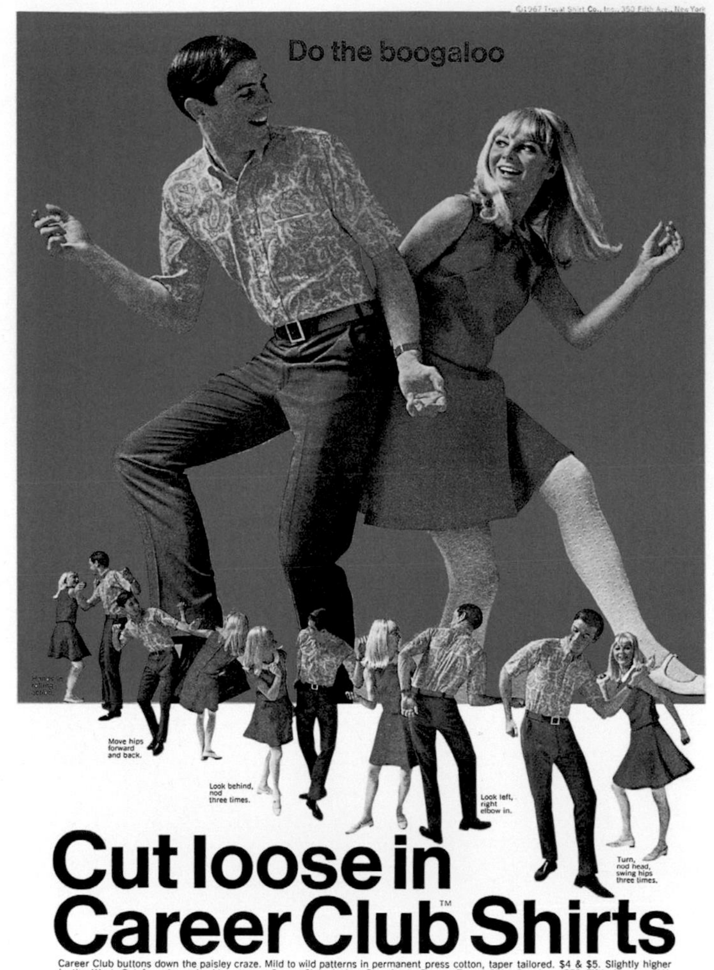

Career Club Shirts, 1967

Career Club ran several ads featuring dancing teens, perhaps in a nod to long-running television dance show *American Bandstand*. From 1952 until 1989, the program spotlighted new musicians and new dances, showcasing several new dance trends including the Stroll, the Circle, and the "Chalypso."

Career Club schaltete einige Anzeigen mit tanzenden Teenagern, vielleicht als Verweis auf die langlebige Fernseh-Tanzshow *American Bandstand*. Von 1952 bis 1989 stellte die Sendung neue Musiker und Tänze vor und präsentierte mehrere neue Tanzstile wie den Stroll, den Circle und den „Chalypso".

Career Club produisit plusieurs visuels publicitaires présentant des adolescents en train de danser, peut-être en référence à *American Bandstand*, une émission de télévision américaine diffusée de 1952 à 1989 qui mettait en vedette de jeunes artistes et des danses inédites, en particulier les nouvelles tendances telles le stroll, le circle et le calypso.

Career Club Shirts, 1967

▸ Puritan Sportswear, 1965

Love him with Puritan Ban-Lon® Brookviews of DuPont Nylon

Textralized yarn, 100% Du Pont nylon

Give him America's favorite knit shirts. Full-Fashioned. Automatic wash and dry. In 25 amorous colors. $8.95 each.

THE PURITAN SPORTSWEAR CORP., 135 W. 50TH ST., NYC

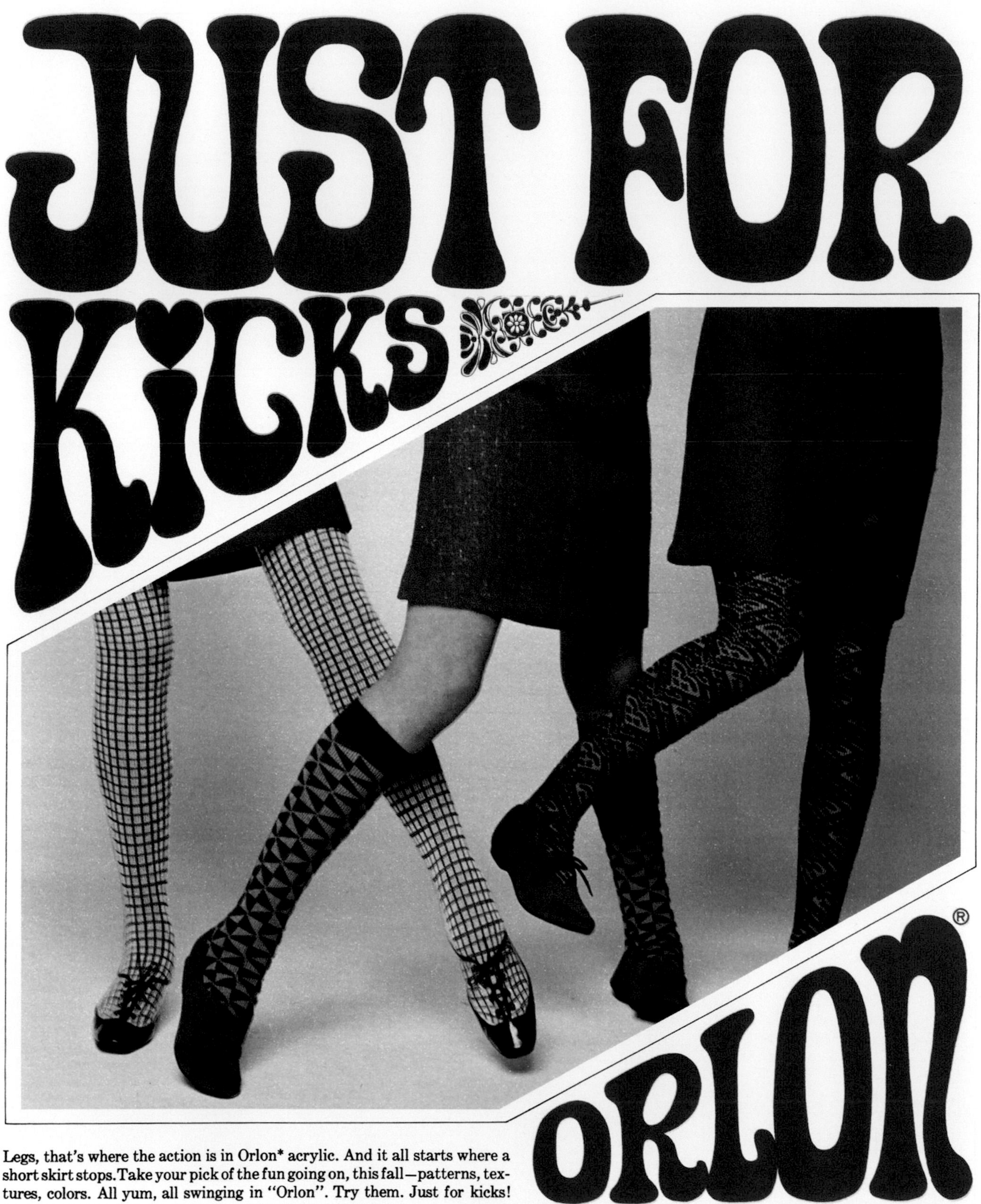

JUST FOR KICKS
ORLON®
Legs, that's where the action is in Orlon* acrylic. And it all starts where a short skirt stops. Take your pick of the fun going on, this fall—patterns, textures, colors. All yum, all swinging in "Orlon". Try them. Just for kicks!
*DU PONT'S REGISTERED TRADEMARK. DU PONT MAKES FIBERS, NOT THE FASHIONS OR STOCKINGS SHOWN.
DU PONT
Better Things for Better Living . . . *through Chemistry*
Seventeen—August 1966
355

DuPont Orlon, 1966

► Alamac Knitting Mills/Bobbie Brooks Sportswear, 1966

nd every great look—
at fabric by
LAMAC

fashion-stretc

Exquisite Form Lingerie/Rudi Gernreich Young Happenings, 1966

Celanese Nylon/Sea B, Inc. Swimwear, 1967 ◂

There are some men a hat won't help

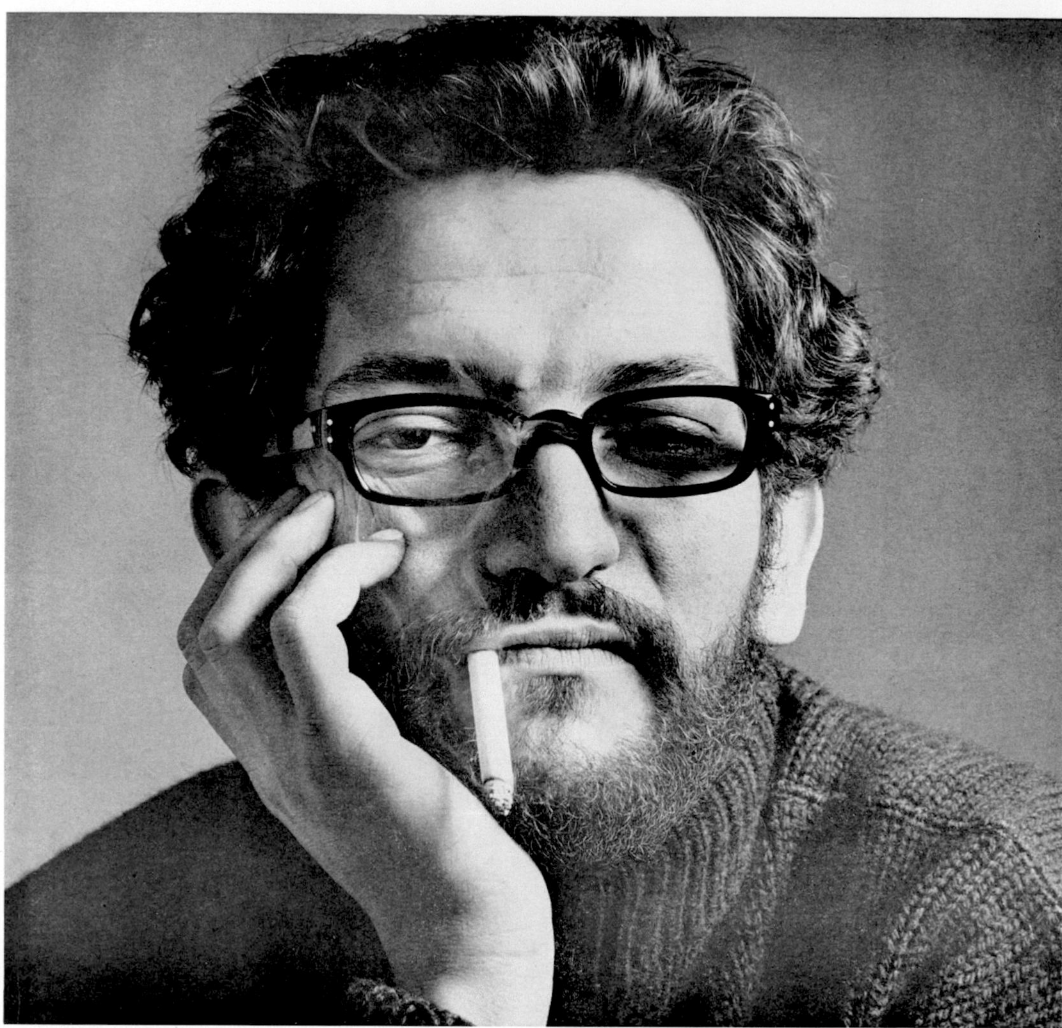

If you look anything like the fellow in the picture, you can stop reading right now. Wearing a hat won't do a thing for you.

No miracles happen when you put on a hat, but it can make the rough, competitive road between you and the top a little easier to travel.

You look more of a man with a hat on, and the men who run things have a deeply ingrained executive habit of reserving responsible jobs for those young men who look mature enough to handle them.

They may be right, or they may be wrong, but there's no denying that they're in charge. So it pays to humor them. Most business executives we've talked to prefer to hire men who wear hats.

We don't imply that going bareheaded marks you for failure. In the long run, it's what's under the hat that counts. Wearing a hat is just one of those little things that make it easier for a young man to get to where he wants to go.

You say you're in a hurry? Where's your hat?

A little friendly advice to young men in a hurry, published in the selfish interests of the hat industry by the Hat Corporation of America, 530 Fifth Avenue, New York 36, New York.

Hat Corporation of America, 1961

Although hatmakers were attempting to use humor to encourage more men to wear hats, by 1961 the fashion had changed, thanks in great part to U.S. president John F. Kennedy, who often appeared hatless in public. At one time, hats were part of a man's everyday wardrobe; a fashionable man would change his hats with the season and the social setting.

Auch wenn die Huthersteller mit Humor versuchten, mehr Männer zum Tragen von Hüten zu animieren, so hatte sich im Jahr 1961 die Mode geändert. Das war nicht zuletzt dem amerikanischen Präsidenten John F. Kennedy zuzuschreiben, der oft ohne Hut in der Öffentlichkeit auftrat. Einst waren Hüte Bestandteil der alltäglichen Herrengarderobe gewesen; ein modebewusster Mann wechselte sie entsprechend der Jahreszeit und den gesellschaftlichen Anlässen.

Les fabricants de chapeaux tentèrent de recourir à l'humour pour inciter plus d'hommes à porter leurs produits mais, en 1961, la mode avait changé, notamment parce que le président américain John F. Kennedy apparaissait souvent tête nue en public. Autrefois, le chapeau faisait partie intégrante de la garde-robe masculine ; un homme à la mode devait changer de chapeau en fonction de la saison et de l'occasion.

▸ Knox Hats, 1962

▸▸ Keds Shoes, 1960

come to the Fair in KEDS

Light as balloons. Cool as grass. Keds are wonderful to wear anywhere, and the *only* pair to wear to the Fair. Keds feel so great no matter how long or far you walk in them. What's their secret?

Only Keds have an exclusive shockproofed arch cushion, a thick heel cushion and a full cushion innersole, all molded together in one lasting, inseparable comfort cushion. What a marvelous feelin

CHAMPION

BIG LEAGUER

LOOK FOR THE BLUE LABEL®

U.S. Keds®

The Shoe of Champions

See Kolonel Keds fly in 'Leonidoff's Wonder World' at the N.Y. World's Fair Amphitheatre!

hey're fair to your feet

d Keds not only feel better, they fit better, and take the most wash and wear
en when you toss them in a machine. So why not be fair to all the feet in your
nily? Outfit them all in the great new '64 Keds. They're the fairest of all.

LOOK FOR THE BLUE LABEL*

U.S. Keds

*Both U. S. Keds and the blue label are registered trademarks of

United States Rubber

Rockefeller Center, New York 20, New York ■ In Canada: Dominion Rubber Company, Ltd.

305

GRASSHOPPER

COURT KING

* Both U. S. Keds and the blue label are registered trademarks of

US RUBBER

United States Rubber

ROCKEFELLER CENTER, NEW YORK 20, NEW YORK

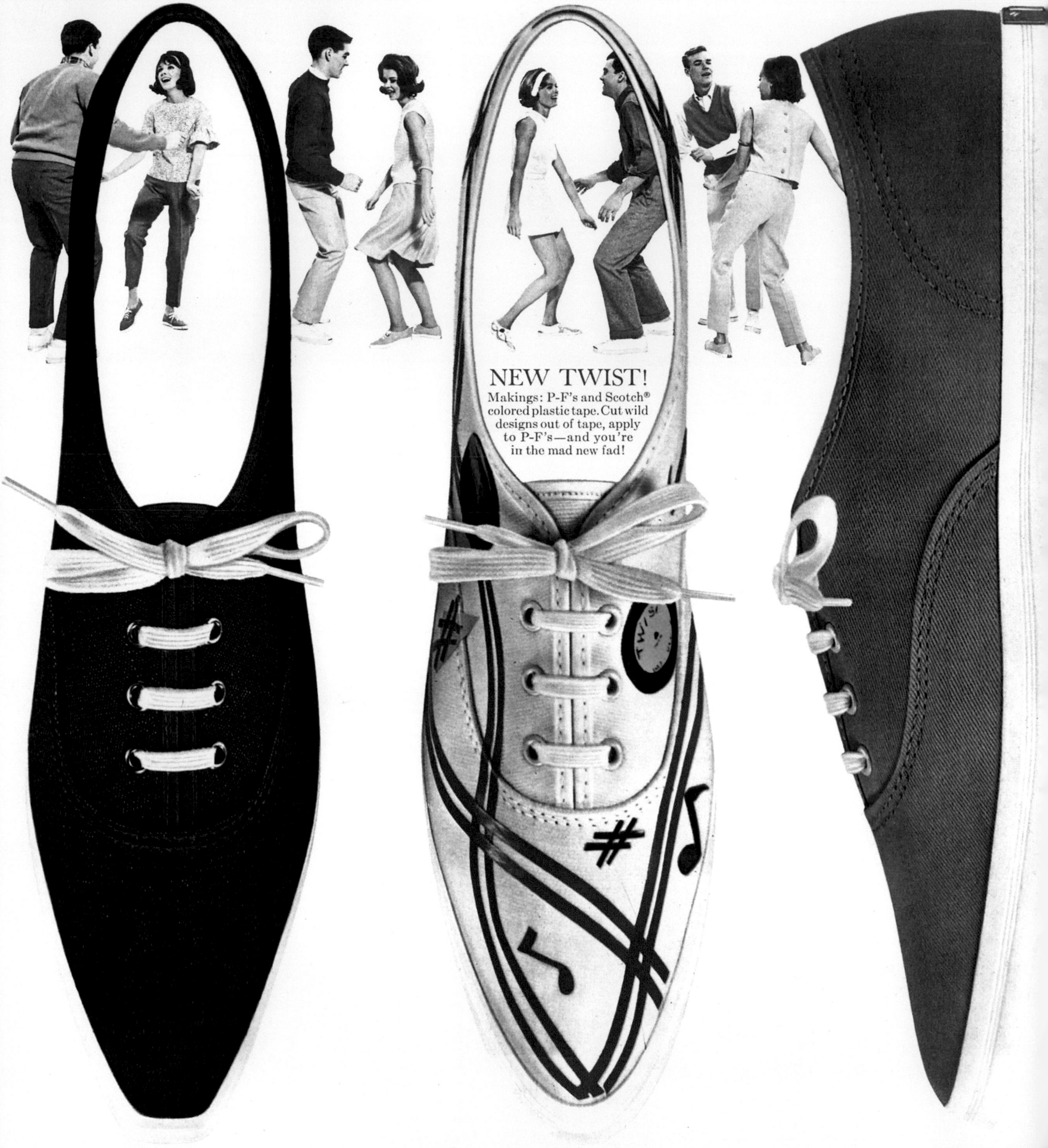

NEW TWIST!
Makings: P-F's and Scotch® colored plastic tape. Cut wild designs out of tape, apply to P-F's—and you're in the mad new fad!

THE FANCY FOOTWORK YOU MADE FAMOUS—

Who made the sneaker *the* shoe? You! And who made it beautifully better? B.F.Goodrich and Hood. Look: square toes and taper toes, adding tomorrow's touch of fashion to the classic look of the sneaker. And, of course, P-F's® have the exclusive Posture Foundation wedge built right into the heel. Does great things for foot and leg muscles, whether you're dancing dervishly or simply rushing into a morning class. P-F's—the real things—the McCoys—the sneakers that *started* it all!

See your favorite BFG or Hood Footwear dealer or write: President's Office, The B.F.Goodrich Company, Akron 18, Ohio.

Quality at your feet

BROWN SHOE COMPANY

Air Step®

Discover that wonderful walking-on-Air Step feeling

in these soft alabaster pigskins with light flexibility and gently tapered toes.

PIXIE

FLAPPER

The Shoe With The Magic Sole – It's Cushioned

To bring you shoes that represent America's biggest dollar's worth today, we use leather as well as a wide variety of materials including fiber and plastic products, textiles and metals—all of which have been thoroughly tested in Brown Shoe Company's Quality Control Laboratories. ... Air Step Division, Brown Shoe Company, St. Louis, Missouri. Also manufactured in Canada by Brown Shoe Company of Canada, Ltd., Perth, Ontario.

SHOES ILLUSTRATED 13.99

Other styles, 9.99 to 14.99
Higher Denver West and Canada

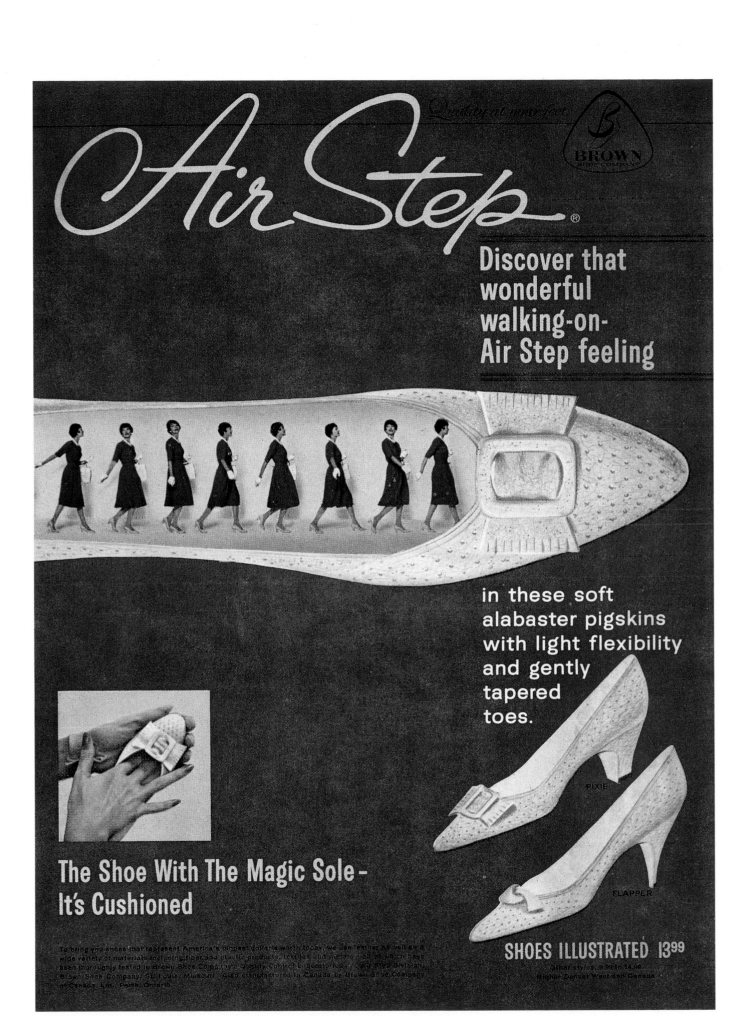

Air Step Shoes, 1961

PF Flyer Sneakers/B. F. Goodrich Company, 1962 ◂

bur-mil Cameo
SHAPEMAKER STRETCH STOCKINGS
BEAUTY
veil your
legs in new
loveliness
FIT
stretch
precisely to fit
oh so nicely
WEAR
so economical—
outwear most
sheer nylons
Burlington Hosiery Co.
A Division of Burlington Industries

Bur-Mil
QUALITY

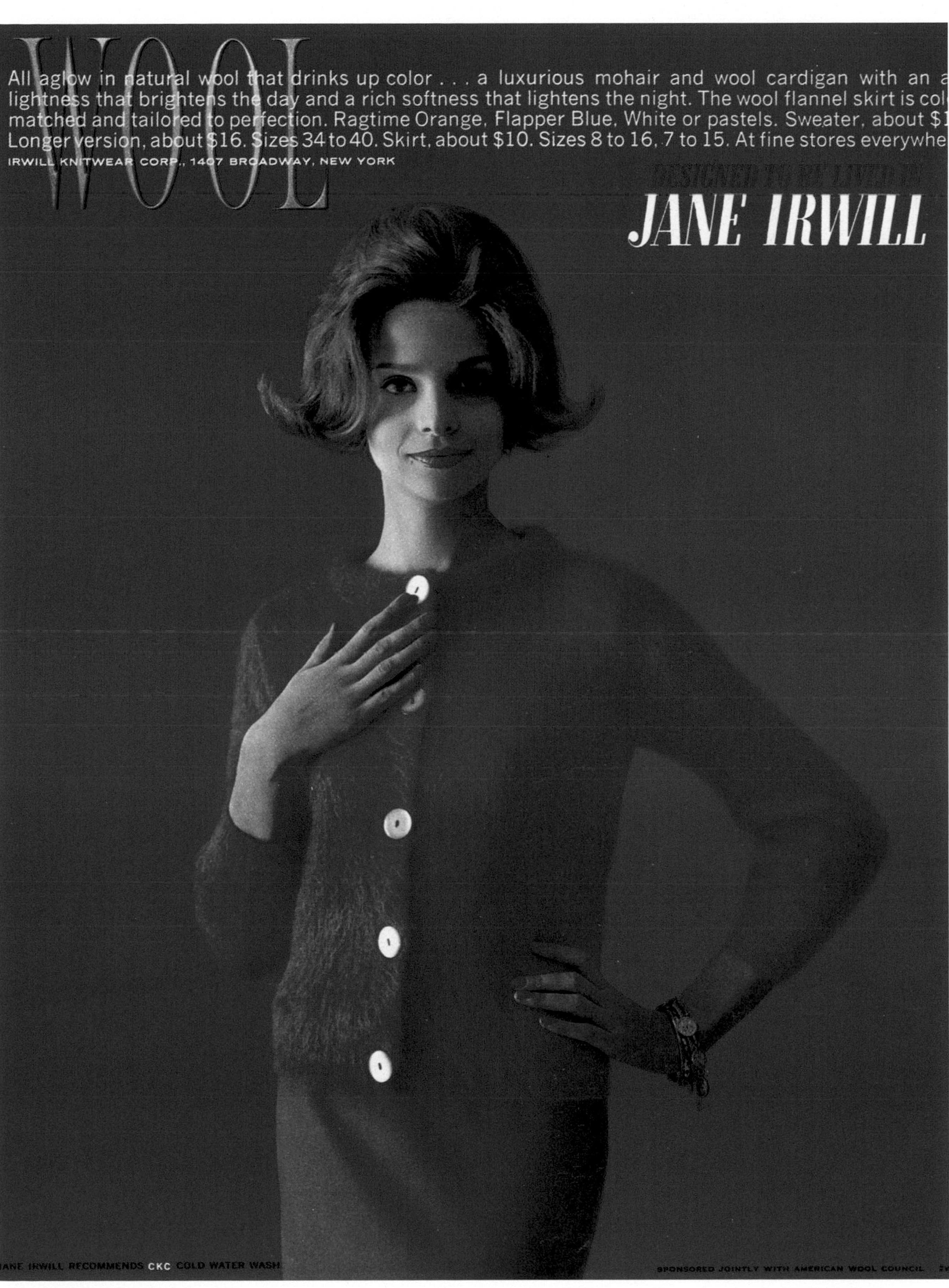

WOOL
All aglow in natural wool that drinks up color . . . a luxurious mohair and wool cardigan with an
lightness that brightens the day and a rich softness that lightens the night. The wool flannel skirt is co
matched and tailored to perfection. Ragtime Orange, Flapper Blue, White or pastels. Sweater, about $
Longer version, about $16. Sizes 34 to 40. Skirt, about $10. Sizes 8 to 16, 7 to 15. At fine stores everywhe
IRWILL KNITWEAR CORP., 1407 BROADWAY, NEW YORK
JANE IRWILL
JANE IRWILL RECOMMENDS CKC COLD WATER WASH
SPONSORED JOINTLY WITH AMERICAN WOOL COUNCIL

Jane Irwill Knitwear/American Wool Council, 1961

Cameo Stockings, 1961 ◂

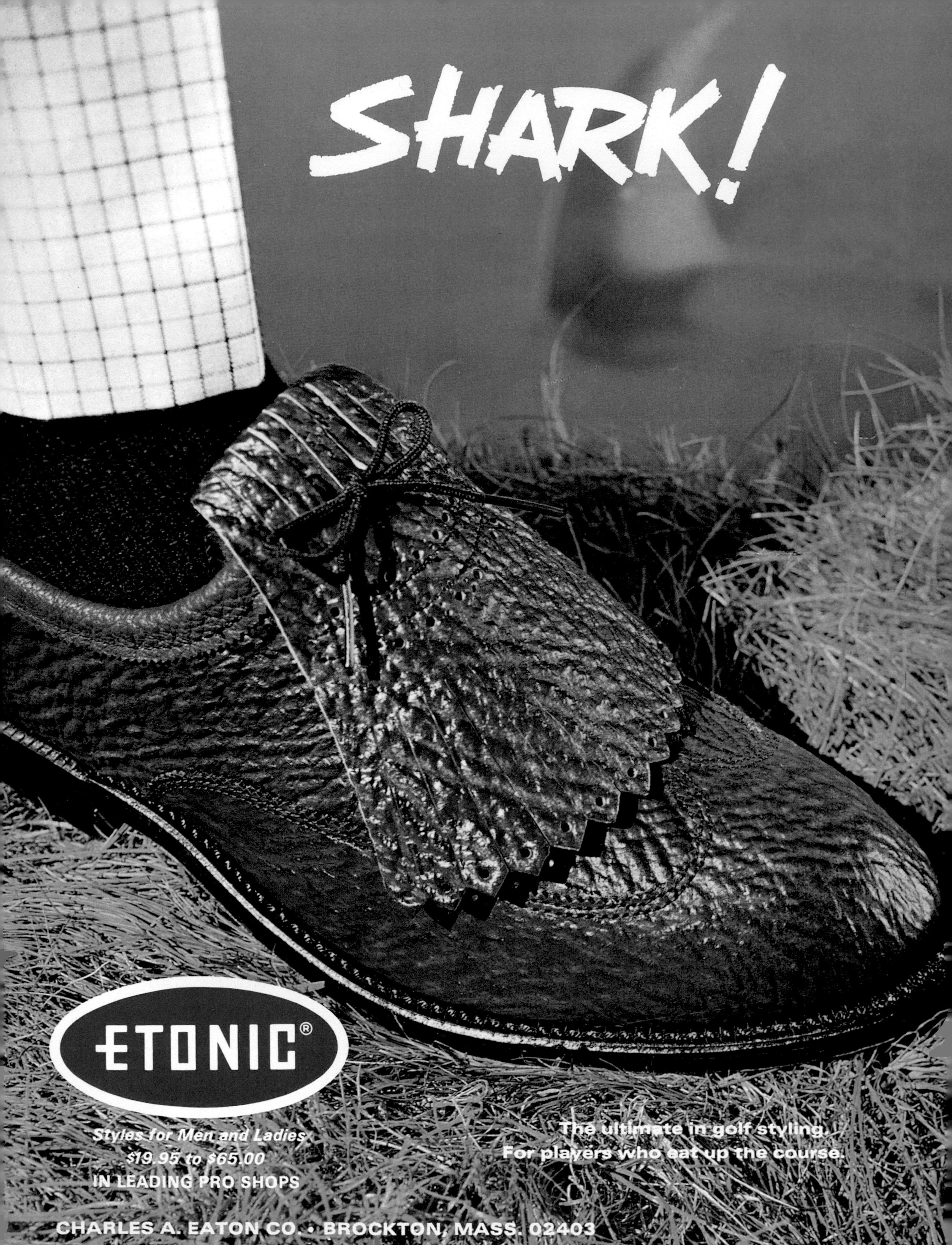
SHARK!
ETONIC®
Styles for Men and Ladies
$19.95 to $65.00
IN LEADING PRO SHOPS
The ultimate in golf styling.
For players who eat up the course.
CHARLES A. EATON CO. • BROCKTON, MASS. 02403

SWIMSUITS · SPORTSWEAR · SWEATERS · FOOTWEAR
jantzen
International
sports club
sportswear for sportsmen
FRANK GIFFORD
BOB COUSY
BOBBY HULL
JERRY WEST
JISC
PAUL HORNUNG
TERRY BAKER
DAVE MARR
JOHN SEVERSON

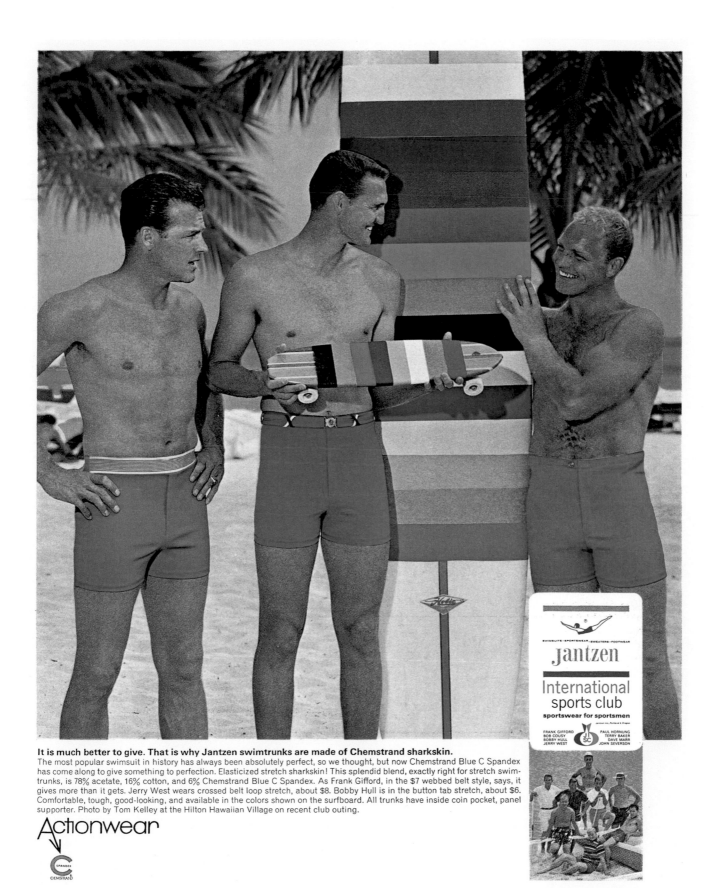

It is much better to give. That is why Jantzen swimtrunks are made of Chemstrand sharkskin.
The most popular swimsuit in history has always been absolutely perfect, so we thought, but now Chemstrand Blue C Spandex has come along to give something to perfection. Elasticized stretch sharkskin! This splendid blend, exactly right for stretch swimtrunks, is 78% acetate, 16% cotton, and 6% Chemstrand Blue C Spandex. As Frank Gifford, in the $7 webbed belt style, says, it gives more than it gets. Jerry West wears crossed belt loop stretch, about $8. Bobby Hull is in the button tab stretch, about $6. Comfortable, tough, good-looking, and available in the colors shown on the surfboard. All trunks have inside coin pocket, panel supporter. Photo by Tom Kelley at the Hilton Hawaiian Village on recent club outing.

Jantzen Swimwear, 1966

Etonic Shoes, 1969 ◂

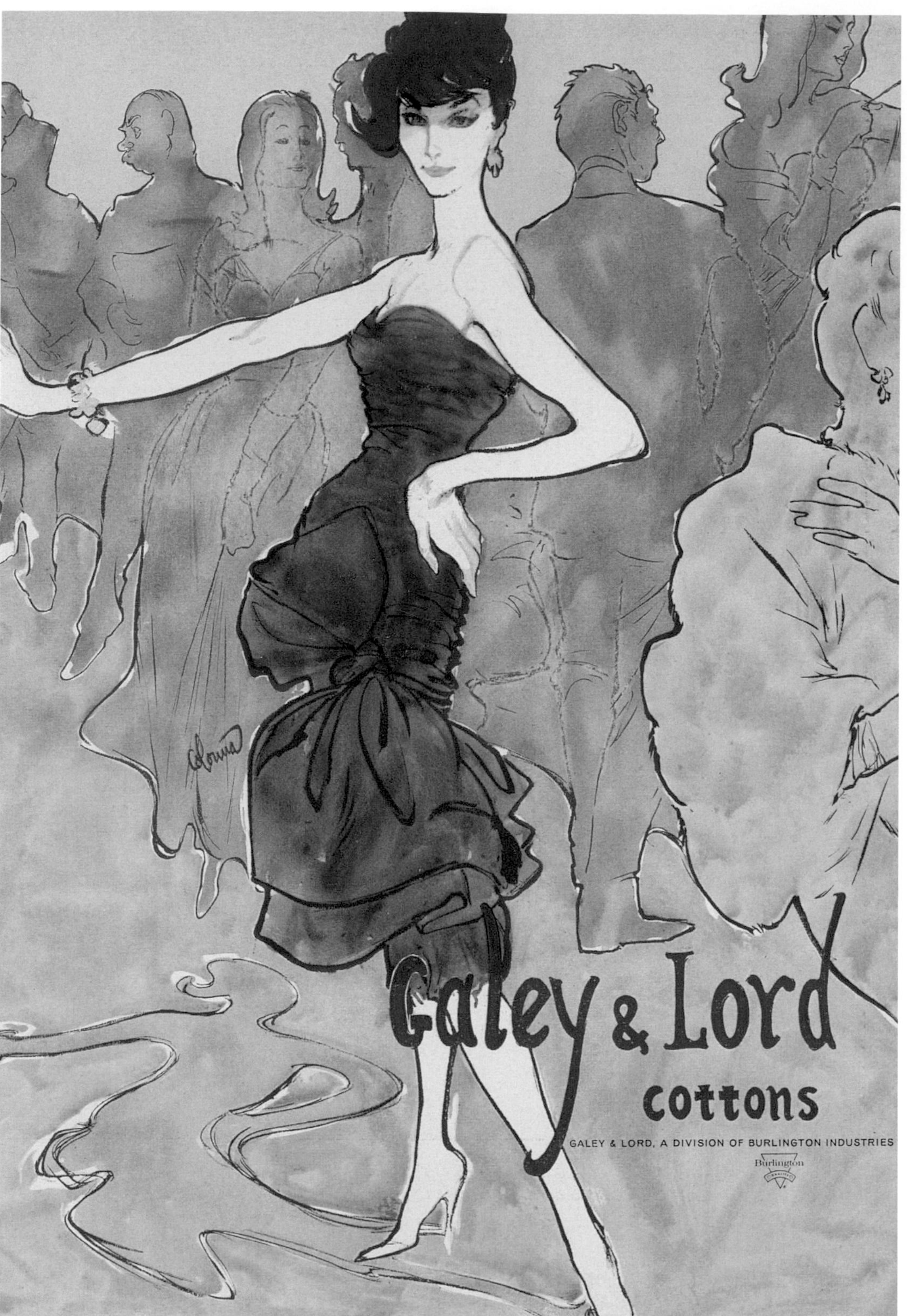

▸ Unknown, 1968

British model Twiggy (née Leslie Hornby) had a look that was distinctively different from the glamorous models of the '50s and early '60s. Her slight frame and gamine looks were a perfect match with the mod styles of the decade.

Das britische Model Twiggy (geb. Leslie Hornby) hatte einen Look, der sich unverwechselbar von den glamourösen Models der 50er und frühen 60er unterschied. Ihre schmächtige Gestalt und knabenhafte Erscheinung passten perfekt zur Mod-Mode der Dekade.

Le mannequin britannique Twiggy (née Leslie Hornby) avait un physique très différent des modèles glamour des années 50 et du début des années 60. Sa frête ossature et son physique de garçon manqué correspondaient parfaitement aux vêtements modernes de la décennie.

Galey & Lord Cottons, 1960

Leslie Hornby found someone she can lean on
EG. TM KLOPMAN MILLS, INC
®REG. TM DU PONT

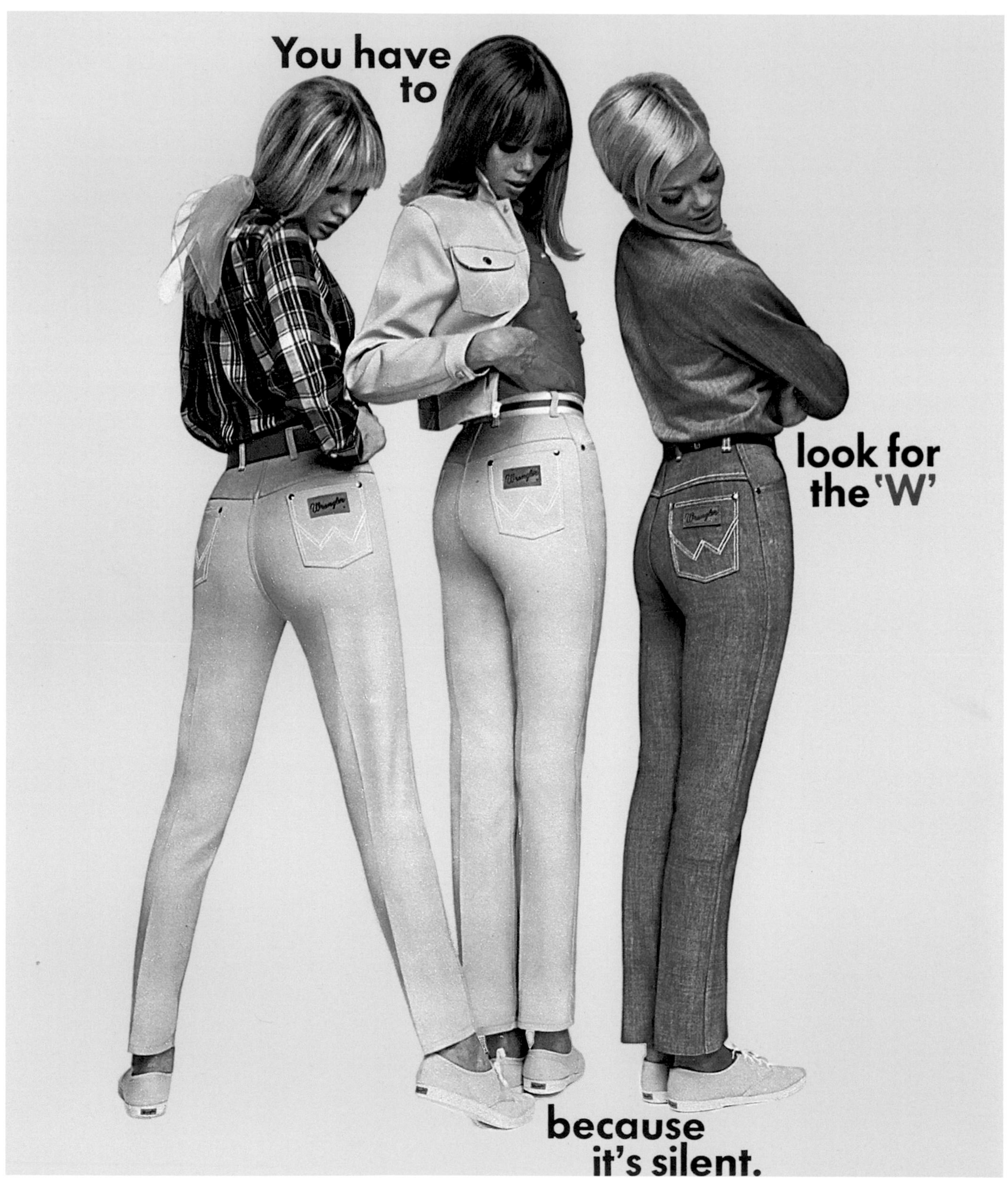

Wrangler Jeans, 1966

► Wrangler Jeans, 1964

the Wrangler® Stretch is the dance to do

Say goodbye to the Monkey, Chicken, Hully Gully and Watusi, too. This new dance really moves. You'll recognize the beat and love it. The inspiration for the whole craze—believe it or not—is a pair of jeans!

The jeans—we should say the jeans—are Wrangler jeans, of course. The only part of the Old West today's generation thinks is worth keeping. They're tough as tumbleweed, trim as a rawhide thong and pre shrunk to boot. What makes Wrangler jeans absolutely irreplaceable though, is that they fit so well they move like part of you. That's how they made the jump so easily from the saddle to the dance floor.

Okay now, if you're ready to do the Wrangler Stretch, get on your horse and head for the nearest Wrangler dealer. He'll give you free copies of the words and music and instructions on what steps to take. You might also ask him how to get a 45 rpm record of the whole bash. Get a pair of Wrangler jeans while you're there.

This is your night to Stretch!

Wrangler for guys: jeans, stretch jeans and regular, walking shorts, western shirts and socks. Wrangler for girls: jamaicas, knee pants, jeans, stretch and regular, in a range of colors, with coordinated shirts. For guys and girls: Wrangler western jackets. Wrangler is a division of Blue Bell, Inc., 350 Fifth Ave., New York, N.Y. 10001.

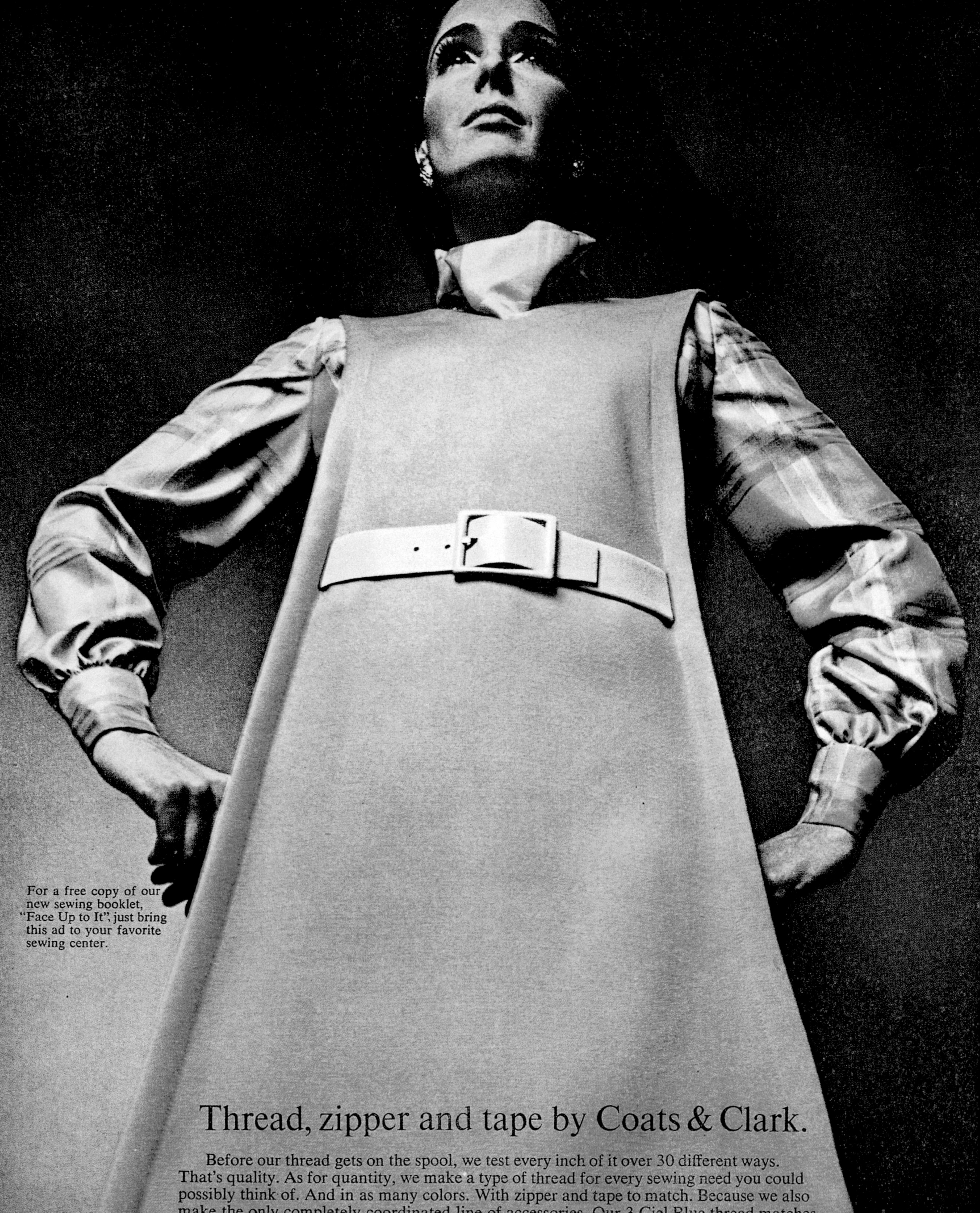
For a free copy of our new sewing booklet, "Face Up to It", just bring this ad to your favorite sewing center.
Thread, zipper and tape by Coats & Clark.
Before our thread gets on the spool, we test every inch of it over 30 different ways. That's quality. As for quantity, we make a type of thread for every sewing need you could possibly think of. And in as many colors. With zipper and tape to match. Because we also make the only completely coordinated line of accessories. Our 3 Ciel Blue thread matches our 3 Ciel Blue tape matches our 3 Ciel Blue zipper. Just ask for us by number. Like they did for Butterick Pattern No. 5250.

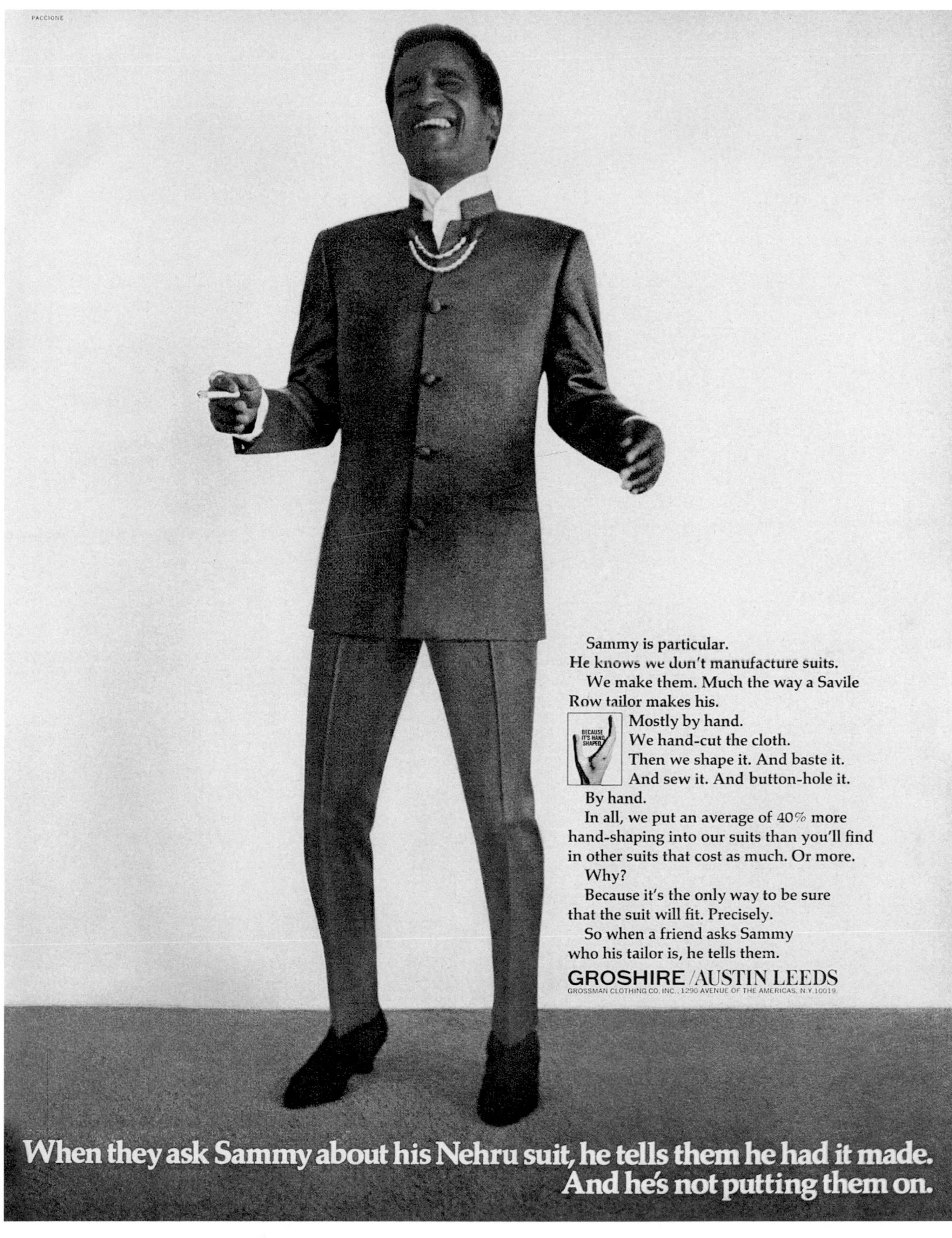

PACCIONE
Sammy is particular.
He knows we don't manufacture suits.
We make them. Much the way a Savile Row tailor makes his.
BECAUSE IT'S HAND SHAPED
Mostly by hand.
We hand-cut the cloth.
Then we shape it. And baste it.
And sew it. And button-hole it.
By hand.
In all, we put an average of 40% more hand-shaping into our suits than you'll find in other suits that cost as much. Or more.
Why?
Because it's the only way to be sure that the suit will fit. Precisely.
So when a friend asks Sammy who his tailor is, he tells them.
GROSHIRE/AUSTIN LEEDS
GROSSMAN CLOTHING CO. INC., 1290 AVENUE OF THE AMERICAS, N.Y. 10019.
When they ask Sammy about his Nehru suit, he tells them he had it made.
And he's not putting them on.

Groshire-Austin Leeds Suits, 1968

Menswear became more experimental in the 1960s, with designers searching for styles from around the globe that could be translated into cuts that would be recognizable to mainstream audiences. Groshire appealed to a sophisticated audience by featuring Rat Pack mainstay Sammy Davis, Jr. as the spokesmodel for its edgy, handmade Nehru suits.

Herrenmode wurde in den 1960ern experimentierfreudiger, denn die Designer suchten rund um die Welt nach Trends, die sich in Schnitte umsetzen ließen und auch vom Massenpublikum verstanden wurden. Groshire richtete sich mit Sammy Davis Jr., einer der tragenden Säulen des Rat Pack, als Fürsprecher für seine ausgefallenen, handgenähten Nehru-Anzüge an eine gehobene Klientel.

Dans les années 60, la mode pour homme devint plus expérimentale, avec des créateurs parcourant le monde entier en quête d'idées à traduire sous forme de coupes susceptibles de séduire le grand public. Groshire ciblait une clientèle sophistiquée en engageant Sammy Davis, Jr., pilier du Rat Pack, comme mannequin pour ses costumes avant-gardistes à col Nehru faits main.

Coats & Clark Sewing Products/Butterick Patterns, 1969 ◄

Jonathan Logan Dresses, 1969

In 1966, London designer Mary Quant helped propel the miniskirt into the mainstream, a style which soon earned the moniker the "Chelsea Look." Quant drew inspiration from such predecessors as André Courrèges and Rudi Gernreich, who did much to launch the mod, miniskirted look.

1966 trug die Londoner Designerin Mary Quant dazu bei, den Minirock zu einem Massenphänomen zu machen; der Trend sollte bald den Spitznamen „Chelsea Look" bekommen. Quant holte sich ihre Inspiration bei Vorgängern wie André Courrèges und Rudi Gernreich, die ebenfalls viel für die Verbreitung des Mod Look mit Minirock taten.

En 1966, la créatrice londonienne Mary Quant contribua à la démocratisation de la minijupe, un style rapidement surnommé le « Chelsea Look ». Mary Quant puisa son inspiration auprès de ses prédécesseurs comme André Courrèges et Rudi Gernreich, qui firent beaucoup pour lancer le look court moderne.

Movie Star Lingerie, 1969 ◂

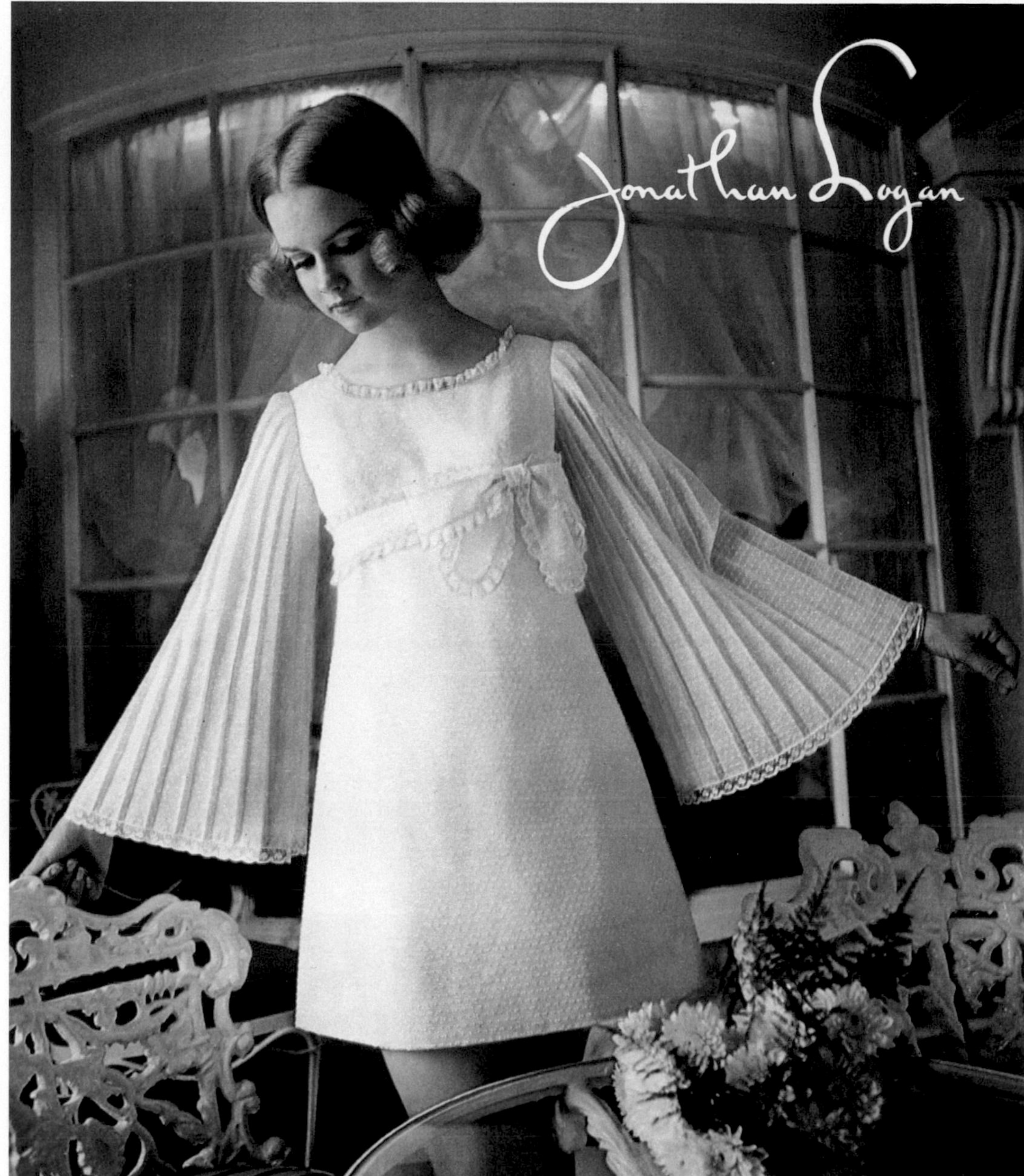

AT THE COTTAGE OF HAMPSHIRE HOUSE

SLIGHTLY HIGHER IN THE WEST

Graduation up your sleeve? And then a round of parties? Here's a fabulous dress with a sleeve for both . . . and a look so deceptively fragile you'll want to wear it on every VIP date all summer long! Voile of Dacron® polyester-cotton with—yes—permanently pleated sleeves. White, as shown only. Junior sizes 5 to 15. About **$26.** *For the store nearest you write Jonathan Logan, 1407 Broadway, New York City, 10018 . . . or call or visit one of the fine stores listed below.*

LORD & TAYLOR, New York; STIX, BAER & FULLER, St. Louis; JORDAN MARSH, Boston; MAISON BLANCHE, New Orleans; NORDSTROM BEST, Seattle & Portland; JACOBSON'S of Michigan; J. W. ROBINSON, Los Angeles; CARSON, PIRIE SCOTT, Chicago; STRAWBRIDGE & CLOTHIER, Philadelphia;

Exquisite Form understands that every figure isn't perfect.
How many times have you seen a bra or girdle that looked terrific on a model, but not so terrific on you?
That's because you're a woman, and a model is a mannequin.
So it's only natural that you may be a little too big here or a little too small there.
Exquisite Form understands.
In fact, the next six pages should convince you that there's only one thing you have to know to meet all your needs.
Our name.
Exquisite Form
We understand a woman's every need.

Exquisite Form Lingerie, 1969

In the mid-'60s, designer Rudi Gernreich created the No-Bra Bra, a sheer bra with little support. The designer went on to work with lingerie label Exquisite Form to create a similar product. The introduction of sheer, no-support bras marked an end to the heavily engineered undergarments of the '50s. The hourglass shape of the previous decade had given way to a more natural silhouette.

Mitte der Sechziger erfand der Designer Rudi Gernreich den No-Bra Bra, einen hauchdünnen BH mit wenig Verstärkung. Zusammen mit dem Dessous-Label Exquisite Form arbeitete der Modeschöpfer an der Idee für ein ähnliches Produkt. Die Einführung zarter, unverstärkter Büstenhalter bedeutete das Ende der technisch aufwändigen Unterwäsche der Fünfziger. Das Sanduhr-Ideal des vorangegangenen Jahrzehnts hatte einer natürlicheren Silhouette Platz gemacht.

Au milieu des années 60, le créateur Rudi Gernreich inventa le No-Bra Bra, un soutien-gorge transparent offrant peu de support. Il travailla ensuite avec la marque de lingerie Exquisite Form pour créer un produit similaire. L'introduction des soutiens-gorge transparents sans armatures marqua la fin des sous-vêtements extrêmement complexes des années 50. Les formes en sablier de la décennie précédente furent supplantées par une silhouette plus naturelle.

▸ Maidenform Bras, 1963

I dreamed I was

HAT BY JOHN FREDERICS

WANTED

in my Maidenform* bra

'FRAME-UP'* new bra with 3-way support

Embroidered panels frame, outline and separate the cups. Extra-firm supports at the sides give you extra uplift. Stretch band at the bottom keeps the bra snug and securely in place. It's a 'Frame-up'—in A, B, C cups.

IT'S A STEAL, AT
$1.59

*REG. U. S. PAT. OFF. ©1963 BY MAIDENFORM, INC., MAKERS OF BRAS, GIRDLES, SWIMSUITS

in my *maidenform* bra*

Arabesque*. . . new Maidenform bra . . . has bias-cut center-of-attraction for *superb* separation . . . insert of elastic for *comfort* . . . floral circular stitching for the most *beautiful* contours!

White in A, B, C cups, just 2.50. Also pre-shaped (light foam lining) 3.50.

*REG. U.S. PAT. OFF. BY MAIDENFORM, INC.—MAKER OF BRAS, GIRDLES AND SWIMSUITS. ©1961

I dreamed I drove them wild
in my maidenform* bra

COUNTERPOINT*... new Maidenform bra made with super-strong Spandex — new, non-rubber elastic that weighs almost nothing at all yet lasts (and controls you) far longer than ordinary elastic. Exclusive "butterfly insert" adjusts size and fit of each cup as it uplifts and separates! Cotton or Spandex back. White. From 2.00.

*REG. U. S. PAT. OFF., ©1961 BY MAIDENFORM, INC.—MAKER OF BRAS, GIRDLES AND SWIMSUITS All Cotton Broadcloth, Acetate, Cotton, Vyrene (Spandex) Elastic.

I dreamed
I barged down the Nile in my *maidenform** *bra*

Sweet Music*... Maidenform dream bra... features spoke-stitched cups for Cleopatra curves! All-elastic band for freedom of fit; reinforced undercups for everlasting uplift. White in A, B, C cups. This and seven other enchanting Sweet Music styles, from 2.50.

*REG. U. S. PAT. OFF. ©1962 BY MAIDENFORM, INC., MAKERS OF BRAS, GIRDLES AND SWIMSUITS

Maidenform Bras, 1961 ◂

By 1962, the Maidenform "I dreamed" campaign was so well known, *Mad* magazine spoofed it in an ad that read, "I dreamed I was arrested for indecent exposure in my Maidenform bra." The company went on to create its equally well-known campaign, "The Maidenform woman, you never know where she'll turn up."

1962 war die Maidenform-Kampagne „I dreamed" schon so bekannt, dass die Zeitschrift *Mad* sie in einer Anzeige aufs Korn nahm, in der es hieß „Mir träumte, ich sei wegen unzüchtigen Auftretens in meinem Maidenform-BH verhaftet worden". Das Unternehmen setzte seine Aktivitäten mit einer bald ebenso bekannten Kampagne fort: „The Maidenform woman, you never know where she'll turn up."

En 1962, la campagne « I dreamed » de Maidenform était si célèbre que le magazine *Mad* la parodia dans une publicité qui disait : « J'ai rêvé qu'on m'arrêtait pour attentat à la pudeur dans mon soutien-gorge Maidenform. » L'entreprise poursuivit en lançant une autre campagne tout aussi célèbre : « Avec la femme Maidenform, on ne sait jamais à quoi s'attendre. »

Maidenform Bras, 1961

Maidenform Bras, 1961

Pick a flower. Power. Do a daisy. Crazy. Plant your stems in panty hose. Stretch nylon crepe fresh from the Hanes hothouse in shocked and whispered tones. For a bloomin' pow wow, buy dozens.

flower pow

Hanes

Hanes Hosiery, 1969

► Berkshire Hosiery, 1966

the panty hose
created specially
for teens
Eye-catchers
PANTY HOSE
The shorter skirts are for you. Show off your legs
and not your stocking tops in the smartest panty hose
made for teens. No girdling. No gartering.
Berkshire styling, Berkshire quality.
only $2.00 a pair
BERKSHIRE
INTERNATIONAL

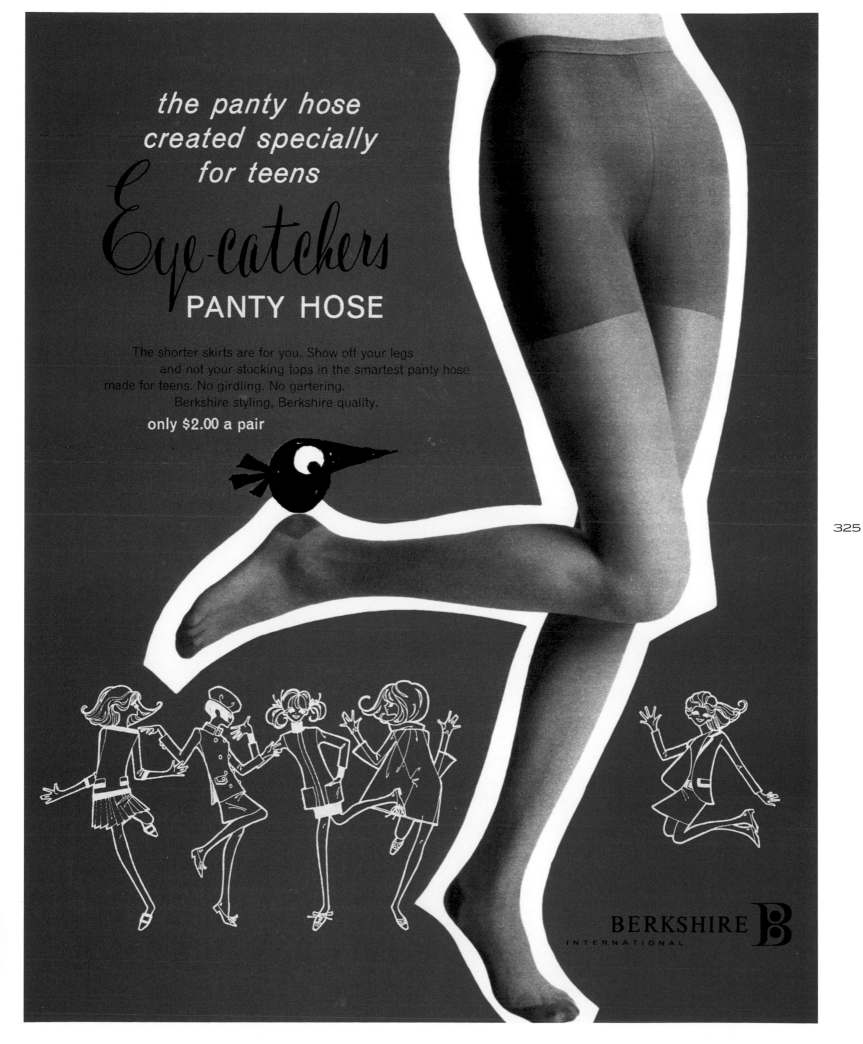

the lass
with the
Pendleton®
air
She's a girl on the go.
Packs 28 hours into 24.
Depends on Pendleton and her
classic 49'ers® (which she
collects like coins, they're nearly
that immortal) to take her *everywhere!*
Fall's fresh crop is bright and bracing:
plaids, tartans, checks, the handsome
herringbone squares pictured. In softest,
loveliest Pendleton virgin wool that simply
refuses to wear out. *Wear your*
49'er belted, with a color-cued Pendleton
skirt, and you're wearing a suit. 17.95
The skirt: 6 panels, half-lining,
knee-pleats fore and aft. 14.95
The sweater: classic short-sleeved slipover,
fine-gauge virgin wool. 7.95
And now, all sweaters mothproof too.
Country clothes by Pendleton

Learn a step (the Frug). Go to an "in" place. Wear a crepe with a flounce (McCall's Pattern 7565). And you have the latest word in nightlife: Discothèque. Discothèque is a club or hideaway where the accent is on hully-gullying and the beat comes from records, or discs (as in French). Of course, the dress is very important. It must be little and black and very expensive looking. Psst! You can make one for yourself. McCall's has created the Dress. In the deepest black crepe, it's slim like a chemise with thin spaghetti straps for glamour and a short, flounced skirt for dancing. The Dress is perfect for any little evening you're out with the "ins." Sew McCall's 7565 and go discothèque. But definitely!

McCall's Patterns

Seventeen—November, 1964

219

McCall's Patterns, 1964

Pendleton Sportswear, 1960 ◂

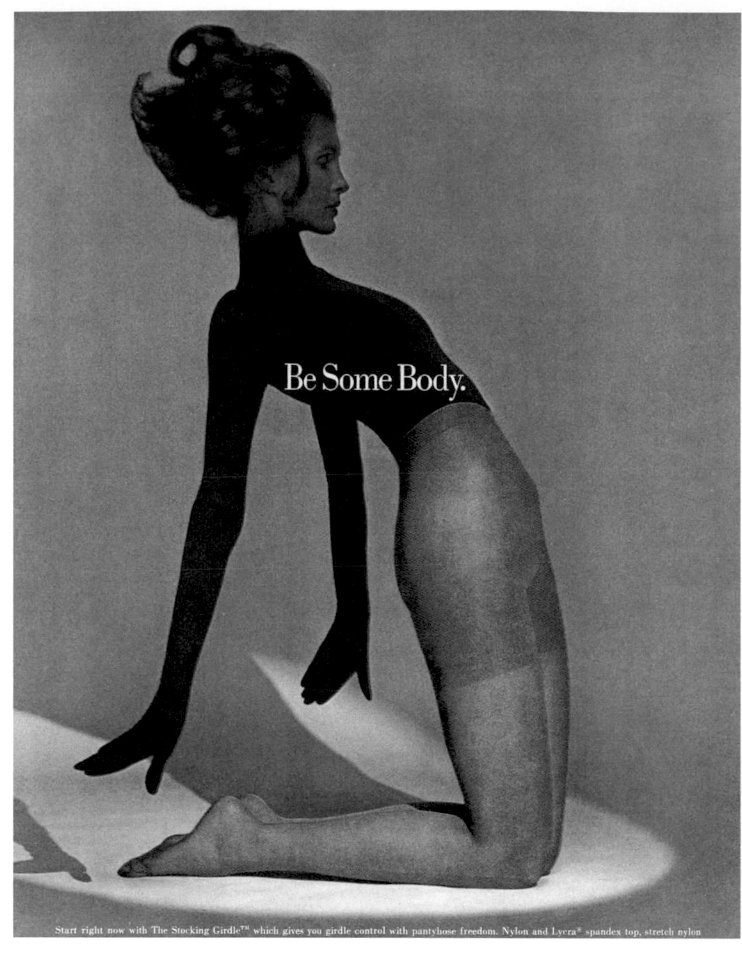

Be Some Body.
Start right now with The Stocking Girdle™ which gives you girdle control with pantyhose freedom. Nylon and Lycra® spandex top, stretch nylon

Waistline pantie or girdle, $7.50. In white, black, beige, blue. (In Canada, too.) Other Double Play™ slimwear briefs, panties, corselettes from $5.95. Better washed in Warner Wash, 10 oz. $1.50.
Now there's a girdle with crisscross bands that gives you back the flat tummy of your teens! The Double Play girdle by Warner's®

Formfit Rogers Hosiery, 1969

Warner's Girdles, 1961

► Dune Deck Tackle Tanky/Actionwear Clothing, 1968

►► DuPont Orlon, 1966

Nobody's little girl.
Not when you've got a Dune Deck
Tackle Tanky.

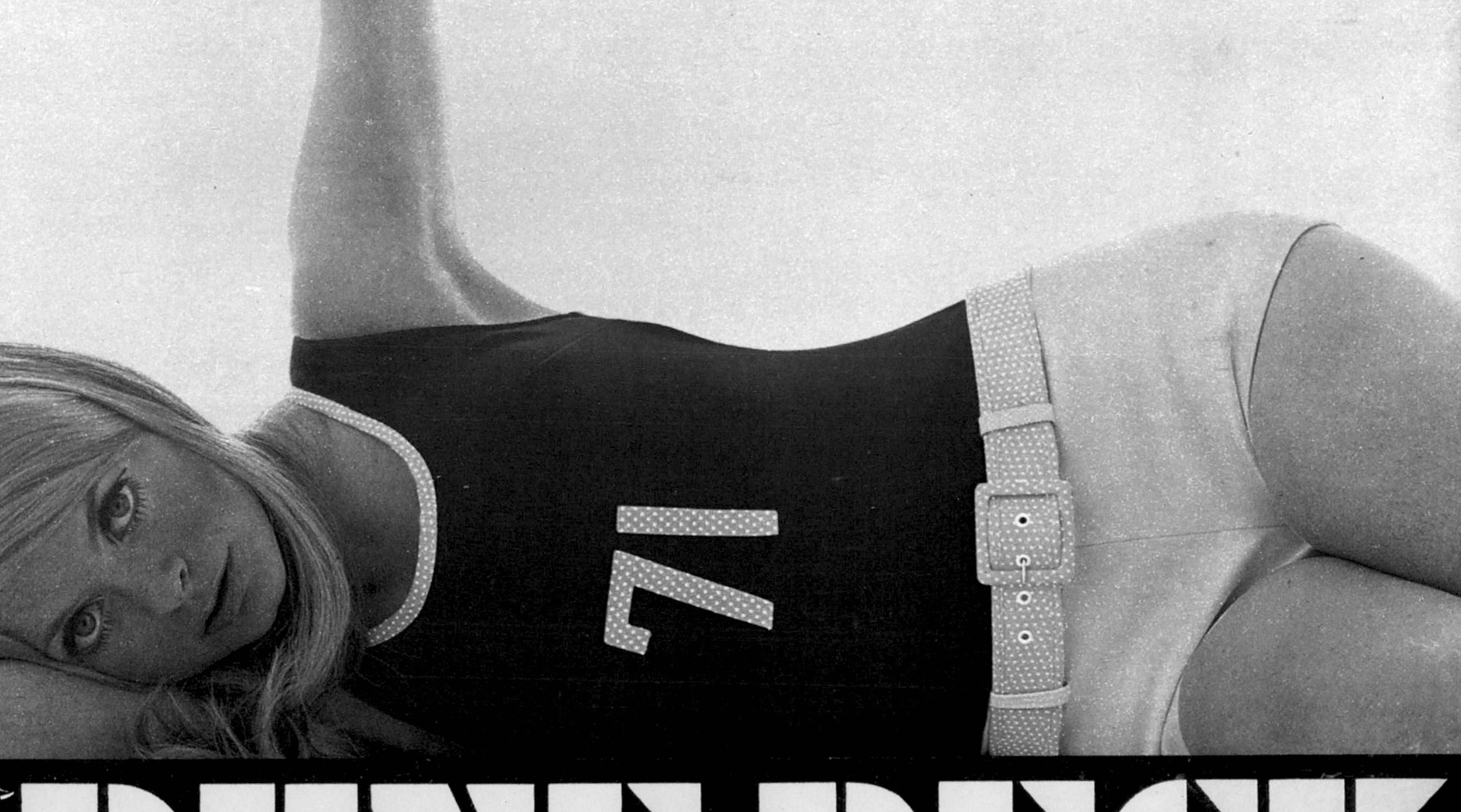

DUNE DECK®

Swimduds and Sunduds

Actionwear™

Tackle Tanky with polka dot numbers and belt. Of 100% stretch blue "C"® nylon, tested and approved for girls who move. At victorious stores or write Dune Deck, 1407 Broadway, N.Y.C. 10018/ in Canada: 1470 Peel St., Montreal, Quebec. American Dune Deck Sportswear Corp.®

Monsanto

THE DESIGNER MOST IDENTIFIED WITH THE DISCO YEARS – AND ITS CULTURAL EPICENTER, STUDIO 54 IN NEW YORK – WAS HALSTON ... [WHO] PIONEERED A CLEAN, TAILORED LOOK THAT WAS A DRAMATIC DEPARTURE FROM THE BOHEMIAN STYLES OF THE DAY.

DER DESIGNER, DEN MAN AM EHESTEN MIT DEN DISCO-JAHREN ASSOZIIERT – WIE AUCH MIT DEREN KULTURELLEM EPIZENTRUM, DEM NEW YORKER STUDIO 54 – WAR HALSTON ... ER PROPAGIERTE ALS ERSTER EINEN KLAREN, PERFEKT GESCHNEIDERTEN LOOK, DER SICH GERADEZU DRAMATISCH VOM DAMALS AKTUELLEN BOHÈME-CHIC UNTERSCHIED.

HALSTON EST LE COUTURIER LE PLUS TYPIQUE DES ANNEÉS DISCO ET DE LEUR ÉPICENTRE CULTUREL, LE STUDIO 54 À NEW YORK ... IL INVENTE DES TAILLEURS AUX LIGNES ÉPURÉES QUI TRANCHENT NETTEMENT AVEC LES TENUES BOHÈME DE L'ÉPOQUE.

1970-

HIPPIES TO HALSTON
VOM HIPPIE-LOOK ZU HALSTON
DES HIPPIES À HALSTON

Joseph Veno

DEXTER

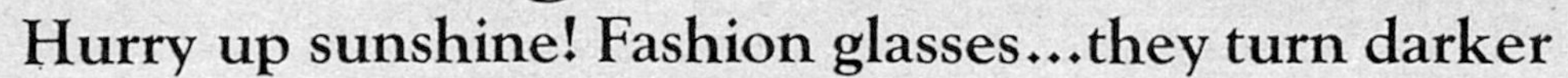
Riviera Brings Fashion to Sunsensor™

Hurry up sunshine! Fashion glasses...they turn darker
as the sun turns brighter
Provocative! Intriguing! And superbly practical!
"Sunsensor"™ lenses adjust to all light
conditions...quickly, smoothly.
Styled to match the life you lead.
Fashion drama...available at
fine stores everywhere...
and exclusive styling
from Riviera.
Riviera®

Dexter Boots, 1971 ◂◂

Riviera Eyewear, 1974 ◂

Adam Briefs, 1976

THE COUNTERCULTURE WENT MAINSTREAM IN THE EARLY 1970s, AS THE RADICAL FASHIONS OF THE '60s—miniskirts, bell-bottoms, and bright graphic prints—were adopted by the masses. The carefully manufactured "natural" look was pervasive in advertising. The culture wars made their way into advertising as products targeting women were pitched with an empowerment message, while those pitched to men took advantage of relaxed standards about sex to capture attention.

In 1971, James Brown recorded "Hot Pants," his ode to short-shorts. That year, Vivienne Westwood opened a store in London called Let It Rock with her boyfriend, music promoter Malcolm McLaren. The two later renamed the store Sex, and, in 1976, Westwood began dressing McLaren's punk band, the Sex Pistols. Surfboard manufacturer Ocean Pacific launched its California-inspired apparel line in 1972, and, the same year, the new athletic footwear company Nike launched. Burt Reynolds's urban cowboy film *Smokey and the Bandit* exceeded box office figures and helped sustain interest in modern Western wear. Diane Keaton pioneered an androgynous look—garbed in men's ties, vests, and trousers—as the title character of Woody Allen's 1977 film, *Annie Hall*.

The most iconic look of the 1970s is the white pantsuit. It was memorably worn by John Travolta in the 1977 film *Saturday Night Fever*. But its roots date back to 1971 and the wedding of Rolling Stones frontman Mick Jagger to Bianca Perez Morena De Macias in Saint-Tropez. The bride and groom both wore white Yves Saint Laurent suits—his was a three-piece pantsuit, hers had a long skirt, which she soon abandoned for pants. The white pantsuit became Bianca Jagger's signature look.

The designer most identified with the disco years—and its cultural epicenter, Studio 54 in New York—was Halston. Born Roy Halston Frowick, the designer got his start in the 1950s as a hatmaker. Jacqueline Kennedy wore one of Halston's pillbox hats at her husband's inauguration. By the '60s, Frowick would make the switch to womenswear, launching his own label in 1968. He pioneered a clean, tailored look that was a dramatic departure from the bohemian styles of the day. His

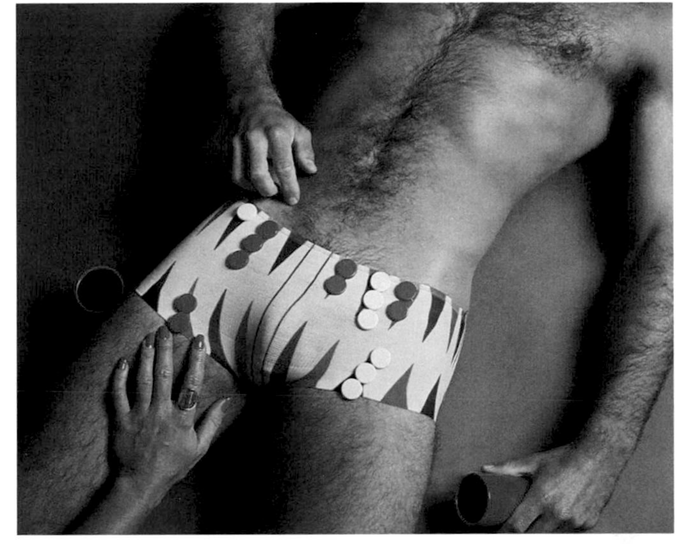

later attempt to take the label to the mass market, however, became his undoing. After he struck a deal to produce a lower-priced line for moderate department store J. C. Penney in 1982, upscale retailer Bergdorf Goodman dropped his collection.

The decade's other pioneering designers include Norma Kamali, who introduced her "sleeping bag" coat in 1975; and Perry Ellis, who launched his Portfolio line that same year. Working women had a new champion in Liz Claiborne, who debuted her first collection in 1976 and soon positioned the brand as affordable clothing for career women.

The end of the decade saw the launch of a new class of designers, including Betsey Johnson, Gianni Versace, and Claude Montana. In 1978, Italian label Diesel opened its doors, and the granddaughter of Mario Prada's venerable but declining leather-goods company took control of Fratelli Prada. Miuccia Prada had her sights on the global market, and she would start with simple, stylish, nylon backpacks that suited the needs of modern women.

1971

1971 Women don halterneck catsuits—often in bright, exotic prints

Frauen tragen schulterfreie Catsuits—oft mit grellen, exotischen Mustern

Les femmes adoptent la combinaison-pantalon moulante à dos nu, souvent ornée d'imprimés exotiques aux couleurs vives

1971 James Brown records "Hot Pants"; fashion follows

James Brown nimmt den Song „Hot Pants" auf; die Mode folgt ihm

James Brown enregistre son ode aux mini-shorts, « Hot Pants » ; la mode suit

1971 Disco era inspires oversize butterfly collars for men

Die Disco-Ära ist Inspiration für die überdimensionalen Schmetterlingskrägen für Herren

L'ère du disco inspire la mode du col pelle à tarte chez les hommes

1972 Ralph Lauren debuts mesh shirt with polo-pony logo in 24 colors

Ralph Lauren präsentiert erstmals ein Mesh-Shirt mit Polo-Pony-Logo in 24 Farben

Ralph Lauren lance ses polos avec logo de poney en 24 couleurs

DIE PROTESTKULTUR WURDE ANFANG DER 1970ER ZUM MAINSTREAM, ALS AUCH DIE BREITE MASSE DIE RADIKALEN TRENDS DER SECHZIGER – MINIRÖCKE, SCHLAGHOSEN UND LEUCHTEND BUNTE GRAFISCHE MUSTER – ÜBERNAHM. Der sorgsam erzeugte „natürliche" Look dominierte die Werbung. Der Geschlechterkampf fand auch in der Werbebranche statt, wo Produkte mit weiblicher Zielgruppe mit emanzipatorischer Message versehen wurden, während solche für Männer durch einen lockeren Umgang mit dem Thema Sex um Aufmerksamkeit buhlten.

1971 nahm James Brown „Hot Pants" auf, seine Hymne an die Ultra-Shorts. Im selben Jahr eröffnete Vivienne Westwood in London gemeinsam mit ihrem Freund, dem Musik-Promoter Malcolm McLaren, einen Laden namens Let It Rock. Später benannten die beiden ihn in Sex um, und 1976 begann Westwood, McLarens Punkband Sex Pistols auszustatten. Der Surfbretthersteller Ocean Pacific kam mit seiner kalifornisch geprägten Funktionskleidung 1972 auf den Markt; im selben Jahr trat auch das Sportschuh-Unternehmen Nike auf den Plan. Burt Reynolds Asphalt-Cowboy-Film *Smokey and the Bandit* übertraf alle Erwartungen an den Kinokassen und hielt das Interesse an modernen Westernklamotten wach. Diane Keaton fungierte dagegen als Pionierin eines androgynen Looks – mit Krawatte, Weste und Anzughose – und zwar als Titelfigur in Woody Allens *Annie Hall* von 1977.

Das ikonografischste Outfit der 1970er war allerdings der weiße Hosenanzug. Unvergessen bleibt John Travolta darin in Saturday Night Fever 1977. Seine Anfänge reichen jedoch zurück ins Jahr 1971 und zur Hochzeit von Rolling-Stones-Frontman Mick Jagger mit Bianca Perez Morena De Macias in Saint-Tropez. Braut und Bräutigam trugen beide weiße Ensembles von Yves Saint Laurent – er einen dreiteiligen Anzug, sie ein Kostüm mit langem Rock, den sie jedoch bald gegen eine Hose tauschte. Denn der weiße Hosenanzug avancierte zu Bianca Jaggers Markenzeichen.

Der Designer, den man am ehesten mit den Discojahren assoziiert – wie auch mit deren kulturellem Epizentrum, dem New Yorker Studio 54 – war Halston. Geboren als Roy Halston Frowick begann er seine Karriere in den 1950ern als Hutmacher. So trug etwa Jacqueline Kennedy bei der Amtseinführung ihres Mannes eine Pillbox von Halston. Ab den Sechzigern verlegte sich Frowick auf Damenmode und startete 1968 sein eigenes Label. Er propagierte als erster einen klaren, perfekt geschneiderten Look, der sich geradezu dramatisch vom damals aktuellen Bohème-Chic unterschied. Der spätere Versuch, sein Label massentauglich zu machen, wurde ihm jedoch zum Verhängnis. Nachdem er 1982 den Zuschlag für eine preiswerte Linie im Auftrag der Kette J.C. Penney erhalten hatte, nahm das Nobelkaufhaus Bergdorf Goodman seine Kollektion aus dem Verkauf.

Zu den übrigen Designpionieren der Dekade gehörte Norma Kamali, die 1975 ihren „Schlafsack"-Mantel präsentierte, wie auch Perry Ellis, der im selben Jahr seine Portfolio-Linie herausbrachte. Berufstätige Frauen fanden in Liz Claiborne eine neue Favoritin, die ihre erste Kollektion 1976 vorstellte und ihre Marke bald als bezahlbares Label für Karrierefrauen positionierte.

Am Ende des Jahrzehnts erlebte man den Auftritt einer neuen Klasse von Designern wie Betsey Johnson, Gianni Versace und Claude Montana. 1978 öffnete die italienische Marke Diesel ihre Läden, und die Enkelin von Mario Prada übernahm die Verantwortung für die ehrenwerte, aber im Niedergang begriffene Lederwarenfabrik Fratelli Prada. Miuccia Prada hatte den Weltmarkt im Blick und startete mit schlichten, eleganten Nylonrucksäcken, die den Bedürfnissen moderner Frauen entsprachen.

1975

1975 Staple of both hippie and disco cultures, bell-bottoms reach new widths

Als Markenzeichen sowohl der Hippie- wie der Disco-Szene erreichen Schlaghosen neue Weiten

Emblème des cultures hippie et disco, les pantalons à pattes d'éléphant ne cessent de s'élargir

1976 Italian boutique Fiorucci opens in New York, becoming "daytime Studio 54"

Die in New York eröffnete italienische Boutique Fiorucci wird zum „Studio 54 für tagsüber"

La boutique italienne Fiorucci ouvre à New York et devient le « Studio 54 » de jour

1977 Diane Keaton's menswear-influenced wardrobe in *Annie Hall* spawns imitators

Diane Keatons maskuline Garderobe in *Annie Hall* findet Nachahmerinnen

La garde-robe masculine de Diane Keaton dans *Annie Hall* inspire de nombreuses femmes

1977 Bob Rush founds Le Tigre as American answer to French polo shirt

Bob Rush gründet Le Tigre als amerikanische Antwort auf das französische Poloshirt

Bob Rush commercialise les chemises Le Tigre, réponse de l'Amérique au polo français

BPEAK

YSL Jeans, 1977 ◄◄

Puritan Sportswear, 1971 ◄

AU DÉBUT DES ANNÉES 70, LA CONTRE-CULTURE SE DÉMOCRATISE QUAND LA RUE ADOPTE LES TENUES RADICALES DE LA DÉCENNIE PRÉCÉDENTE : MINIJUPES, PANTALONS À PATTES D'ÉLÉPHANT ET IMPRIMÉS GRAPHIQUES AUX COULEURS VIVES. Ce look « nature » pourtant soigneusement étudié est omniprésent dans la publicité. Les combats sociaux transparaissent dans la publicité qui vend les produits destinés aux femmes avec un message d'émancipation, tandis que ceux qui s'adressent aux hommes tirent parti de références à la libération sexuelle pour attirer leur attention.

En 1971, James Brown enregistre « Hot Pants », son ode aux mini-shorts. La même année, Vivienne Westwood ouvre à Londres une boutique appelée Let It Rock avec son petit ami, le producteur de musique Malcolm McLaren. Ils rebaptisent ensuite leur boutique Sex et, en 1976, Vivienne Westwood commence à habiller le groupe punk de McLaren, les Sex Pistols. Le fabricant de planches de surf Ocean Pacific lance sa ligne de vêtements d'inspiration californienne en 1972, et la même année assiste à la création de la nouvelle entreprise de chaussures de sport Nike. *Cours après moi Shérif*, le film de cow-boy urbain avec Burt Reynolds, explose au box-office et contribue à susciter de l'intérêt pour les tenues western modernes. Diane Keaton arbore un nouveau look androgyne – avec cravates, gilets et pantalons d'homme – dans le rôle-titre du film *Annie Hall* de Woody Allen en 1977.

Le look le plus emblématique des années 70 reste le costume blanc, mémorable de John Travolta dans le film *Saturday Night Fever* en 1977. Ses racines remontent pourtant à 1971 et au mariage tropézien de Mick Jagger, leader des Rolling Stones, avec Bianca Perez Morena De Macias. Les mariés étaient tous deux habillés en blanc par Yves Saint Laurent : lui dans un costume trois pièces, elle dans une jupe longue qu'elle abandonnera rapidement au profit d'un pantalon. Le tailleur-pantalon blanc devient l'image de marque de Bianca Jagger.

Halston est le couturier le plus typique des années disco et de leur épicentre culturel, le Studio 54 à New York. Né Roy Halston Frowick, il avait débuté sa carrière en tant que chapelier dans les années 50. Lors de l'investiture de son mari, Jacqueline Kennedy portait l'un des petits chapeaux sans bord de Halston. Dans les années 60, Frowick s'était lancé dans la mode pour femme, créant sa propre griffe en 1968. Il invente des tailleurs aux lignes épurées qui tranchent nettement avec les tenues bohème de l'époque. Sa dernière tentative pour commercialiser sa collection sur le marché de masse cause toutefois sa perte. Après avoir signé un contrat pour produire une ligne moins chère avec le grand magasin J. C. Penney en 1982, le détaillant haut de gamme Bergdorf Goodman renonce à sa collection.

Parmi les autres couturiers innovants de la décennie, Norma Kamali lance son manteau « sac de couchage » en 1975 et Perry Ellis présent, la même année, sa ligne Portfolio. Les femmes qui travaillent trouvent un nouveau soutien en la personne de Liz Claiborne, qui commercialise sa première collection en 1976 et positionne rapidement sa marque comme celle des vêtements abordables pour femmes actives.

La fin de la décennie voit à l'arrivée d'une nouvelle génération de créateurs de mode, dont Betsey Johnson, Gianni Versace et Claude Montana. La marque italienne Diesel est fondée en 1978, et la petite-fille de Mario Prada, propriétaire d'une entreprise de maroquinerie respectable mais sur le déclin, reprend la direction de Fratelli Prada. Miuccia Prada vise le marché mondial et commence par proposer des sacs à dos en nylon simples et élégants qui répondent aux besoins des femmes modernes.

1978

1978 Banana Republic debuts khakis and other safari-inspired wear

Banana Republic startet mit Khakis und anderer vom Safaristil inspirierter Kleidung

Banana Republic lance les pantalons de treillis et autres vêtements d'inspiration safari

1978 Velcro introduced

Der Klettverschluss Velcro kommt auf den Markt

Commercialisation du Velcro

BETSEY JOHNSON.

1978 Betsey Johnson launches and opens first retail store in Soho

Betsey Johnson promotet und eröffnet ihren ersten Laden in Soho

Betsey Johnson ouvre sa première boutique à Soho

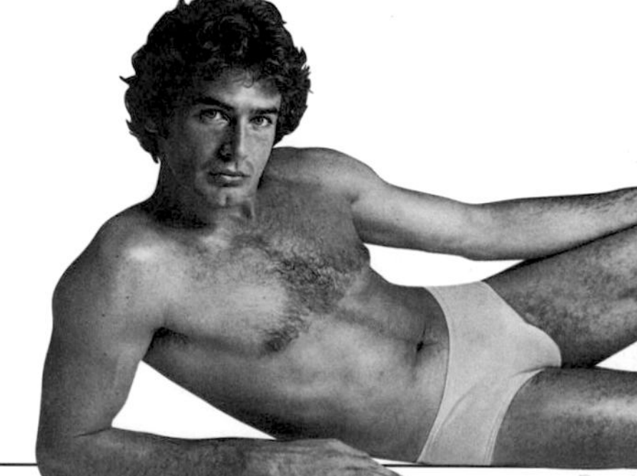

1978 Continental briefs become popular for men

Slips von Continental sind bei Männern gefragt

Le slip Continental devient à la mode chez les hommes

How to get a second glance.
Wear Career Club Shirts.
New exclusive dobby pattern from our BELGRAVE SQUARE collection. Long point collar with just the right angle of spread. Permanent press blend of 65% Fortrel® polyester, 35% cotton. Career Club priced at $8.50.

Career Club Shirt Co., Inc., 350 Fifth Avenue, New York 10001

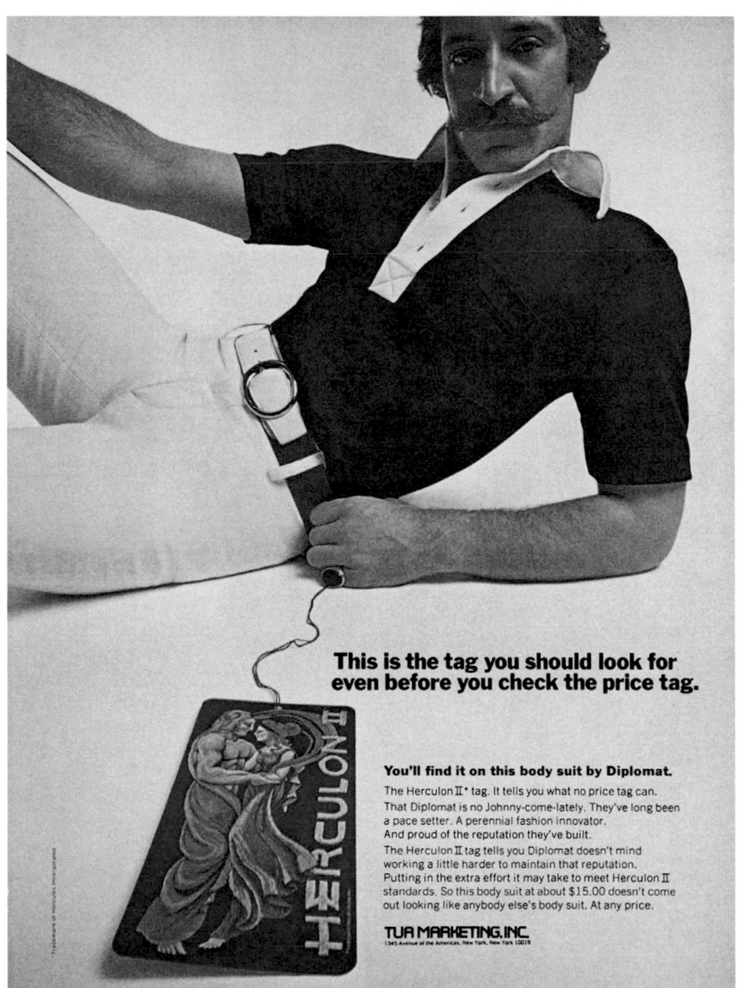

HERCULON II
This is the tag you should look for even before you check the price tag.
You'll find it on this body suit by Diplomat.
The Herculon II* tag. It tells you what no price tag can.
That Diplomat is no Johnny-come-lately. They've long been a pace setter. A perennial fashion innovator.
And proud of the reputation they've built.
The Herculon II tag tells you Diplomat doesn't mind working a little harder to maintain that reputation. Putting in the extra effort it may take to meet Herculon II standards. So this body suit at about $15.00 doesn't come out looking like anybody else's body suit. At any price.
TUA MARKETING, INC.
1345 Avenue of the Americas, New York, New York 10019

Career Club, 1972

Herculon II/Diplomat Menswear, 1973

▸ Arrow Shirts, 1971

The Eternal Shirt.

There's a shirt you can wear today that men wore sixty years ago. It won't make you look old. Or corny. Or out of style.

To the contrary, you'll look quite dashing in it. Just like the man who made it famous. The handsome young Arrow Collar Man.

He was the model for this shirt back in 1905. And he captured the heart of America. All the men wanted to look like him. All the young ladies just plain wanted him. Such was the magic of his boldly striped shirt.

And that magic is alive today. For we've recreated the shirts the Arrow Collar Man wore to glory. In Dacron® polyester and cotton. And Sanforized-Plus-2. They're as colorful now as they were sixty years ago.

But that's no surprise. Once you're a classic, you're always a classic.

Arrow

A division of Cluett, Peabody & Co., Inc.

The Nostalgia Collection by Arrow, the colorful white shirt company.

Introducing Oleg Cassini's tennis whites. In smashing colors.

Oleg Cassini, avid tennis player.
Oleg Cassini, top fashion designer.
Who else could have created a smashing collection like the Oleg Cassini Tennis Club?

The *designer* in Cassini created the smashing colors and a sporting harmony in men's and women's outfits never before seen on the court.

But the *tennis player* in Cassini created the *fit*. It's pure tennis and ready for action. Every warm-up suit, sweater, jacket, dress, skirt, shirt and pair of shorts designed to *give* luxuriously. And cut to flatter too, like a Cassini original.

It doesn't look like ordinary tenniswear because it isn't. It's the Oleg Cassini Tennis Club.

And you're invited to join this season at a fine store near you.

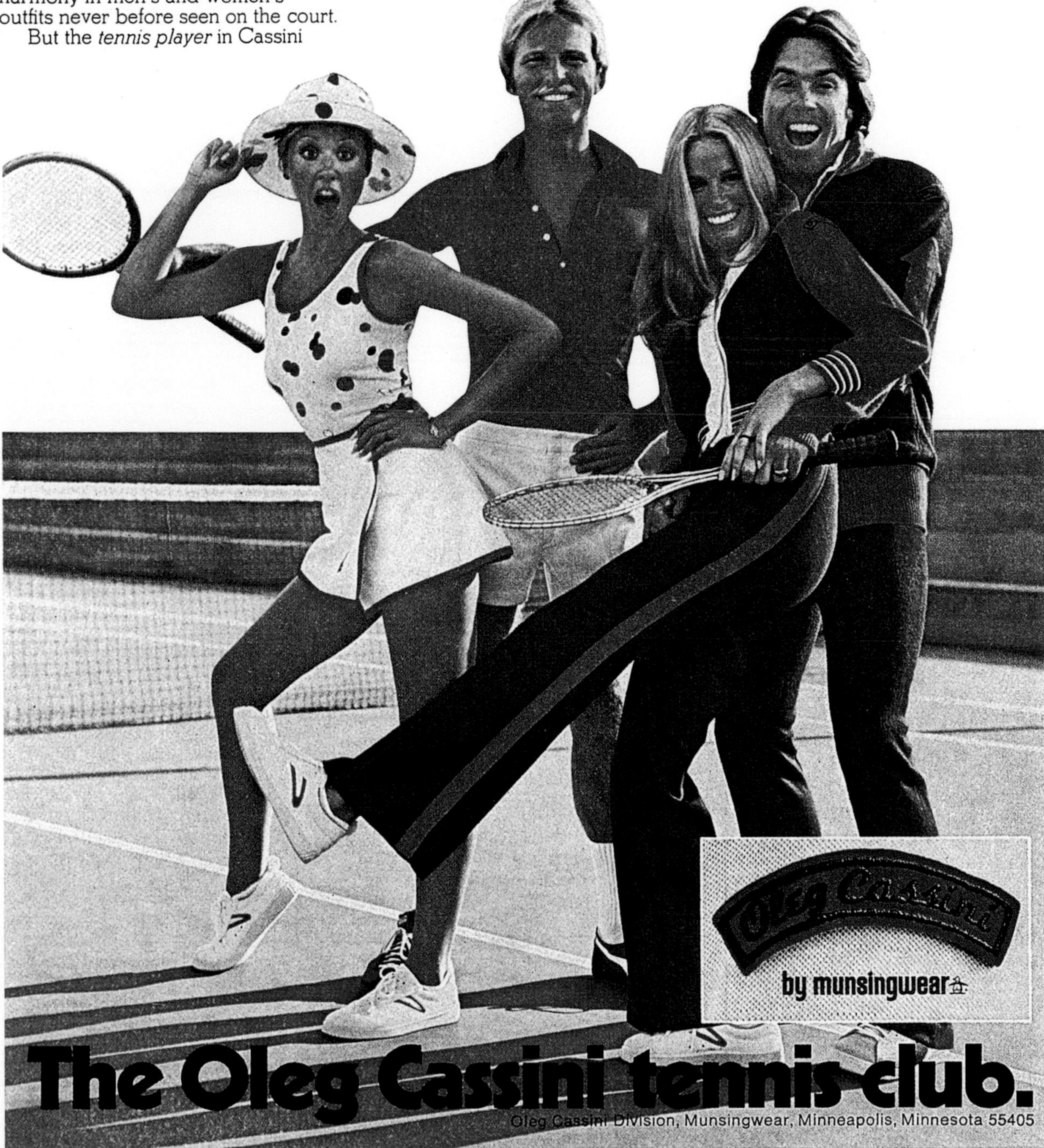

Oleg Cassini
by munsingwear
The Oleg Cassini tennis club.
Oleg Cassini Division, Munsingwear, Minneapolis, Minnesota 55405

Oleg Cassini Tennis Club, 1974

Adidas Warm Ups/Keyrolan Fabrics, 1977 ◂

A direct hit from the Christian Dior sunglass collection.

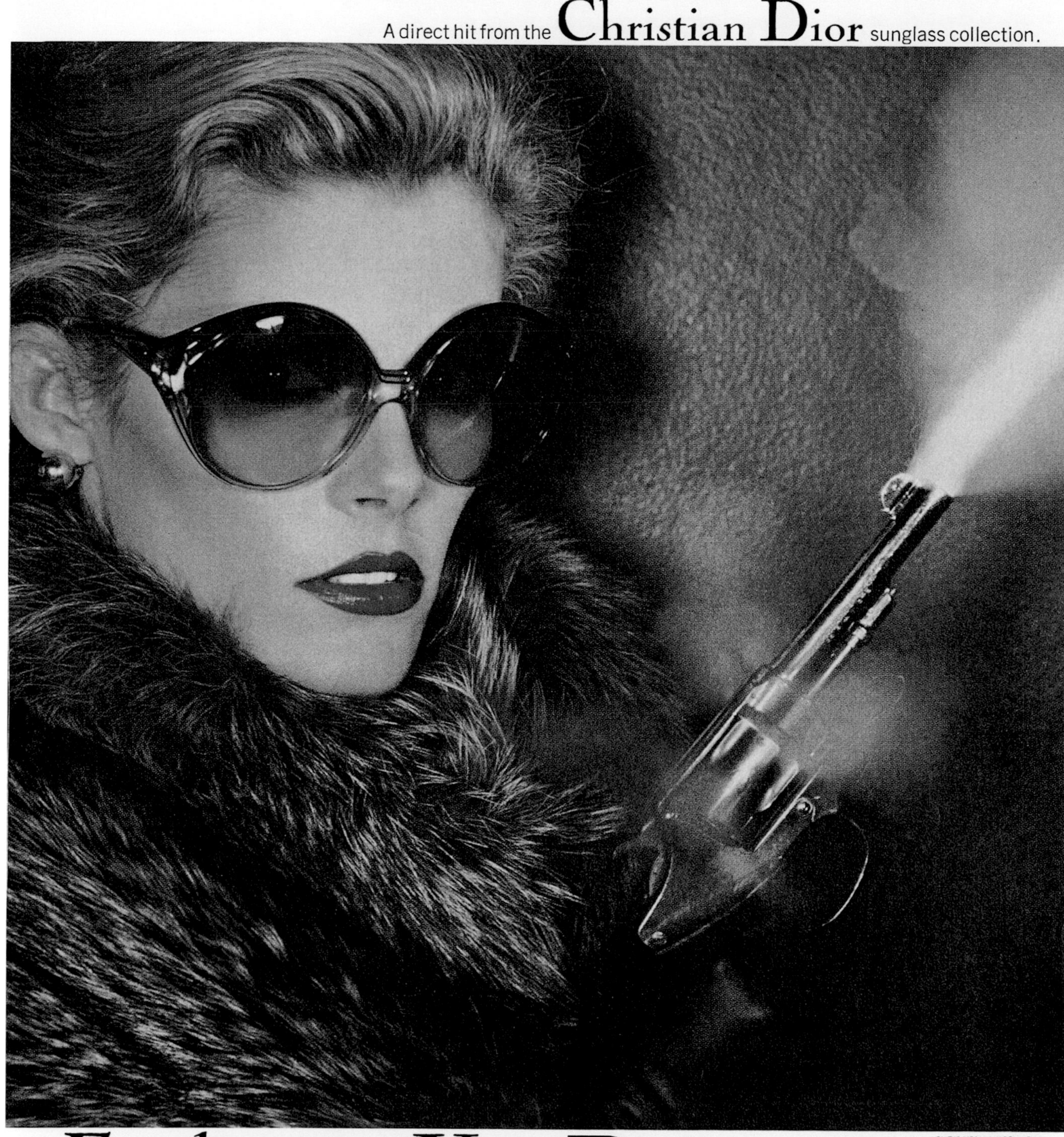

Explosive is Your Dior.

346

Christian Dior Eyewear, 1977

► Christian Dior Swimwear, 1977

VON WANGENHEIM

Electrifying is Your Dior.

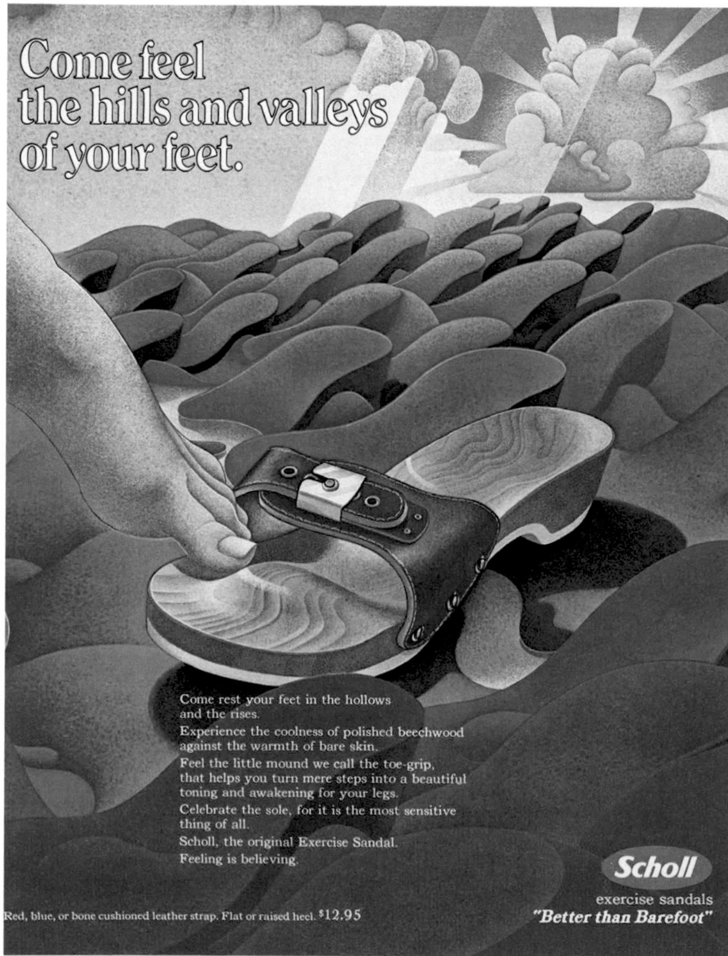

Come feel
the hills and valleys
of your feet.
Come rest your feet in the hollows
and the rises.
Experience the coolness of polished beechwood
against the warmth of bare skin.
Feel the little mound we call the toe-grip,
that helps you turn mere steps into a beautiful
toning and awakening for your legs.
Celebrate the sole, for it is the most sensitive
thing of all.
Scholl, the original Exercise Sandal.
Feeling is believing.
Scholl
exercise sandals
"Better than Barefoot"
Red, blue, or bone cushioned leather strap. Flat or raised heel. $12.95

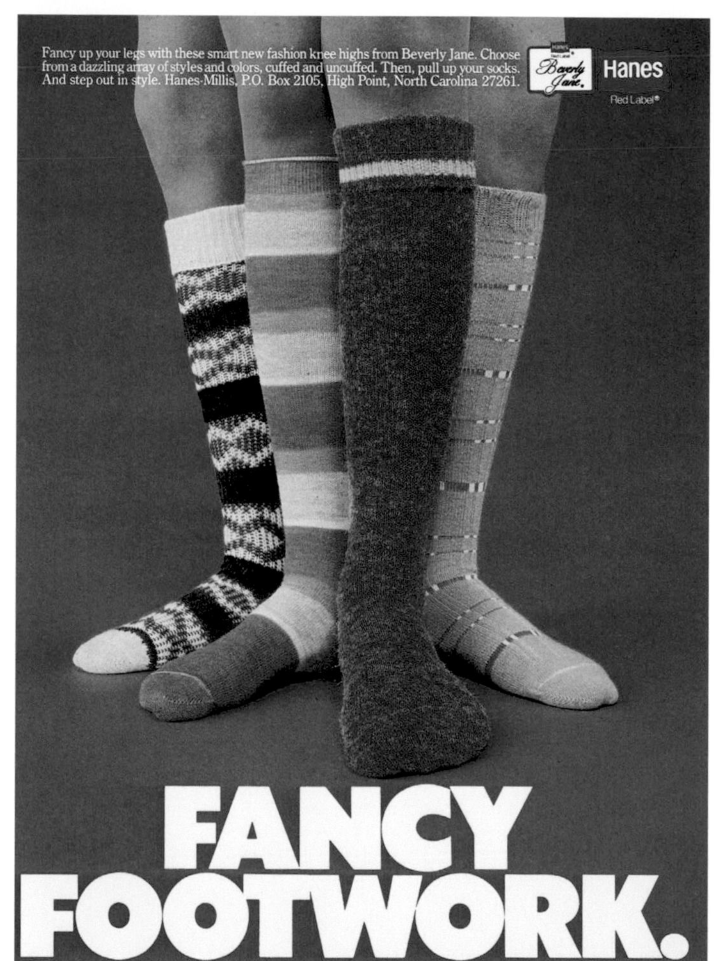

Fancy up your legs with these smart new fashion knee highs from Beverly Jane. Choose
from a dazzling array of styles and colors, cuffed and uncuffed. Then, pull up your socks.
And step out in style. Hanes-Millis, P.O. Box 2105, High Point, North Carolina 27261.
Beverly Jane
Hanes
Red Label®
FANCY
FOOTWORK.

Scholl Excercise Sandal, 1974

Beverly Jane/Hanes Socks, 1977

► Sears, Roebuck and Co. Department Store, 1970

Catch a Clog (or two or three)

We did!

Lazy, crazy clogs. Our deliberately cloppy, frankly floppy, sorta shoes. The fun thing to wear with long pants, short skirts, bare legs and so-what moods. Catch a clog—this season's big oaf of a shoe—at most Sears, Roebuck and Co. stores. Also available in the spring and summer catalog.

The Shoe Place at Sears

the fashion stop

GET TO THE BOTTOM OF THINGS

COOL WHITES
Nothing goes with the hot, new summer fashions like Bostonian Cool Whites. They're crisp. Fresh. And designed with snap by Ambros. We've got the whole, cool collection. The squashy crinkle patent zip boot. And the softest textured calfskin demi-boot and slipon. All on the hot new, high heel. Come in and turn on your summer wardrobe today.
Bostonians
COOL WHITES
a) 27.95
b) 35.00
c) 37.50
American Express Card, Master Charge or BankAmericard
you can depend on
DESMOND'S

All shoes are not created equal.
The booted-front Commodore slip-on by
Johnston & Murphy

Desmond's Footwear, 1972

Johnston & Murphy Shoes, 1971

Tempos Shoes, 1973 ◂

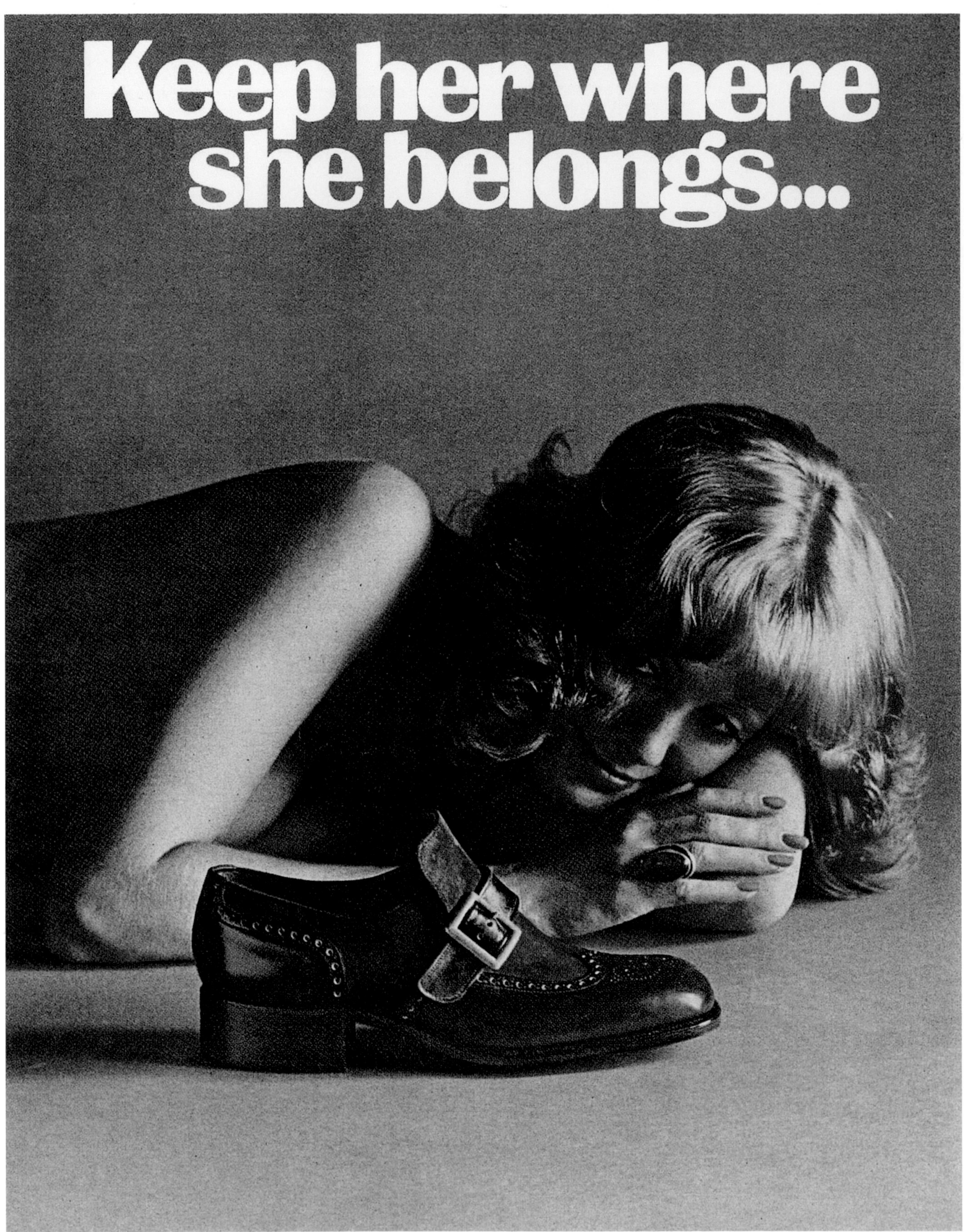
Keep her where
she belongs...

Weyenberg Massagic Shoes, 1972

▸ Flagg Bros. Footwear, 1972

rise on!
STAR SPANGLE
Brushed olive, beige and gold suede lace-up. Platform sole. Star-studded eyelets. Newest "rise on" curved maxi heel covered in beige suede. Style #1766.
Only $18.99 by mail.
BIG MUTHA
Smooth red and black leather platform lace-up. Scalloped leather accents. Black enameled eyelets. Newest "rise on" curved maxi heel covered in red leather. Style #1043.
Only $18.99 by mail.
THE BROTHER
Newest platform lace-up! Smooth black and brown leather. New flared "rise on" maxi heel. Potato toe. Style #1751.
Only $15.99 by mail.
RIPPLE RED
Smooth red and black lace-up. Newest platform sole. Scalloped leather accents. New "rise on" curved maxi heel. Style #1740.
Only $17.99 by mail.
GRAY GHOST
Newest platform lace-up. Shiny black leather and gray suede. "Rise on" flared maxi heel. Style #1742.
Only $16.99 by mail.
REBEL ROUSER
Soft black leather boot piped in red. Platform sole. Side zipper. New "rise on" curved maxi heel covered in red leather. Style #6106.
Only $19.99 by mail.
Order today by mail!
FLAGG BROS.
Send order to: Flagg Bros. P.O. Box 3642 Dept. E-4 Nashville Tennessee 37217
CHECK HERE FOR FREE COLOR CATALOG!
PRINT NAME
ADDRESS
ZIP
CITY
STATE
STYLE NUMBER
SIZE (D width only)
STYLE NUMBER
SIZE (D width only)
(If money order, add $1.25 for uniform postage fees and insurance. For C.O.D., send $1.00 deposit.) No C.O.D.'s to A.P.O. and F.P.O. or outside the U.S.A.
C.O.D.
MONEY ORDER
Your neighborhood Flagg Bros. store carries these and hundreds of other ahead of the times styles.

You'll get a boot out of this. $5.88 a pair.

Where can you possibly find hook and eyelet lace-up boots, with side zippers, stretch shiny vinyl uppers, 1½ inch man-made heel, man-made soles, 16 inches high for $5.88 a pair? At Wards. If you're ready for a boot, we're ready for you. In brown, black and white.

Open a Wards "Charg-All" account. It makes shopping simpler in our stores and catalogs.

MONTGOMERY WARD

Wards. The unexpected.

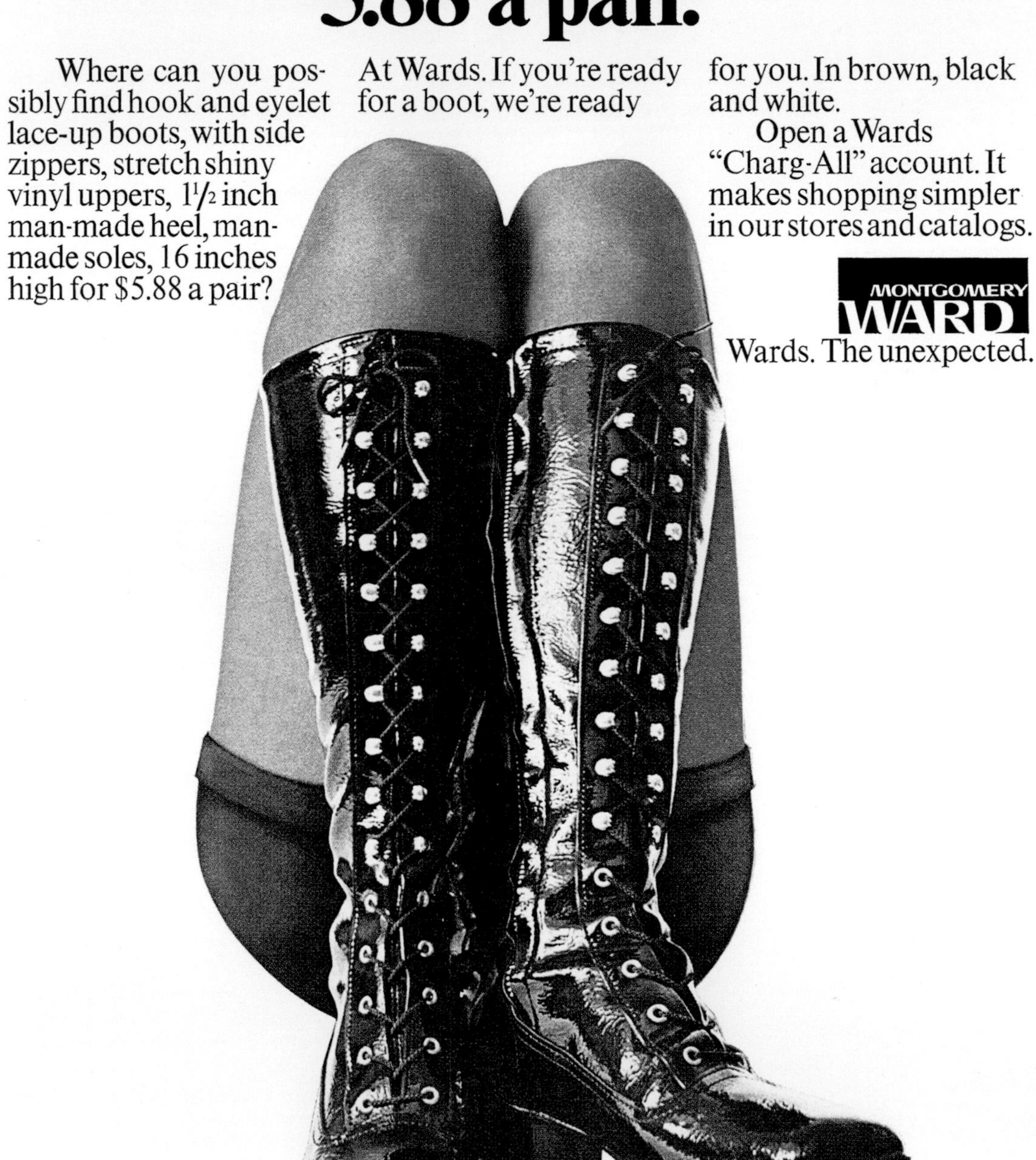

Montgomery Ward Department Store, 1971

The Olympic Pacesetters
Look at the feet and your eyes will convince you that more olympic athletes wear adidas than all other brands combined.
The secret is that adidas makes the right shoe for the right event.
adidas®
—the original 3-stripe shoe.
ADISTAR 2000
MONTREAL 76
adidas

Adidas Athletic Shoes, 1976

It doesn't cost a million to feel like a million.

► Blackglama Furs, 1973

Pearl Bailey was one of several famous faces – including Judy Garland and Ray Charles – featured in the long-standing Blackglama furs "Legends" campaign, which debuted in 1968.

Pearl Bailey war eines von mehreren berühmten Gesichtern – darunter auch Judy Garland und Ray Charles – in der langlebigen Kampagne „Legends" für Blackglama-Pelze, die 1968 startete.

Outre Judy Garland et Ray Charles, Pearl Bailey compta parmi les nombreux visages célèbres qui prêtèrent leur image à la longue campagne « Legends » des fourrures Blackglama, lancée en 1968.

American Fur Industries, 1972

What becomes a Legend most?

BLACKGLAMA® IS THE WORLD'S FINEST NATURAL DARK RANCH MINK BRED ONLY IN AMERICA BY THE GREAT LAKES MINK MEN

Happy Legs Sportswear, 1973 ◄

Happy Legs used the risqué slogan "What to wear on Sunday when you won't be home until Monday" throughout the 1970s, exploiting the relaxed sexual mores of the era.

Happy Legs benutzte den gewagten Slogan "Was Sie am Sonntag tragen sollten, wenn Sie nicht vor Montag nach Hause kommen" die 1970er Jahre hindurch und spielte damit auf die gelockerten sexuellen Gewohnheiten jener Ära an.

Happy Legs utilisa l'audacieux slogan « Que porter le dimanche quand on ne rentrera pas avant lundi » tout au long des années 70, reflétant le libéralisme sexuel de l'époque.

Thom McAn Boots, 1971

If you'd like to find the nearest Thom McAn store, just look on the opposite page.

360

Classic White Knits–Casually sophisticated. That sums up this Lee trend-setter featuring a shirt jacket (about $30) with epaulets and enamel-like buttons and matching slacks (about $20). Both are defined twill double-knits of non-glitter 100% Dacron® polyester. The sports shirt (about $17) tops off another great "Tops & Bottoms" idea from The Lee Company, 640 Fifth Ave., N.Y., N.Y. 10019.
Lee
A company of V corporation

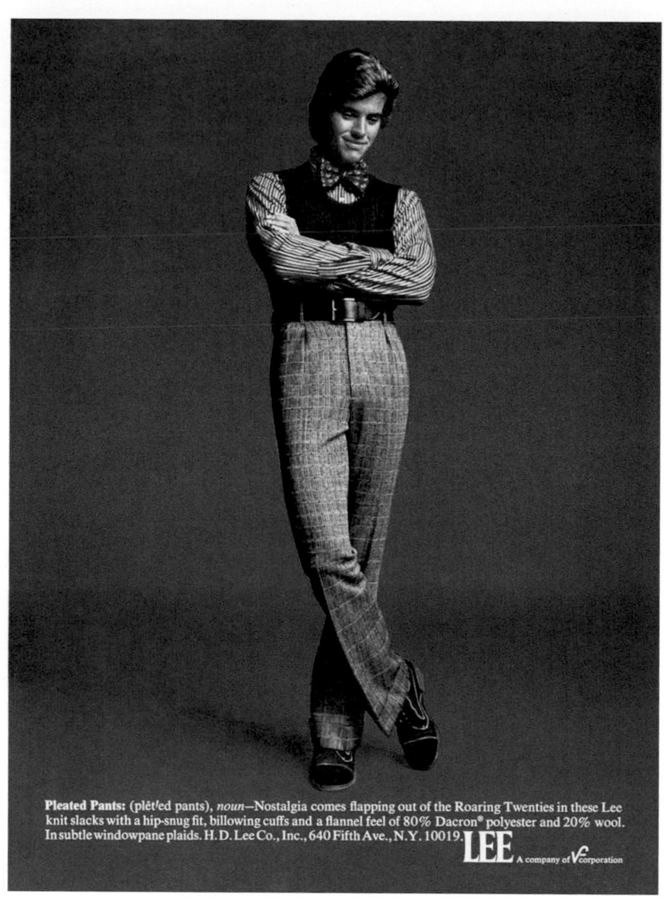

Pleated Pants: (plēt'ed pants), *noun*–Nostalgia comes flapping out of the Roaring Twenties in these Lee knit slacks with a hip-snug fit, billowing cuffs and a flannel feel of 80% Dacron® polyester and 20% wool. In subtle windowpane plaids. H. D. Lee Co., Inc., 640 Fifth Ave., N.Y. 10019.
LEE
A company of V corporation

► Jump Suits, Ltd., 1976

In the 1970s, jumpsuits made the jump from workwear staple to men's fashion item. It was a short-lived trend for men, but the style soon made its way into women's fashion, where it has remained off and on ever since. The white leisure suit, on the other hand, was a mainstay of the era, reaching its pinnacle with *Saturday Night Fever* star John Travolta. Even classic American denim brand Lee got into the trend with its own version in white double knit.

In den 1970ern gelang dem Overall der Sprung von der Arbeitskleidung zum Modeartikel für Herren. Es war zwar nur ein kurzlebiger Trend, aber er schaffte es rasch auch in die Damenmode, wo er seither immer mal wieder gefragt ist. Als weißer Freizeitanzug erreichte er den Gipfel der Popularität mit John Travolta als Star in *Saturday Night Fever*. Selbst die klassische amerikanische Jeansmarke Lee sprang mit einem eigenen Modell aus weißem Double Knit auf den Zug auf.

Dans les années 70, salopettes et combinaisons, à l'origine vêtements d'ouvrier, firent une incursion dans la mode masculine. Ce fut une tendance éphémère chez les hommes, mais on la retrouva rapidement dans la mode pour femme, où la combinaison n'a jamais cessé d'apparaître et de disparaître depuis. A l'opposé, le costume blanc marqua cette époque, sa popularité culminant grâce à John Travolta dans *Saturday Night Fever*. Même Lee, marque de jean américain classique, surfa sur cette tendance en proposant sa propre version en maille blanche doublée.

Lee Knits, 1975

Lee Slacks, 1972

our name says it all.

Jump Suits, Ltd. began it all. And today, seven years later, is still a jump ahead.
Designing Jumpsuits in the newest, most natural fabrics.
Designing Jumpsuits which are young, hip, tight and sexy.
Designing jumpsuits which are made to fit.
When it comes to jumpsuits, we were first in fashion . . . . and we still are!

JUMP SUITS®
LTD.

A Division Of
BRIGHT
GROUP™

5526 E. Mockingbird / Dallas, Texas 75206
Telephone 214/826-8100
WRITE TO US FOR NEAREST DEALER AND CATALOG.

The tie for the shirt by Hathaway.

The sound of Jazz: Hathaway's Cabaret Plaid.

It's bold and beautiful! Like the vibrant tones from an Armstrong or Beiderbecke. Syncopated checks over checks create real added dimension in this stunning Cabaret Plaid, and the sheik, Rutland collar is a perfect set-up for a contemporary bow tie. The shirt is a weave of Durable Press polyester and cotton, priced at $16.00. For the store nearest you, write C. F. Hathaway Company, Waterville, Maine 04901, a division of Warnaco, Inc.

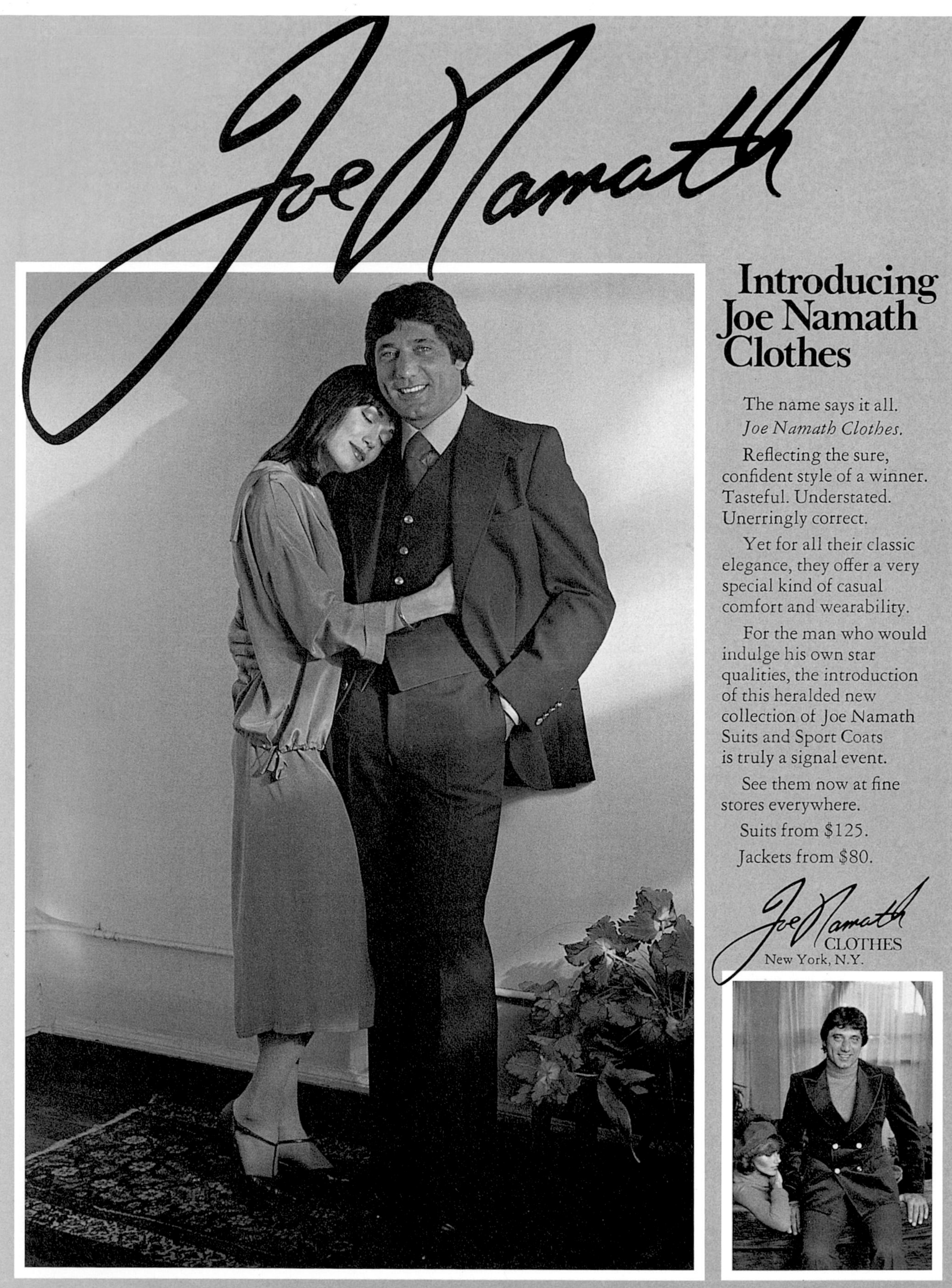

Joe Namath
Introducing Joe Namath Clothes
The name says it all. Joe Namath Clothes.
Reflecting the sure, confident style of a winner. Tasteful. Understated. Unerringly correct.
Yet for all their classic elegance, they offer a very special kind of casual comfort and wearability.
For the man who would indulge his own star qualities, the introduction of this heralded new collection of Joe Namath Suits and Sport Coats is truly a signal event.
See them now at fine stores everywhere.
Suits from $125.
Jackets from $80.
Joe Namath CLOTHES
New York, N.Y.

Joe Namath Clothes, 1977

Hathaway Shirts, 1973 ◂

Jockey International, Inc., Kenosha, Wisconsin 53140

TAKE AWAY THEIR UNIFORMS AND WHO ARE THEY.

JOCKEY® BRAND

Steve Garvey: Dual Purpose Underwear-Swimwear; **Brad Park**: Slim Guy, Nylon Boxer and T-Shirt; **Lou Brock**: Life* International Scandia Mesh A-Shirt/Brief; **Vic Hadfield**: International Skants,* Metre Brief; **Fred Dryer**: Dual Purpose Sport Short; **Craig Morton**: International Skants,* Tropez Brief; **Terry Metcalf**: Nylon A-Shirt/Brief; **Ed Marinaro**: Life* Bosun Shirt/Slim Guy Brief; **Jim McMillian**: Life* Denim Brief/A-Shirt.
Where to buy it? See page 189

Jockey Underwear, 1976

This 1976 Jockey underwear campaign was targeted at both the traditionally male sports market and women, who, as the predominant family shoppers, were making the ultimate purchasing decisions.

Diese Unterwäsche-Kampagne von Jockey aus dem Jahr 1976 zielte sowohl auf den traditionell männlichen Sportartikelmarkt ab wie auch auf die Frauen, die als die tonangebenden Einkäuferinnen der Familie letztlich die Kaufentscheidungen treffen.

Cette campagne de 1976 pour les sous-vêtements Jockey ciblait à la fois le marché sportswear masculin traditionnel et les femmes : comme c'étaient généralement elles qui faisaient les courses, elles prenaient donc les décisions d'achat finales.

► Dingo Boots, 1977

O.J. DINGO
The man's all legs and knows everything about feet. Listen:
"Boots have to look great — but they also have to be made for whatever you're going to be doing in them. That's why, when you say boots, you gotta say Dingo®."
Like O.J. Simpson, we mean what we say, and what we say is: Nobody Puts Leather Together Like Dingo.
dingo®
Nobody Puts Leather Together Like Dingo.

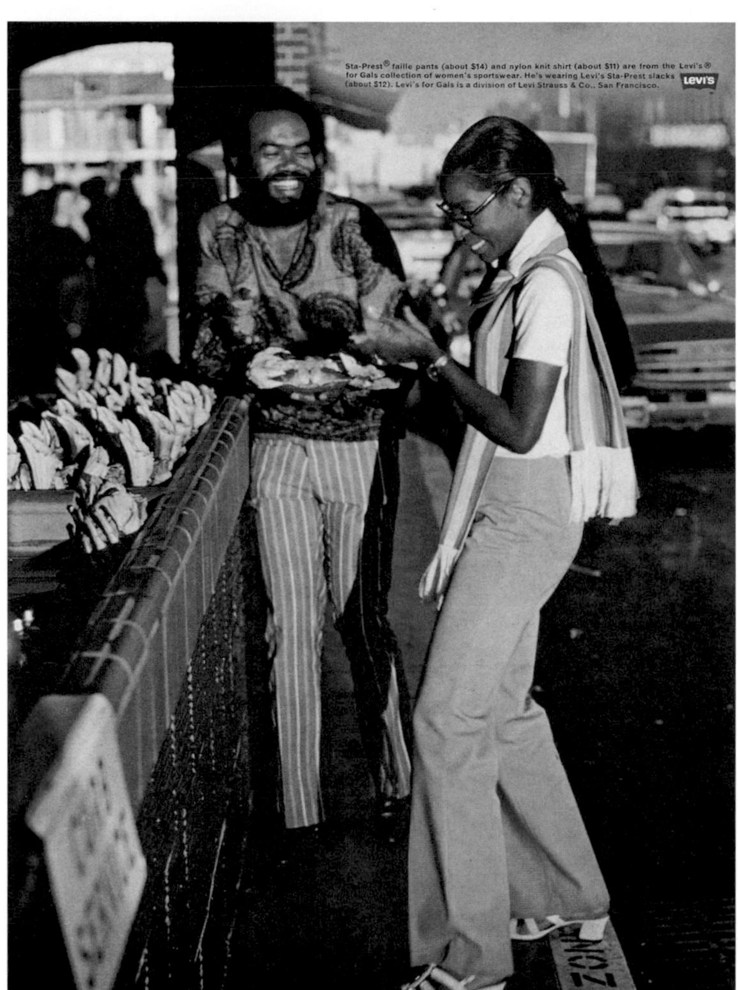

Levi's Sportswear, 1971

Levi's Sportswear, 1970

► Wrangler Jeans & Sportswear, 1971

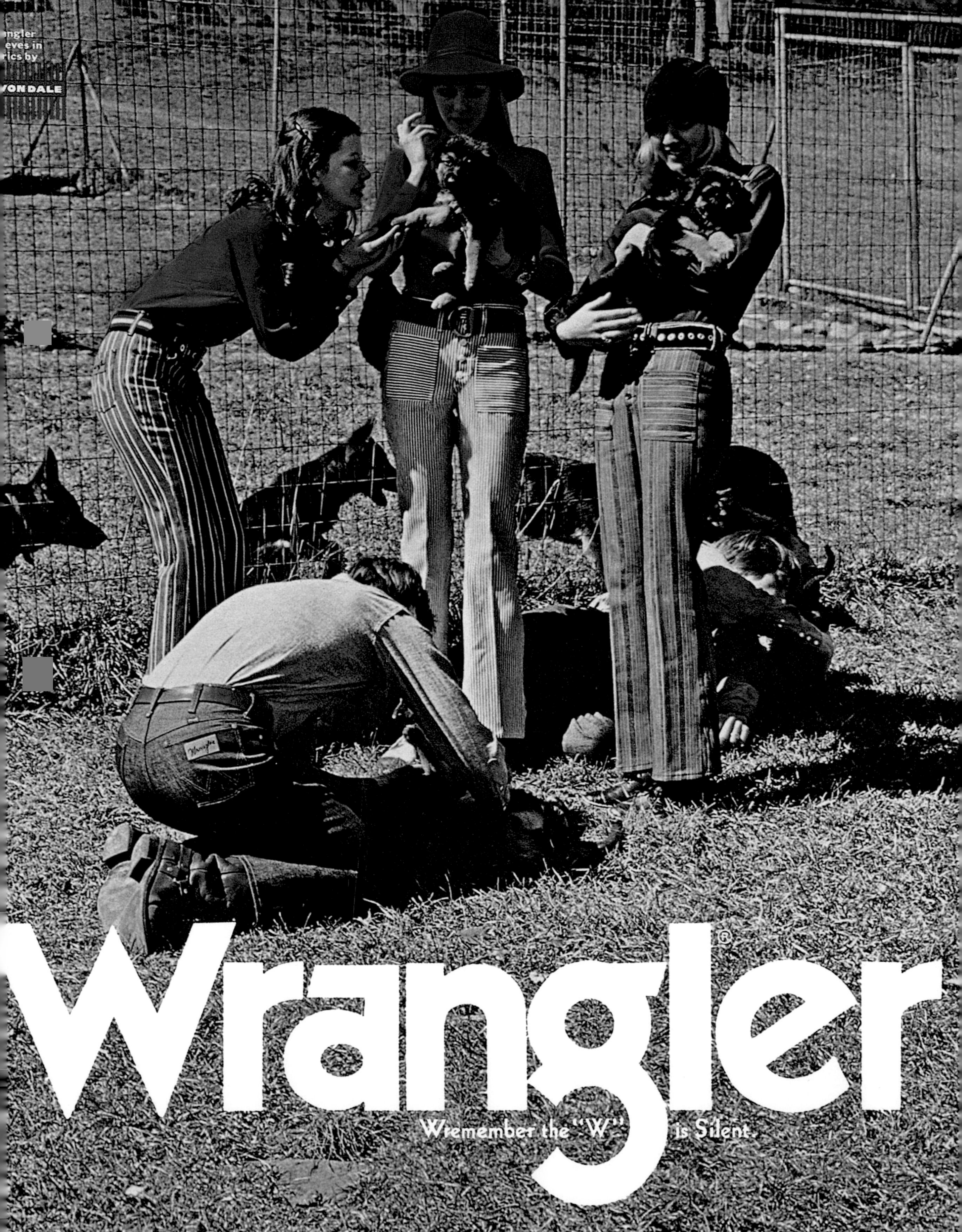
Wrangler®
Wremember the "W" is Silent.

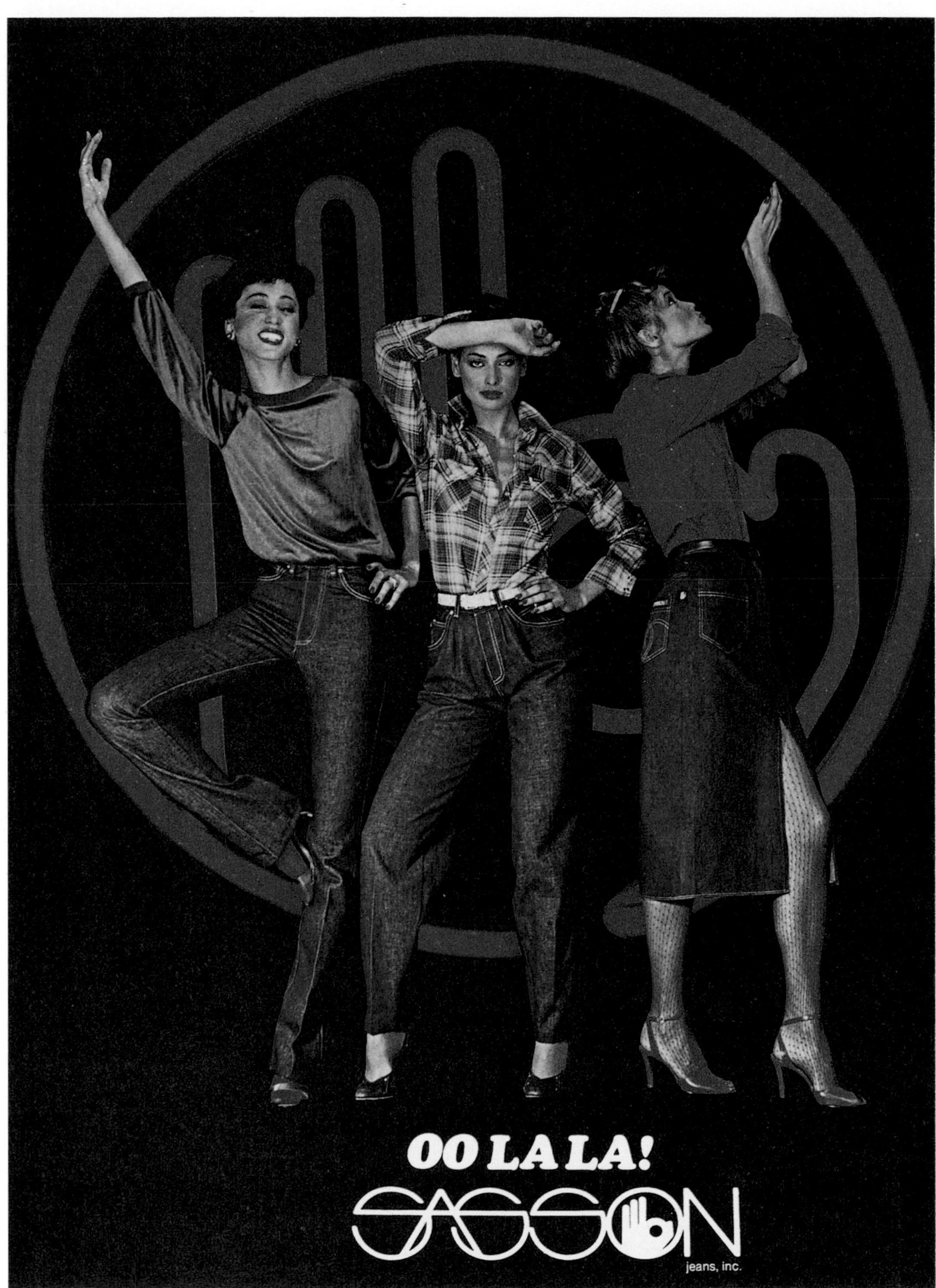

Sasson Jeans, 1979

Paul Guez, the man who went on to launch Antik Denim, was behind Sasson Jeans, one of the pioneers of designer denim. The company's "Oo la la!" campaign reached the height of its popularity with a TV commercial that featured members of the New York Rangers hockey team, wearing the jeans in an ice rink, tunelessly singing the jingle.

Paul Guez, der später Antik Denim starten sollte, war auch der Drahtzieher bei Sasson Jeans, einem der Pioniere im Bereich Designerjeans. Die „Oo la la!"-Kampagne der Firma erreichte den Gipfel ihrer Popularität mit einem TV-Spot, der Mitglieder des Hockeyteams der New York Rangers zeigt, die die Jeans auf einem Eislaufplatz tragen, während sie völlig schief den Jingle singen.

Pionnier du jean de créateur, Paul Guez créa aussi Sasson Jeans avant de lancer Antik Denim. La campagne « Oo la la! » atteignit des sommets de popularité grâce à un spot TV présentant des joueurs de l'équipe de hockey des New York Rangers qui portaient les jeans sur une patinoire et reprenaient la rengaine en chantant faux.

► Jesus Jeans, 1976

Thou shalt not have any other jeans but me.

Foto Toscani

jesus
jeans

THE JORDACHE LOOK
JORDACHE®
JORDACHE
JORDACHE®
Designer Jeans by R. Jordache
Showroom: 110 E.9 th St., L.A., CA 90079 213.624.1992
Available In San Francisco at:
Emporium, Grodins, I. Magnin, J. Magnin,
Liberty House, Macy's, Roos Atkins.
Available In Los Angeles at:
Alroe, Apropos Look, The Broadway, Bullock's,
Double-up Stores, Fred Segal Jeans, I. Magnin,
Inspiration, J. Magnin, J.W. Robinson,
Nobby, Peaches, Pigeon,
Rix Rack Inc., The Corral,
Wild West Stores, Windsor Fashion.

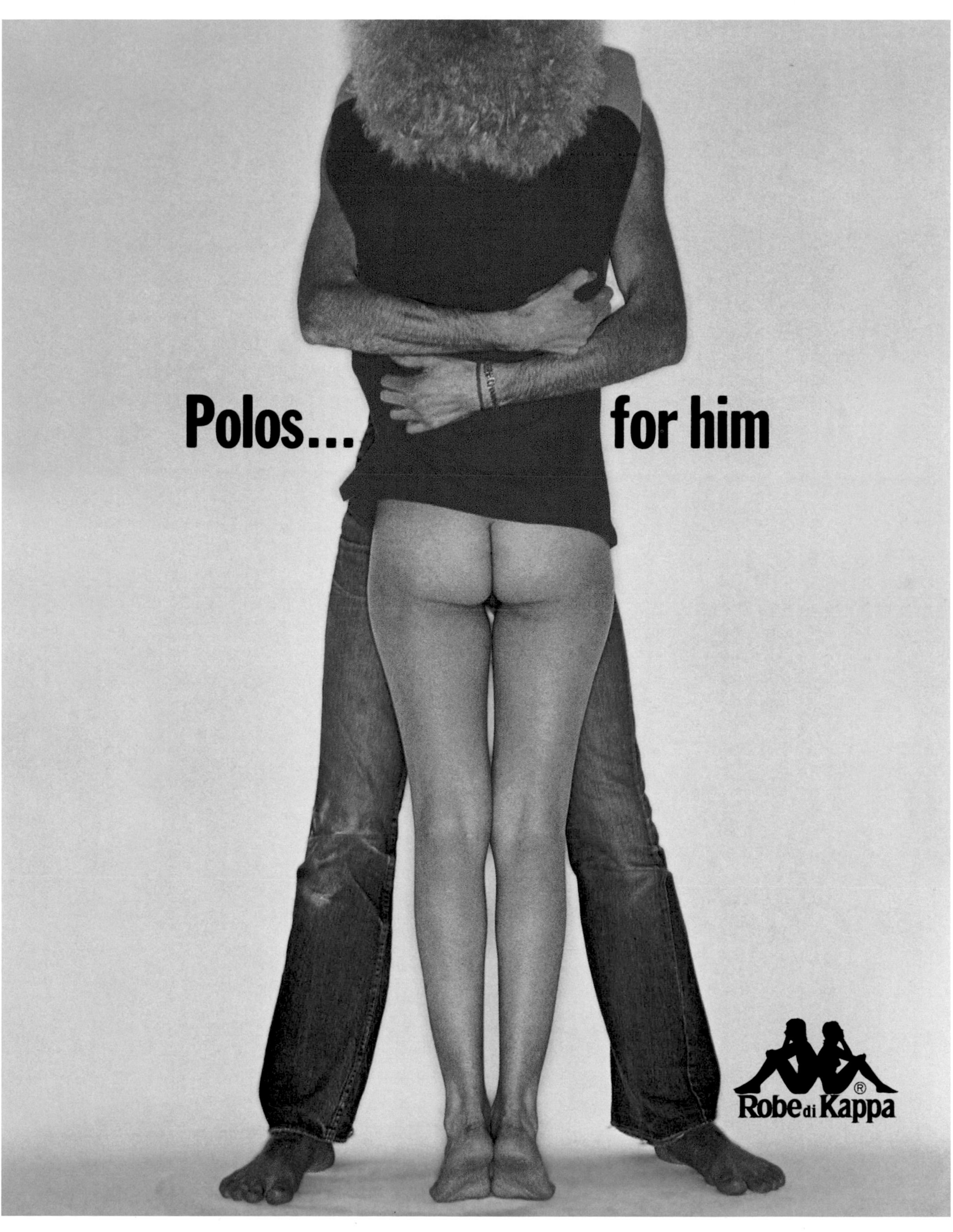

Robe di Kappa Menswear, 1976

Jordache Jeans, 1979 ◂

HENRY IV
When we have shuffled off this
Mortal coil,
give us pause.
ACT III. SC 1
Nothing is better than Landlubber® clothes.

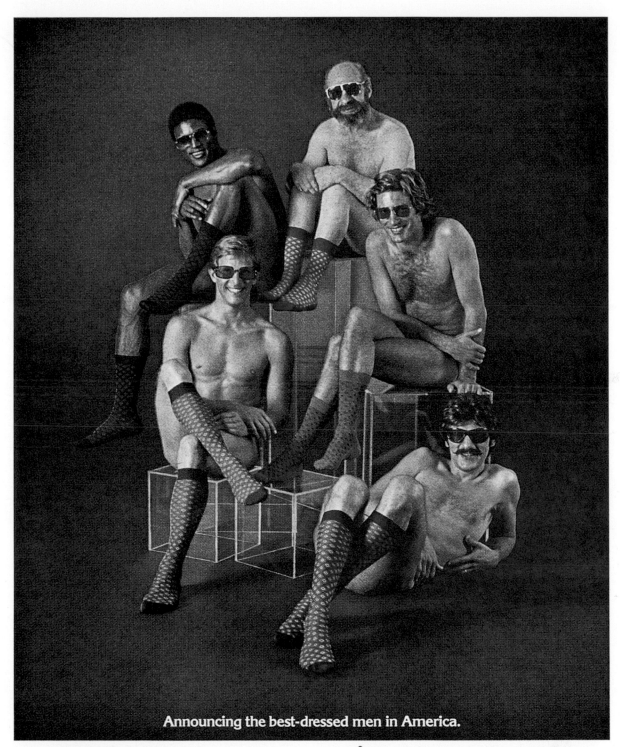

Announcing the best-dressed men in America.

You're looking at a revolution.

The most influential men in America are breaking out of their socks—out of their old, blah, boring, one-color, no-style socks.

At Interwoven/Esquire Socks, we saw it coming all the way. That's why we make the great fashion socks that are making it happen.

In lots of great colors and lengths. All in the first Ban-Lon® pattern socks ever made. They feel softer and fit better than any sock you've ever worn.

That's why we dress the best-dressed men in America. Or anywhere.

KR
Another fine product of Kayser-Roth

Interwoven Socks, 1972

Landlubber Menswear, 1971 ◂

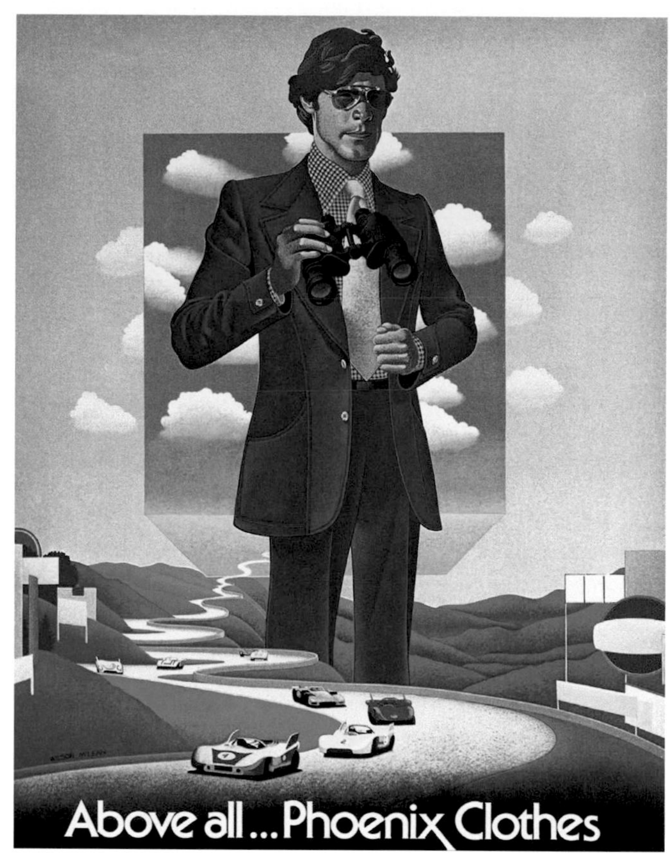

PG's Menswear, 1975

Phoenix Clothes Menswear, 1974

► Geoffrey Beene Menswear, 1974

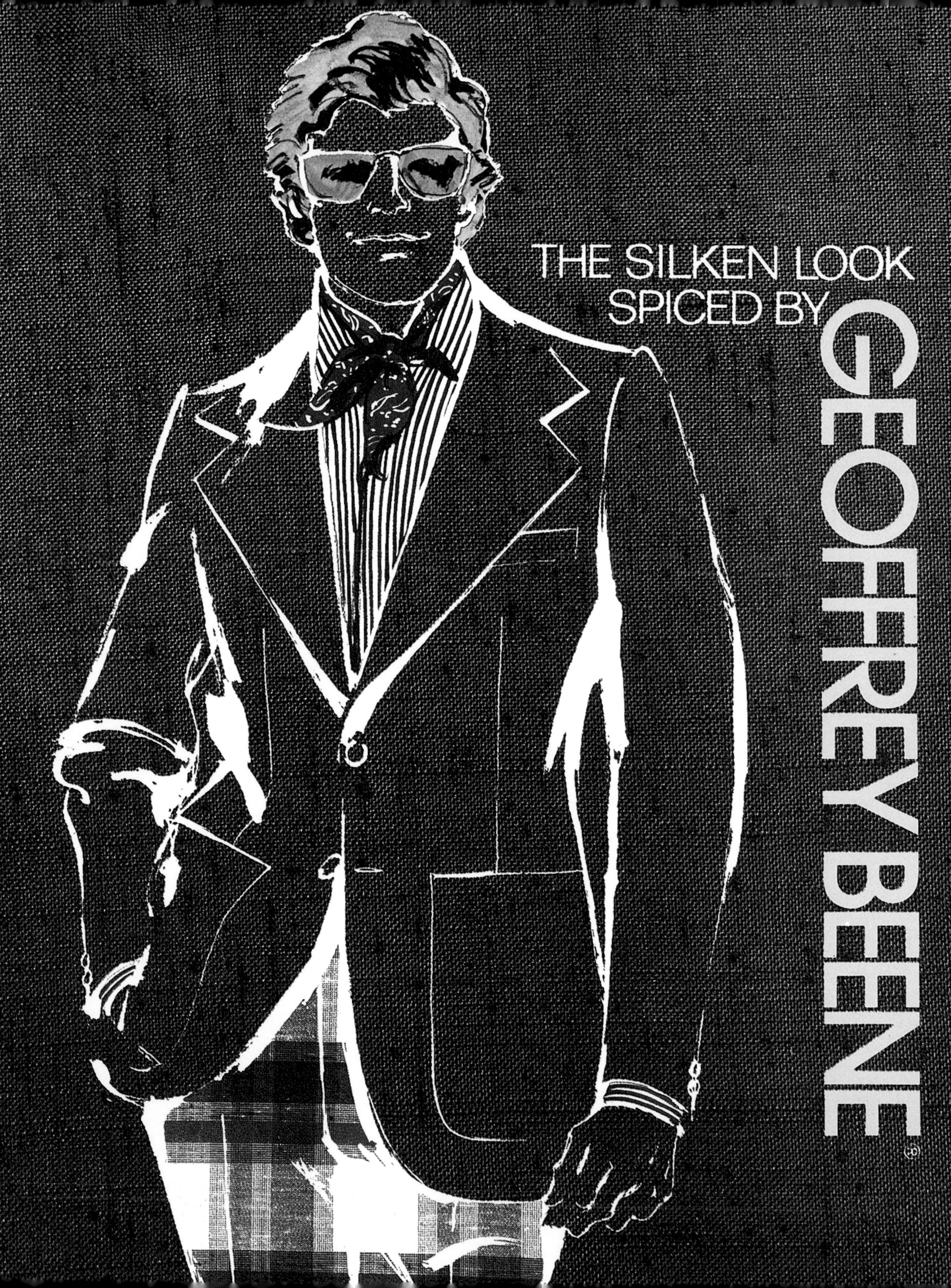
THE SILKEN LOOK
SPICED BY
GEOFFREY BEENE

Make your legs look good.
And feel good, too.
With Sheer Energy® Pantyhose. Our sheer smooth yarn makes your legs look good. Our all-day massage™ makes your legs feel good.
So get into sheer, smooth Sheer Energy. (Now you can get 'em in our Queensize, too.)
SHEER ENERGY
SHEER ENERGY
PANTYHOSE

L'eggs Sheer Energy Hosiery, 1977 ◄

T-shirt and underwear manufacturer Hanes introduced its L'eggs brand pantyhose in 1970, selling the product in distinctive plastic egg-shaped containers in grocery stores and pharmacies. The company launched its Sheer Energy brand three years later, with the claim that the style would give the wearer added energy to get her through her busy day.

Der T-Shirt- und Wäschehersteller Hanes stellte 1970 seine Strumpfhose der Marke L'eggs vor, wobei das Produkt im unverwechselbaren eiförmigen Plastikbehälter in Lebensmittelläden und Apotheken verkauft wurde. Seine Marke Sheer Energy brachte das Unternehmen drei Jahre später heraus, und zwar mit der Behauptung, sie würde ihrer Trägerin zusätzliche Energie für ihren anstrengenden Alltag schenken.

Le fabricant de T-shirts et de sous-vêtements Hanes lança sa marque de collants L'eggs en 1970. Les produits étaient vendus dans des boîtes en plastique originales en forme d'œuf dans les épiceries et les pharmacies. L'entreprise introduisit sa marque Sheer Energy trois ans plus tard, proclamant que ses collants donnaient aux femmes plus d'énergie pour assumer leurs journées surchargées.

Fruit of the Loom Hosiery, 1978

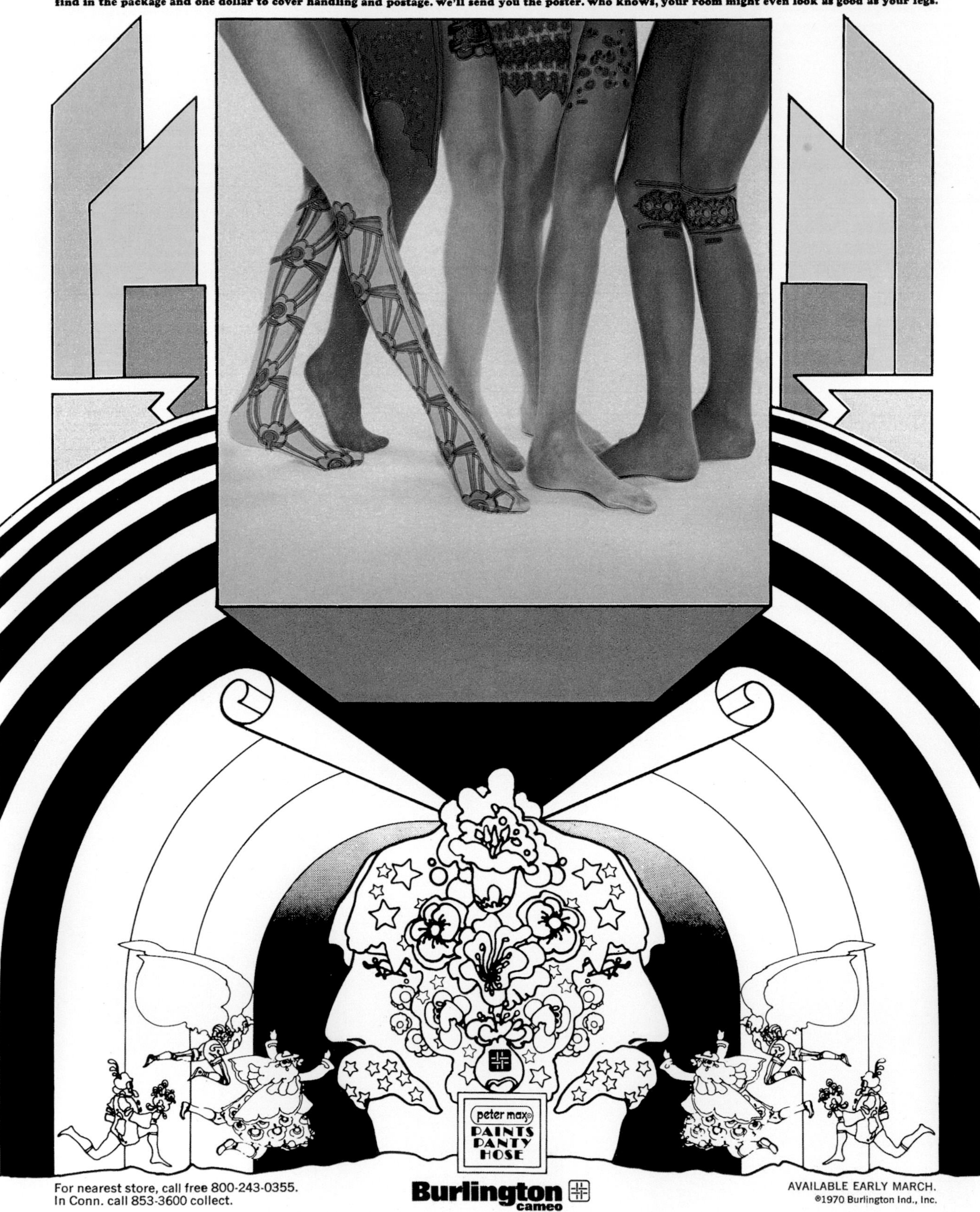

Peter Max paints panty hose for Burlington-Cameo.
they come in three proportioned-to-fit sizes, $8.00 each. body stockings, too. one size only, in 2 peter max original designs [not shown]. cost $10.00 each. buy the panty hose or body stockings and you get a coupon for a peter max poster. [it's a copy of this page blown up to poster size 24"x36".] send us the coupon you'll find in the package and one dollar to cover handling and postage. we'll send you the poster. who knows, your room might even look as good as your legs.
peter max
PAINTS
PANTY
HOSE
For nearest store, call free 800-243-0355.
In Conn. call 853-3600 collect.
Burlington
cameo
AVAILABLE EARLY MARCH.
©1970 Burlington Ind., Inc.

Burlington-Cameo Hosiery, 1970

▸ Funky Womenswear/Silesta Polyester, 1978

▸▸ Jantzen Swimwear, 1976

ENTERTAINERS.

Modern Art

Jantzen sets
the new direction
for swimwear in these
soft, stylish knits.
An action brief of
DuPont ANTRON® nylon
and LYCRA® spandex,
a shirt of ANTRON.
They're pure "Body Art"™—
from just one of the
collections that makes
Jantzen #1 in swimwear.

Jantzen®

A source of pride

JANTZEN INC., PORTLAND, OREGON 97208

The
now action
in fashion.
DU PONT
Lycra®

VENERABLE DENIM LABELS LIKE LEVI'S FOUND THEMSELVES FACED WITH A NEW WAVE OF COMPETITION WHEN BROOKE SHIELDS PUT HERSELF AND CALVIN KLEIN VERY DEFINITIVELY ON THE MAP BY DECLARING THAT NOTHING CAME BETWEEN HER AND HER CALVINS.

EHRWÜRDIGE JEANSLABELS WIE LEVI'S WURDEN MIT EINER WELLE NEUER KONKURRENTEN KONFRONTIERT, ALS BROOKE SHIELDS EIN ZEICHEN FÜR SICH UND CALVIN KLEIN SETZTE, INDEM SIE ERKLÄRTE, IHR KÄME SCHLICHTWEG NICHTS ZWISCHEN SIE UND IHRE CALVINS.

LES MARQUES DE JEANS ÉTABLIES DE LONGUE DATE COMME LEVI'S SONT CONFRONTÉES À UNE NOUVELLE FORME DE CONCURRENCE QUAND BROOKE SHIELDS FAIT SA GLOIRE ET CELLE DE CALVIN KLEIN EN DÉCLARANT NE RIEN PORTER SOUS SON JEAN CALVIN.

1980

PUNK, POP, AND POWER SUITS

PUNK, POP UND POWER SUITS

PUNK, POP ET POWER SUITS

-1989

JORDACHE®
Millers Outpost®

Jordache Jeans, 1988 ◂

Converse All Star Sports Shoes, 1987

MTV LAUNCHED ITS ALL-MUSIC VIDEO CABLE NETWORK IN 1981, BRINGING ROCK-STAR STYLE INTO THE LIVING ROOM. Overnight, rock stars had to look the part—projecting an image that reflected their music and resonated with their fans. No one did that better than Madonna, a little-known up-and-comer until the first MTV Video Music Awards in 1984, when many music fans got their first glimpse of the future material girl. Dressed in a lingerie-inspired wedding dress, Madonna stunned the crowd as she writhed across the stage while performing her hit, "Like a Virgin." The following year, the film *Desperately Seeking Susan* put the spotlight on Madonna's vintage-chic style.

The music industry exploded with new genres and new style-setters, from Michael Jackson's leather jackets to Pat Benatar's leotards and legwarmers. Meanwhile, rap music was just beginning to break, and with it came new street-inspired fashions. But it wasn't all rock 'n' roll in the '80s.

Early on, disco gave way to the chaste preppy looks of Ralph Lauren's lifestyle empire. The '80s saw Liz Claiborne go public and quickly grow into a mega brand; former Anne Klein designer Donna Karan took up where Claiborne left off, carving out a new niche for professional women: minimalist and professional. This became the decade of the "power suit," as more women entered the workforce and strong U.S. and Japanese economies put the spotlight on the business class. Giorgio Armani's impeccably tailored suits came to the fore, thanks in no small part to the 1980 film *American Gigolo*, in which Richard Gere memorably contemplates his vast Armani wardrobe in the opening scene.

It was also the decade of the avant-garde designer, including Jean-Paul Gaultier and Martin Margiela. Japanese designers Yohji Yamamoto and Comme des Garçons' Rei Kawakubo began showing their collections in Paris, and a new avant-garde design movement was born in Brussels. The Antwerp Six included Ann Demeulemeester and Dries Van Noten. Miuccia Prada launched her first ready-to-wear collection for Prada, and Karl Lagerfeld became the designer for Chanel.

For the masses, sportswear put the emphasis on "sports." A fitness craze led by actress Jane Fonda led to aerobics-inspired fashions filtering into daily dress. Norma Kamali took the look to a stylish new level with her sweatshirt collection. Nike set a new standard for celebrity endorsements by brokering a deal with Chicago Bulls rookie Michael Jordan to introduce the Air Jordan shoe.

Venerable denim labels like Levi's found themselves faced with a new wave of competition when Brooke Shields put herself and Calvin Klein very definitively on the map by declaring that nothing came between her and her Calvins. Los Angeles became a center for youth fashions from soon-to-be giant Guess and rival denim brands Z. Cavaricci and Bugle Boy. L.A. Gear joined the sneaker movement with an emphasis on Valley Girl style; and new brand Cross Colours took advantage of the burgeoning rap movement, taking urban streetwear to the mainstream.

1980

1980 In denim cutoffs, *Dukes of Hazzard* TV star sparks "Daisy Duke" trend

Mit ihren abgeschnittenen Jeans setzt der Star der TV-Serie *Dukes of Hazzard* den „Daisy Duke"-Trend

Dans ses mini-shorts en jean, la star de la série *Shérif, fais-moi peur* lance la tendance « Daisy Duke »

1980 Giorgio Armani's designs appear in *American Gigolo*

Giorgio Armanis Kreationen sind in *American Gigolo* zu sehen

Le film *American Gigolo* met à l'honneur les créations de Giorgio Armani

1981 Vivienne Westwood launches her first eponymous collection in London

Vivienne Westwood bringt in London ihre erste, nach ihr benannte Kollektion heraus

Vivienne Westwood lance sa première collection éponyme à Londres

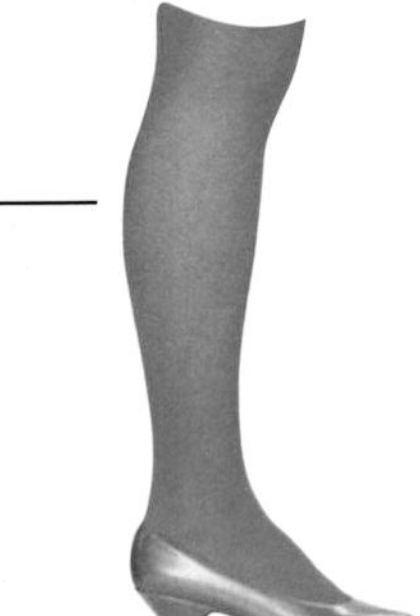

1982 Frank Zappa and 14-year-old daughter Moon Unit immortalize "Valley Girls"

Frank Zappa und seine 14-jährige Tochter Moon Unit machen „Valley Girls" unsterblich

Frank Zappa et sa fille de 14 ans Moon Unit égratignent les Américaines matérialistes et égocentriques dans leur chanson « Valley Girls »

MTV STARTETE 1981 SEINEN MUSIKVIDEO-SENDER UND BRACHTE SO DAS ROCKSTAR-STYLING DIREKT INS WOHNZIMMER. Quasi über Nacht waren die Rockstars plötzlich gefordert – hatten sie doch ein Image zu vermitteln, das ihrer Musik entsprach und zugleich bei ihren Fans ankam. Das gelang niemandem besser als Madonna, einer bis zu den ersten MTV Video Music Awards 1984 kaum bekannten Newcomerin; damals bekamen viele Musikfans einen ersten Eindruck vom künftigen Material Girl. In einem an Spitzenunterwäsche erinnernden Hochzeitskleid überwältigte Madonna das Publikum, als sie sich zu ihrem Hit „Like a Virgin" auf der Bühne wand. Im Jahr darauf brachte der Film *Susan verzweifelt gesucht* Madonnas Vintage-Chic noch stärker ins Rampenlicht.

Die Musikindustrie überschlug sich mit neuen Genres und Trendsettern, von Michael Jackson in seinen Lederjacken bis hin zu Pat Benatar in Trikot und Beinwärmern. Rap war gerade im Entstehen begriffen und damit auch eine neue, von der Kultur der Straße inspirierte Mode. Allerdings war in den 80ern nicht alles Rock'n'Roll. Schon früh machte die Discomode den keuschen, braven Looks des Lifestyle-Imperiums von Ralph Lauren Platz. Liz Claiborne wurde massentauglich und zu einer Megamarke; die bis dato für Anne Klein tätige Designerin Donna Karan füllte die Lücke, die Claiborne hinterließ, und schuf sich eine neue Nische für Karrierefrauen: minimalistisch und professionell. Es war das Jahrzehnt der sogenannten Power Suits, als zunehmend Frauen ins Berufsleben traten und die florierende amerikanische und japanische Wirtschaft die Aufmerksamkeit auf die Business Class lenkten. Giorgio Armanis tadellos sitzende Anzüge rückten ins Blickfeld, was zu keinem geringen Anteil dem Film *American Gigolo* von 1980 zu verdanken ist: In der ersten unvergesslichen Szene sieht man Richard Gere versunken vor seiner riesigen Armani-Garderobe.

Es war aber auch das Jahrzehnt der Avantgarde-Designer, u. a. Jean-Paul Gaultier und Martin Margiela. Die japanischen Modeschöpfer Yohji Yamamoto und Rei Kawakubo von Comme des Garçons begannen, ihre Kollektionen in Paris zu zeigen, und in Brüssel entstand eine neue avantgardistische Designbewegung. Zu den Antwerp Six zählten u.a. Ann Demeulemeester und Dries Van Noten. Miuccia Prada präsentierte ihre erste Prêt-à-porter-Kollektion für Prada, und Karl Lagerfeld wurde Designer bei Chanel.

Die breite Masse nahm den Begriff Sportswear ernst. Angeführt von der Schauspielerin Jane Fonda setzte ein Fitness-Wahn ein, der Modetrends aus dem Aerobic in die Alltagsmode einfließen ließ. Norma Kamali brachte den Look mit ihrer Sweatshirt-Kollektion auf ein neues elegantes Niveau. Nike setzte Maßstäbe in der Verpflichtung Prominenter, als man einen Deal mit Michael Jordan, damals Neuling bei den Chicago Bulls, abschloss, um den Schuh Air Jordan vorzustellen.

Ehrwürdige Jeanslabels wie Levi's wurden mit einer Welle neuer Konkurrenten konfrontiert, als Brooke Shields ein Zeichen für sich und Calvin Klein setzte, indem sie erklärte, ihr käme schlichtweg nichts zwischen sie und ihre Calvins. Los Angeles wurde ein Zentrum der jugendlichen Mode des sich rasch zu einem Branchenriesen entwickelnden Labels Guess und konkurrierender Jeansmarken wie Z. Cavaricci und Bugle Boy. L.A. Gear schloss sich dem Turnschuhtrend mit dem Schwerpunkt auf Valley-Girl-Mode an; und das neue Label Cross Colours nutzte die aufblühende Rap-Bewegung, um urbane Streetwear massentauglich zu machen.

1983

1983 Swatch releases cheap and chic watches

Swatch bringt preiswerte, schicke Uhren auf den Markt

Swatch lance ses montres chics et bon marché

1983 Karl Lagerfeld revivifies Chanel brand with racy new edge

Karl Lagerfeld sorgt mit gewagten Innovationen für die Wiederbelebung der Marke Chanel

Karl Lagerfeld fait revivre la marque Chanel grâce à un nouveau style racé

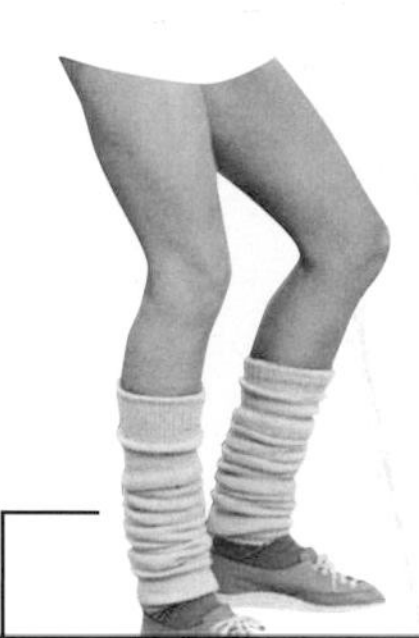

1983 Teen girls don leg warmers after seeing films *Fame* and *Flashdance*

Teeniemädchen tragen Beinwärmer, nachdem sie die Filme *Fame – Der Weg zum Ruhm* und *Flashdance* gesehen haben

Les adolescentes adoptent les jambières repérées dans les films *Fame* et *Flashdance*

1984 Madonna performs at first MTV Video Music Awards in vintage garb

Madonna tritt bei den ersten MTV Video Music Awards in Vintage-Kleidern auf

Madonna se produit aux premiers MTV Video Music Awards en costume vintage

MISSONI
836. Madison Avenue New York, N.Y.

© PETER

Missoni Menswear, 1983 ◄◄

Neo Max Sportswear, 1987 ◄

►► Benetton Sportswear, 1984

EN 1981, MTV LANCE SA CHAÎNE CÂBLÉE ENTIÈREMENT CONSACRÉE AUX VIDÉOCLIPS ET LE STYLE DES ROCK-STARS ENTRE DANS LES FOYERS AMÉRICAINS. Du jour au lendemain, les stars du rock se doivent de projeter une image fidèle à leur musique et qui résonne auprès de leurs fans. Personne n'y excelle mieux que Madonna, chanteuse alors méconnue mais prometteuse. Quand elle vient recevoir son premier MTV Video Music Awards en 1984, elle offre à de nombreux amateurs de musique pop un aperçu de la future « material girl ». Vêtue d'une robe de mariée très lingerie, Madonna stupéfait le public lorsqu'elle se contorsionne sur scène en chantant son tube « Like a Virgin ». L'année suivante, le film *Recherche Susan Désespérément* attire l'attention sur son style vintage chic.

L'industrie de la musique explose grâce à de nouveaux genres et de nouvelles figures de mode, entre Michael Jackson et ses blousons en cuir, et Pat Benatar en collants de danse et jambières. Parallèlement, le rap qui commence à peine à percer lance les nouvelles tendances repérées dans la rue. Pourtant, tout n'est pas que rock'n'roll dans les années 80. Très tôt, le disco fait place aux chastes looks BCBG de l'empire Ralph Lauren. Désormais cotée en bourse, la marque de Liz Claiborne devient une énorme entreprise; Donna Karan, anciennement styliste chez Anne Klein, reprend le terrain cédé par Liz Claiborne, se forgeant une nouvelle niche avec des vêtements minimalistes au look professionnel pour femmes actives. Alors qu'un nombre croissant de femmes accède au monde du travail et que les économies fortes des Etats-Unis et du Japon mettent en avant hommes et femmes d'affaires, c'est la décennie du « power suit », ce fameux tailleur aux épaules structurées. Les coupes impeccables de Giorgio Armani occupent le devant de la scène, un succès en grande partie dû au film *American Gigolo* de 1980, avec cette mémorable scène d'ouverture où Richard Gere contemple sa vaste garde-robe Armani.

C'est aussi la décennie des couturiers d'avant-garde, dont Jean Paul Gaultier et Martin Margiela. Les créateurs japonais Yohji Yamamoto et Rei Kawakubo de Comme des Garçons commencent à présenter leurs collections à Paris tandis qu'un mouvement de création très pointu émerge à Bruxelles. Les « six d'Anvers » font connaître Ann Demeulemeester et Dries Van Noten. Miuccia Prada lance sa première collection de prêt-à-porter pour Prada, et Karl Lagerfeld devient directeur de la création chez Chanel.

Pour le grand public, le sportswear semble s'adapter enfin au sport. La folie du fitness et de l'aérobic déclenchée par l'actrice Jane Fonda voit naître des créations qui s'infiltrent dans les tenues du quotidien. Norma Kamali hisse ce look vers de nouveaux sommets d'élégance grâce à sa collection de sweat-shirts. Nike établit une référence publicitaire sans précédent en signant un contrat avec Michael Jordan, le petit nouveau des Chicago Bulls, pour lancer ses baskets Air Jordan.

Les marques de jeans établies de longue date comme Levi's sont confrontées à une nouvelle forme de concurrence quand Brooke Shields fait sa gloire et celle de Calvin Klein en déclarant ne rien porter sous son jean Calvin. Los Angeles devient la plaque tournante de la mode jeune, du futur géant Guess aux marques rivales Z. Cavaricci et Bugle Boy. L.A. Gear surfe sur la tendance des tennis pour femme en optant pour le style « Valley Girl » ; et la nouvelle griffe Cross Colours mise sur le mouvement rap émergent en démocratisant le streetwear.

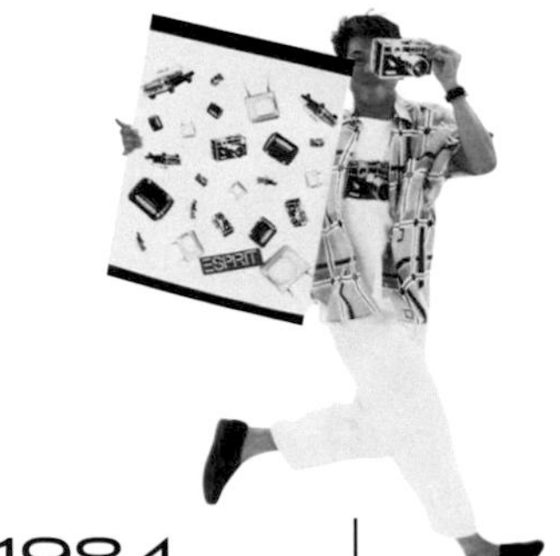

1984

1984 San Francisco-based Esprit launches "Real People" ad campaign

Die Firma Esprit mit Sitz in San Francisco startet ihre Werbekampagne „Real People"

La société Esprit basée à San Francisco lance sa campagne publicitaire « Real People »

1986 Run-D.M.C. immortalize their love for their sneakers in hit song "My Adidas"

Run-D.M.C. machen ihr Faible für Turnschuhe in dem Hit „My Adidas" unsterblich

Run-D.M.C. immortalise sa passion des baskets dans le tube « My Adidas »

1989 Adopting trend from Japan, streetwear goes from fitted to oversize nearly overnight

Einem japanischen Trend folgend ändert sich die Alltagsmode praktisch über Nacht von figurnah zu oversized

Pratiquement du jour au lendemain, le streetwear abandonne les coupes ajustées au profit des modèles surdimensionnés, une tendance venue du Japon

1989 Claudia Schiffer among first top models to appear in Guess ads

Claudia Schiffer ist eines der ersten Topmodels in den Guess-Anzeigen

Claudia Schiffer figure parmi les premières top-modèles à poser pour les publicités Guess

benetton
Benetton has all the colors in the world.

392

Bill Blass Womenswear, 1985

Gianni Versace Ready-to-Wear, 1985

Italian designer Gianni Versace launched his first collection in 1978. By 1982, he had landed the Cutty Sark and L'Occhio d'Oro fashion awards.

Der italienische Designer Gianni Versace brachte 1978 seine erste Kollektion heraus. 1982 hatte er bereits die Mode-Preise Cutty Sark und L'Occhio d'Oro erhalten.

Le créateur de mode italien Gianni Versace lança sa première collection en 1978. En 1982, il remporta les prix Cutty Sark et L'Occhio d'Oro.

► Gianni Versace Ready-to-Wear, 1981

LEVI'S
LEVI STRAUSS

©1985 Converse Inc.

LIMOUSINES FOR YOUR FEET.

Converse All Stars.® The original canvas high tops and oxfords in eighteen fun and flashy colors and prints for people who want to go places in style.

CONVERSE
Reach for the stars

Converse All Star Sports Shoes, 1985

Levi's Jeans, 1984 ◂

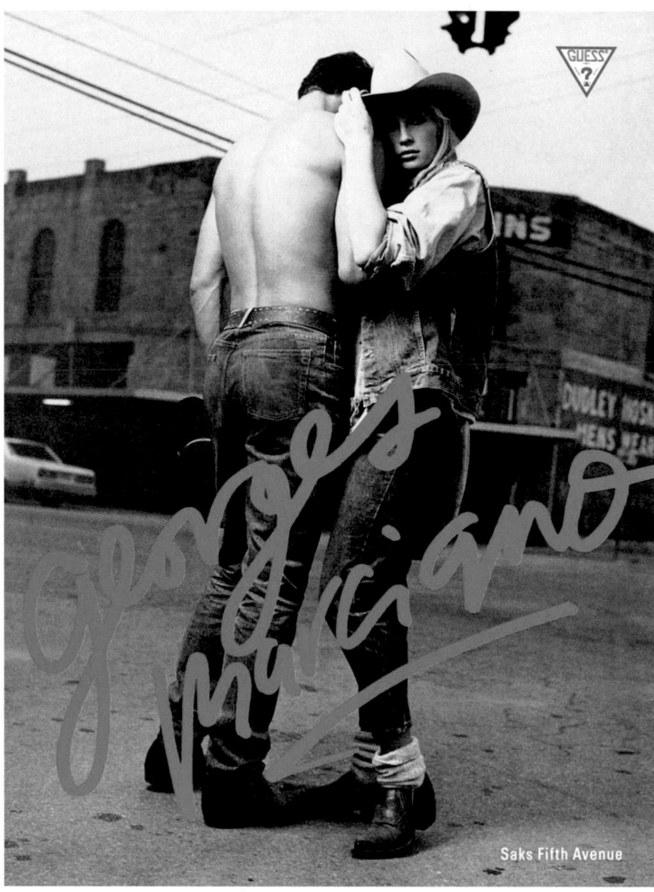

► Georges Marciano/Guess Jeans, 1985

Frederique van der Wal was one of the first models for Guess ad campaigns. Over the next 20 years, Guess ads would go on to feature such models as Claudia Schiffer, Carré Otis, Eva Herzigova, Laetitia Casta, Carla Bruni, Naomi Campbell, and Anna Nicole Smith; and such photographers as Wayne Maser, Ellen von Unwerth, Neil Kirk, and others.

Frederique van der Wal war eines der ersten Models der Werbekampagne für Guess. Im Verlauf der nächsten 20 Jahre folgen Guess-Anzeigen mit Models wie Claudia Schiffer, Carré Otis, Eva Herzigova, Laetitia Casta, Carla Bruni, Naomi Campbell und Anna Nicole Smith; die Fotografen waren u. a. Wayne Maser, Ellen von Unwerth und Neil Kirk.

Frederique van der Wal compta parmi les premiers mannequins à poser pour les campagnes publicitaires de Guess. Au cours des 20 années suivantes, les publicités Guess allaient engager de top-modèles telles que Claudia Schiffer, Carré Otis, Eva Herzigova, Laetitia Casta, Carla Bruni, Naomi Campbell et Anna Nicole Smith, photographiées par Wayne Maser, Ellen von Unwerth, Neil Kirk, entre autres.

Georges Marciano/Guess Jeans, 1986

Georges Marciano/Guess Jeans, 1986

JOCHEN FREY

L.A. Eyeworks, 1984

L.A. Eyeworks began running its "Great Faces" campaign in 1981. With a memorable tagline, "A face is like a work of art. It deserves a great frame," the ads have featured many familiar faces, including Paul Reubens, Andy Warhol, Stephen Sprouse, and Iman.

L.A. Eyeworks begann 1981 mit der Kampagne „Great Faces". Dazu gehörte der bemerkenswerte Slogan: Eine Gesicht ist wie ein Kunstwerk. Es vedient einen großartigen Rahmen. In den Anzeigen wurden viele bekannte Gesichter präsentiert, u. a. Paul Reubens, Andy Warhol, Stephen Sprouse und Iman.

L.A. Eyeworks lança sa campagne « Great Faces » en 1981. Avec l'inoubliable slogan « Un visage est comme une œuvre d'art, il mérite un beau cadre », ses publicités utilisèrent de nombreux visages célèbres, dont ceux de Paul Reubens, Andy Warhol, Stephen Sprouse et Iman.

Betsey Johnson Womenswear, 1985 ◂

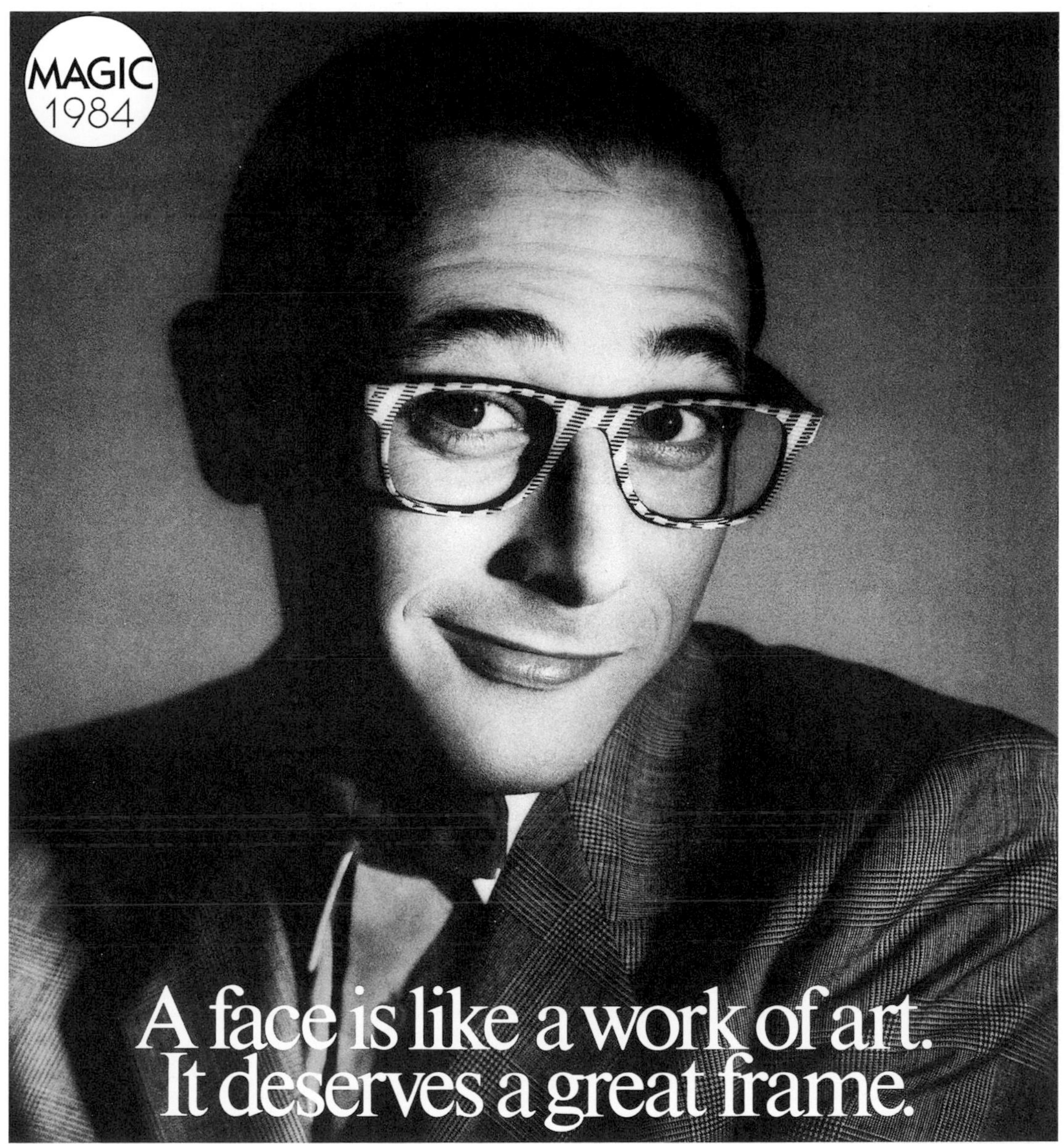

There has never been a frame quite like "The Beat." It was designed by l.a. Eyeworks, made in France and comes in dozens of textures, patterns and colors. Everything from matte crystal to buffalo horn to pink and black rayure (shown above). "The Beat" is available with many colored lenses and all prescriptions are filled in our own laboratory. Send $1 for a color catalog featuring "The Beat" and other designs by l.a. Eyeworks.

l.a. Eyeworks
7407 MELROSE. LOS ANGELES. CA 90046

Glasses shown: The Beat. Designed by l.a. Eyeworks. Face: Pee Wee Herman. Photographer: Greg Gorman. © 1984, l.a. Eyeworks, Los Angeles, CA 90046. Available at Barneys New York; Bendel's; Bergdorf-Goodman; Bullock's; Carson, Pirie Scott; Charavari; Foley's; I. Magnin; Jerry Magnin; McInerny; Neiman Marcus; Robinson's; Sointu; Theodore; Ultimo; Wilkes Bashford. For wholesale inquiries contact Three, 7407 Melrose Avenue, Los Angeles, CA 90046. 213/653-8176.

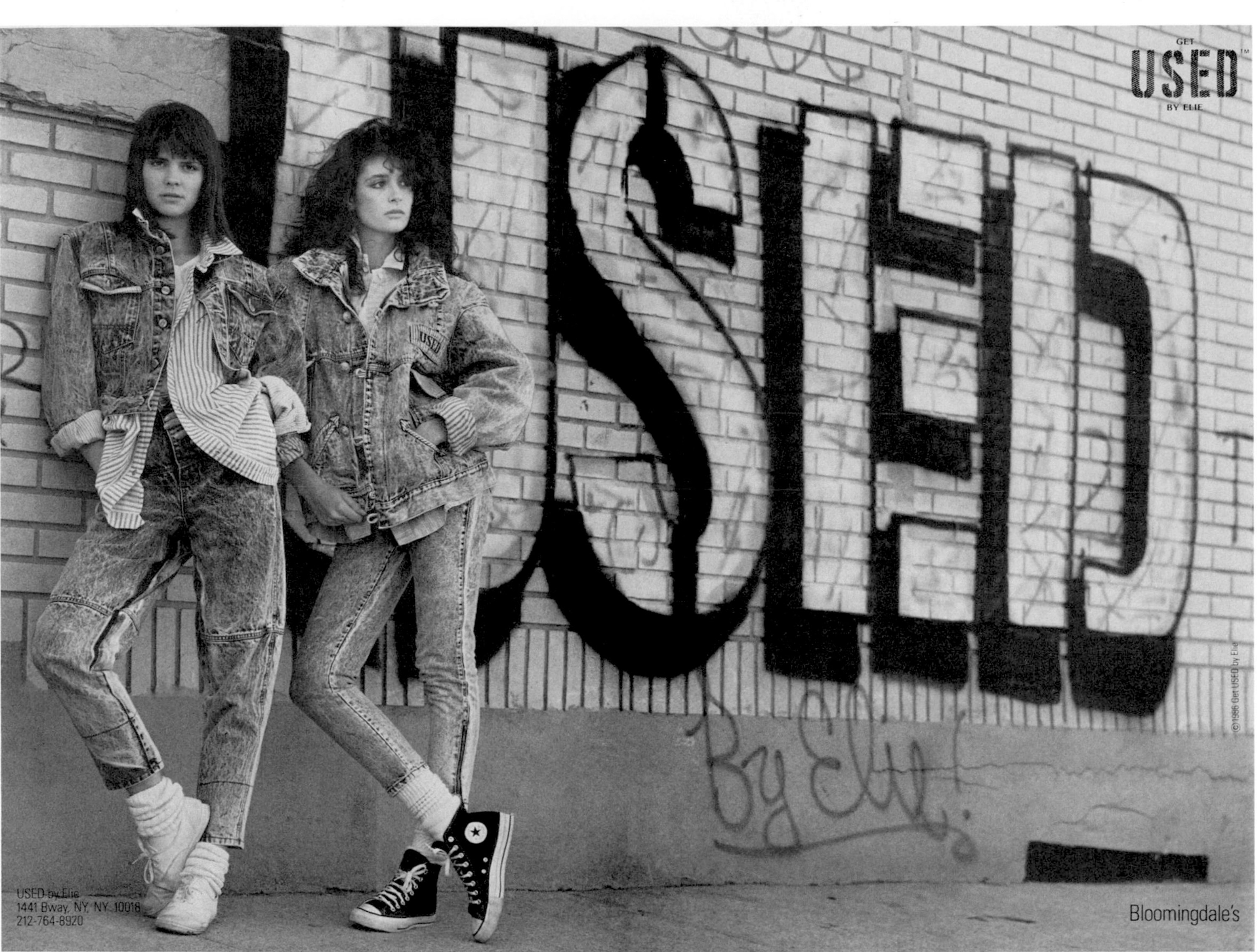

400

► Brittania Jeans, 1988

Used Jeans, 1986

BRITTANIA®

"I LIVE IN BRITTANIA"

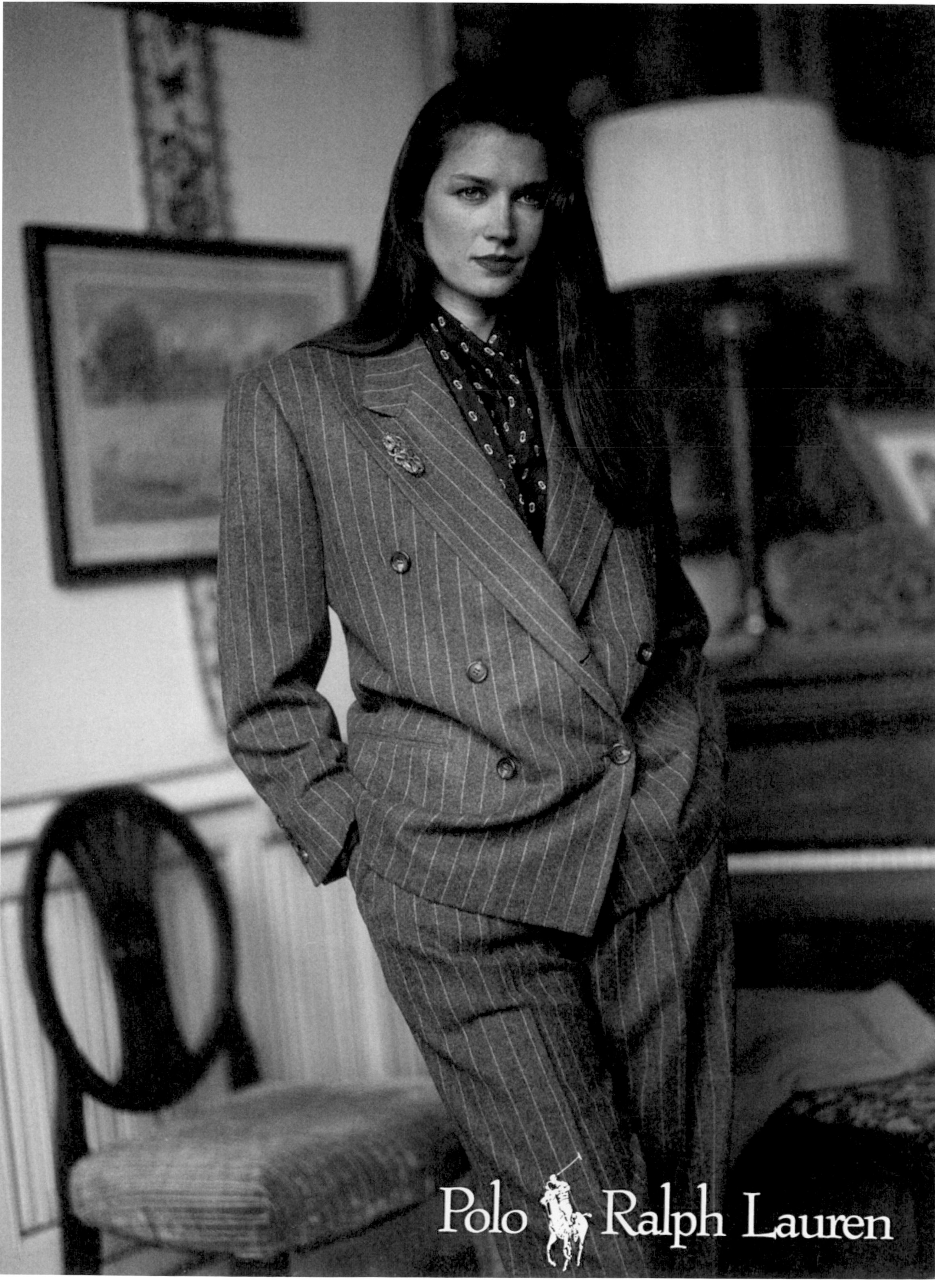
Polo Ralph Lauren

Polo Ralph Lauren, 1986

Ralph Lauren started in the late 1960s as a menswear retailer. By the 1980s, his company had grown to include women's and children's apparel, and would soon expand further into many licensed categories. The company's ads underscored the brand's position as an upscale lifestyle brand.

Ralph Lauren begann in den späten 1960ern als Einzelhändler für Herrenmode. In den 80ern war sein Unternehmen deutlich gewachsen und umfasste nun auch Damen- und Kinderbekleidung. Bald sollte sich sein Geschäft noch in viele lizensierte Kategorien ausdehnen. Die Anzeigen unterstrichen die Stellung der Marke als Label für den gehobenen Lebensstil.

Ralph Lauren débuta sa carrière à la fin des années 60 en tant que vendeur de vêtements pour homme. Au début des années 80, son entreprise s'était diversifiée dans la mode pour femme et pour enfant, avant de développer de nombreuses catégories sous licence. Les publicités de la marque soulignaient son positionnement haut de gamme.

Polo Ralph Lauren, 1984 ◄

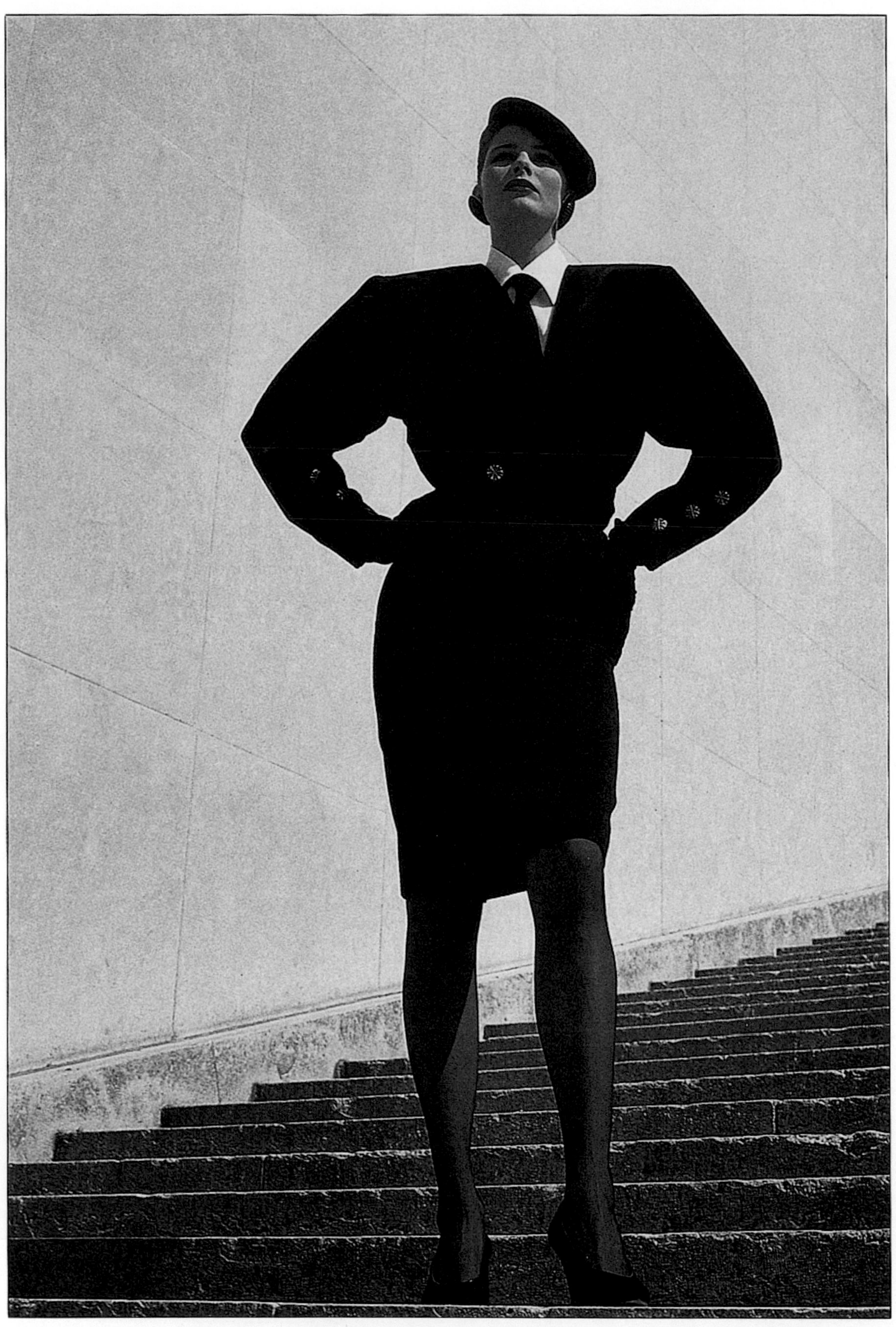

SAINT LAURENT
rive gauche

Yves Saint Laurent Rive Gauche, 1985

CHANEL

Chanel Ready-to-Wear, 1988

Gap pocket-t as worn by
KIM BASINGER, actress
POWER.
GAP

The Gap Sportswear, 1989 ◂

Formerly a small clothing shop in San Francisco, The Gap began its "Fall into the Gap" ad campaign in 1974 and eventually became the number one retailer in America. It upgraded its look in 1988 with what would become a long-running "Individuals of Style" campaign, which featured celebrities from actress Kim Basinger to beat novelist William S. Burroughs photographed by top photographers from Annie Leibovitz to Herb Ritts.

Der ehemals kleine Klamottenladen in San Francisco namens The Gap begann seine Kampagne „Fall into the Gap" 1974 und wurde schließlich zur Nummer 1 unter den Textil-Einzelhändlern Amerikas. 1988 polierte man sein Image mit der sich als langlebig erweisenden Kampagne „Individuals of Style" auf. In deren Rahmen präsentierte man Promis, angefangen bei der Schauspielerin Kim Basinger bis hin zum Beatpoeten William S. Burroughs, fotografiert von Spitzenfotografen wie Annie Leibovitz oder Herb Ritts.

The Gap, une petite boutique de vêtements de San Francisco, lança sa campagne « Fall into the Gap » en 1974 et finit par devenir le détaillant numéro un des Etats-Unis. La marque réactualisa son look en 1988 avec ce qui allait devenir la longue campagne « Individuals of Style ». Celle-ci présentait des célébrités, de l'actrice Kim Basinger au romancier de la beat generation William S. Burroughs, immortalisées par des photographes de renom, d'Annie Leibovitz à Herb Ritts.

The Gap Sportswear, 1989

Calvin Klein Underwear, 1985

Calvin Klein Underwear, 1983

▸ Christian Dior Underwear, 1983

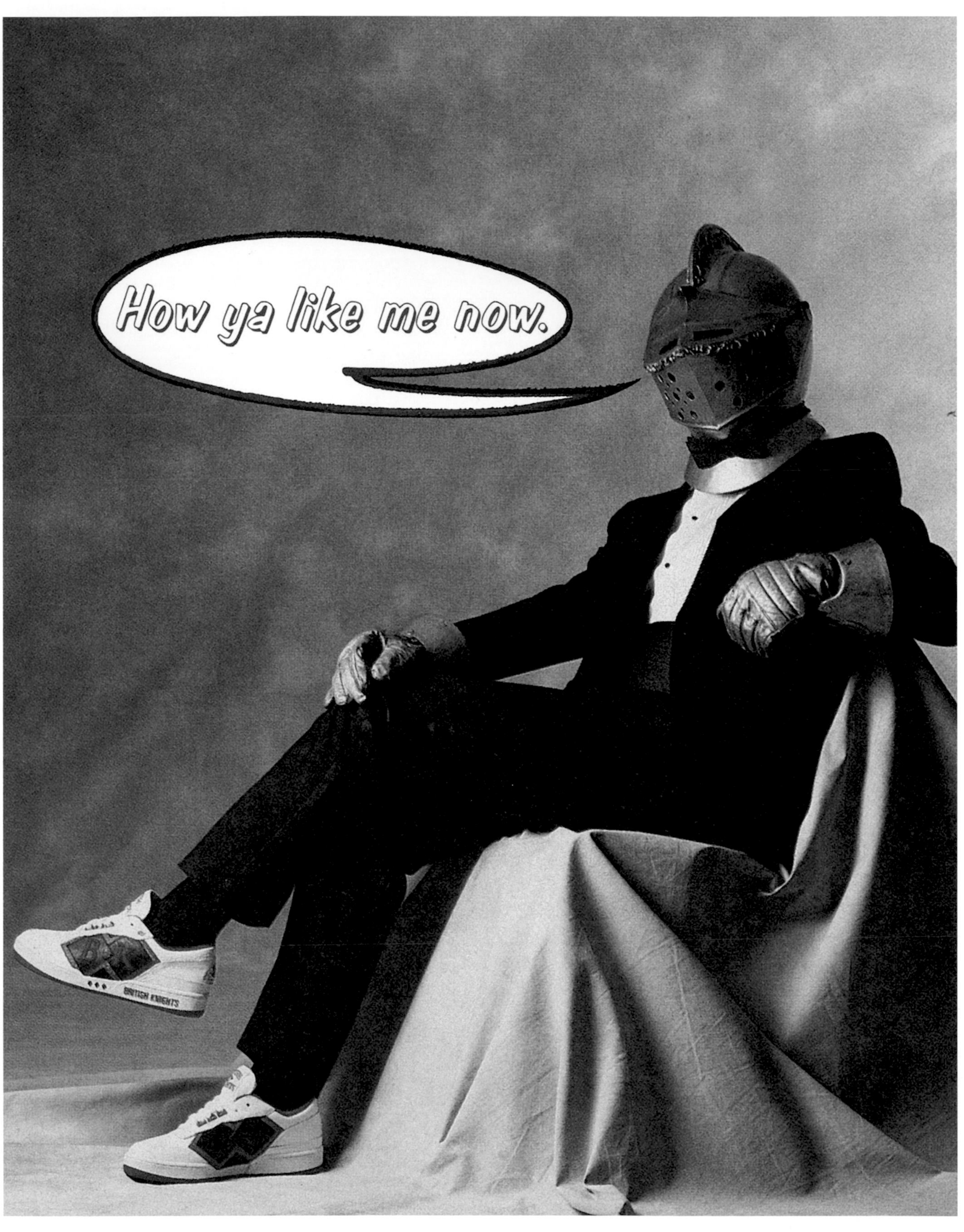

British Knights Athletic Shoes, 1988

► Jump Athletic Shoes, 1988

THE ONLY WAY TO GET HIGHER IS ILLEGAL.

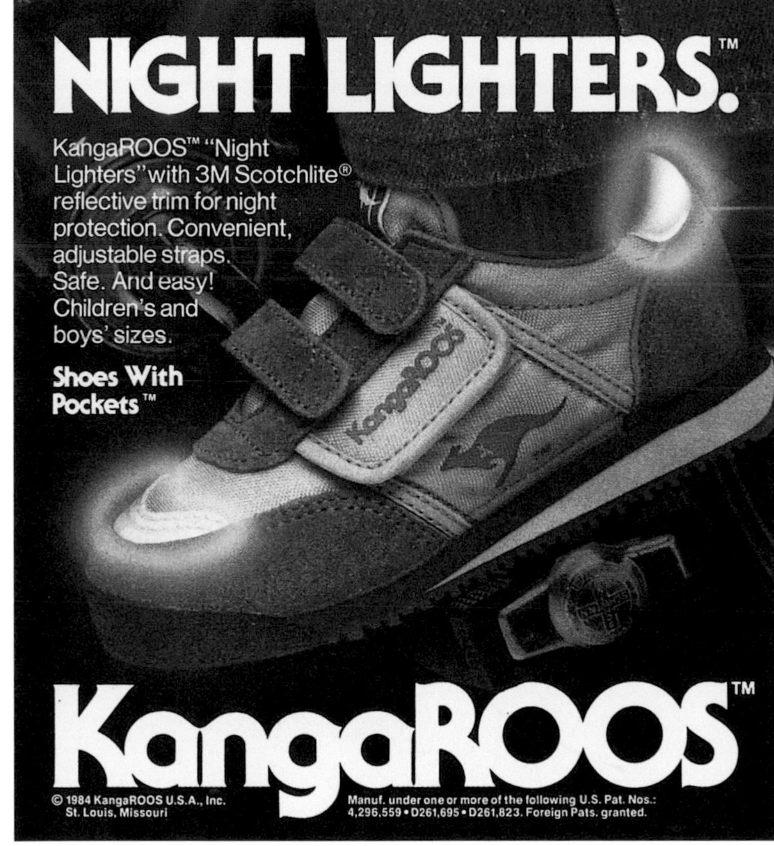

KangaRoos Athletic Shoes, 1984

Reebok Athletic Shoes, 1985

Bass Shoes, 1984 ◂

► Vans Breakers, 1984

Founded in 1966, Orange County, California, shoe company Vans tapped into the growing skateboard culture by aligning itself with professional skaters in the early '70s. The shoe company's distinctive checkerboard slip-on style was featured in the popular 1982 film *Fast Times at Ridgemont High*, boosting the brand's association with the counterculture.

Die 1966 in Orange County, Kalifornien, gegründete Schuhfabrik Vans nutzte die wachsende Skateboard-Szene, indem sie sich in den frühen 70ern mit professionellen Skatern zusammentat. Das Modell zum Reinschlüpfen im typischen Schachbrettmuster wurde in dem populären Film *Ich glaub', ich steh' im Wald* präsentiert und verlieh der Gleichsetzung der Marke mit der Subkultur enormen Auftrieb.

Fondé en 1966 à Orange County en Californie, le fabricant de chaussures Vans misa sur la culture skate florissante en collaborant avec des skateurs professionnels au début des années 70. Le célèbre modèle à damier sans lacet de l'entreprise apparut dans le film à succès de 1982 *Fast Times at Ridgemont High*, consolidant l'association de la marque avec la contre-culture.

L.A. Gear Athletic Shoes, 1988

BREAKING OUT

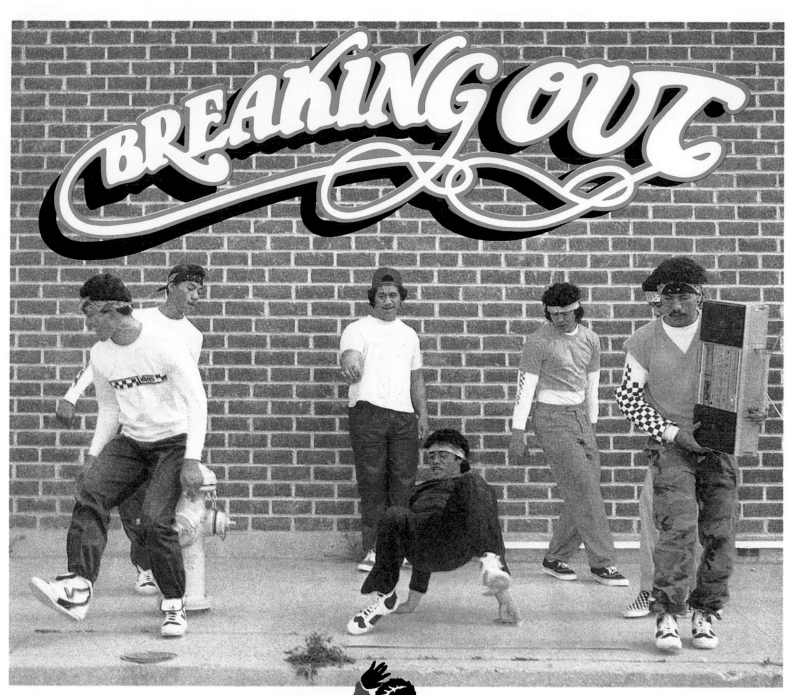

Man, I need VANS™

Breakers

Only For The Elite!

Complete this form if shoes are unavailable at your local VANS dealer

QUANTITY	STYLE NO. (Indicate #438 or #439)	SIZE	WIDTH (N/M/W)	PRICE
		☐ Boys ☐ Mens ☐ Womens		
		☐ Boys ☐ Mens ☐ Womens		
			TOTAL	$

Specify your correct shoe size & width in Mens, Womens or Boys
(Color is as shown in photo)

Style #438 Price: **$45.00**
Style #439 Price: **$43.00**

Add $2.50 For Shipping & Handling Per Pair. All orders must be pre-paid. Personal checks or money orders accepted. Allow 2–3 weeks for delivery.

Please Complete Form In Full And Mail To

VANS
P.O. Box 729
Anaheim, CA 92805
Attn: JUNE TAPP

NAME ______
ADDRESS ______
CITY ______ STATE ______ ZIP ______
TELEPHONE # (   ) ______

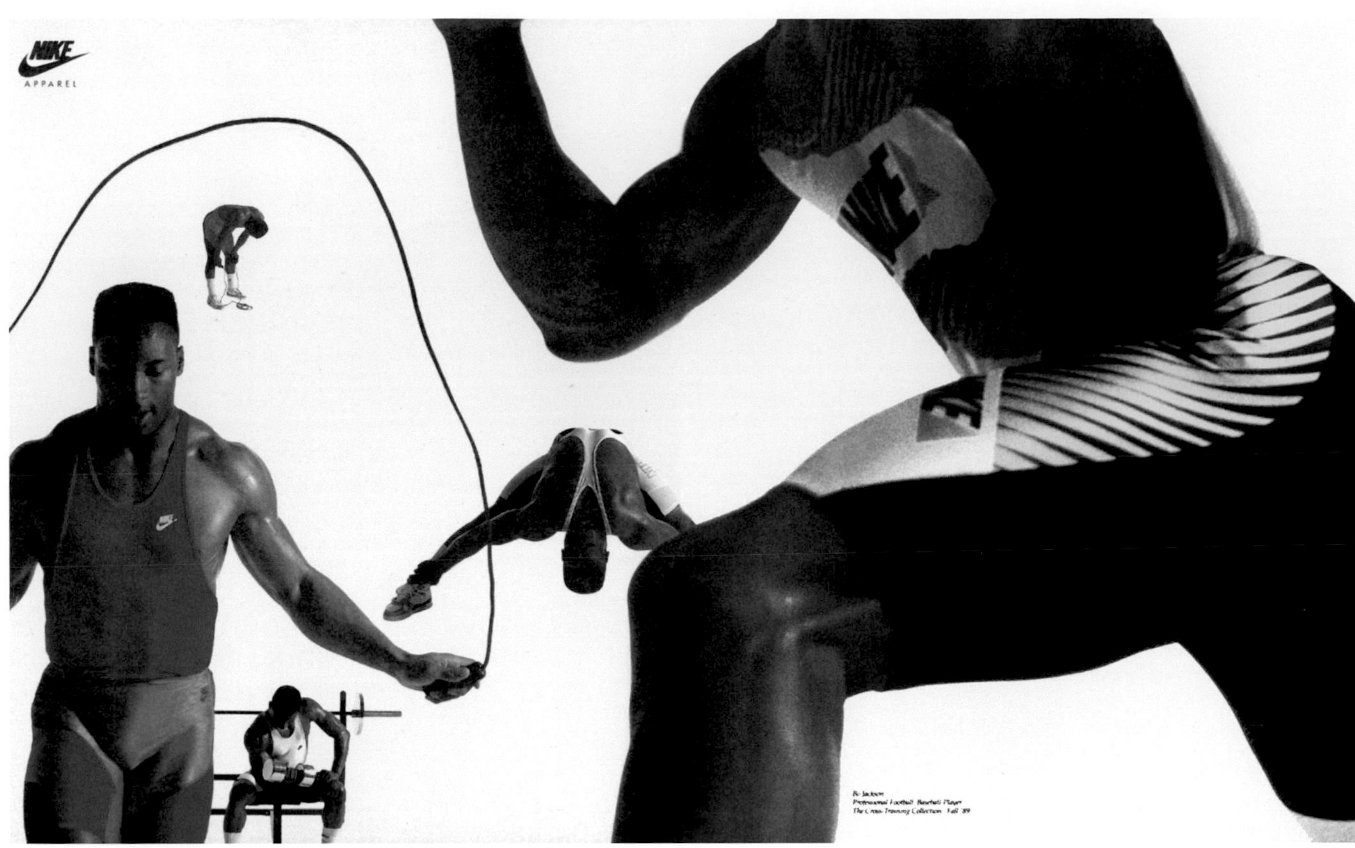

► Nike Athletic Shoes, 1988

Nike's "Just Do It" campaign launched in 1988 and quickly drew pot shots from competitors such as ASICS, who groused, "Just Doing it Doesn't Do It."

Nikes „Just Do It"-Kampagne startete 1988 und sorgte rasch für Attacken von Konkurrenten wie ASICS, der nörgelte: „Just Doing it Doesn't Do It."

Lancée en 1988, la campagne « Just Do It » de Nike s'attira rapidement les foudres de ses concurrents, tels qu'ASICS qui lui rétorqua : « Just Doing it Doesn't Do It ».

Nike Sportswear, 1989

JUST DO IT.

TRENDS WOULD NO LONGER TRICKLE DOWN FROM DESIGNER COLLECTIONS TO THE MASSES, AND WITH A WIDE WORLD HUNGRY FOR BRAND NAMES, SAVVY DESIGNERS BEGAN LAUNCHING LOWER-PRICED SECONDARY LINES, DENIM COLLECTIONS, AND ACCESSORIES TO ATTRACT WIDER AUDIENCES.

LES TENDANCES DES COLLECTIONS NE SE TRADUISENT PLUS DANS LA MODE GRAND PUBLIC. ALORS QUE LE MONDE ENTIER SEMBLE OBSÉDÉ PAR LES MARQUES, CERTAINS CRÉATEURS ONT LE FLAIR DE LANCER DES LIGNES SECONDAIRES, DES COLLECTIONS EN DENIM ET DES GAMMES D'ACCESSOIARES MOINS ONÉREUSES POUR ATTIRER UNE PLUS LARGE CLIENTÈLE.

TRENDS WÜRDEN NICHT LÄNGER LANGSAM AUS DESIGNERKOLLEKTIONEN IN DIE MASSENPRODUKTION DURCHSICKERN, UND ANGESICHTS DER WELTWEITEN GIER NACH MARKENNAMEN BEGANNEN SCHLAUE DESIGNER MIT GÜNSTIGEREN ZWEITLINIEN, JEANS-KOLLEKTIONEN UND ACCESSOIRES FÜR EIN BREITERES PUBLIKUM AUF DEN MARKT ZU DRÄNGEN.

1990-

HIP-HOP MEETS HAUTE COUTURE

HIP-HOP TRIFFT HAUTE COUTURE

LE HIP-HOP RENCONTRE LA HAUTE COUTURE

GUESS®
USA
WASHED
?
JEANS

GUESS
LEGWEAR

Guess Hosiery, 1992 ◄◄

D&G Dolce&Gabbana Womenswear, 1997 ◄

Levi's Sportswear, 1998

THE 1990s OPENED WITH AN ANTI-FASHION BACKLASH – ALBEIT SHORT-LIVED – FUELED BY THE GRUNGE MUSIC SCENE growing in America's Pacific Northwest. Classic Levi's, Doc Martens boots, and battered plaid flannel shirts became the youth uniform. But the movement did not last long, and, by 1993, a new medium emerged that would accelerate the speed of information around the world.

Even in its infancy, the Internet promised to deliver instantaneous access to news. Fashion magazines were slow to adapt to the new medium, and advertisers were unsure how to capitalize on its potential, but it was clear that the Web would soon deliver a virtual front-row seat to the latest fashion collections. Trends would no longer trickle down from designer collections to the masses, and with a wide world hungry for brand names, savvy designers began launching lower-priced secondary lines, denim collections, and accessories to attract wider audiences.

At the center of the fashion shift were Tom Ford, who had been promoted to Gucci creative director in 1994, to revive the Italian luxury label's image, and Miuccia Prada. With her minimalist fashions, Prada gave women—and eventually men—a reason to get dressed up again. The designer also helped kick off the "it" bag craze with its leather-trimmed nylon backpack. (The bag was first released in the early 1980s, but when the backpack was featured on the runway with the 1989 launch of Prada's ready-to-wear collection, the style took off and became a ubiquitous accessory of the 1990s.)

Ford, meanwhile, took a moribund luxury brand and gave it a luxury makeover, updating pieces from Gucci's archives and showcasing the luxe look in ads photographed by Mario Testino. In addition to overtly sexy imagery, Gucci ads excelled at highlighting one well-branded "must-have" item: the must-have bag, or the must-have sunglasses.

Fashion was having a pop-culture close-up, as well. In 1992, British TV viewers tuned in to *Absolutely Fabulous* to watch the antics of fashion publicist Edina and her sidekick Patsy. An attempt to translate the hit show for the American audience failed, as did Robert Altman's fictitious sendup of

Paris Fashion Week, *Prêt-à-Porter*. But *Unzipped*, the 1995 documentary following the months leading up to the release of Isaac Mizrahi's fall 1994 runway show, was a modest hit which turned Mizrahi into an overnight star.

The counterculture flourished in the rave music scene and with music festivals like Perry Farrell's Lollapalooza, which drew crowds of tattooed and pierced teens. The graphic T-Shirt has its roots in this era, with companies like Freshjive taking a swipe at America's consumer culture with its Tide-logo T. Denim makers were touting relaxed-fit styles, while the hip-hop scene was super-sizing everything from jeans to T-shirts. Within the rave scene and deejay culture, the look for denim was the elephant-bell jean—the most extreme styles had leg openings up to 50 inches around. But as the decade came to a close, denim prepared for another major shift. In 1999, Los Angeles designer Daniella Clarke launched her Frankie B. label, creating the ultra-low-rise jean, a look that would take denim into the next century.

1990

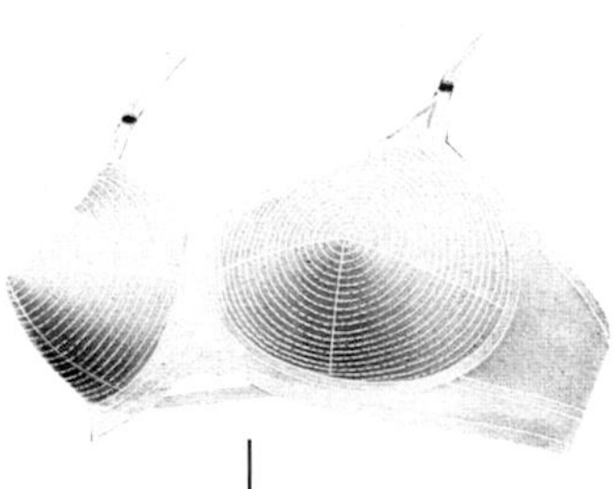

1990 Madonna brings back the bullet bra, or cone bra, on her Blonde Ambition tour

Madonna bringt auf ihrer Blonde-Ambition-Tour den Spitz-BH wieder ins Bewusstsein

Madonna remet à la mode le soutien-gorge « à obus » lors de sa tournée Blonde Ambition

1991 Doc Martens and plaid flannel shirts hallmark of grunge fashion

Doc Martens und karierte Flanellhemden sind die Markenzeichen der Grunge-Mode

Les Doc Martens et la chemise à carreaux en flanelle symbolisent la mode grunge

1991 Gucci creative director Tom Ford revives label's double-G logo

Guccis Creative Director Tom Ford belebt das Logo mit dem Doppel-G neu

Tom Ford, le directeur de la création Gucci, ressuscite le logo en double G de la griffe

1992 Calvin Klein begins creating provocative ads with Bruce Weber and Herb Ritts

Calvin Klein beginnt provokative Anzeigenkampagne mit Bruce Weber und Herb Ritts

Calvin Klein commence à concevoir des campagnes provocantes avec Bruce Weber et Herb Ritts

DIE 1990ER BEGANNEN MIT EINER KURZLEBIGEN ANTI-MODE-BEWEGUNG, AUSGELÖST VON DER GRUNGE-MUSIKSZENE, DIE IN AMERIKAS NORDWESTEN ENTSTANDEN WAR. Klassische Levi's, Stiefel von Doc Martens und schäbige karierte Flanellhemden wurden zur Uniform der Jugendlichen. Der Trend hielt allerdings nicht lange an, und ab 1993 machte ein neues Medium Furore, das die Informationsgeschwindigkeit rund um die Welt enorm beschleunigen sollte. Selbst in seinen Kindertagen versprach das Internet bereits unverzüglichen Nachrichtenzugang. Modemagazine adaptierten das neue Medium nur zögerlich, und auch die Werbebranche war sich nicht sicher, wie sie dieses Potenzial für sich nutzen sollte; klar war jedoch, dass das Web im Hinblick auf die neuesten Kollektionen bald für einen virtuellen Platz in der ersten Reihe gut sein würde. Trends sollten nicht länger langsam aus Designerkollektionen in die Massenproduktion durchsickern, daher begannen schlaue Designer angesichts der weltweiten Gier nach Markennamen mit günstigeren Zweitlinien, Jeanskollektionen und Accessoires für ein breiteres Publikum auf den Markt zu drängen.

Im Zentrum dieser Veränderungen im Modebereich standen Tom Ford, den man 1994 als Creative Director zu Gucci geholt hatte, um das Image des italienischen Luxuslabels neu zu beleben, und Miuccia Prada. Mit ihren minimalistischen Kreationen gab Prada Frauen – und schließlich auch Männern – wieder einen Grund, sich aufzustylen. Die Designerin trug auch zum Beginn des Hypes um die sogenannte „It"-Bag bei, und zwar in Gestalt des mit Leder gesäumten Nylonrucksacks. (Die Tasche kam Anfang der 1980er erstmals auf den Markt, doch setzte sie sich erst durch, als sie 1989 zusammen mit Pradas Prêt-à-porter-Kollektion auf dem Laufsteg präsentiert wurde, von da aus avancierte sie schließlich zum allgegenwärtigen Accessoire der 1990er.)

Ford nahm sich inzwischen des todgeweihten Luxuslabels Gucci an und verpasste ihm ein Luxus-Lifting, indem er Stücke aus den Gucci-Archiven modernisierte und den Luxus-Look mit von Mario Testino fotografierten Anzeigen groß herausstellte. Neben der eindeutig sexuellen Bildsprache waren die Gucci-Anzeigen auch perfekt darin, ein die Marke unverkennbar repräsentierendes Must-have zu betonen: die Tasche oder die Sonnenbrille, die man einfach haben muss.

Auch die Popkultur unterzog die Mode einer näheren Betrachtung. 1992 schalteten britische Fernsehzuschauer *Absolutely Fabulous* ein, um sich die Possen der Modejournalistin Edina und ihres Handlangers Patsy zu Gemüte zu führen. Der Versuch, die Erfolgs-Show für das amerikanische Publikum zu adaptieren, scheiterte ebenso wie *Prêt-à-Porter*, Robert Altmans fiktive Doku über die Pariser Modewoche. Dagegen war *Unzipped*, eine Dokumentation von 1995 über die Monate vor der Präsentation von Isaac Mizrahis Laufstegpremiere seiner Herbstkollektion 1994, ein regelrechter Hit, der Mizrahi über Nacht zum Star machte.

Die Gegenkultur blühte in Gestalt der Rave-Szene und im Rahmen von Musikfestivals wie Perry Farrells Lollapalooza, das massenhaft tätowierte und gepiercte Teenies anlockte. Das grafisch gestaltete T-Shirt hat seine Wurzeln in dieser Zeit, als Firmen wie Freshjive mit seinem Tide-Logo-Shirt Amerikas Konsumkultur aufs Korn nahmen. Jeanshersteller propagierten bequeme Schnitte, während die Hip-Hop-Szene von der Jeans bis zum T-Shirt alles in Übergrößen einführte. Innerhalb der Raver- und Deejay-Szene waren Elephant-Bell-Jeans gefragt – die extremsten Schnitte hatten knapp 1,30 m Beinumfang. Doch gegen Ende des Jahrzehnts bereitete sich der Jeansmarkt auf eine weitere große Neuerung vor: 1999 startete die Designerin Daniella Clarke aus Los Angeles ihr Label Frankie B. mit einer ultratiefen Hüftjeans – ein Look, der die Denimmode gleich bis ins nächste Jahrhundert prägen sollte.

1992

1992 Prada launches Miu Miu

Prada präsentiert erstmals Miu Miu

Prada lance la collection Miu Miu

FUBU

1992 Urban streetwear brand FUBU (For Us By Us) launches in New York

Die Streetwear-Marke FUBU (For Us By Us) wird in New York eingeführt

Lancement de la marque de streetwear urbain FUBU (For Us By Us) à New York

1994 Donatella Versace takes reins at Versace after murder of brother Gianni

Donatella Versace übernimmt nach dem Mord an ihrem Bruder Gianni die Leitung von Versace

Donatella Versace reprend les rênes de Versace après l'assassinat de son frère Gianni

1994 Uma Thurman's crisp white shirt in *Pulp Fiction* revives the minimalist staple

Uma Thurmans gestärktes weißes Hemd in *Pulp Fiction* bringt minimalistische Basics wieder in Mode

Le chemisier blanc d'Uma Thurman dans *Pulp Fiction* remet le minimalisme au goût du jour

Louis Vuitton Bags, 1997 ◄◄

Victoria's Secret Lingerie, 1992 ◄

LES ANNÉES 90 S'OUVRENT SUR UN MOUVEMENT ANTI-MODE DE COURTE DURÉE ALIMENTÉ PAR LA SCÈNE GRUNGE QUI SE DÉVELOPPE AU NORD DE LA CÔTE OUEST AMÉRICAINE. Le jean Levi's classique, les bottes Doc Martens et les chemises à carreaux en flanelle élimée deviennent l'uniforme des ados, bien que cette tendance s'essouffle rapidement. En 1993, l'émergence d'un nouveau média accélère la vitesse de l'information dans le monde entier. Même à ses débuts, Internet promet déjà un accès instantané à l'actualité. Les magazines de mode tardent à se mettre en ligne et les publicitaires ne savent pas vraiment comment exploiter le potentiel du Web, mais il est évident qu'il permettra bientôt de découvrir les tout derniers défilés de mode aux premières loges. Les tendances des collections ne se traduisent plus dans la mode grand public. Alors que le monde entier semble obsédé par les marques, certains créateurs ont le flair de lancer des lignes secondaires, des collections en denim et des gammes d'accessoires moins onéreuses pour attirer une plus large clientèle.

Cette transformation de la mode est principalement due à Tom Ford, promu au poste de directeur de la création de Gucci en 1994 pour réactualiser l'image de la griffe italienne de luxe, mais aussi à Miuccia Prada: avec ses vêtements minimalistes, elle donne aux femmes – puis aux hommes – une bonne raison de redevenir élégantes. La créatrice contribue également à lancer la folie des sacs à main grâce à son sac à dos en nylon passepoilé de cuir (d'abord introduit au début des années 80, ce modèle décolle vraiment en 1989 lors de son apparition sur le podium du défilé de la première collection de prêt-à-porter Prada, devenant un accessoire omniprésent dans les années 90).

De son côté, Tom Ford ressuscite une marque de luxe moribonde en modernisant les pièces des archives Gucci, soutenu par les visuels publicitaires du photographe Mario Testino comme vitrine de son look luxueux. Outre une imagerie ouvertement sexy, les publicités Gucci excellent quand il s'agit de vendre un *must* siglé, qu'il s'agisse d'un sac à main ou de lunettes de soleil.

La mode, elle aussi, se détourne de la culture pop. En 1992, les téléspectateurs anglais regardent *Absolutely Fabulous* pour suivre les aventures déjantées de l'attachée de presse en mode Edina et de son acolyte Patsy. L'adaptation américaine de la série ne touche pas son public, tout comme la parodie de la semaine de la mode parisienne réalisée par Robert Altman, *Prêt-à-Porter*. Mais en 1995, le documentaire *Dégrafées, déboutonnées, dézippées* qui retrace les mois de travail précédant le défilé automne 1994 d'Isaac Mizrahi remporte un joli succès qui fait de ce créateur une star du jour au lendemain.

La scène alternative prospère grâce à la musique électro et aux festivals tels que le Lollapalooza de Perry Farrell qui attire des foules de jeunes tatoués et piercés. Cette période voit naître le T-shirt graphique, des entreprises comme Freshjive s'appropriant la société de consommation avec un T-shirt qui revisite le logo de Tide, une grande marque de lessive américaine. Les fabricants de jeans imposent les coupes décontractées, tandis que la mouvance hip-hop surdimensionne tous les vêtements, des jeans aux T-shirts. Au sein de la culture rave et du milieu des DJ, le jean se porte à pattes d'éléphant, les modèles les plus extrêmes arborant des ourlets de 130 centimètres de circonférence. A l'approche du nouveau millénaire, le denim s'apprête à connaître une autre révolution. En 1999, la créatrice de Los Angeles Daniella Clarke lance sa griffe Frankie B. et innove avec le jean à taille ultra-basse, le look qui fera entrer le jean dans le 21ème siècle.

1994 Touting its engineered fit, Wonderbra launches in U.S.

Wonderbra propagiert in einer US-Kampagne seine ausgereifte Passform

Revendiquant une coupe ampliforme, le Wonderbra est commercialisé aux États-Unis

1996 *Swingers* film reflects mid-decade vintage fashion trends

Der Film *Swingers* spiegelt die Vintage-Mode-Trends um die Mitte des Jahrzehnts

Le film *Swingers* reflète la folie du vintage qui s'empare de la mode

1997 Bruce Weber creates notorious imagery for new Abercrombie & Fitch catalog

Bruce Weber entwirft die berühmten Bilder für den neuen Katalog von Abercrombie & Fitch

Bruce Weber devient le photographe exclusif du nouveau catalogue Abercrombie & Fitch

1998 Manolo Blahnik shoes star in *Sex and the City* television series

Schuhe von Manolo Blahnik genießen in der Fernsehserie *Sex and the City* Kultcharakter

Les chaussures Manolo Blahnik jouent un rôle de premier plan dans la série télévisée *Sex & the City*

Diesel Jeans and Workwear, 1994

Italian brand Diesel began working with Swedish ad agency DDB Paradiset, a division of DDB Needham Worldwide, in 1991, together launching an international campaign that blended humor with social issues. The DDB campaigns twice won the grand prix in the Cannes Press & Poster competition.

Das italienische Label Diesel begann 1991 mit der schwedischen Werbeagentur DDB Paradiset, einer Sparte von DDB Needham Worldwide, zusammenzuarbeiten; gemeinsam präsentierte man schließlich eine internationale Kampagne, die Humor mit sozialpolitischen Themen verband. Die DDB-Kampagnen gewannen zweimal den Grand Prix in Cannes im Wettbewerb Press & Poster.

En 1991, la marque italienne Diesel commença à travailler avec l'agence de publicité suédoise DDB Paradiset, une division de DDB Needham Worldwide, sur une campagne internationale mêlant humour et questions de société. Les campagnes DDB ont remporté deux fois le Grand Prix du concours Cannes Press & Poster.

Charles David Shoes by Nathalie M., 1997◂

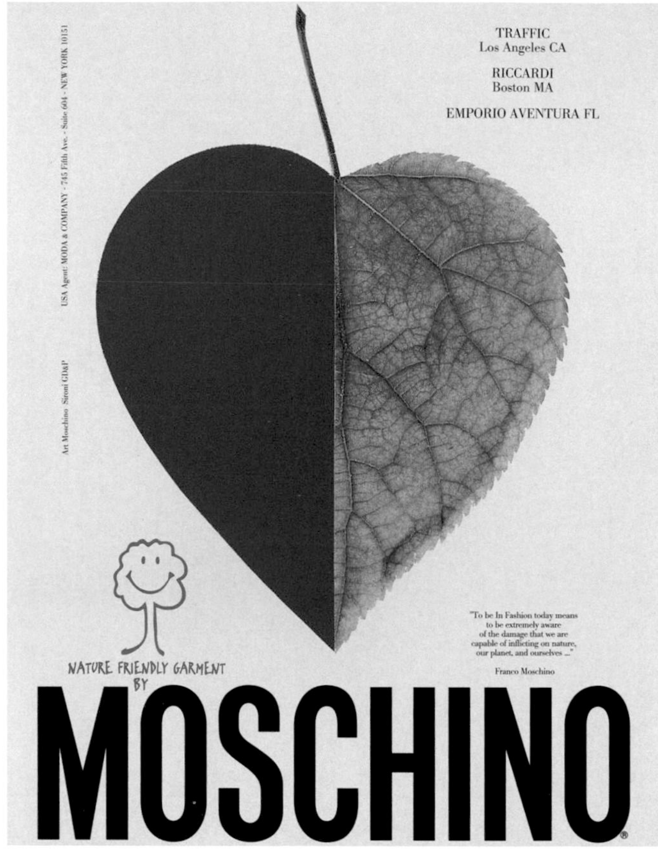

Moschino Jeans, 1996

The heart logo is a recurring theme for the irreverent Italian label Moschino, which was founded by former Versace illustrator Franco Moschino in 1983. Four years later, the designer followed up with the denim line Moschino Jeans, which has since been renamed Love Moschino.

Das Herz-Logo ist ein immer wiederkehrendes Motiv des italienischen Labels Moschino, das der ehemalige Illustrator bei Versace, Franco Moschino, 1983 gegründet hatte. Vier Jahre später ließ der Designer die Denimlinie Moschino Jeans folgen, die inzwischen in Love Moschino umgetauft wurde.

Le logo en cœur est un thème récurrent pour l'irrévérente marque italienne Moschino, fondée en 1983 par Franco Moschino, anciennement styliste chez Versace. Quatre ans plus tard, le créateur lança sa collection en denim Moschino Jeans, rebaptisée depuis Love Moschino.

Moschino Jeans, 1994

► Esprit Sportswear, 1993

ESPRIT
© Esprit de Corp. 1993 For more information call 1.800.777.8765. Photo: P. Sirota

Cross Colours Sportswear, 1993

The urban streetwear market was a largely untapped niche in the 1980s, addressed primarily by established athletic-apparel brands. Los Angeles–based Cross Colours launched in the late '80s with much fanfare and soon landed in large U.S. department stores. The company fell victim to its own success, failing to keep up with the demands of rapid expansion, but it paved the way for other brands like FUBU and Phat Farm.

Der Markt für urbane Streetwear war in den 1980ern noch eine weitgehend unbeachtete Nische, um die sich vornehmlich etablierte Sportmodenhersteller kümmerten. Die Firma Cross Colours mit Sitz in Los Angeles trat in den späten 80ern mit großem Tamtam auf den Plan und etablierte sich bald in den großen amerikanischen Kaufhäusern. Letztlich fiel das Unternehmen allerdings seinem eigenen Erfolg zum Opfer, weil es ihm nicht gelang, den Anforderungen der raschen Expansion zu genügen, dafür ebnete es zumindest anderen Marken wie FUBU und Phat Farm den Weg.

Dans les années 80, le marché du streetwear était encore une niche largement inexploitée et principalement occupée par des marques de sportswear bien établies. La griffe Cross Colours de Los Angeles fut lancée en fanfare à la fin des années 80 et rapidement distribuée dans les grands magasins américains. Victime de son succès, l'entreprise ne réussit pas à suivre les exigences d'une expansion aussi rapide, mais essuya les plâtres pour d'autres marques telles que FUBU et Phat Farm.

Lucky Jeans, 1997 ◄

Versus Ready-to-Wear, 1996

► Gaultier Jeans, 1997

Gaultier
Jean's
I
PIN-UP
BOY

Miu Miu Ready-to-Wear, 1997

Miuccia Prada took over her grandfather's leather-goods company in 1978, launching a ready-to-wear line in 1989. In 1992, the company launched its diffusion line, Miu Miu – the designer's nickname. In the mid-'90s, the brand shifted from the anti-fashion of grunge to an intellectual and minimalist look that exuded sophisticated luxury.

Miuccia Prada übernahm 1978 die Lederwarenfabrik ihres Großvaters und startete 1989 eine Prêt-à-porter-Linie. 1992 führte man die Nebenlinie Miu Miu ein – benannt nach dem Spitznamen der Designerin. Mitte der 90er wechselte die Marke von der Anti-Mode im Stil von Grunge zu einem intellektuellen und minimalistischen Look, der raffinierten Luxus ausstrahlte.

Miuccia Prada reprit l'entreprise de maroquinerie de son grand-père en 1978 et lança une ligne de prêt-à-porter en 1989. En 1992, la société commercialisa une ligne secondaire baptisée Miu Miu, le surnom de la créatrice. Au milieu des années 90, la marque délaissa l'anti-mode du grunge au profit d'un look intello minimaliste emprunt de luxe et de sophistication.

▸ Versace Signature, 1994

VERSACE
SIGNATURE
NEW YORK BEVERLY HILLS SAN FRANCISCO WASHINGTON HOUSTON SAN DIEGO
CHICAGO LAS VEGAS BAL HARBOUR MEXICO CITY VANCOUVER TORONTO

BOSS
BOSS
JEANS
BOSS
BY I.G. DESIGN
350 Fifth Ave., New York, NY For a retailer nearest you call 212-563-2720

FUBU Jeans, 1999

Following Cross Colours' short-lived success, urban streetwear remained a largely untapped market. Two New York companies stepped in to fill the void. FUBU ("for us by us") launched in 1992 as a hat line and soon expanded to include an expansive, logo-driven collection. Music executive Russell Simmons launched his Phat Farm men's line that same year, followed by a women's line, Baby Phat, in 1999.

Nach Cross Colours kurzlebigem Erfolg blieb der Markt für urbane Streetwear zunächst weitgehend unerschlossen. Dann traten zwei New Yorker Firmen auf den Plan, um die Lücke zu füllen. FUBU („for us by us") startete 1992 als Hutmarke und expandierte bald mit einer breiten, Logo-lastigen Kollektion. Der Musikmanager Russell Simmons kam im selben Jahr mit seiner Herrenlinie Phat Farm auf den Markt, der 1999 die Damenlinie Baby Phat folgte.

Après le succès éphémère de Cross Colours, le marché du streetwear resta largement inexploité. Deux entreprises de New York comblèrent ce vide. Fondée en 1992, la marque FUBU (« for us by us ») proposa d'abord des chapeaux avant de développer toute une collection tournant autour de son logo. La même année, le producteur de hip-hop Russell Simmons lança sa marque pour homme Phat Farm, suivie d'une collection pour femme, Baby Phat, en 1999.

Boss Jeans, 1994 ◂

► Gucci Eyewear, 1998

Under the creative direction of Tom Ford, Italian brand Gucci revived its luxury brand in the 1990s, becoming synonymous with luxury and glamour. Gucci's stylish ads helped propel many of its products to become "must-have" items of the season.

Unter Creative Director Tom Ford etablierte die italienische Marke Gucci sich in den 1990ern neu als Luxuslabel und avancierte zum Synonym für Überfluss und Glamour. Die eleganten Anzeigen halfen, viele Gucci-Produkte zu Kult-objekten der jeweiligen Saison zu machen.

Sous la direction créative de Tom Ford, la maison italienne Gucci ressuscita le prestige de sa marque dans les années 90, devenant synonyme de luxe et de glamour. Les élégantes publicités Gucci contribuèrent au succès de nombreux produits en les imposant comme les incontournables de la saison.

Gucci Bags, 1996

Gucci Boots, 1996

GUCCI
sunwear
bloomingdale's

ON SPRING BREAK

LOOKING FOR LOVE

THE A&F QUARTERLY/SPRING ISSUE AVAILABLE ON FEBRUARY 14 AT ALL ABERCROMBIE & FITCH STORES OR TO ORDER NOW CALL 1 800 432 0

Pepe Jeans
LONDON

Pepe Jeans, 1993

Abercrombie & Fitch catalog, 1998 ◄

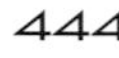

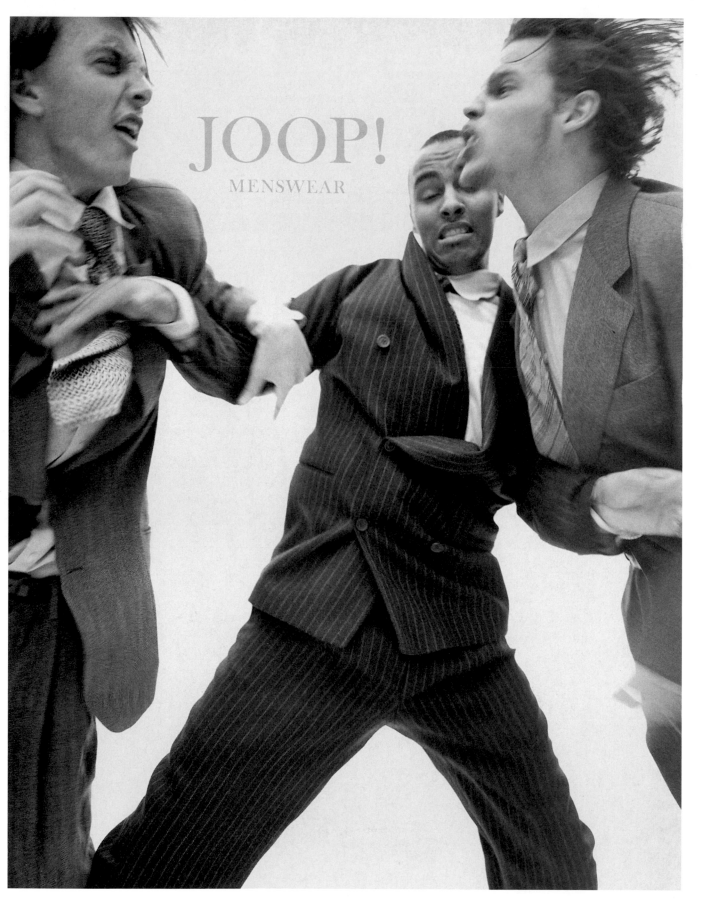

Joop! Menswear, 1994

▸ Guess Jeans, 1990

guess jeans

► Calvin Klein Jeans, 1995

Calvin Klein, no stranger to controversial advertising, found itself faced with a flood of negative press about its 1995 ad campaign, which featured youthful-looking models shot against a wood-paneled wall. Critics likened the ads' look to amateur child pornography, and the campaign was quickly abandoned.

Calvin Klein, dem kontroverse Werbung nicht fremd war, wurde angesichts seiner Anzeigenkampagne von 1995 mit einer Flut von negativen Pressemeldungen konfrontiert. Es ging um sehr jung aussehende Models, die vor einer mit Holzpaneelen verkleideten Wand fotografiert waren. Kritiker verglichen die Anzeigen mit amateurhafter Kinderpornografie, und die Kampagne wurde rasch eingestellt.

Habitué à la controverse, Calvin Klein eut très mauvaise presse en lançant sa campagne publicitaire de 1995 qui mettait en scène de jeunes mannequins photographiés devant un mur en lambris de bois. Les critiques associèrent ce look à celui de la pédophilie amateur et le créateur dut rapidement mettre fin à cette campagne.

Calvin Klein Underwear and Jeans, 1993

Versace Jeans and Underwear, 1998

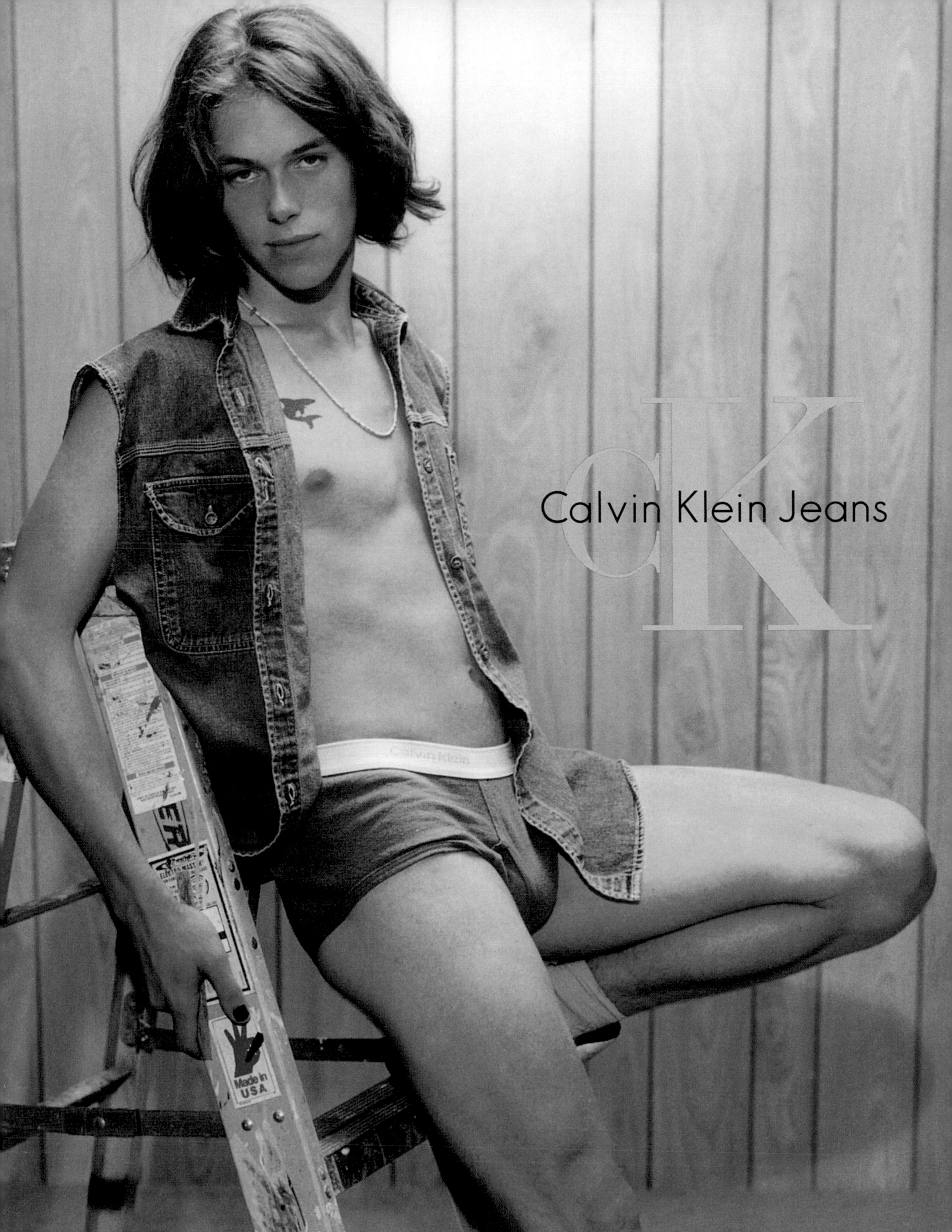

cK
Calvin Klein Jeans
Calvin Klein
Made In
USA

Calvin Klein Underwear, 1994

► Wilke-Rodriguez Sportwear, 1992

AVAILABLE AT BETTER DEPARTMENT AND SPECIALITY STORES NATIONWIDE. FOR LOCATION DETAILS CALL 1-800-992-9406.

AMERICA,
CHANGE
DAILY!

JOE BOXER®
UNDERWEAR, SLEEPWEAR AND HOME FURNISHINGS
AVAILABLE AT BETTER DEPARTMENT STORES AND SPECIALTY SHOPS NATIONWIDE
CONTACT JOE BOXER IN UNDERWEAR CYBERSPACE! INTERNET joeboxer@jboxer.com
JOE BOXER TV IS COMING TO Q2!
TUNE IN THIS FALL FOR THE PREMIERE OF AMERICA'S WACKIEST UNDERWEAR HOUR!

Joe Boxer Underwear, 1994

Joe Boxer founder Nicholas Graham got his start making novelty ties, which soon turned into a successful underwear and loungewear brand known for its whimsical designs and cheeky ads. In 1993, the company sent 100 pairs of its smiley-face boxers to U.S. President Bill Clinton with a note that read, "If you're going to change the country, you've got to change your underwear."

Der Gründer von Joe Boxer, Nicholas Graham, begann mit der Produktion von Spaßkrawatten, etablierte sich allerdings bald als erfolgreiche Marke für Unterwäsche und Freizeitkleidung, die für ihre skurrilen Kreationen und ironischen Anzeigen berühmt war. 1993 schickte die Firma US-Präsident Bill Clinton 100 Boxershorts mit Smileys darauf und dazu den Text: Wenn Sie das Land verändern wollen, müssen Sie bei Ihrer Unterwäsche anfangen.

Nicholas Graham, fondateur de Joe Boxer, démarra sa carrière en fabriquant des cravates fantaisie, une activité qui évolua rapidement vers une marque de sous-vêtements et de loungewear à succès, réputée pour ses créations fantasques et ses publicités provocantes. En 1993, l'entreprise envoya 100 de ses caleçons à smiley au président américain Bill Clinton, avec ce commentaire : « Si vous voulez changer le pays, vous devez changer de caleçon. »

Joe Boxer Underwear, 1993 ◂

452

Lacoste Shirts, 1997

▸ Lacoste Shirts, 1995

THE AUTHENTIC. THE ORIGINAL. MADE IN FRANCE.

LACOSTE EXCLUSIVE BOUTIQUES 206 WORTH AVENUE, PALM BEACH • THE BAL HARBOUR SHOPS, BAL HARBOUR
ALSO AVAILABLE AT SAKS FIFTH AVENUE • BARNEYS NEW YORK • NEIMAN MARCUS, SELECT STORES
FOR ADDITIONAL INFORMATION, CALL 1-800-4-LACOSTE

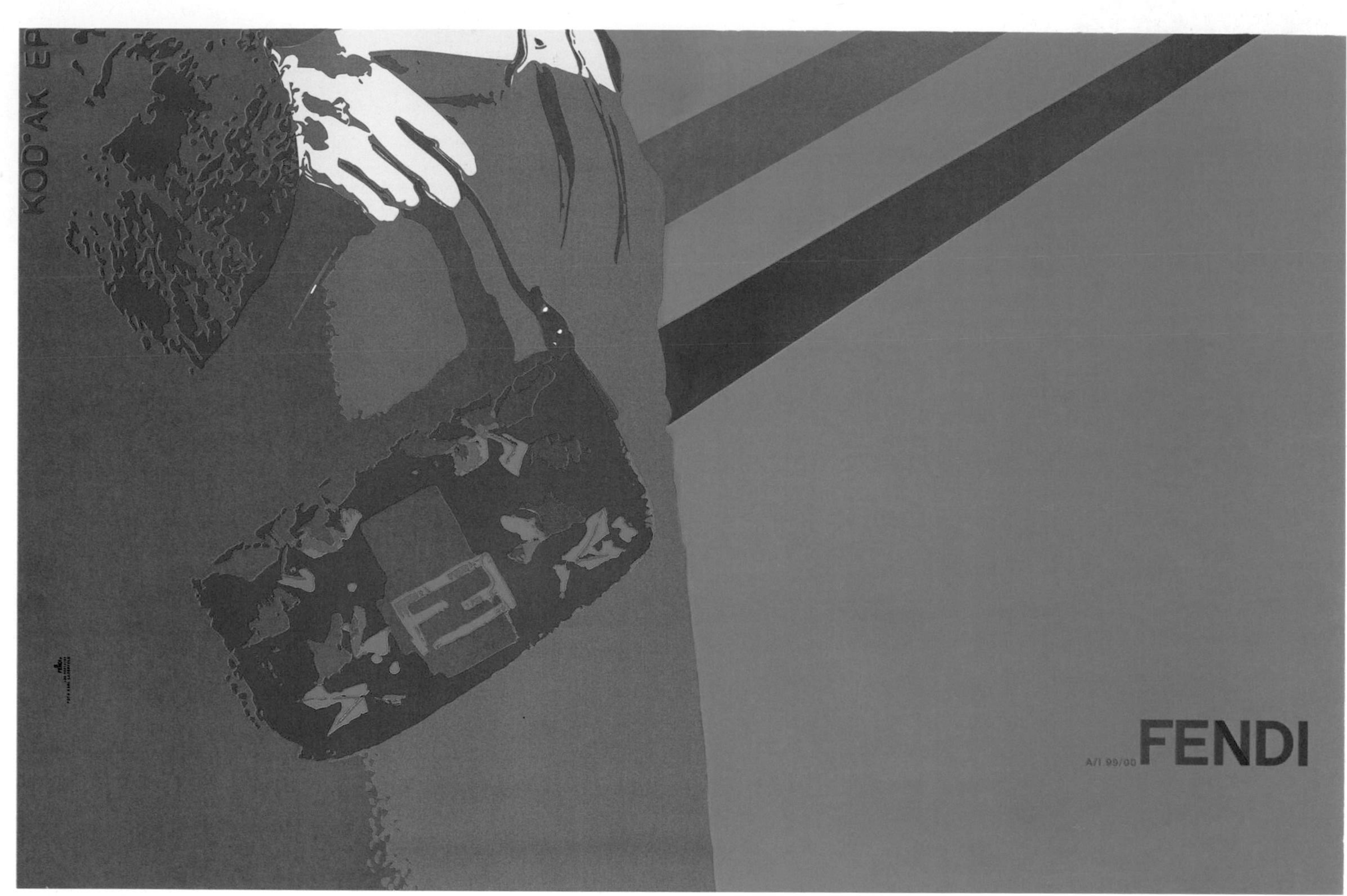

Fendi Bags, 1999

► Yves Saint Laurent Furs, 1996

►► Ermenegildo Zegna Suits, 1996

a
whole
new way
of
walking

PADRINO

marshmallows, platforms and down to earth fashions

SMERLING IMPORTS, INC. 350 Fifth Avenue (Suite 7419) New York, N.Y. 10001

INDEX

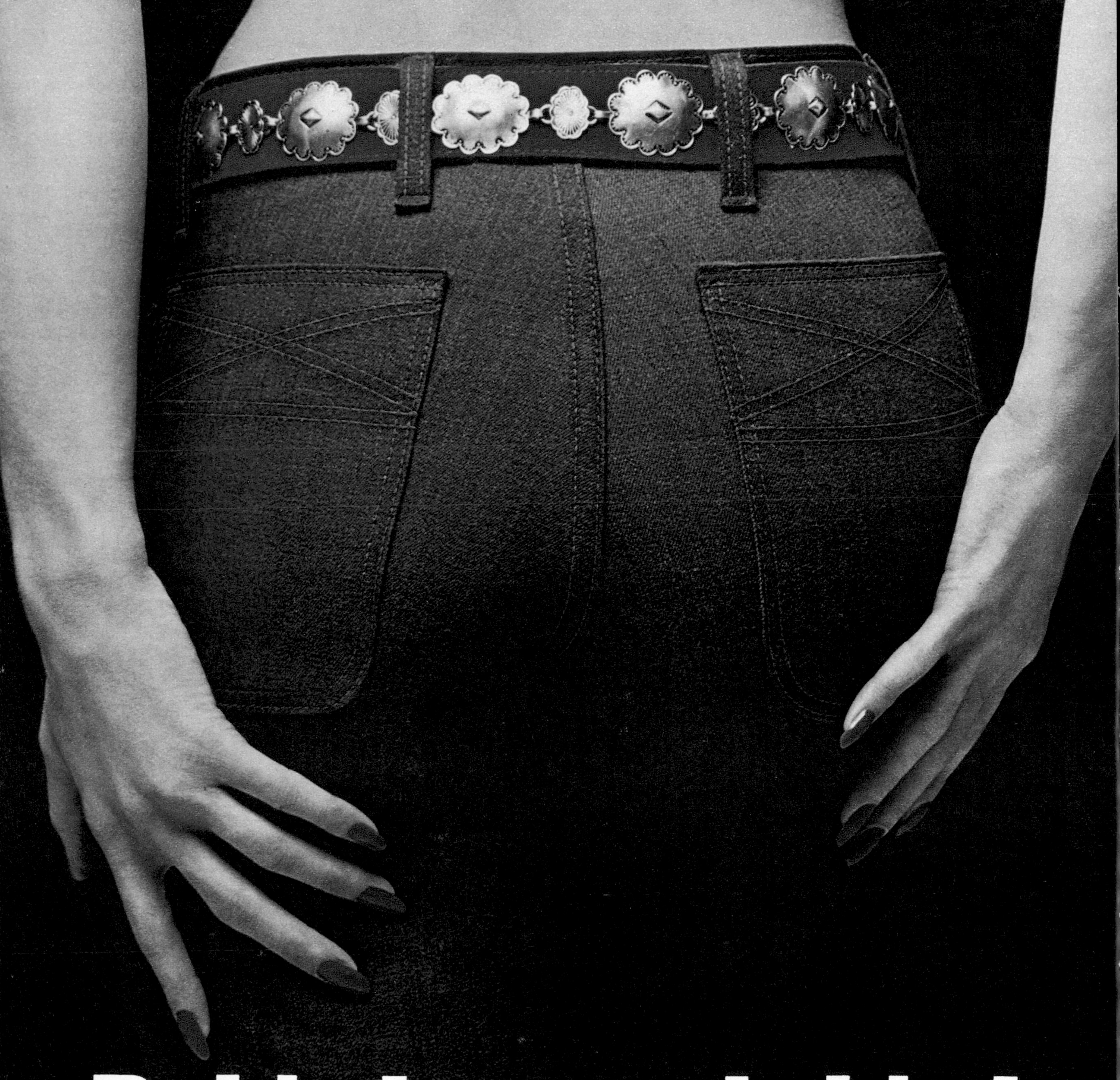
Be kind to your behind.

Padrino Shoes, 1974 ◂◂
Hillbilly Jeans, 1973 ◂

Frontispiece Maidenform Bras, 1954

Timeline image credits: Anne Marie Borle: Lacoste (1933), Polo (1972), Swatch (1983). Blake Roberts: Prada (1978). Burton Holmes Historical Archive, www.burtonholmes.org: Eiffel Tower (1900), Josephine Baker (1926), Charlie Chaplin (1931). Marco Zivny: Nike (1985). Nina Wiener: Missoni (1958), Gucci (1992). Tyler Flatt: Le Tigre (1977).

The publisher would like to thank Mark Haddawy of Resurrection Vintage, Los Angeles and New York for his fact-checking expertise; and Jennifer Patrick, Marco Zivny, Cara Walsh, Christopher Kosek, and Thomas Chung, for their invaluable assistance in getting this book produced.

To stay informed about upcoming TASCHEN titles, please request our magazine at www.taschen.com/magazine or write to TASCHEN, Hohenzollernring 53, D-50672 Cologne, Germany; contact@taschen.com; Fax: +49-221-254919. We will be happy to send you a free copy of our magazine which is filled with information about all of our books.

Hohenzollernring 53, D-50672 Köln
www.taschen.com

Art direction: Josh Baker, Los Angeles
English-language editor & project management: Nina Wiener, Los Angeles
Design and layout: Tyler Flatt with Nina Wiener, Los Angeles
Cover lettering: Michael Doret, Los Angeles
Editorial coordination: Anne Sauvadet and Julia Krumhauer, Cologne; Maurene Goo, Los Angeles
Production: Ute Wachendorf, Cologne
German translation: Henriette Zeltner, Munich
French translation: Claire Le Breton, Paris

Printed in China
ISBN 978-3-8365-1461-3

Gabrielle Chanel
PARIS
SHEER ENERGY
PANTYHOSE
benetton